Data Mining with SQL Server 2005

ZhaoHui Tang and
Jamie MacLennan

Wiley Publishing, Inc.

Data Mining with SQL Server 2005
Published by
Wiley Publishing, Inc.
10475 Crosspoint Boulevard
Indianapolis, IN 46256
www.wiley.com

To everyone in my extended family

—ZhaoHui Tang

To April, my kids, and my Mom and Dad

—Jamie MacLennan

About the Authors

ZhaoHui Tang is a Lead Program Manager in the Microsoft SQL Server Data Mining team. Joining Microsoft in 1999, he has been working on designing the data mining features of SQL Server 2000 and SQL Server 2005. He has spoken in many academic and industrial conferences including VLDB, KDD, TechED, PASS, etc. He has published a number of articles for database and data mining journals. Prior to Microsoft, he worked as a researcher at INRIA and Prism lab in Paris and led a team performing data-mining projects at Sema Group. He got his Ph.D. from the University of Versailles, France in 1996.

Jamie MacLennan is the Development Lead for the Data Mining Engine in SQL Server. He has been designing and implementing data mining functionality in collaboration with Microsoft Research since he joined Microsoft in 1999. In addition to developing the product, he regularly speaks on data mining at conferences worldwide, writes papers and articles about SQL Server Data Mining, and maintains data mining community sites. Prior to joining Microsoft, Jamie worked at Landmark Graphics, Inc. (division of Halliburton) on oil & gas exploration software and at Micrografx, Inc. on flowcharting and presentation graphics software. He studied undergraduate computer science at Cornell University.

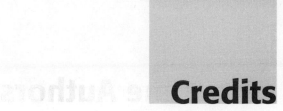

Credits

Acquisitions Editor
Robert Elliot

Development Editor
Sydney Jones

Production Editor
Pamela Hanley

Copy Editor
Foxxe Editorial

Editorial Manager
Mary Beth Wakefield

**Vice President & Executive Group
Publisher**
Richard Swadley

Vice President and Publisher
Joseph B. Wikert

Project Coordinator
Ryan Steffen

Graphics and Production Specialists
Carrie A. Foster
Lauren Goddard
Jennifer Heleine
Stephanie D. Jumper

Quality Control Technician
Joe Niesen

Proofreading and Indexing
TECHBOOKS Production Services

Contents

Foreword

Database systems have had great success during the past two decades. More and more data are being collected and saved in databases—a database with a pedabyte of data is no longer uncommon. Finding useful information in these databases has become an important focus of many enterprises; and more and more attention has turned to data mining as a key component to such information discovery. Data-mining algorithms and visualization tools are being used to find important patterns in data and to create useful forecasts. This technology is being applied in virtually all business sections including banking, telecommunication, manufacturing, marketing, and e-commerce.

Data-mining algorithms and visualization tools were introduced in SQL Server 2000. Since then, most relational database systems now include data mining features in their product. Data mining in SQL Server 2005 is the next big step in the integration of data-mining and database technologies—a culmination of five years of intensive collaboration between the SQL Server product team and Microsoft Research. Engineers and researchers from these two organizations have worked together to bring both classic and new, cutting-edge data mining tools to SQL Server. The authors, ZhaoHui Tang and Jamie MacLennan, have been the key drivers of this collaboration.

This book is an invaluable companion to SQL Server 2005 Data Mining. The authors explain the basic principles of each algorithm and visualization tool, and provide many hands-on examples. I am certain that many database developers, database administrators, IT professionals, and students of data mining will benefit from this book.

David Heckerman
Research Manager
Microsoft Research, Redmond

Acknowledgments

First of all we would like to acknowledge the help from our colleagues in the data mining team and other parts of the Business Intelligence organization in Microsoft SQL Server. In addition to creating the best data-mining package on the planet, most of them gave up some of their free time to review the text and sample code. Thanks go to: Peter Kim, Bogdan Crivat, Raman Iyer, Wayne Guan, Scott Oveson, Raymond Balint, Liu Tang, Dana Cristofor, Ariel Netz, Marin Bezic, Ashvini Sharma, Amir Netz, and Bill Baker.

SQL Server 2005 Data Mining is a product jointly developed by Microsoft SQL Server Group and Microsoft Research. We would like to specially thank our colleagues at Microsoft Research, particularly those in the Machine Learning and Applied Statistics (MLAS) Group, headed by Research Manager David Heckerman. We would like to thank David Heckerman, Jesper Lind, Alexei Bocharov, Chris Meek, Bo Thiesson, Max Chickering, Hang Li, Yunbo Cao, Ye Zhang and Carl Kadie for their contribution.

We also would like to thank to our early adopters of SQL Server 2005 Data Mining. These loyal users are the first ones who read our chapters and played with our product. These people include Jim Yang, Ying Li, Teresa Mah, Jim Yang, Xiaobin Dong, Paul Bradley, Brian Burdick, DaChuan Yang and JiaWei Han.

We would like to give special thanks to Bob Elliot, acquisition editor at Wiley, for his support and patience for this long due book. We would like to thank Sydney Jones for her countless hours spent editing this book.

An extra-special thanks goes from Jamie to his wife April, who pushed him through the hard spots, inspired him when ideas ran low by helping him bring clarity to the issues by presenting them in her own special light, and made him stay up late at night to finish chapters when the deadlines came near. I love you, honey.

Introduction to Data Mining

Data mining is getting more and more attention in today's business organizations. You may often hear people saying, "we should segment our customers using data mining tools," "data mining will increase customer satisfaction," or even "our competitors are using data mining to gain market share — we need to catch up!"

So, what is data mining and what benefits will using it bring you? How can you leverage this technology to solve your daily business problems? What are the technologies behind data mining? What is the life cycle of a typical data mining project? In this chapter, we will answer all these questions and give you an extended introduction to the data mining world.

In this chapter, you will learn about:

- A definition of data mining
- Determining which business problems can be solved with data mining
- Data mining tasks
- Using various data mining techniques
- Data mining flow
- The data mining project life cycle
- Current data mining standards
- A few new trends in data mining

What Is Data Mining

Data mining is a key member in the Business Intelligence (BI) product family, together with Online Analytical Processing (OLAP), enterprise reporting and ETL.

Data mining is about analyzing data and finding hidden patterns using automatic or semiautomatic means. During the past decade, large volumes of data have been accumulated and stored in databases. Much of this data comes from business software, such as financial applications, Enterprise Resource Management (ERP), Customer Relationship Management (CRM), and Web logs. The result of this data collection is that organizations have become data-rich and knowledge-poor. The collections of data have become so vast and are increasing so rapidly in size that the practical use of these stores of data has become limited. The main purpose of data mining is to extract patterns from the data at hand, increase its intrinsic value and transfer the data to knowledge.

You may wonder, why can't we dig out the knowledge by using SQL queries? In other words, you may wonder what the fundamental differences between data mining and relational database technologies are. Let's have a look of the following example.

Figure 1.1 displays a relational table containing a list of high school graduates. The table records information such as gender, IQ, the level of parental encouragement, and the parental income of each student along with that student's intention to attend college. Someone asks you a question: What drives high school graduates to attend college?

You may write a query to find out how many male students attend college versus how many female students do. You may also write a query to determine the impact of the Parent Encouragement column. But what about male students who are encouraged by their parents? Or female students who are not encouraged by their parents? You would need to write hundreds of these queries to cover all the possible combinations. Data in numerical forms, such as that in Parent Income or IQ, is even more difficult to analyze. You would need to choose arbitrary ranges in these numeric values. What if there are hundreds of columns in your table? You would quickly end up with an impossible to manage number of SQL queries to answer a basic question about the meaning of your data.

In contrast, the data mining approach to this question is rather simple. All you need to do is select the right data mining algorithm and specify the column usage, meaning the input columns and the predictable columns (which are the targets for the analysis). A decision tree model would work well to determine the importance of parental encouragement in a student's decision to continue to college. You would select IQ, Gender, Parent Income, and Parent Encouragement as the input columns and College Plans as the predictable column. As the decision tree algorithm scans the data, it analyzes the impact of each input attribute related to the target and selects the most significant attribute to split. Each split divides the dataset into two subsets so that the value distribution of CollegePlans is as different as possible among these two subsets. This process is repeated recursively on each subset until the tree is completely built. Once the training process is complete, you can view the discovered patterns by browsing the tree.

Figure 1.2 shows a decision tree for the College Plan dataset. Each path from the root node to a leaf node forms a rule. Now, we can say that students with an IQ greater than 100 and who are encouraged by their parents have a 94% probability of attending college. We have extracted knowledge from the data.

As exemplified in Figure 1.2, data mining applies algorithms, such as decision trees, clustering, association, time series, and so on, to a dataset and analyzes its contents. This analysis produces patterns, which can be explored for valuable information. Depending on the underlying algorithm, these patterns can be in the form of trees, rules, clusters, or simply a set of mathematical formulas. The information found in the patterns can be used for reporting, as a guide to marketing strategies, and, most importantly, for prediction. For example, based on the rules produced by the previous decision tree, you can predict with significant accuracy whether high school students who are not represented in the original dataset will attend college.

Gender	ParentIncome	IQ	ParentEncouragement	CollegePlans
Male	46580	100	Not Encouraged	No
Male	39687	121	Not Encouraged	No
Male	63482	102	Encouraged	Yes
Female	40454	129	Not Encouraged	No
Male	7333	86	Not Encouraged	No
Female	17617	105	Not Encouraged	No
Male	33540	110	Not Encouraged	No
Male	48171	102	Not Encouraged	Yes
Male	33356	79	Not Encouraged	No
Male	73325	120	Encouraged	Yes
Male	33153	112	Not Encouraged	No
Male	10331	94	Not Encouraged	No
Female	33505	106	Not Encouraged	Yes
Female	30052	76	Encouraged	Yes
Male	24579	105	Not Encouraged	No
Male	37497	72	Not Encouraged	No
Male	31572	98	Encouraged	No
Female	41979	138	Not Encouraged	No
Female	11151	61	Not Encouraged	No
Female	9532	86	Encouraged	No
Male	73580	124	Encouraged	Yes
Female	70149	104	Encouraged	No
Male	44316	122	Encouraged	Yes
Male	14915	100	Not Encouraged	No
Male	52417	68	Encouraged	No

Figure 1.1   Student table

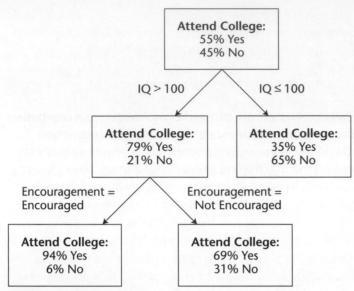

Figure 1.2 Decision tree

Data mining provides a lot of business value for enterprises. Why are we interested in data mining now? The following are a number of reasons:

A large amount of available data: Over the last decade, the price of hardware, especially hard disk space, has dropped dramatically. In conjunction with this, enterprises have gathered huge amounts of data through many applications. With all of this data to explore, enterprises want to be able to find hidden patterns to help guide their business strategies.

Increasing competition: Competition is high as a result of modern marketing and distribution channels such as the Internet and telecommunications. Enterprises are facing worldwide competition, and the key to business success is the ability to retain existing customers and acquire new ones. Data mining contains technologies that allow enterprises to analyze factors that affect these issues.

Technology ready: Data mining technologies previously existed only in the academic sphere, but now many of these technologies have matured and are ready to be applied in industry. Algorithms are more accurate, are more efficient and can handle increasingly complicated data. In addition, data mining application programming interfaces (APIs) are being standardized, which will allow developers to build better data mining applications.

Business Problems for Data Mining

Data mining techniques can be applied to many applications, answering various types of businesses questions. The following list illustrates a few typical problems that can be solved using data mining:

Churn analysis: Which customers are most likely to switch to a competitor? The telecom, banking, and insurance industries are facing severe competition these days. On average, each new mobile phone subscriber costs phone companies over 200 dollars in marketing investment. Every business would like to retain as many customers as possible. Churn analysis can help marketing managers understand the reason for customer churn, improve customer relations, and eventually increase customer loyalty.

Cross-selling: What products are customers likely to purchase? Cross-selling is an important business challenge for retailers. Many retailers, especially online retailers, use this feature to increase their sales. For example, if you go to online bookstores such as Amazon.com or Barnes andNoble.com to purchase a book, you may notice that the Web site gives you a set of recommendations about related books. These recommendations can be derived from data mining analysis.

Fraud detection: Is this insurance claim fraudulent? Insurance companies process thousands of claims a day. It is impossible for them to investigate each case. Data mining can help to identify those claims that are more likely to be false.

Risk management: Should the loan be approved for this customer? This is the most common question in the banking scenario. Data mining techniques can be used to score the customer's risk level, helping the manager make an appropriate decision for each application.

Customer segmentation: Who are my customers? Customer segmentation helps marketing managers understand the different profiles of customers and take appropriate marketing actions based on the segments.

Targeted ads: What banner ads should be displayed to a specific visitor? Web retailers and portal sites like to personalize their content for their Web customers. Using customers' navigation or online purchase patterns, these sites can use data mining solutions to display targeted advertisements to their customers' navigators.

Sales forecast: How many cases of wines will I sell next week in this store? What will the inventory level be in one month? Data mining forecasting techniques can be used to answer these types of time-related questions.

Data Mining Tasks

Data mining can be used to solve hundreds of business problems. Based on the nature of these problems, we can group them into the following data mining tasks.

Classification

Classification is one of the most popular data mining tasks. Business problems like churn analysis, risk management and ad targeting usually involve classification.

Classification refers to assigning cases into categories based on a predictable attribute. Each case contains a set of attributes, one of which is the *class* attribute (predictable attribute). The task requires finding a model that describes the class attribute as a function of input attributes. In the College Plans dataset previously described, the *class* is the College Plans attribute with two states: Yes and No. To train a classification model, you need to know the class value of input cases in the training dataset, which are usually the historical data. Data mining algorithms that require a target to learn against are considered *supervised* algorithms.

Typical classification algorithms include decision trees, neural network, and Naïve Bayes.

Clustering

Clustering is also called segmentation. It is used to identify natural groupings of cases based on a set of attributes. Cases within the same group have more or less similar attribute values.

Figure 1.3 displays a simple customer dataset containing two attributes: age and income. The clustering algorithm groups the dataset into three segments based on these two attributes. Cluster 1 contains the younger population with a low income. Cluster 2 contains middle-aged customers with higher incomes. Cluster 3 is a group of senior individuals with a relatively low income.

Clustering is an *unsupervised* data mining task. No single attribute is used to guide the training process. All input attributes are treated equally. Most clustering algorithms build the model through a number of iterations and stop when the model converges, that is, when the boundaries of these segments are stabilized.

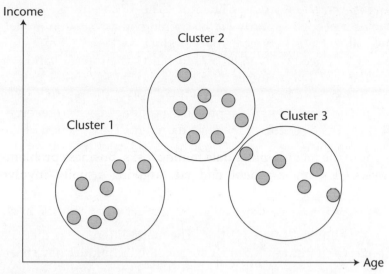

Figure 1.3   Clustering

Association

Association is another popular data mining task. Association is also called market basket analysis. A typical association business problem is to analyze a sales transaction table and identify those products often sold in the same shopping basket. The common usage of association is to identify common sets of items (frequent itemsets) and rules for the purpose of cross-selling.

In terms of association, each product, or more generally, each attribute/value pair is considered an item. The association task has two goals: to find frequent itemsets and to find association rules.

Most association type algorithms find frequent itemsets by scanning the dataset multiple times. The frequency threshold (support) is defined by the user before processing the model. For example, support = 2% means that the model analyzes only items that appear in at least 2% of shopping carts. A frequent itemset may look like {Product = "Pepsi", Product = "Chips", Product = "Juice"}. Each itemset has a size, which is the number of items that it contains. The size of this particular itemset is 3.

Apart from identifying frequent itemsets based on support, most association type algorithms also find rules. An association rule has the form A, B => C with a probability, where A, B, C are all frequent item sets. The probability is also referred to as the *confidence* in data mining literature. The probability is a threshold value that the user needs to specify before training an association model. For example, the following is a typical rule: Product = "Pepsi", Product = "Chips" => Product = "Juice" with an 80% probability. The interpretation of this rule is straightforward. If a customer buys Pepsi and chips, there is an 80% chance that he or she may also buy juice. Figure 1.4 displays the product association patterns. Each node in the figure represents a product, each edge represents the relationship. The direction of the edge represents the direction of the prediction. For example, the edge from Milk to Cheese indicates that those who purchase milk might also purchase cheese.

Regression

The regression task is similar to classification. The main difference is that the predictable attribute is a continuous number. Regression techniques have been widely studied for centuries in the field of statistics. Linear regression and logistic regression are the most popular regression methods. Other regression techniques include regression trees and neural networks.

Regression tasks can solve many business problems. For example, they can be used to predict coupon redemption rates based on the face value, distribution method, and distribution volume, or to predict wind velocities based on temperature, air pressure, and humidity.

Forecasting

Forecasting is yet another important data mining task. What will the stock value of MSFT be tomorrow? What will the sales amount of Pepsi be next month? Forecasting can help to answer these questions. It usually takes as an input time series dataset, for example a sequence of numbers with an attribute representing time. The time series data typically contains adjacent observations, which are order-dependant. Forecasting techniques deal with general trends, periodicity, and noisy noise filtering. The most popular time series technique is ARIMA, which stands for AutoRegressive Integrated Moving Average model.

Figure 1.5 contains two curves. The solid line curve is the actual time series data on Microsoft stock value, while the dotted curve is a time series model based on the moving average forecasting technique.

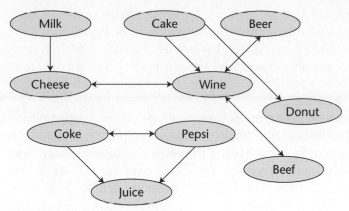

Figure 1.4   Products association

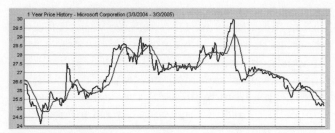

Figure 1.5   Time series

Sequence Analysis

Sequence analysis is used to find patterns in a discrete series. A sequence is composed of a series of discrete values (or states). For example, a DNA sequence is a long series composed of four different states: A, G, C, and T. A Web click sequence contains a series of URLs. Customer purchases can also be modeled as sequence data. For example, a customer first buys a computer, then speakers, and finally a Webcam. Both sequence and time series data contain adjacent observations that are dependant. The difference is that the sequence series contains discrete states, while the time series contains continuous numbers.

Sequence and association data are similar in the sense that each individual case contains a set of items or states. The difference between sequence and association models is that sequence models analyze the state transitions, while the association model considers each item in a shopping cart to be equal and independent. With the sequence model, buying a computer before buying speakers is a different sequence than buying speakers before a computer. With an association algorithm, these are considered to be the same itemset.

Figure 1.6 displays Web click sequences. Each node is a URL category. Each line has a direction, representing a transition between two URLs. Each transition is associated with a weight, representing the probability of the transition between one URL and the other.

Sequence analysis is a relatively new data mining task. It is becoming more important mainly due to two types of applications: Web log analysis and DNA analysis. There are several different sequence techniques available today such as Markov chains. Researchers are actively exploring new algorithms in this field. Figure 1.6 displays the state transitions among a set of URL categories based on Web click data.

Deviation Analysis

Deviation analysis is for finding those rare cases that behave very differently from others. It is also called outlier detection, which refers to the detection of significant changes from previously observed behavior. Deviation analysis can be used in many applications. The most common one is credit card fraud detection. To identify abnormal cases from millions of transactions is a very challenging task. Other applications include network intrusion detection, manufacture error analysis, and so on.

There is no standard technique for deviation analysis. It is still an actively researched topic. Usually analysts employ some modified versions of decision trees, clustering, or neural network algorithms for this task. In order to generate significant rules, analysts need to oversample the anomaly cases in the training dataset.

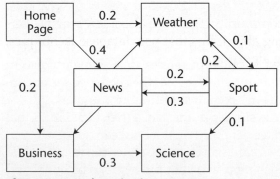

Figure 1.6   Web navigation sequence

Data Mining Techniques

Although data mining as a term is relatively new, most data mining techniques have existed for years. If we look at the roots of those popular data mining algorithms, we find that they are mainly derived from three fields: statistics, machine learning, and database.

Most of data mining tasks listed in the previous section have been addressed in the statistics community. A number of data mining algorithms, including regression, time series, and decision trees, were invented by statisticians. Regression techniques have existed for centuries. Time series algorithms have been studied for decades. The decision tree algorithm is one of the more recent techniques, dating from the mid-1980s.

Data mining focuses on automatic or semiautomatic pattern discovery. Several machine learning algorithms have been applied to data mining. Neural networks are one of these techniques and are excellent for classification and regression, especially when the attribute relationships are nonlinear. The genetic algorithm is yet another machine learning technique. It simulates the natural evolution process by working with a set of candidates and a survival (fitness) function. The survival function repeatedly selects the most suitable candidates for the next generation. Genetic algorithms can be used for classification and clustering tasks. They can also be used in conjunction with other algorithms, for instance, helping a neural network to find the best set of weights among neurons.

A database is the third technical source for data mining. Traditional statistics assumes that all the data can be loaded into memory for statistical analysis. Unfortunately, this is not always the case in the modern world. Database experts know how to handle large amounts of data that do not fit in memory, for example, finding association rules in a fact table containing millions of sales transactions. As a matter of fact, the most efficient association algorithms come from the database research community. There are also a few scalable versions of classification and clustering algorithms that use database techniques, including the Microsoft Clustering algorithm.

Data Flow

Data mining is one key member in the data warehouse family. Where does data mining fit in terms of the overall flow of data in a typical business scenario? Figure 1.7 illustrates a typical enterprise data flow to which data mining can be applied in various stages.

A business application stores transaction data in an online transaction processing (OLTP) database. The OLTP data is extracted, transformed and loaded into data warehouse on a regular basis. The schema of the data warehouse is generally different from an OLTP schema. A typical data warehouse schema has the form of a star or snowflake, with fact tables (transaction tables) in the middle of the schema, surrounded by a set of dimension tables. Once the data warehouse is populated, OLAP cubes can be built on the warehouse data.

Where can data mining add value in this typical enterprise data flow? First, and most commonly, data mining can be applied to the data warehouse where data has already been cleaned. The patterns discovered by mining models can be presented to marketing managers through reports. Usually in small enterprises there is no data warehouse. Consequently, people directly mine OLTP tables (usually by making a copy of the related tables on a separate database).

Data mining may have a direct link to business applications, most commonly through predictions. Embedding data mining features within business applications is becoming more and more common. In a Web cross-selling scenario, once a Web customer places a product in the shopping cart, a data mining prediction query is executed to get a list of recommended products based on association analysis.

Data mining can also be applied to analyze OLAP cubes. A cube is a multi-dimensional database with many dimensions and measures. Large dimensions may have millions of members. The total number of cells in a cube is exponential to the number of dimensions and members in a dimension. It becomes difficult to find interesting patterns manually. Data mining techniques can be applied to discover hidden patterns in a cube. For example, an association algorithm can be applied to a sales cube, analyzing customer purchase patterns for a specific region and time period. We can apply data mining techniques to forecast the measures such as store sales and profit. Another example is clustering. Data mining can group customers based on dimension properties and measures. Data mining can not only find patterns in a cube but also reorganize cube design. For instance, we can create a new customer dimension based on the results of the clustering model, grouping customers of the same cluster together in the new dimension.

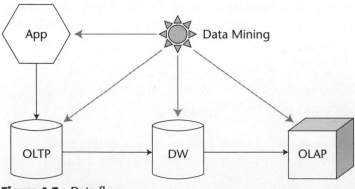

Figure 1.7   Data flow

Data Mining Project Cycle

What is the life cycle of a data mining project? What are the challenging steps? Who should be involved in a data mining project? To answer these questions, let's go over a typical data mining project step by step.

Step 1: Data Collection

The first step of data mining is usually data collection. Business data is stored in many systems across an enterprise. For example, there are hundreds of OLTP databases and over 70 data warehouses inside Microsoft. The first step is to pull the relevant data to a database or a data mart where the data analysis is applied. For instance, if you want to analyze the Web click stream and your company has a dozen Web servers, the first step is to download the Web log data from each Web server.

Sometimes you might be lucky. The data warehouse on the subject of your analysis already exists. However, the data in the data warehouse may not be rich enough. You may still need to gather data from other sources. Suppose that there is a click stream data warehouse containing all the Web clicks on the Web site of your company. You have basic information about customers' navigation patterns. However, because there is not much demographic information about your Web visitors, you may need to purchase or gather some demographic data from other sources in order to build a more accurate model.

After the data is collected, you can sample the data to reduce the volume of the training dataset. In many cases, the patterns contained in 50,000 customers are the same as in 1 million customers.

Step 2: Data Cleaning and Transformation

Data cleaning and transformation is the most resource-intensive step in a data mining project. The purpose of data cleaning is to remove noise and irrelevant information out of the dataset. The purpose of data transformation is to modify the source data into different formats in terms of data types and values. There are various techniques you can apply to data cleaning and transformation, including:

Data type transform: This is the simplest data transform. An example is transforming a Boolean column type to integer. The reason for this transform is that some data mining algorithms perform better on integer data, while others prefer Boolean data.

Continuous column transform: For continuous data such as that in Income and Age columns, a typical transform is to bin the data into buckets. For example, you may want to bin Age into five predefined age groups. Apart from binning, techniques such as normalization are popular for transforming continuous data. Normalization maps all numerical values to a number between 0 and 1 (or –1 to 1) to ensure that large numbers do not dominate smaller numbers during the analysis.

Grouping: Sometimes there are too many distinct values (states) for a discrete column. You need to group these values into a few groups to reduce the model's complexity. For example, the column Profession may have tens of different values such as Software Engineer, Telecom Engineer, Mechanical Engineer, Consultant, and so on. You can group various engineering professions by using a single value: Engineer. Grouping also makes the model easier to interpret.

Aggregation: Aggregation is yet another important transform. Suppose that there is a table containing the telephone call detail records (CDR) for each customer, and your goal is to segment customers based on their monthly phone usage. Since the CDR information is too detailed for the model, you need to aggregate all the calls into a few derived attributes such as total number of calls and the average call duration. These derived attributes can later be used in the model.

Missing value handling: Most datasets contain missing values. There are a number of causes for missing data. For instance, you may have two customer tables coming from two OLTP databases. Merging these tables can result in missing values, since table definitions are not exactly the same. In another example, your customer demographic table may have a column for age. But customers don't always like to give you this information during the registration. You may have a table of daily closing values for the stock MSFT. Because the stock market closes on weekends, there will be null values for those dates in the table. Addressing missing values is an important issue. There are a few ways to deal with this problem. You may replace the missing values with the most popular value (constant). If you don't know a customer's age, you can replace it with the average age of all the customers. When a record has too many missing values, you may simply remove it. For more advanced cases, you can build a mining model using those complete cases, and then apply the model to predict the most likely value for each missing case.

Removing outliers: Outliers are abnormal cases in a dataset. Abnormal cases affect the quality of a model. For example, suppose that you want to build a customer segmentation model based on customer telephone usage (average duration, total number of calls, monthly invoice, international calls, and so on) There are a few customers (0.5%) who behave very differently. Some of these customers live aboard and use roaming all the time. If you include those abnormal cases in the model, you may end up by creating a model with majority of customers in one segment and a few other very small segments containing only these outliers. The best way to deal with outliers is to simply remove them before the analysis. You can remove outliers based on an individual attribute; for instance, removing 0.5% customers with highest or lowest income. You may remove outliers based on a set of attributes. In this case, you can use a clustering algorithm. Many clustering algorithms, including Microsoft Clustering, group outliers into a few particular clusters.

There are many other data-cleaning and transformation techniques, and there are many tools available in the market. SQL Server Integration Services (SSIS) provides a set of transforms covering most of the tasks listed here.

Step 3: Model Building

Once the data is cleaned and the variables are transformed, we can start to build models. Before building any model, we need to understand the goal of the data mining project and the type of the data mining task. Is this project a classification task, an association task or a segmentation task? In this stage, we need to team up with business analysts with domain knowledge. For example, if we mine telecom data, we should team up with marketing people who understand the telecom business.

Model building is the core of data mining, though it is not as time- and resource-intensive as data transformation. Once you understand the type of data mining task, it is relatively easy to pick the right algorithms. For each data mining task, there are a few suitable algorithms. In many cases, you won't know which algorithm is the best fit for the data before model training. The accuracy of the algorithm depends on the nature of the data such as the number of states of the predictable attribute, the value distribution of each attribute, the relationships among attributes, and so on. For example, if the relationship among all input attributes and predictable attributes were linear, the decision tree algorithm would be a very good choice. If the relationships among attributes are more complicated, then the neural network algorithm should be considered.

The correct approach is to build multiple models using different algorithms and then compare the accuracy of these models using some tool, such as a lift chart, which is described in the next step. Even for the same algorithm, you may need to build multiple models using different parameter settings in order to fine-tune the model's accuracy.

Step 4: Model Assessment

In the model-building stage, we build a set of models using different algorithms and parameter settings. So what is the best model in terms of accuracy? How do you evaluate these models? There are a few popular tools to evaluate the quality of a model. The most well-known one is the lift chart. It uses a trained model to predict the values of the testing dataset. Based on the predicted value and probability, it graphically displays the model in a chart. We will give a better description of lift charts in Chapter 3.

In the model assessment stage, not only do you use tools to evaluate the model accuracy but you also need to discuss the meaning of discovered patterns with business analysts. For example, if you build an association model on a dataset, you may find rules such as *Relationship = Husband => Gender = Male with 100% confidence*. Although the rule is valid, it doesn't contain any business value. It is very important to work with business analysts who have the proper domain knowledge in order to validate the discoveries.

Sometimes the model doesn't contain useful patterns. This may occur for a couple of reasons. One is that the data is completely random. While it is possible to have random data, in most cases, real datasets do contain rich information. The second reason, which is more likely, is that the set of variables in the model is not the best one to use. You may need to repeat the data-cleaning and transformation step in order to derive more meaningful variables. Data mining is a cyclic process; it usually takes a few iterations to find the right model.

Step 5: Reporting

Reporting is an important delivery channel for data mining findings. In many organizations, the goal of data miners is to deliver reports to the marketing executives. Most data mining tools have reporting features that allow users to generate predefined reports from mining models with textual or graphic outputs. There are two types of reports: reports about the findings (patterns) and reports about the prediction or forecast.

Step 6: Prediction (Scoring)

In many data mining projects, finding patterns is just half of the work; the final goal is to use these models for prediction. Prediction is also called scoring in data mining terminology. To give predictions, we need to have a trained model and a set of new cases. Consider a banking scenario in which you have built a model about loan risk evaluation. Every day there are thousands of new loan applications. You can use the risk evaluation model to predict the potential risk for each of these loan applications.

Step 7: Application Integration

Embedding data mining into business applications is about applying intelligence back to business, that is, closing the analysis loop. According to Gartner Research, in the next few years, more and more business applications will embed a data mining component as a value-added. For example, CRM applications may have data mining features that group customers into segments. ERP applications may have data mining features to forecast production. An online bookstore can give customers real-time recommendations on books. Integrating data mining features, especially a real-time prediction component into applications is one of the important steps of data mining projects. This is the key step for bringing data mining into mass usage.

Step 8: Model Management

It is challenging to maintain the status of mining models. Each mining model has a life cycle. In some businesses, patterns are relatively stable and models don't require frequent retraining. But in many businesses patterns vary frequently. For example, in online bookstores, new books appear every day. This means that new association rules appear every day. The duration of a mining model is limited. A new version of the model must be created frequently. Ultimately, determining the model's accuracy and creating new versions of the model should be accomplished by using automated processes.

Like any data, mining models also have security issues. Mining models contain patterns. Many of these patterns are the summary of sensitive data. We need to maintain the read, write, and prediction rights for different user profiles. Mining models should be treated as first-class citizens in a database, where administrators can assign and revoke user access rights to these models.

Data Mining and the Current Market

In this section, we give an overview of the current data mining market and discuss a few major vendors in this field.

Data Mining Market Size

Giga Research estimates the size of the market for data mining to have passed the billion dollar mark, including software and services (consulting and service bureau). Other research organizations disagree and make more conservative estimations of its market size, from $200 to $700 million. However, one research conclusion is shared by various analysts: the data mining market is the fastest growing business intelligence component (reporting, OLAP, packaged data marts, and so on). Data mining currently represents about 15% of the business intelligence market. It is evolving from transitional horizontal packages toward embedded data mining applications, integrated with CRM, ERP, or other business applications.

Major Vendors and Products

There are hundreds of data mining product and consulting companies. KDNuggets (kdnuggets.com) has an extended list of most of these companies and their products in the data mining field. Here we list a few the major data mining product companies.

SAS: SAS is probably the largest data mining product vendor in terms of the market share. SAS has been in the statistics field for decades. SAS Base contains a very rich set of statistical functions that can be used for all sorts of data analysis. It also has a powerful script language called SAS Script. SAS Enterprise Miner was introduced in 1997. It provides the user with a graphical flow environment for model building, and it has a set of popular data mining algorithms, including decision trees, neural network, regression, association, and so on. It also supports text mining.

SPSS: SPSS is another major statistics company. It has a number of data mining products including SPSS base and Answer Tree (decision trees). SPSS acquired a British company ISL in late 1998 and inherited the Clementine data mining package. Clementine was one of the first companies to introduce the data mining flow concept, allowing users to clean data, transform data, and train models in the same workflow environment. Clementine also has tools to manage data mining project cycle.

IBM: IBM has a data mining product called Intelligent Miner, developed by an IBM German subsidiary. Intelligent Miner contains a set of algorithms and visualization tools. Intelligent Miner exports mining models in Predictive Modeling Markup Language (PMML), which was defined by the Data Mining Group (DMG), an industry organization. PMML documents are Extensible Markup Language (XML) files containing the descriptions of model patterns and statistics of training dataset. These files can be loaded by DB2 database for prediction purpose.

Microsoft Corporation: Microsoft was the first major database vendor to include data mining features in a relational database. SQL Server 2000, released in September 2000, contains two patented data mining algorithms: Microsoft Decision Trees and Microsoft Clustering. Apart from these algorithms, the most important data mining feature is the implementation of OLE DB for Data Mining. OLE DB for Data Mining is an industry standard that defines a SQL-style data mining language and a set of schema rowsets targeted at database developers. This API makes it very easy to embed data mining components, especially prediction features, into user applications. We will detail the OLE DB for Data Mining API in a later chapter.

Oracle: Oracle 9i shipped in 2000, containing a couple of data mining algorithms based on association and Naïve Bayes. Oracle 10g includes many more data mining tools and algorithms. Oracle also incorporated the Java Data Mining API, which is a Java package for data mining tasks.

Angoss: Angoss' KnowledgeSTUDIO is a data mining tool that includes the power to build decision trees, cluster analysis, and several predictive models, allowing users to mine and understand their data from many different perspectives. It includes powerful data visualization tools to support and explain the discoveries. Angoss also has a set of content viewer controls, which work with data mining algorithms in SQL Server 2000. Its algorithms can also be plugged into the SQL Server platform.

KXEN: KXEN is a data mining software provider based in France. It has a number of data mining algorithms, including SVM, regression, time series, segmentation, and so forth. It also provides data mining solutions for OLAP cubes. It developed an Excel add-in that allows users to do data mining in a familiar Excel environment.

Current Issues and Challenges

Although data mining has been talked about more frequently in recent years, it is still a relatively small market. Most data mining users are the data analysts of large businesses in the sector of finance, telecom, and insurance. Data mining is still considered as an optional high-end feature. Because it seems to be too sophisticated for most developers to understand, very few business applications include data mining features.

Data mining is not yet a main stream technology, although it has the potential to bring added value to almost any kind of business application. There are a few challenges to overcome before data mining will become a mass technology:

Proprietary horizontal packages without a standard API: The majority of the data mining products available in the market are horizontal packages. These tools include a few data mining algorithms, a graphic interface for model building, some data extraction and transformation functions, and a reporting tool. Some products also include their own storage engines with special formats. Because there are so many different components, it is hard to find a good product with satisfactory features across all these areas. Most products are strong in data mining algorithms, but relatively weak in other components. Probably the biggest issue is that these products are proprietary systems. There is no dominant standard API. Thus, it is hard for developers to integrate the results of data mining with standard reporting tools or use model prediction functions in applications.

Analyst-oriented instead of developer-oriented: Most data mining products are oriented toward data analysts, most likely statisticians. Many data mining products originate from statistical packages with hundreds of statistical functions, requiring users to have strong mathematical backgrounds. To make data mining a main stream technology, we need to help millions of application developers who know more about database technologies and less about math to apply data mining techniques in an easy way.

Limited user education: Data analysis is becoming more and more important. However, most developers are not familiar with data analysis techniques. Accordingly we need to improve user education in this area.

Limited algorithm features: Most data mining algorithms are quite general. It is easy to generate hundreds of rules using these algorithms; however, most of these rules may be just common sense. Integrating subjects of interest and domain knowledge with the algorithm is still an open issue. Some new areas such as DNA sequence analysis require more advanced techniques than just horizontal data mining packages. There is still a lot of research to do on data mining algorithms.

Data Mining Standards

Data mining is a relatively new field. You can compare today's data mining market with the database market about 20 years ago, when there was no relational concept or SQL. Each vendor had its own propriety storage format, and there was no easy way to query different data sources. During the past few years, data mining vendors have begun to recognize similar issues in the data mining field and have made some effort to standardize the data mining metadata, APIs and content formats. These efforts are mostly led by industrial bodies or independent data mining software vendors. In this section, we will give you a high-level overview of these data mining standards.

OLE DB for DM and XML for Analysis

Data Mining (OLE DB for DM) was initialized by Microsoft in 1999 and supported by a number of data mining vendors including Angoss, KXEN, and Megaputer. OLE DB for Data Mining doesn't define any new COM or OLE DB interfaces. Instead, it defines powerful data mining languages for model creation, training, and prediction. It also defines a set of schema rowsets, which store the metadata for mining models and mining algorithms. The key philosophy of OLE DB for Data Mining is to map relational concepts to data mining by leveraging SQL and OLE DB. In the specification, a mining model is considered to be a first-class object, just like a relational table. All the operations on mining models are relational. Prediction is a special joint query between a mining model and a relational table. Developers can connect to the data mining algorithms provider through ADO, in the same way that they connect to a database server. Through the Command object, a prediction query can be defined and executed. The query results are presented in the form of a record set. It is very natural for database developers to learn the concept of OLE DB for DM.

XML for Analysis is another industrial standard initialized by Microsoft in 2001 and owned by XML/A Council. The council is co-chaired by Microsoft and two other major BI vendors: Hyperion and SAS. A dozen of BI vendors are the members of the council. The XML/A Council is in charge of the definition of XML for Analysis Specification. This standard leverages technologies from OLE DB for OLAP and OLE DB for Data Mining, supporting the OLAP Query Language (MDX) and the data mining query language Data Mining eXtensions (DMX). It allows consumer applications to query OLAP and data mining servers through the XML Simple Object Access Protocol (SOAP) across different platforms. We will explain the details of OLE DB for DM and XML for Analysis in later chapters.

SQL/Multimedia for Data Mining

ISO SQL/Multimedia (SQL MM) is structured as multipart SQL extensions covering framework, full text, spatial data, images and data mining. The data mining section was proposed by IBM. The key concept is to define a set of user-defined types and methods in a database for the purpose of data mining. These types and methods can then be used in database queries.

Figure 1.8 shows an overview of user-defined types for model training, test and application. The user-defined type DM_MiningData is an abstraction of source data contained in tables or views. It also stores the metadata needed to access the data source. The DM_MiningSchema type defines the input fields used by data mining training, test, or application runs. The data mining field type defines how a field should be handled by the data mining techniques. For instance, a field can be declared as categorical. DM_ClasTask is a data mining task type. There are four data mining types supported by SQL/MM for DM, including association, clustering, classification, and regression. There is also a set of methods defined for these tasks for the purpose of model training and parameter setting.

DM_ClasModel is a mining model type that is an abstraction for a classification type of mining model. It provides methods to access the model properties as well as methods to apply (predict) or to test the model. DM_ClasTestResult is a data mining test result type. It is used to hold the result information of a test run computed for a data mining model. Finally, the DM_ApplicationData type is defined as a container for data used to apply a mining model. Basically, it is an abstraction for a set of values with associated names representing a single row of input data. The result of model application is stored in the result type such as DM_ClasResult.

The following is an example of creating a classification mining model based on these user-defined types:

```
With MyData As (
    DM_MiningData::DM_defMiningData('CT')
)
Insert into MT (ID, TASK)
Values (
1, DM_ClasTask::DM_defClasTask) (
    MyData, NULL,
    (
      (new DM_ClasSettings())
      .DM_clasUseSchema(MyData.DM_genMiningSchema())
    ).DM_clasSetTarget('r')
)
)
```

The preceding statement does the following tasks:

1. Creates a DM_MiningData value using the DM_defMiningData method

2. Creates a DM_MiningSchema value using the DM_genMiningSchema of the DM_MiningData type

3. Creates a DM_ClasSettings value using the default constructor and assign the DM_MiningSchema value as the schema to use

4. Declares column named "r" as a predictable field

5. Creates a DM_ClasTask value using the DM_defClasTask method

6. Stores the newly created DM_ClasTask value in table MT

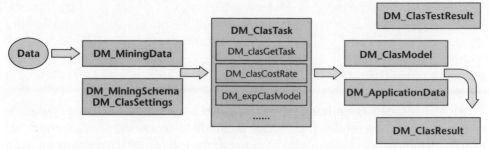

Figure 1.8   Overview of user-defined types for model training, testing, and application

The following statement invokes the training for the classification model using the task value in the MT table. The trained model is stored in the MM table with two columns: ID and Model. It can later be used for the application and test run.

```
Insert Into MM (ID, MODEL)
Values (1, MyTask.DM_buildClasModel())
```

Java Data Mining API

The Java Data Mining API (JSR-73 API) is a Java package for data mining. JSR 73 work is led by Oracle. The goal is to allow Java applications to communicate with data mining engines to build, test, and apply mining models.

JSR-73 separates source data (physical data) and logical data concepts. Source data can be any relational data or text files. There are three key sources: individual record case (single case), single-record case table (simple table) and multirecord case table. A multirecord case table is more like a transaction table, and each case has multiple records. Logical data contains a set of logical attributes. A logical attribute is an abstraction of a physical attribute and contains the definition of content type such as categorical, ordinal, or numerical.

Another important class in JSR 73 is schema, which is a folder for storing named mining objects. Schema is maintained in metadata repository.

JSR 73 defines a set of Java classes for different data mining tasks such as classification and clustering. Each task contains a set of methods for prediction, validation, and other purposes. Users can also specify the type of the mining model settings, such as cost matrix.

The code in Listing 1.1 creates a mining model using JSR:

```
//Get a connection.
javax.datamining.ConnectionSpec spec =
    connectionFactory.createConnectionSpec("myDMS", "me", "myPass");
```

Listing 1.1   Mining model using JSR *(continued)*

```
javax.datamining,Connection dmsCom =
    connectionFactory.getConnection (spec);

//Set schema
dmsCon.setCurrentSchema("mySchema";

//Create and populate PhysicalData object
String uri = new String ("...customer.data");
PhysicalDataSet data = new PhysicalDataSet (uri);
Data.getMetadata();

//Create LogicalData object
LogicalData ld = new LogicalData (data);
//Specify logical attribute
LogicalAttribute income = ld.getAttribute ("income");
Income.setAttributeType(AttributeType.numerical);

//Create FunctionSettings.
FunctionSettings settings = new
    ClassficationSettings(ld, "credit_risk");
Settings.setCostMatrix(costs);

//Create the build task.
buildTask = new BuildTask(data, settings, "myModel");
dmsCon.addObject("myBuildTask", buildTask);
dmsCon.save();

//Execute the task.
ExecutetionHandle handle = dmsCon.execute(task);
Handle.waitForCompletion();

//Access the model.
Model model = (Model)dmsCon;getObject("myModel")
```

Listing 1.1 *(continued)*

Predictive Model Markup Language

Predictive Model Markup Language (PMML) is defined by an industrial organization called Data Mining Group (DMG, dmg.org). DMG includes most of
major data mining product vendors. SAS, SPSS, IBM, Microsoft, Oracle, and a
few others are the members of DMG. The goal of PMML is to define a standard
XML format for persisting mining model content. Without PMML, mining models are application-dependent, system-dependent, and architecture-dependent.
PMML standardizes the model content for common data mining algorithms,
eases the model deployment, and allows models to be exchanged among various software packages.

Because each data mining algorithm has different types of content, the formats of the XML documents needed to persist these contents are different. PMML defines the XML representation for a set of popular data mining algorithm contents, including decision trees, regression, neuron network, clustering, and so on. For example, PMML for the Decision Tree algorithms specifies tags to describe tree topology, node splitting condition, node statistics, and so on.

Apart from its algorithm part, a PMML document also has sections to hold a data dictionary, statistics, transformations, and so on. The following is a list of components in a PMML document:

Data dictionary: The data dictionary contains definitions for fields as used in mining models. It specifies the types and value ranges.

Mining schema: The mining schema is a subset of the fields as defined in the data dictionary. Each model contains one mining schema that lists fields as used in that model.

Transformation dictionary: The transformation dictionary contains descriptions of mining fields derived by using transformations such as aggregation and binning.

Statistics: This section contains the statistics of training dataset.

Taxonomy: Taxonomy is the section for defining attribute hierarchies. For example, the attributes Country, State, and City form a geographic hierarchy.

One or more PMML models: The section describes the content of the mining model. It is algorithm-specific.

PMML supports the content definition for following mining algorithms:

- Polynomial regression
- Logistic regression
- General regression
- Center-based clusters
- Density-based clusters
- Trees
- Associations
- Neural nets
- Naïve Bayes
- Sequences
- Text model
- Vector machine

While OLE DB for DM, SQL MM/DM, and JSR 73 are more or less competing against each other, PMML remains in a neutral position. It is not a programming interface for data mining; instead, it focuses on the model content. All the major data mining vendors support the PMML standard. There are two advantages to PMML. The first one is about model interchange, that is, a model created by using an algorithm of product A can be loaded by product B. The second advantage of PMML is the ease of deployment. It is rather simple to deploy an XML document to different servers and platforms. More information about PMML can be found at dmg.org. Listing 1.2 is the extraction of a PMML document for a decision tree model.

```xml
<?xml version="1.0" ?>
  <PMML version="3.0" >
    <Header copyright="www.dmg.org" description="A very small binary
tree model to show structure."/>
    <DataDictionary numberOfFields="5" >
      <DataField name="temperature" optype="continuous"/>
      <DataField name="humidity" optype="continuous"/>
      <DataField name="windy" optype="categorical" >
        <Value value="true"/>
        <Value value="false"/>
      </DataField>
      <DataField name="outlook" optype="categorical" >
        <Value value="sunny"/>
        <Value value="overcast"/>
        <Value value="rain"/>
      </DataField>
      <DataField name="whatIdo" optype="categorical" >
        <Value value="will play"/>
        <Value value="may play"/>
        <Value value="no play"/>
      </DataField>
    </DataDictionary>
    <TreeModel modelName="golfing" functionName="classification">
      <MiningSchema>
        <MiningField name="temperature"/>
        <MiningField name="humidity"/>
        <MiningField name="windy"/>
        <MiningField name="outlook"/>
        <MiningField name="whatIdo" usageType="predicted"/>
      </MiningSchema>
      <Node score="will play">
        <True/>
        <Node score="will play">
          <SimplePredicate field="outlook" operator="equal"
value="sunny"/>
          <Node score="will play">
            <CompoundPredicate booleanOperator="and" >
```

Listing 1.2   Extraction of a PMML document for a decision tree model

```
                    <SimplePredicate field="temperature" operator="lessThan"
value="90" />
                    <SimplePredicate field="temperature"
operator="greaterThan" value="50" />
                </CompoundPredicate>
                <Node score="will play" >
                    <SimplePredicate field="humidity" operator="lessThan"
value="80" />
                </Node>
                <Node score="no play" >
                    <SimplePredicate field="humidity"
operator="greaterOrEqual" value="80" />
                </Node>
            </Node>
          </Node>
          <Node score="no play" >
            <CompoundPredicate booleanOperator="or" >
                <SimplePredicate field="temperature"
operator="greaterOrEqual" value="90"/>
                <SimplePredicate field="temperature"
operator="lessOrEqual" value="50" />
            </CompoundPredicate>
          </Node>
        </Node>
        <Node score="may play" >
          <CompoundPredicate booleanOperator="or" >
            <SimplePredicate field="outlook" operator="equal"
value="overcast" />
            <SimplePredicate field="outlook" operator="equal"
value="rain" />
          </CompoundPredicate>
          <Node score="may play" >
            <CompoundPredicate booleanOperator="and" >
                <SimplePredicate field="temperature"
operator="greaterThan" value="60" />
                <SimplePredicate field="temperature" operator="lessThan"
value="100" />
                <SimplePredicate field="outlook" operator="equal"
value="overcast" />
                <SimplePredicate field="humidity" operator="lessThan"
value="70" />
                <SimplePredicate field="windy" operator="equal"
value="false" />
            </CompoundPredicate>
          </Node>
          <Node score="no play" >
            <CompoundPredicate booleanOperator="and" >
                <SimplePredicate field="outlook" operator="equal"
value="rain" />
```

Listing 1.2 *(continued)*

```
            <SimplePredicate field="humidity" operator="lessThan"
  value="70" />
            </CompoundPredicate>
          </Node>
        </Node>
      </Node>
    </TreeModel>
  </PMML>
```

Listing 1.2 *(continued)*

Crisp-DM

The Crisp-DM data mining methodology was initialized by three companies: SPSS (ISL by then), NCR, and DaimlerChrysler in 1996. It was later sponsored by the European Community research fund. By August 2000, version 1.0 of Crisp-DM was published.

Crisp-DM does not describe a particular data mining technique; rather it focuses on the process of a data mining project's life cycle.

The Crisp-DM methodology can be described in terms of a hierarchical process model, consisting of sets of tasks described at four levels of abstraction: phase, generic task, specialized task, and process instance.

Phase: The topic level of the process is called phase. For example, business understanding is the first phase of the data mining process.

Generic task: Generic task is the general description of tasks under each phase. This level is still quite abstract, for example, data cleaning is a generic task.

Specialized task: Specialized task describes how generic tasks can be carried out in certain specific situation. For example, the data cleansing task has special tasks such as cleaning numeric values and cleaning categorical values.

Process instances: Process instances is the lowest level of task, and contains records of actions, decisions, and the results of an actual data mining engagement. Figure 1.9 displays the life cycle of major phases of a data mining project. The project consists of six phases. The sequence of the phases is not always ordered. Moving back and forth between different phases is often required in a data mining project.

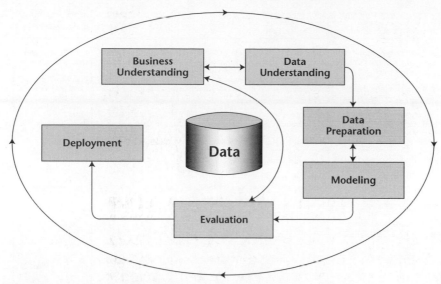

Figure 1.9 Phases of CRISP-DM reference model

Figure 1.10 describes an outline of the phases accompanied by generic tasks (bold) and outputs (italic). These tasks are quite straightforward. For example, the first phase is Business Understanding. In this phase of the project, there are four generic tasks: determine business objectives, assess situation, determine data mining goals, and produce the project plan.

In the determine business objectives task, there are three outputs: background, business objectives, and business success criteria. Crisp-DM further defines the detail for each output.

Common Warehouse Metadata

CWM stands for Common Warehouse Metadata (CWM) and it is led by the OMG CWM Working Group (IBM, Unisys, NCR, and a few other vendors). It addresses the metadata definition issue for the business intelligence field, including OALP, data mining, transformation, and so on. The goal of CWM is to solve the metadata management and integration problem for data warehouses, thus allowing different applications to be easily integrated in a heterogeneous environment.

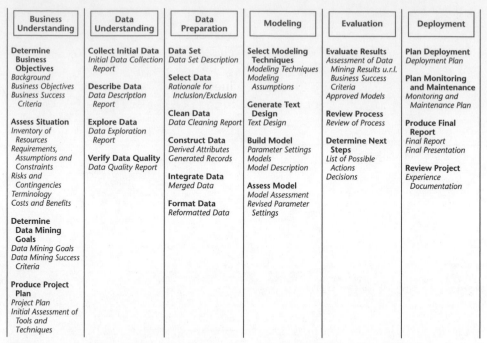

Figure 1.10 Generic tasks and outputs of the CRISP-DM reference model

CWM is a complete specification of the syntax and semantics needed to export/import data warehouse metadata and meta models. It mainly includes:

- CWM Meta model (defined in UML)
- Interchange format for shared warehouse metadata (CWM DTD)
- Interchange format for the CWM Meta model (CWM XML)
- Access API for shared warehouse metadata (CWM IDL)

In the CWM specification, there is a data mining package that defines meta models for data mining.

Figure 1.11 presents the meta model related to the Model conceptual area. It consists of a representation of the `MiningModel`; the `MiningSettings`, which drive the construction of the model; the `ApplicationInput Specification`, which specifies the set of input attributes for the model; and the `MiningModelResult`, which represents the result set produced by the testing or application of a generated model.

Apart from the Model conceptual area, there are other two conceptual areas: Settings and Attributes. The Settings conceptual area mainly focuses on the data mining algorithm parameter settings. There are four subclasses of mining settings: StatisticsSettings, ClusteringSettings, Supervised MiningSettings, and AssociationrulesSettings. The Supervised MiningSettings subclass has two subclasses: ClassificationSettings and RegressionSettings.

The Attributes conceptual area defines two subclasses of the Mining attribute: NumericAttribute and CategoricalAttribute.

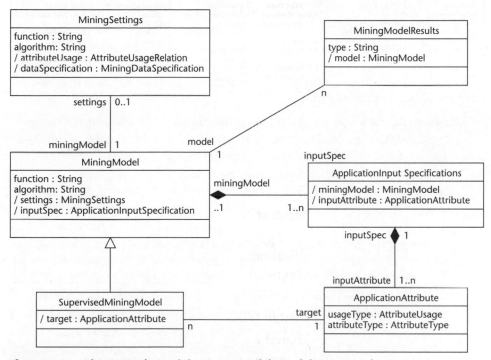

Figure 1.11 The CWM data mining meta model: Model conceptual area

New Trends in Data Mining

Data mining is relatively young compared to database technology. It is still considered a niche and emerging market. One of the reasons for this designation is that most of the data mining packages are targeted toward statisticians or data miners. Application developers find it too challenging to master these technologies. More recently a number of data mining vendors, including Microsoft, realized this and initialized data mining APIs that are directed toward the developer communities. We believe that in the next few years there will be more and more developers who will be able to build mining models, and as a consequence a large number of applications will include data mining features.

We foresee the following trends in data mining area over the next few years:

Embedded data mining: More and more business applications will include data mining features, in particular the prediction feature, for added value. For example, the CRM application will allow users to forecast product sales. Online retailers will recommend products to customers for cross-selling purposes. This will be due largely to the fact that industrial data mining APIs, such as OLE DB for Data Mining, enable database and application developers to use data mining features and embed them in a line of business applications. Embedded data mining will increase the overall size of data mining market.

Data mining packages for vertical applications: Data mining is becoming popular as major database vendors add it to their database management system (DBMS) packages. Data mining can be applied to almost every sector. Today, major data mining markets exist in finance, insurance, and telecom. There is a growing need for specialized data mining techniques to solve business problems in many vertical sectors. For example, in the health care field, we need special data mining techniques to analyze DNA sequences. In network security applications, we need real time training algorithms to detect network intrusion. We need nontraditional data mining techniques to analyze the unstructured data in the World Wide Web. Text mining is yet another vertical sector to which we need to apply data mining. Traditional horizontal data mining packages are too general to solve these problems. We foresee there will be more new data mining packages specialized for these vertical sectors.

Products consolidation: Hundreds of software vendors are providing horizontal data mining packages. Many packages include only one or two algorithms. The data mining market is still very fragmented. Just as with other software sectors, consolidation is inevitable. Small vendors will find more competitive pressure in the horizontal market, especially when major database vendors add data mining features to DBMSs.

PMML: Although big vendors, such as Microsoft, Oracle, IBM, and SAS, are competing on various data mining APIs, they are all member of the same club: the DMG (Data Mining Group). They all support PMML as the model persistence format. PMML offers many advantages in terms of model exchange and model deployment. Because it is an XML document, it is also editable by advanced users. PMML will become more popular in the near future.

Summary

In this chapter, we have given you an extended introduction to data mining. By now, you should know the basics of data mining. There's nothing magic about it; it is about discovering hidden patterns from historical datasets and applying these patterns for predictions. There are a handful of data mining tasks, including classification, regression, association, clustering, forecasting, fraud detection, and visualization. These tasks cover hundreds of business scenarios. You learned the basic concepts of the set of data mining techniques and the typical life cycle of a data mining project.

The chapter also told you about the current data mining market and major product vendors. You learned about new standards in this field and the trends for data mining over the next few years.

OLE DB for Data Mining

In this chapter, you take a closer look at the OLE DB for Data Mining specification, an industry standard initialized by Microsoft and supported by a number of data mining vendors. OLE DB for Data Mining was introduced in July 2000. It is derived from two key database technologies: OLE DB and SQL. You will find that this standard adopts many relational database concepts and applies them to the data mining field. The core part of the standard defines Data Mining eXtensions (DMX), a SQL-style query language for data mining. The specification also includes a list of predefined prediction functions and a set of schema rowsets. The schema rowsets allow your applications to discover mining models and mining services dynamically. After reading this chapter, you should be able to write data mining queries.

This chapter is organized as the follows. We will first give a little background information of OLE DB and OLE DB for Data Mining API. We will then explain a set of key concepts for data mining. The main part of this chapter teaches you the syntax of the data mining query language. The last part of the chapter explains the new extensions on DMX, including the concept of mining structure.

In this chapter, you will be introduced to:

- OLE DB

- The key concepts in OLE DB for Data Mining.

- DMX queries including model creation, training, and prediction.

Introducing OLE DB

Object Linking and Embedding (OLE) DB is based on the Microsoft Component Object Model (COM) infrastructure. It was introduced in the mid-1990s. The main purpose of OLE DB is to provide a standard way to access tabular data. Before OLE DB, the most popular way to access a relational database was through Open Database Connectivity (ODBC), an API-based on SQL C Level Interface standard. ODBC provides an easy way to query different types of relational databases.

However, most data is not stored in relational databases. Just think about the types of data you use on a regular basis. The data is found in text files, emails, Excel spreadsheets, Word documents, and so on. You want to access all of this data in a way similar to the way you access relational data, ideally through the same API. OLE DB was introduced for this purpose. It includes the SQL functionality as well as interfaces suitable for gaining access to other data sources. OLE DB identifies common characteristics among different data providers and services, and defines common interfaces to expose those characteristics. For example, OLE DB defines the standard IRowset interface, which provides a way to navigate through tabular data. The tabular data can be obtained by querying underlying source data through the appropriate OLE DB driver.

Figure 2.1 shows an overview of the architecture of OLE DB. OLE DB providers implement a set of predefined interfaces on top of native data storage software such as DBMSs, ISAM, text file, mail data, or Excel. Consumer applications can access these data sources in a same way, directly through OLE DB or indirectly through Active Data Objects (ADO). ADO is a high-level interface on top of OLE DB that most applications developers use. Since the release of the Microsoft .Net framework, ADO has been replaced by ADO.Net in the managed code world. ADO.Net includes an OLE DB.Net–managed provider, which communicates with the unmanaged OLE DB provider to access source data just as ADO does.

OLE DB defines a set of interfaces. These interfaces are implemented by objects. Figure 2.2 shows the four core objects in OLE DB: the Data Source object, the Session object, the Command object and the Rowset object.

- The Data Source object is a COM object through which the consumer connects to a provider's underlying data store. Each OLE DB provider implements its own data source object class. To connect to an OLE DB provider, the consumer application needs to instantiate this class first. The Data Source object implements the IDBCreateSession interface. It can also support interfaces for describing metadata information.

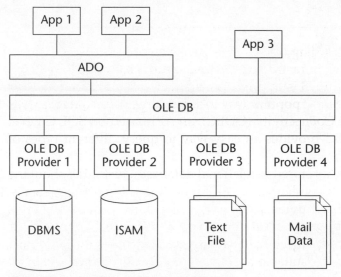

Figure 2.1   OLE DB architecture overview

- The Session object provides a context for a transaction. Using the `IDBCreateSession` interface, a data source object may create a number of sessions. The Session object implements the `IDBCreate Command` interface.

- If a provider supports executing queries, it implements a Command object. The Command object can be obtained from the `IDBCreate Session` interface of a Session object. A Command object is a container for a text command. A text command usually contains a `Select` statement. After executing the command, it returns a rowset containing the query result. The Command object implements the `ICommand` interface to formulate, prepare, and execute queries.

- The Rowset object is the central object that enables all OLE DB data providers to expose data in a tabular form. Conceptually, a rowset is a set of rows in which each row has columns of data. Users can navigate the rowset to get different rows of data. Query results are returned to the user application in the form of rowsets.

In the Analysis Services of SQL Server 2000, there are two OLE DB providers, one for the OLAP server and the other for the Data Mining server. User applications can access data mining and OLAP storage using ADO/ADO.Net or OLE DB directly, in the same way that they access relational data. These two providers wrap the result of OLAP and data mining queries into a tabular format. In SQL Server 2005, these two providers are unified with the OLE DB Provider for Microsoft Analysis Service version 9.0.

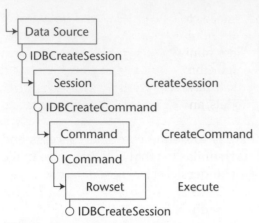

Figure 2.2   OLE DB core objects

Why OLE DB for Data Mining?

Although some of the data mining technologies have existed since the 1960s, the term *data mining* is relatively new. Before the OLE DB for Data Mining (OLE DB for DM) API was introduced in July 2000, the data mining market was very fragmented. You can compare it with the database market in the 1970s, before relational concepts existed. There were no standard concepts for mining models, model training, and making predictions. For many people, data mining was just a set of algorithms, just as in the old days people thought databases were no more than hierarchical data structures for storing data. Data mining was a high-end tool available to only those Ph.D.s in statistics or machine learning, not for database developers.

There have been many data mining products on the market since late 1990s. Each of these independent data mining software vendors (ISVs) has its own proprietary way of building data mining applications. Most data mining packages on the market include their own algorithms, their own storage formats for model patterns, their own data-cleansing tools, and even their own reporting tools. Data mining has been an isolated software package, not part of the data warehouse.

Besides lacking standard concepts for data mining, there has been no standard programming API. It has been very difficult to integrate the result of data mining with user applications to close the analysis loop. Most data mining products don't have APIs. It is very painful to integrate data mining features with many business applications. Some data mining products generate source code for decision trees or neural networks. The generated code includes trained parameters of models, for example, the coefficients for neural networks. To deploy a mining model, this source code needs to be compiled and linked with user applications. As a consequence, data mining projects are totally vendor locked. If you choose product A for a data mining project, and later you find that product B has a better time series algorithm, you have to start the project from the beginning, since different products have different tools for transforming data, different formats for storing models, and different APIs for integrating them with user applications.

The goal of OLE DB for Data Mining is to define common concepts and common APIs for the data mining world, similar to what SQL has done in the database world. The API should be easily understood by most database developers, not only by those with a Ph.D. in statistics. In July 1999, OLE DB for Data Mining was launched by Microsoft with many data mining ISVs. One year later, OLE DB for Data Mining API Version 1.0 was finalized and published on Microsoft Web site. The OLE DB for Data Mining API defines common data mining concepts such as mining models, model training, model content, model prediction, and so on. OLE DB for Data Mining also defines a query language for data mining. The syntax of this query language is similar to SQL. Since the standard was published, a number of data mining vendors, including Microsoft, Megaputer, Angoss, KXEN, and DBMiner, have developed their own OLE DB for Data Mining providers.

User applications can connect to different data mining providers through OLE DB or ADO connections, as illustrated in Figure 2.3. Each OLE DB for DM provider has a set of data mining algorithms. These algorithms can access any tabular source data through OLE DB. Source data can be stored in various formats, such as relational databases, OLAP cubes, text files, and email documents.

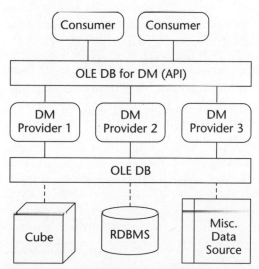

Figure 2.3 OLE DB DM architecture overview

ADDING ALGORITHMS TO SQL SERVER ANALYSIS SERVICE

In SQL Server 2000 Service Pack 1, a new component called Provider Aggregator was added to Analysis Services. This component aggregates other providers to provide a unified set of schema rowsets for metadata. Consumer applications can connect to the MSOLAP provider and query the set of unified schema rowsets to discover the combined set of algorithms that Microsoft and other companies provided. MSOLAP dispatches DMX queries to different providers based on the model algorithm.

In SQL Server 2005, Microsoft provides a lower-level interface than OLE DB for Data Mining Provider Aggregator. This lower-level interface is called the Algorithm Plug-In Framework. With this API, algorithm developers no longer need to implement the DMX parsers and schema rowsets. The Microsoft data mining provider parses the query, provides tokenized data to the third-party algorithms, and calls the third-party algorithms' training or prediction functions. This largely simplifies the development effort for adding algorithms to SQL Server Analysis Services.

Exploring the Basic Concepts in OLE DB for Data Mining

OLE DB for Data Mining defines the common concepts for a number of data mining objects. We will explain these concepts in this section.

Case

Data mining is about analyzing cases — a *case* is the basic entity of information. It contains a set of *attributes*, such as Gender and Age. Attributes are also called *variables* in statistical terms. An attribute can have a set of possible values, called its *state*. For example, the attribute Gender has two states: Male and Female.

A case can be simple. For example, when you use customer demographic information to analyze customer loan risk, each case is a customer. It also corresponds to a row in the customer table.

Or a case can be more complicated. For example, when you analyze customer purchasing behavior based on the customers' demographic data as well as purchase history, each case is a customer together with the list of products the customer has purchased. This type of case is *a nested case*. A nested case contains at least one table column. Figure 2.4 shows a few nested cases of customer with their purchase histories.

In OLE DB for Data Mining, a data mining algorithm provider *consumes* cases. If a case is a nested case, data mining algorithms require the case to be input with hierarchical rowset format.

Cust ID	Gender	Income	Marital Status	Purchases	
				Product	Quantity
1	Male	23000	Single	Milk	1
				Cheese	1
				Beer	2
2	Female	79200	Married	Milk	8
				Pepsi	6
				Cake	1
3	Male	42000	Married	Cheese	2
				Juice	2

Figure 2.4 Three nested customer cases

NOTE The concept of nested cases proposed in OLE DB for Data Mining is extremely important . It helps you model complicated cases with one-to-many relationships. It adds lots of expressive power for model building. Without the nested case concept, you would need to pivot the nested table to case level attributes during the data transformation stage. This could be a very challenging task. Because most relational databases have limitations on the total number of columns in a table, if you have lots of different products in the case, as displayed in Figure 2.4, you may not be able to pivot the entire purchase table.

The Case Key

The case key is the attribute that uniquely identifies each case. A case key is often the primary key of a relational table. Sometimes a case may have composite case key. For example, FirstName and LastName can both be indicated as the case key.

The Nested Key

Although the case key can be considered as the primary key in the relational terminology, the nested key is very different from the foreign key. The case key is just an identifier and doesn't contain any patterns (often ignored by data mining algorithm), whereas the nested key is the most important attribute of the nested part of the case. Other attributes in the nested part are used to describe the nested key. For example, if a model is designed to learn patterns about customer purchasing behavior, the nested key is the *product*. *Quantity* describes the product purchase. The nested key is not an identifier; it contains useful information about patterns. For example, we can use the nested key Product as input to predict the case-level attribute Gender.

Case Tables and Nested Tables

A case table is the table containing the case information that's related to the flat part of the case. A nested table is the table that contains information related to the nested part of the case. A nested table is often a transaction table, for example, purchase history, and Web navigation logs. A nested table can be joined with the case table using the case key. To join the case table and nested table to produce hierarchical rowset, OLE DB defines an operator Shape. We will describe the syntax of the Shape operator in the following sections.

> **TIP** For those of you who are familiar with data warehouse and OLAP concepts, a case table is usually a dimension table, whereas a nested table is a fact table.

Scalar Columns and Table Columns

A column in a mining model is similar to a column in a relational table; it's also called a *variable* or *attribute* in statistical terminology. Depending on the usage, a data mining model can have four types of columns: key, input, predictable, or a column that's both input and predictable. The predictable column is the target of the mining model. Most data mining models use the set of input columns to predict an output column. Some algorithms, such as clustering, don't require predictable columns. In this case, the mining model may contain only input columns.

There are two kinds of column structures: *scalar* and *table*. Most columns are scalar columns. Each scalar column of an individual record has a single value. For example, *Gender* and *Age* are scalar columns. A table column is a special column. A table column embeds a table inside the column. For example, *Purchases* is a table column. It stores the purchase information for each customer. It contains a table of two columns: *Product* and *Quantity*. OLE DB has the hierarchical rowset concept. The flat parts of the rowsets are the scalar columns, while the hierarchical parts are table columns.

The Data Mining Model

A data mining model, or mining model, can be thought of as a relational table. It contains key columns, input columns, and predictable columns. Each model is associated with a data mining algorithm on which the model is trained. Training a mining model means finding patterns in the training dataset by using specified data mining algorithms with proper algorithm parameters. After training, the data mining model stores patterns that the data mining algorithm discovered about the dataset.

While a relational table is a container of records, a data mining model is a container of patterns.

Model Creation

The concept of model creation simply deals with creating an empty data mining model, similar to the way we create a new table.

Model Training

Model training is also called model processing. It is used to invoke the data mining algorithm to uncover knowledge about the training dataset. After training, patterns are stored in the mining model.

Model Prediction

The model prediction is used for applying trained mining model patterns to the new dataset and predicting the potential value of predictable columns for each new case.

DMX

The most important contribution of the OLE DB for Data Mining specification is the definition of a data mining query language. This language is called DMX, which stands for Data Mining eXtensions. Without a good query language, it is very challenging to integrate data mining functions such as prediction with user applications. The data mining query language defined in OLE DB for DM adopts mainly relational concepts, and its syntax is based on SQL. As a database developer, you will find that it is fairly easy to learn this query language.

Three Steps of Data Mining

Before showing you the language, we will review the three basic steps of data mining, as illustrated in Figure 2.5.

The first step is to create a mining model. This is similar to creating a table in relational database. A mining model definition includes a number of input columns, predictable columns, and an associated algorithm. A mining model is a container similar to a relational table. It is used to store patterns discovered by data mining algorithms.

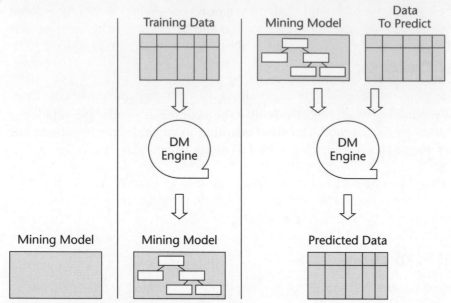

Figure 2.5 The three steps of data mining

The second step of the data mining is model training (also called processing). In this step, we feed historical data to the data mining engine, for example, existing customers' demographics and their credit risk information. In the training step, the data mining algorithm starts to analyze the input data. Depending on the efficiency of an algorithm, it may scan the dataset in one or more iterations to find correlations among attribute values. Training steps are usually time-consuming. But in most cases, mining models are trained in batches weekly or monthly. After training, patterns are stored in the mining model. You can browse the model content using content viewers such as the Decision Tree viewer and Cluster viewer (we will explain these viewers in later algorithm chapters).

The third step of data mining process is prediction. In order to predict, we need a trained mining model and a new dataset. During the prediction, the data mining engine applies rules it found in the training step to the new dataset and assigns the prediction result for each input case. The prediction process is usually quite simple. For most algorithms, prediction is very fast and can be executed in real time. There are two types of prediction queries: batch and singleton. A batch query has multiple input cases, which are stored in a table. A singleton query has only one input case, which is constructed on the fly (the case is not persisted in database).

In this section, we will go over the core part of this language for model creation, training, and prediction. The examples are based on the following schema of a mini-data-mart of a supermarket (see Figure 2.6). There are two tables in the schema: a customer table and a purchase table. The customer table contains customer demographic information and customers' store membership card. The purchase table is the fact table about customer shopping transactions.

Step 1: Model Creation

Because the mining model is considered to be a container similar to a relational table, the statement for model creation is similar to the table creation statement and uses the `Create` command. The following is example of mining model creation:

```
Create mining model MemberCard_Prediction
(
CustomerId long key,
Gender      text    discrete,
Age          long   continuous,
Profession  text    discrete,
Income       long   continuous,
HouseOwner  text    discrete,
MemberCard  text     discrete predict
)
Using Microsoft_Decision_Trees
```

The model here uses `Gender, Age, Profession, HasChildren` and `HouseOwner` to predict the type of membership card that a customer will have. The algorithm applied for the model is Microsoft Decision Trees. The statement is very similar to the table creation statement in SQL. You may have noticed a few differences to SQL. For example, for each column, the statement specifies not only the data type, but also `Continuous` or `Discrete`. These are called content types. Content types tell the algorithm the right way to model the column.

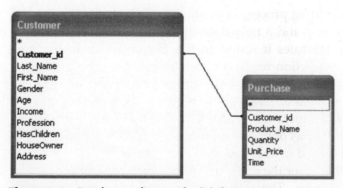

Figure 2.6   Database schema of mini-data-mart

Often, algorithms work better if we can give the distribution information of the column values. For example, if we know that the age of the customers follows a normal distribution, we can specify the Age column as follows:

```
Age        long    normal continuous
```

Usually data mining algorithms have parameters for tuning the model. For example, the Microsoft Decision Trees algorithm has a parameter called `Minimum_Support` that specifies the minimum cases any leaf node must contain. The user can specify algorithm parameters at the end of the creation statement.

```
. . .
Using Microsoft_Decision_Trees(Minimum_Support=50)
```

Some algorithms, such as Microsoft Decision Trees, support multiple predictable columns. For example, a mining model can predict both `MemberCard` and `HouseOwner`. The following model builds two decision trees. One uses `Gender`, `Age`, `Profession`, `HasChildren`, and `HouseOwner` to predict `MemberCard`, the other uses `Gender`, `Age`, `Profession`, `HasChildren`, `MemberCard` to predict `HouseOwner`.

```
Create mining model MemberCard_Prediction
(
CustomerId long key,
Gender      text    discrete,
Age         int     continuous,
Profession  text    discrete,
Income      long    continuous,
HouseOwner  text    discrete predict,
MemberCard  text    discrete predict
}
Using Microsoft_Decision_Trees
```

In the previous model, if you want `MemberCard` to be used only as predictable, not as input to predict `HouseOwner`, you can use the keyword `Predict_Only`.

```
MemberCard   text    discrete predict_only
```

Sometimes there are dependencies among attributes. For example, in the customer table, there are two attributes: `City` and `State`. The `State` attribute depends on the attribute `City` (if `City` is Seattle, `State` must be Washington). This information is very useful. For example, when there are too many cities, some algorithms may decide to group some cities together based their states. In DMX, there is a `Related To` keyword that is used to specify the dependencies among attributes.

METHODS FOR DESCRETIZATION

Microsoft OLE DB for DM provider contains several methods for discretization.

◆ **Clusters:** This finds buckets by performing single-dimensional clustering on the input values using the K-means algorithm. It uses gaussian distributions.

◆ **EqualAreas:** This examines the distribution of values across the population and creates bucket ranges such that that the total population is distributed equally across the buckets. In other words, if the distribution of continuous values were plotted as a curve, the areas under the curve covered by each bucket range would be equal. This is useful when there are a large number of duplicate values.

◆ **Thresholds:** This breaks the input range of continuous values into buckets based on the inflection (turning) points in their distribution curve — these are the points where the gradient changes direction. If the number of points is more than the requested number of buckets, *N*, it sorts by height and selects the first *N*. This can only be used for numeric columns.

◆ **Automatic:** If this is selected, it tries obtaining the requested number of buckets by applying the above discretization methods in the following order: Clusters, EqualAreas and Thresholds. It uses the first method that gets closest to the number of buckets specified.

```
City    text  discrete,
State text   discrete related to City
```

For numeric columns such as Age, sometimes you might want to cut it into *n* buckets. In DMX, there is a function `discretized` *(discretization method, buckets number)* with two parameters. The first one is the method used for discretization. The second parameter is the number of buckets to be grouped by. For example, the following column definition grouped `Age` into five buckets using the `Equal_Areas` method:

```
Income long  discretized (Equal_Areas, 5)
```

You can also specify:

```
Income long  discretized
```

It uses the default discretization method to bin `Income` into five buckets.

As you have learned, nested case is a very important concept in DMX. It adds much express power for building mining models. Predictable attributes can be the case-level attributes as well as nested-level attributes. For example, you can build models that use customer demographic information to predict the list of products in which the customer may be interested. You can also build models that predict a customer's demographic information based on the list of products that he or she buys. Other models can be built to analyze product associations for cross-selling using nested cases. The following are some sample models built with nested cases:

```
Create mining model MemberCard_Prediction
(
CustomerId long key,
Gender      text    discrete,
Income      long    continuous,
MemberCard  text    discrete predict,
Purchase table (
     ProductName text key,
     Quantitylong continuous
)
)
Using Microsoft_Decision_Trees
```

The preceding model uses Gender, Income, and the list of the purchased products and their associated quantities to predict the MemberCard.

```
Create mining model MarketBasketModel
(
CustomerId long key,
Gender      text    discrete,
Income      long    continuous,
MemberCard  text    discrete,
Purchase table Predict_Only (
     ProductName text key,
     Quantitylong continuous
)
)
Using Microsoft_Decision_Trees
```

When a nested table is marked as predict or predict_only, the nested key and its associated nested attributes are all predictable. The previous model uses Gender, Income, and MemberCard to predict the list of products a customer may be interested in and the quantity for each product.

Now, we want to build another model, which not only uses the demographic information to predict a list of potential products a customer may buy, but also uses the list of products a customer has already bought. For example, suppose that there is a strong correlation between cheese and milk for female customers. A female customer that has cheese in her shopping cart is very likely to buy milk. To build such a model, you just need to slightly change the previous mining model by replacing the Predict_Only keyword with Predict for the Purchase table column.

UNDERSTANDING NESTED KEYS

You should have a clear understanding of nested keys before going further. Each nested key is modeled as an attribute. For example, if there are 200 different products in the nested table, it will generate 200 attributes for the mining algorithm. (Each product is a binary attribute.) If the Quantity column is also used as an input, it will generate 200 attributes related to product quantities, including Quantity of Milk, Quantity of Cake, Quantity of Juice, and so forth.

You should limit the number of columns in the nested table. It may generate too many useless attributes for your model. In many cases, you need only one attribute in the nested table, which is the nested key.

Step 2: Model Training

Model training is also called model processing. During the training stage, data mining algorithms consume input cases and analyze correlations among attribute values. After the training, mining models are populated with patterns. Thus the syntax for a mining model training statement is the same as the Insert statement for relational table:

```
Insert into <mining model name>
          [ <mapped model columns>]
  <source data query>
```

In most cases, <Source data query> is a Select query from a relational database. Because most DM providers are embedded within the relational database management system (RDBMS) containing the source data, the <source data query> needs to read data from other data sources. In OLE DB, the OpenRowset statement supports querying data from a data source through an OLE DB provider. The syntax for the OpenRowset statement is the following:

```
OpenRowset('Provider_Name', 'Provider_String', 'DB Query')
```

Provider_Name is an OLE DB provider name, for example, MSSQL for Microsoft SQL Server, Jet for Access. OLE DB drivers are available for almost any data sources (text file, Oracle, DB2, Sybase, and so on)

Provider_String is the connection string for the provider.

DB Query is the SQL query supported by the provider. The query returns a rowset.

The following is a training statement for the MemberCard_Prediction model. The data source is stored in an SQL Server database on myserver machine.

```
Insert into MemberCard_Prediction
( CustomerId, Gender, Age, Profession, Income, HouseOwner, MemberCard)
OpenRowset('sqloledb', 'myserver';'mylogin';'mypwd',
'Select CustomerId, gender, age, profession, income, houseowner,
membercard From customers')
```

The previous model training statement has exactly the same syntax required to insert data into a relational table. The only difference is that the object name is a mining model.

If a mining model contains nested tables, the model training syntax is more complicated in <source data query> part. DMX uses the Data Shaping Service defined in OLE DB to create hierarchical rowsets. Input cases must be shaped to the hierarchical format in order to feed the data mining provider. The Shape command is similar to the join operator, which joins two related rowsets based on the related columns. Shape results in hierarchical rowsets. Each parent row contains some columns that represent child rows. For example, after shaping customer and purchases rowsets using the CustomerId key, the result rowsets has the structure displayed in Figure 2.4. The following is a training statement with a nested table using Shape provider.

```
Insert into MarketBasketModel ( CustomerId, Gender, Income, MemberCard,
Purchases(skip, ProductName, Quantity) )
OPENROWSET('MSDataShape', 'data provider=SQLOLEDB;
Server=myserver;UID=mylogin; PWD=mypwd',
 'Shape
   { Select CustomerId, Gender, Income, MemberCard From Customers }
  Append (
   { Select CustomerId, ProductName, Quantity From Purchases }
  Relate CustomerId to CustomerId ) as Purchases')
```

NOTE You may have noticed that the training statement is independent of the mining model algorithm. It is based purely on the definition of the mining structure.

NOTE As you may have noticed, OpenRowset statement requires user to put login and password in clear text if not using integrated security. This causes security concerns. In SQL Server 2005, the OpenRowset statement is turned off by default. If you want to issue OpenRowset queries for date mining, you need to set the Analysis Services server property AllowAdhocOpenRowsetQueries to be True.

SQL Server 2005 proposes a new statement called OpenQuery, which is similar to OpenRowset. The main difference is instead of specifying login and password in the statement, it uses an existing data source object in the AS database as a parameter. The following is an example of OpenQuery:

```
Insert into MemberCard_Prediction
( CustomerId, Gender, Age, Profession, Income, HouseOwner, MemberCard)
OpenQuery('mydatasource',
'Select CustomerId, gender, age, profession, income, houseowner,
membercard From customers')
```

Step 3: Model Prediction

Prediction discovers information about unknown cases using patterns found from historical data. Prediction is an important step in the data mining process. It is often the final goal of a data mining project. It is also considered to be the method for closing the analysis loop. The training step is time-consuming because it requires multiple passes through the historical dataset to find patterns. Prediction is a simple and efficient task for most data mining algorithms. For example, you can think of prediction for the decision tree algorithm as dropping a case from the tree root node. The case falls to a leaf node, following the splitting condition at each intermediate node. This is a very simple process that requires only a few predicate evaluations and can be done in real time. While mining models are trained once a month, predictions are executed frequently. For example, a Web site personalizes the advertisement banner according to the user's profile. When each user hits the Web site, a prediction query is executed to get the list of targeted advertisements. Another example is an insurance quote, each quote is a prediction. A call center executes tens of thousands of prediction queries each day.

Understanding Prediction Joins

To predict, we need to have two inputs: a trained mining model and a set of new cases. In DMX, a mining model is considered the same as a relational table. Conceptually, a trained mining model can be considered a truth table. A *truth table* is a term in the electronics field. It contains all the combinations of possible input attribute values and the predictable column value associated with a probability. In the MemberCard_Prediction model, a truth table contains all the value combinations of Gender, Income, HouseOwner, Marital Status, and Member Card, with a probability assigned for each row. For example, there is a row in the truth table: Gender (Male), Income (20000), HouseOwner (Yes), Marital Status(Single), MemberCard(Gold) with Probability(10%). If there is a new customer with the exact the same profile, we can predict that the customer has 10% probability of having a gold membership. When there is a continuous attribute, such as Income, the truth table has an infinite number of rows. Of course, a mining model doesn't store the patterns in the format of truth table, though conceptually they are similar.

In Figure 2.7, the table on the right is a truth table. The left table is a new customer table with demographic information. We want to know the most likely type of membership card for each of these new customers. The typical relational method to get the membership card of each new customer is to *join* these two tables together. The join condition is the input column mappings. We adopt the relational join operator for making data mining predictions. However, it is a special kind of join with a mining model and a table; we call it *Prediction Join*.

Query Syntax for Prediction

The query syntax of a prediction join is the same as the syntax of a join query in SQL. There are three parts: the `Select` expression, the `On` condition, and the `Where` clause. The `Select` expression is a set of comma-separated expressions, each of which can be a column from an input table, a predictable column from the mining model, or a prediction function. The select expression can have sub-`select`-clause, which we will explain this later in this section.

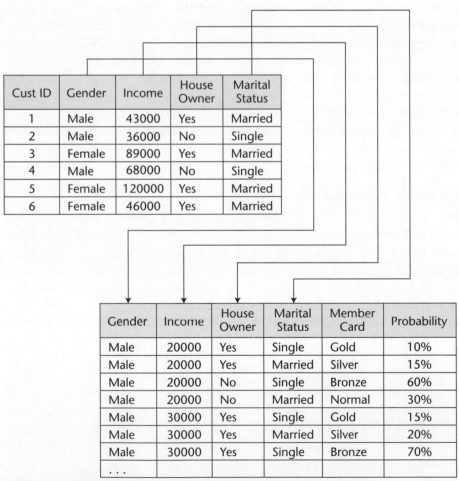

Cust ID	Gender	Income	House Owner	Marital Status
1	Male	43000	Yes	Married
2	Male	36000	No	Single
3	Female	89000	Yes	Married
4	Male	68000	No	Single
5	Female	120000	Yes	Married
6	Female	46000	Yes	Married

Gender	Income	House Owner	Marital Status	Member Card	Probability
Male	20000	Yes	Single	Gold	10%
Male	20000	Yes	Married	Silver	15%
Male	20000	No	Single	Bronze	60%
Male	20000	No	Married	Normal	30%
Male	30000	Yes	Single	Gold	15%
Male	30000	Yes	Married	Silver	20%
Male	30000	Yes	Single	Bronze	70%
. . .					

Figure 2.7   Prediction join between a mining model and a table

The on condition specifies the column mapping between the mining model and input table. For example:

```
Select ...
From ...
On MemberCard_Prediction.age= NewCustomer.age
And MemberCard_Prediction.gender= NewCustomer.gender ...
```

Sometimes new input cases don't have all the attributes that a mining model is trained from. For example, a new customer table contains most demographic information except customer age. In this case, the On clause doesn't specify the mapping of Age column. This is still a valid prediction query. The data mining algorithm provider decides how to execute the prediction without complete input information. Some algorithms may treat missing information as informative, that is, a valid input state; other algorithms may treat missing as noninformative, that is, to be ignored. Of course, the prediction result is less accurate without all the input attributes.

The Where clause is the filter that limits the number of cases returned by the prediction query. Filter conditions can be set on input columns as well as on prediction functions. For example:

```
Where NewCustomer.age > 30
And PredictProbability(MemberCard, 'Gold')>0.75
```

This Where clause limits the query results. It returns only those customers older than 30 and with prediction certainty of gold membership card greater than 0.75. PredictProbability is a prediction function. We will explain these functions later in the section.

A Prediction Query Example

The following is an example of prediction query used to predict the type of customer membership card.

```
Select T.CustomerID, T.LastName, M.MemberCard
From MemberCard_Prediction Prediction Join
OpenRowset('Provider=Microsoft.Jet.OLEDB', 'data
source=c:\customer.mdb', 'select * from customers') as T
On MemberCard_Prediction.Gender= T.Gender
And MemberCard_Prediction.Age = T.Age
And MemberCard_Prediction.Profession = T.Profession
And MemberCard_Prediction.Incom = T.Income
And MemberCard_Prediction.HouseOwner=T.HouseOwner
Where NewCustomer.age > 30
```

If the column names of the input table are the same as the column names in the mining model, we can use a Natural Prediction Join statement without specifying the On clause.

```
Select T.CustomerID, T.LastName, MemberCard_Prediction.MemberCard
From MemberCard_Prediction Natural Prediction Join
OpenRowset('Provider=Microsoft.Jet.OLEDB', 'data
source=c:\customer.mdb', 'select * from customers') as T
```

Prediction Functions

DMX defines a set of prediction functions. Some of these functions return simple scalar values, while others return a table of details, including information such as statistics.

Prediction Functions on Scalar Columns

Scalar predict functions return scalar values. The most important prediction function is `Predict` (`Predict` can also return table values, which we will discuss later). When a scalar column is given to the `Predict` function, the result is a scalar value. For example the following function returns the data shown in Table 2.1:

```
Select T.CustomerID, Predict(MemberCard), PredictProbability(MemberCard)
as Proba
...
```

Directly selecting a predictable column from a mining model is a shortcut for using `Predict` with the predictable column as parameter, that is, `Select MemberCard` is same as `Select Predict(MemberCard)`.

Sometimes we may want to know if the prediction result is in a "Missing" state (Null state). For example, in the mining model there is a rule: for male customers with a low income and who are younger than 25, the membership card information is missing with a probability of 0.60. We may want the prediction result to include the Missing state. To do this, we need to add the `INCLUDE_NULL` option in the prediction function (The default behavior is `EXCLUDE_NULL`, which means the missing state is not represented in the result).

```
Select T.CustomerID, Predict(MemberCard, INCLUDE_NULL),
```

`PredictProbability` returns the probability of the predicted state. Sometimes we want to know the probability of a given state, such as "Gold" member card, instead of the most likely one. We can add the state value as a parameter of the `PredictProbability` function. For example the following function returns the data shown in Table 2.2.

```
Select T.CustomerID, PredictProbability(MemberCard, 'Gold') as
Proba_Gold
```

Table 2.1   Query Result

CUSTOMER ID	MEMBERCARD	PROBA
1	Gold	0.75
2	Silver	0.68
. . .		

Table 2.2   Query Result

CUSTOMER ID	PROBA_GOLD
1	0.75
2	0.25
. . .	

Besides `Predict`, there are many other prediction functions such as `PredictProbability`, `PredictSupport`, `Cluster`, and so on. Table 2.3 provides a short description of scalar prediction functions:

Table 2.3   Prediction Functions on Scalar Columns

FUNCTION	RETURN VALUE	DESCRIPTION
`Predict (<scalar column reference>, options, . . .)`	Scare value	General prediction function to modify the behavior of predictions for scalar values, such as including a missing state. Returns the "best" value, given the options, for the specified scalar column.
`PredictSupport (<scalar column reference>)`	Scalar value	Count of cases in support of the predicted value.
`PredictVariance (<scalar column reference >)`	Scalar value	Variance describing the distribution for which the value of `Predict` is the mean (generally for continuous attributes).
`PredictStdev (<scalar column reference >)`	Scalar value	Square root of `PredictVariance`.
`PredictProbability (<scalar column reference >,<value>)`	Scalar value	Likelihood that `Predict` is the correct value. If value specified, it returns the probability of the given state of value.

(continued)

Table 2.3   *(continued)*

FUNCTION	RETURN VALUE	DESCRIPTION
PredictProbability Variance (`<scalar column reference >, <value>`)	Scalar value	Expresses certainty in the value of PredictVariance.
PredictProbability Stdev (`<scalar column reference >, <value>`)	Scalar value	Square root of **PredictProbabilityVariance**.
PredictTimeSeries (`<column reference>, <n1>,<n2>`)	Table value	Returns the predicted value of the next *n* time slices in a table format.
Cluster()	Scalar value or `<cluster column reference>`	Cluster identifier that the input case belongs to with the highest probability. It also can be used as a `<cluster column reference>` for a **PredictHistogram** function.
ClusterDistance (`[ClusterID_expr]`)	Scalar value	Distance from the center of the cluster that is identified by `ClusterID_expr` or the highest probability cluster.
ClusterProbability (`[ClusterID_expr]`)	Scalar value	Probability that the input case belongs to the cluster that is identified by `ClusterID_expr` or the highest probability cluster.
RangeMid (`<scalar column reference>`)	Scalar value	Gives the midpoint of the predicted bucket for a discretized column.
RangeMin (`<scalar column reference>`)	Scalar value	Gives the low end of the predicted bucket for a discretized column.
RangeMax (`<scalar column reference>`)	Scalar value	Gives the upper end of the predicted bucket for a discretized column.

PredictHistogram

Sometimes we want the prediction result to contain not only the most likely state but also a histogram with all states and their associated probabilities. For example, in the MemberCard_Prediction model, we would like to know the probabilities of each type of membership cards for a given customer. In DMX, there is a prediction function PredictHistogram, which returns the histogram of each possible value of the predictable column with a probability. PredictHistogram returns a table column, that is, a column that embeds a table. The columns in the embedded table are $Support, $Variance, $Stdev (standard deviation), $Probability, $AdjustedProbability, $Probability Variance, and $ProbabilityStdev.

The following is the example of query result using `PredictHistogram`. Its results are shown in Table 2.4.

```
Select CustomerId, PredictHistogram(MemberCard) as Histogram
```

Table 2.4 Query result of PredictHistogram

CUSTOMERID	HISTOGRAM			
1	MemberCard	$Support	$Probability	...
	Gold	820	0.820	
	Silver	100	0.100	
	Bronze	60	0.060	
	Normal	20	0.020	
	Missing	0	0.000	

Prediction Functions on Table Columns

You just learned the syntax for prediction functions using scalar columns as parameters. A few other prediction functions, such as `PredictAssociation`, `PredictSequence`, and `TopCount`, accept table columns. Some functions support both scalar columns and table columns, such as `PredictTimeSeries` and `Predict`.

RETURNING HIERARCHICAL ROWSETS

Similar to `PredictHistogram`, a few data mining prediction functions return hierarchical rowsets (nested rowsets). The concept of hierarchical rowsets is defined in OLE DB. It provides a way to represent the results in a compact format. The data type for the column containing a nested table is Chapter. While retrieving the query result rowsets, you need to verify the column data type. If it is a Chapter type, you need to retrieve its contents in an inner loop.

You can also flatten the query result by indicating the Flattened keyword in the `Select` clause as follows:

```
Select Flattened CustomerId, PredictHistogram(MemberCard) as
Histogram...
```

In this case, you get query result in flat format without columns with Chapter type. Note, the flatten operation could be inefficient if you have multiple nested tables in a rowsets.

In the previous `MarketBasketModel` example, we can get the list of products a customer may be interested by using the following query:

```
Select CustomerID, gender, PredictAssociation(Purchases)
From MarketBasketModel Prediction Join
     Openrowsets(...)
```

`PredictAssociation(Purchase)` returns a table column. The columns of the table are the same as the columns in the nested part of the model. The number of rows in the table equals the number of nested keys, in this case, the number of different products. Table 2.5 shows the resulting rowsets:

The `Predict` function is a special prediction function. It supports *polymorphism*. Based on the underlying algorithm, the `Predict` function delegates the request to `Predict`, `PredictTimeSeries`, `PredictSequence`, `Predict Association`, and so on. For the previous query, we can use `Predict (Purchases)` instead of `PredictAssociation(Purchases)`.

Sometimes a customer may have already purchased some products. We want to have prediction results for one of the following three cases:

1. The prediction contains the *complete* list of products that the store offers, with associated predicted quantities.

2. The prediction shows what *other* products a customer is likely to buy based on the products the customer has already bought. The reported list should not include the product from the input case.

3. The prediction contains just the predicted Quantity value associated with the products from the input case, or perhaps just the likelihood of each product in the input case. No other products should appear in the output table.

To express these three different cases, we can specify, respectively, one of the following options in the `Predict` function:

- `INCLUSIVE`, which represents the behavior in case 1.
- `EXCLUSIVE` (default option), which causes behavior number 2.
- `INPUT_ONLY`, which ensures that the predicted table contains only the rows supplied by the input (behavior number 3).

Table 2.5 Query result of PredictAssociation

CUSOMTERID	GENDER	PURCHASES	
1	Male	ProductName	Quantity
		Cake	1
		Coke	1

Table 2.5 *(continued)*

CUSOMTERID	GENDER	PURCHASES	
		Milk	3
		Pepsi	4
		Wine	1
		. . .	

Each row in the Purchase table may contain statistics, for example, the support and the probability. This information is stored in the derived columns $Support and $Probability, respectively. The support is the number of cases similar to the given customer in the training dataset (for example, those who bought a particular product and has the same demographic information). The probability indicates how likely it is for a given customer to buy a particular product and is not concerned with the quantity of the product the customer may buy. Be aware that probabilities for different products don't sum to 1, because the customer may buy a number of products. To include these statistics in the result rowset, we add another parameter for the `Predict` function: `INLCUDE_STATISTICS`.

```
Select CustomerId, gender, Predict(Purchase, Include_Statistics,
Input_Only) . . .
```

The result of the previous query is shown in Table 2.6.

Table 2.6 Query result using Include_Statistics

CUSOMTER_ID	GENDER	PURCHASES			
1	Male	ProductName	Quantity	$Support	$Probability
		Milk	3	300	0.32
		Pepsi	2	320	0.34
		Wine	1	200	0.21

Sometimes we need more information than just the purchase probability for each product. We want to know, for example, how likely it is that the customer will buy 1, 2 or 3 units of the product. Conceptually, all this information is included in the `Predict` function. In order to get the probability for each quantity, we can use the `PredictHistogram` function on the Quantity column and use the nested `Select` statement to select from the results of `Predict` function. The `PredictHistogram` function returns the histogram of all quantities and their associated probabilities. These probabilities sum to 1.

```
Select CustomerId, gender,
(Select (ProductName, PredictHistogram(Quantity) As QuantityHistogram
From Predict(Purchase, Include_Statistics) ...
```

The preceding query returns the data shown in Table 2.7.

Table 2.7   Result for Nested Query

CUSTOMERID	GENDER	PURCHASES					
1	Male	Product Name		QuantityHistogram		$Support	$Probability
		Cake	Quantity	$Variance	$Probability	300	0.32
			1	0	0.60		
			2	0	0.20		
			3	0	0.20		
		Coke	Quantity	$Variance	$Probability	320	0.34
			1	0	0.70		
			2	0	0.20		
			3	0	0.10		
		Milk	. . .			200	0.21

The result rowset from Predict table column could be very large, especially when the query uses options, such as INCLUSIVE, INCLUDE_STATITICS, or uses PredictHistogram on nested columns. To solve the problem, DMX introduces the TopX and BottomX family of functions, which operate on nested tables (including those resulting from PredictHistogram, a nested Select or any other expression returning a table). These functions order the records of the nested table by a specified column's value and then truncate the sorted list to a specified length.

For example, the following query uses the TopCount function to retrieve the top two most likely membership cards that may interest the customer:

```
Select CustomerId, TopCount(PredictHistogram(MemberCard), $Probability,
2). . .
```

The following query retrieves the top 10 products the customers is predicted to buy in the largest quantities:

```
Select CustomerId, TopCount(Predict(Purchase, EXCLUSIVE), quantity,
10)...
```

The following query retrieves the top five products the customers is most likely to buy:

```
Select CustomerId, TopCount(Predict(Purchase, EXCLUSIVE), $Probability,
5)...
```

DMX 2.0 proposes a shortcut for the previous query using `TopCount` on the `Predict` function with `$Probability` as the select criteria. The following is the equivalent query using the shortcut.

```
Select CustomerId, Predict(Purchase, 5)...
```

If you want to return the top *n* recommendations based on an adjusted probability instead of probability, you can use the following query:

```
Select CustomerId, Predict(Purchase, 5, $AdjustedProbability)...
```

NOTE `AdjustedProbability` is derived from `Probability`, with adjustment based on some math functions. It usually penalizes most popular states (items). For example, if every customer buys Pepsi, recommending Pepsi to new customer doesn't add too much value. In this case, you may try use `AdjustedProbability`, which penalizes common items such as Pepsi.

As the result of `TopCount` is a table column, we can apply a subselect clause to the result of `TopCount` function (or any prediction function returns table column). The following is an example:

```
Select CustomerId, Gender,  (Select MemberCard, $Probability as Proba
From TopCount(PredictHistogram(MemberCard), $Probability, 2) As
ProbabilityHistogram). . .
```

The result rowset of the previous query is shown in Table 2.8.

Table 2.8 Query Result

CUSTOMERID	GENDER	PROBABILITYHISTOGRAM	
1	Male	MemberCard	Proba
		Gold	0.70
		Silver	0.10
2	Female	MemberCard	Proba
		Gold	0.25
		Silver	0.15

We can also add a `Where` clause to pull out certain records from a nested table. For example, if instead of always getting the "best" prediction for a membership card, suppose that a query only wants to get the probability of having a silver membership card for each customer. We can express this query using the following Select clause:

```
Select CustomerId, (Select $Probability From
PredictHistogram(MemberCard) Where MemberCard='Silver') As
SilverCardProba)...
```

Similar to the query in the MarketBasketAnlysis model, the following query retrieves only the probability for each customer of purchasing Pepsi.

```
Select CustomerId, (Select $Probability From PredictHistogram(Purchase,
INCLUSIVE, INCLUDE_STATISTICS) Where ProductName='Pepsi') As
PepsiPurchaseProba)...
```

Table 2.9 contains a list of prediction functions that operates on table columns. A brief description is also given in the table.

Table 2.9   Prediction Function on Table Columns

FUNCTION	RETURN VALUE	DESCRIPTION
Predict(<table column reference>, options, . . .)	Scare value	When the parameter of a Predict function is a table column, it predicts the information related to the nested table. Possible options include EXCLUDE_NULL, INCLUDE_NULL, INCLUSIVE, EXCLUSIVE, INPUT_ONLY, and INCLUDE_STATISTICS.
TopCount(<table expr>, <rank expr >, <n-items>)	<table expr>	Return the first <n-items> rows in a decreasing order of <rank expr >.
TopSum(<table expr>, <rank expr >, <sum>)	<table expr>	Return the first *n* rows in a decreasing order of <rank expr> such that the sum of the <rank column reference> values is at least <sum>.
TopPercent(<table expr>, <rank expr >, <percent>)	<table expr>	Return the first *n* rows in a decreasing order of <rank expr> such that the sum of the <rank expr> values is at least the given percentage of the total sum of <rank expr> values.

Table 2.9 *(continued)*

FUNCTION	RETURN VALUE	DESCRIPTION
`PredictTimeSeries` `(<table expr>,` `<n1>, <n2>)`	`<table expr>`	Returns the predicted value of the next n time slices in a table.
`PredictSequence` `(<table expr>,` `<n1>, <n2>)`	`<table expr>`	Returns the sequence of states of next *n* steps in a table.
`PredictAssociation` `(<table expr>, <n>)`	`<table expr>`	Returns *n* most likely associated item.

Singleton Queries

Sometimes, the input case for prediction doesn't exist in a database table. For example, suppose that an insurance company wants to give a quote to a customer over the phone or that an online retail site wants to recommend products based on the list of products a customer has already chosen in the shopping cart. In these cases, the customer data may not yet be recorded in the database. To make a prediction in these cases, DMX provides the syntax for a singleton prediction query. The singleton query allows sets of constant values to be used in place of the <source data query> for the prediction join query. The following is an example of singleton prediction query using the Member Card_Prediction model:

```
Select CustomerId, MemberCard
From MemberCard_Prediction m Prediction Join
(Select 'Male' As gender, '35' As age, 'Engineer' As Profession,'60000'
As Income, 'Yes' As HouseOwner) As customer
On m.gender = customer.gender
...
```

It is also possible to construct a singleton query with a nested table. The following is an example of prediction against MarketBasketAnalysis model based on the items in a customer's shopping cart:

```
Select CustomerId, Predict(Purchase, 5)
From MarketBasketAnalysis m Prediction Join
(Select 'Male' As gender, '60000' As Income, 'Silver' As MemberCard,
(Select 'Cake' As ProductName, 1 As Quantity
Union Select 'Milk' As Product Name, 2 As Quantity) as Purchase) As
customer
On   m.gender = customer.gender
```

```
And  m.Income = customer.Income
And  m.MemberCard = customer.MemberCard
And  m.Purchase.ProductName = customer.Purchase.ProductName
And  m.Purchase.Quantity   = customer.Purchase.Quantity
```

Making Predictions Using Content Only

One of the initial steps in training a mining model is to gather marginal statistics, for example, counting the number of customers with gold, silver, bronze member cards. DMX allows us to make predictions based on the marginal statistics of model content.

The following queries return the most popular member card: Bronze.

```
Select Predict(MemberCard)
From MemberCard_Prediction
```

or

```
Select MemberCard
From MemberCard_Prediction
```

You can also query nonpredictable columns. The following query returns the distinct values of Gender in the training dataset.

```
Select Distinct Gender
From MemberCard
```

The following query returns the most popular three products based on customer purchases:

```
Select Predict(Purchase, 3)
From MarketBasketAnalysis
```

NATURAL PREDICTION JOINS

If the column names of the input case match the column names of the mining model, you don't need to specify the On clause in the Prediction Join query. Instead, you can use *Natural* Prediction Join. It works for both the batch prediction query and the singleton prediction query. For example:

```
Select CustomerId, MemberCard
From MemberCard_Prediction Natural Prediction Join
(Select 'Male' As gender, '35' As age, 'Engineer' As
Profession,'60000' As Income, 'Yes' As HouseOwner) As customer
```

Drilling through the Model's Content

The drill-through concept in DMX means getting the source data from the model's content. For example, from a tree model, you can get all the source cases classified in a given node of the tree. This type of query is based on Model.Cases.

The following query returns all the training dataset:

```
Select * from MyModel.Cases
```

The following query returns those cases classified in Node 001 (including all the descendants of Node 001):

```
Select * from MyModel.Cases
Where IsInNode('0001')
```

Model.Sample_Cases is similar to Model.Cases; the only difference is that Model.Sample_Cases returns the sample cases instead of full training cases. The sample cases are not necessarily real input cases. These cases can be generated based on the model's pattern.

Content Query

A Content query is a type of query that retrieves the content of a trained mining model. The model content represents the patterns a data mining algorithm discovered from the training dataset. These patterns are stored in tabular format. You can use the following query to select the tabular data from a mining model:

```
Select * from MyModel.Content
```

We will discuss the details of returned columns and give more examples of content query in the "Understanding Schema Rowsets" section. Based on the information retrieved from the content query, you should be able to display the patterns graphically.

Understanding Schema Rowsets

In addition to the DMX language, OLE DB for DM has defined a set of schema rowsets. In OLE DB, the schema for an object is a description of the object's structure; it is the metadata. A schema rowset is an OLE DB rowset that encapsulates the descriptions for all objects of particular type within the database. Each row in the rowset corresponds to an individual object. The individual properties of the objects are stored in columns.

OLE DB also provides a mechanism, called restriction, to filter schema rowsets based upon the content of certain columns. For each schema rowset, a set of restriction columns is specified.

In summary, schema rowsets are global tables for metadata. In the case of data mining, metadata includes algorithms, mining models, model columns, model contents, and so on. The metadata allows user applications to discover dynamically the list of data mining algorithms and the list of objects different data mining providers generated. There are seven schema rowsets defined by OLE DB for DM:

- `Mining_Services`
- `Mining_Service_Parameters`
- `Mining_Models`
- `Mining_Columns`
- `Mining_Model_Content`
- `Mining_Functions`
- `Mining_Model_PMML`

All the schema rowsets support restrictions on certain columns. This means your program can query the schema rowsets with certain criteria.

The Mining_Services Schema Rowset

The `Mining_Services` schema rowset stores the description of the list of algorithms (services) registered in the server. These algorithms may or may not come from the same data mining provider.

Different algorithms are capable of different types of data mining tasks. They may also differ in the type of data they support. The list of algorithms, their usage, their limitations, and their capabilities are all exposed in the `Mining_Services` schema rowset. Table 2.10 describes a few important columns in `Mining_Services` schema rowset.

Table 2.10 Mining_Services Schema Rowset

COLUMN NAME	TYPE INDICATOR	DESCRIPTION
SEVICE_NAME	DBTYPE_WSTR	The name of the algorithm. Provider-specific. Used with the CREATE MINING MODEL command to specify algorithm.

Table 2.10 *(continued)*

COLUMN NAME	TYPE INDICATOR	DESCRIPTION
SEVICE_TYPE_ID	DBTYPE_UI4	A bitmask that describes mining service types. The list includes known popular mining services, such as the following: classification, clustering, association, sequence, and so forth.
PRDICTED_CONTENT	DBTYPE_WSTR	The attribute types that can be predicted. This is a comma-delimited list of content types.
SPORTED_DISTRIBUTION_ FLAGS	DBTYPE_WSTR	A comma-delimited list of one or more of the distribution such as Normal, Log_normal, Uniform, Uniform.
SUPORTED_INPUT_ CONTENT_TYPES	DBTYPE_WSTR	A comma-delimited list of one or more of the following: KEY, DISCRETE, CONTINUOUS, DISCRETIZED, ORDERED, SEQUENCE_TIME, CYCLICAL, PROBABILITY, VARIANCE, STDEV, SUPPORT, PROBABILITY_VARIANCE, PROBABILITY_STDEV, ORDER, SEQUENCE, TABLE.
SUPPORTED_PREDICTION_ CONTENT_TYPES	DBTYPE_WSTR	Same as above.
TRAINING_COMPLEXITY	DBTYPE_I4	Indication of expected time for training (high, medium, low).
PREDICTION_COMPLEXITY	DBTYPE_I4	Indication of expected time for prediction (high, medium, low).
ALLOW_INCREMENTAL_ INSERT	DBTYPE_BOOL	True if additional Insert into statements are allowed after the initial training.

The Service_Parameters Schema Rowset

The `Service_Parameters` schema rowset is a simple schema rowset. (See Table 2.11.) It provides a list of parameters for each registered data mining algorithm and their default values. These parameters can be used in the model creation statement.

Table 2.11 Service_Parameters Schema Rowset

COLUMN NAME	TYPE INDICATOR	DESCRIPTION
SERVICE_NAME	DBTYPE_WSTR	The name of the algorithm. Provider-specific.
PARAMETER_NAME	DBTYPE_WSTR	The name of the parameter.
PARAMETER_TYPE	DBTYPE_WSTR	Data type of parameter (DBTYPE).
IS_REQUIRED	DBTYPE_BOOL	If true, the parameter is required.
DESCRIPTION	DBTYPE_WSTR	Text describing the purpose and format of the parameter.

The Mining_Models Schema Rowset

Data mining models are exposed in the `Mining_Models` schema rowset. This rowset stores information such as the mining model's name, the associated algorithm, creation data, and so on. Table 2.12 lists some of the important columns in this schema rowset.

Table 2.12 Mining_Models Schema Rowset

COLUMN NAME	TYPE INDICATOR	DESCRIPTION
MODEL_NAME	DBTYPE_WSTR	Model name. This column cannot contain NULL.
SERVICE_TYPE_ID	DBTYPE_UI4	A bitmask that describes mining service types.
SERVICE_NAME	DBTYPE_WSTR	A provider-specific name that describes the algorithm used to generate the model.
CREATION_STATEMENT	DBTYPE_WSTR	Optional. The statement used to create the original data mining model.

Table 2.12 *(continued)*

COLUMN NAME	TYPE INDICATOR	DESCRIPTION
PREDICTION_ENTITY	DBTYPE_WSTR	A comma-delimited list indicating which columns the model can predict.
IS_POPULATED	DBTYPE_BOOL	Indicates is the model is trained.

The Mining_Columns Schema Rowset

The Mining_Columns schema rowset stores information about each column of mining models. The column information includes the column name, data type, distribution flag, content type, and so on. The distribution flag describes the column's value distribution. For example, if the Age column of the customers table follows a normal distribution, the user can specify this information during the model creation statement. The content type gives a column's specific content information. Content types include key, discrete, discretized, continuous, time key, sequence key, and so on.

Table 2.13 describes some important columns in the Mining_Columns schema rowset:

Table 2.13 Mining_Columns Schema Rowset

COLUMN NAME	TYPE INDICATOR	DESCRIPTION
COLUMN_NAME	DBTYPE_WSTR	The name of the column; this might not be unique. If this cannot be determined, a NULL is returned.
DISTRIBUTION_FLAG	DBTYPE_WSTR	The distribution of column values such as normal, log_normal, uniform, poisson, and so forth.
CONTENT_TYPE	DBTYPE_WSTR	Content type can be key, discrete, continuous, discretized, key sequence, key time, and so forth.
RELATED_ATTRIBUTE	DBTYPE_WSTR	This is the name of the target column that the current column either relates to or is a special property of.

The Mining_Model_Content Schema Rowset

The `Mining_Model_Content` schema rowset is probably the most important schema rowset. It stores the content of a mining model, meaning the patterns that data mining algorithms have discovered on the training datasets. These patterns are restructured in the tabular format so it can be stored in this rowset.

A few of the important columns in `Mining_Model_Content` schema rowsets include Model_Name, Node_Name, Node_Parent, Node_Rule, and Node_Distribution. Model_Name stores the name of a mining model. Node_Name is the name of a node. Each row in the schema rowset has a unique node name. Depending on the type of the algorithm, a node may represent different kinds of information. For example, for the decision tree model, each node is a tree node; for the clustering model, each node is a cluster; for the association model, each node is a frequent itemset or a rule. Node_Parent points to the parent node. Node_Rule gives an XML description of the rule embedded in the node. For example, in the case of decision tree, Node_Rule describes the tree node splitting information. The format used in the XML descriptions is based on the PMML standard if possible. (The PMML standard doesn't define content for all data mining algorithms.) Node_Distribution is a table column; it embeds another table (a distribution table). The distribution table stores the statistics or additional information for the current node. In the case of a decision tree, it contains associated statistics of the current node. It is probably the most important column in this schema rowset.

Table 2.14 lists some of the important columns in Mining_Model_Content schema rowset.

Table 2.14   Mining_Model_Content Schema Rowset

COLUMN NAME	TYPE INDICATOR	DESCRIPTION
MODEL_NAME	DBTYPE_WSTR	Name of the model.
ATTRIBUTE_NAME	DBTYPE_WSTR	Name(s) of the attribute(s) corresponding to this node. For a model node, this would be a list of predictable attributes. For a leaf distribution node, this would be a single attribute that the distribution corresponds to.
NODE_NAME	DBTYPE_WSTR	Name of the node.
NODE_TYPE	DBTYPE_I4	The type of the node. For example, cluster node, tree leaf node, model root node, and so forth.

Table 2.14 *(continued)*

COLUMN NAME	TYPE INDICATOR	DESCRIPTION
PARENT_UNIQUE_ NAME	DBTYPE_WSTR	Unique name of the node's parent. NULL is returned for any nodes at the root level. For providers that generate unique names by qualification, each component of this name is delimited.
NODE_DESCRIPTION	DBTYPE_WSTR	A human-readable description of the node.
NODE_RULE	DBTYPE_WSTR	An XML description of the rule embedded in the node. The format of the XML string is based on the PMML standard.
MARGINAL_RULE	DBTYPE_WSTR	An XML description of the rule moving to the node from the parent node.
NODE_PROBABILITY	DBTYPE_R8	The probability for reaching the node.
MARGINAL_ PROBABILITY	DBTYPE_R8	The probability of reaching the node from the parent node.
DISTRIBUTION	DBTYPE_HCHAPTER	A table containing the probability histogram of the node.
SUPPORT	DBTYPE_R8	Number of cases in support of this node.

Table 2.15 gives the columns information of distribution table:

Table 2.15 Distribution Chapter Layout

COLUMN NAME	TYPE INDICATOR	DESCRIPTION
ATTRIBUTE_NAME	DBTYPE_WSTR	Name of the attribute
ATTRIBUTE_VALUE	DBTYPE_VARIANT	The attribute value represented as a variant
SUPPORT	DBTYPE_ R8	The number of cases that support this attribute value
PROBABILITY	DBTYPE_R8	The probability of an occurrence of this attribute value
VARIANCE	DBTYPE_ R8	The variance of this attribute value

Figure 2.8 displays a `Mining_Model_Content` schema rowset with a single decision tree model `MemberCard_Prediction`. There are five rows in the schema rowset. These five rows actually represent five nodes in a decision tree as displayed in Figure 2.8.

> **TIP** All Microsoft content viewers (tree viewers, cluster viewers, and so on) are purely based on the information in the content schema rowsets. You can also develop your own content viewers. It is a relatively simple task. You may find a couple of thin client browsers in Microsoft's data mining newsgroup.

Model Name	Attribute	Node Name	Node Caption	Node Parent	Distribution			. . .
MemberCard _Prediction	Member Card	A	Yes	O	Gold	200	. . .	
					Silver	100		
					. . .			
MemberCard _Prediction	Member Card	B	Income ≥ = 50000	A	Gold	150	. . .	
					Silver	80		
					. . .			
MemberCard _Prediction	Member Card	C	Income < 50000	A	Gold	50	. . .	
					Silver	20		
					. . .			
MemberCard _Prediction	Member Card	D	HouseOwner = 'Yes'	B	Gold	120	. . .	
					Silver	30		
					. . .			
MemberCard _Prediction	Member Card	E	HouseOwner = 'No'	B	Gold	30	. . .	
					Silver	50		
					. . .			

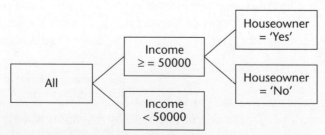

Figure 2.8   Content schema rowset containing a decision tree model

Some special data mining algorithms may require specific columns to store their patterns. The OLE DB for DM specification allows data mining providers to add additional columns for all schema rowsets. For example, Microsoft's data mining provider adds a number of columns in a number of schema rowsets; these columns' names start from MSOLAP_*.

We mentioned the schema rowsets restriction earlier. Now we will give you an example of how to use the restriction.

Suppose that there are lots of mining models in your database. The size of the content schema rowsets is huge. You want to retrieve only those rows of a given model. The following C# code connects to Analysis Service through the MSOLAP90 provider using ADO.Net, queries the Mining_Content schema rowsets, and returns only those rows of the mining model MemberCard_Prediciton in a DataTable object.

```
string myConnectionString = "Provider=MSOLAP90;Data
Source=localhost;Initial Catalog=MyDatabase";
OleDbConnection connection = new OleDbConnection(myConnectionString);
connection.Open();
Guid contentSchema = new Guid("{3add8a76-d8b9-11d2-8d2a-00e029154fde}");
DataTable dt =  connection.GetOleDbSchemaTable(contentSchema,new
object[] {"MyDatabase", null, "MemberCard_Prediction"});;
```

The set of restriction columns in Mining Content schema rowsets are CATALOG_NAME, SCHEMA_NAME, MODEL_NAME, ATTRIBUTE_NAME, NODE_NAME, NODE_UNIQUE_NAME, NODE_TYPE, NODE_GUID, and NODE_CAPTION. The restrictions are specified in an object array following the restriction column order.

The Query_Content Schema Rowset

Applications may want to query the Mining_Model_Content schema rowset for various purposes, for example, to write a customized tree viewer, or to get the list of association rules programmatically. There is one special type of DMX query for model content. We call this type of query *content query*.

The following content query retrieves everything from the content schema rowset. It returns a rowset; one of the columns of the rowset contains an embedded table for distribution.

```
Select * from MemberCard_Prediction.Content
```

The content schema rowset could become very large as it may contain many mining models, and some mining models may contain lots of patterns. We can use the Where condition to restrict the query result. The following query retrieves only the content for all the tree leaf nodes of MemberCard_Prediction model.

```
Select * from MemberCard_Prediction.Content
Where Node_Type = 4
```

`Note_Type` = 4 means that leaf level nodes in decision tree model content. A decision tree mining model may contain multiple trees (we will explain this in the Chapter 5). You can use the following query to retrieve all the nodes in a particular tree:

```
Select * from MemberCard_Prediction.Content
Where Attribute_Name = 'MemberCard'
```

The previous query returns the model content about `MemberCard_ Prediction`. The number of rows the result rowset contains is the number of nodes of the decision tree. Each node includes a distribution table that contains the statistics of each type of membership card. To be even more specific, we can specify that the content of the distribution table contain only gold membership card statistics using the following nested query:

```
Select (Select [Support] From Node_Distribution
Where Attribute_Value = 'Gold')
```

Sometimes, we may need to update the model content manually. For example, change the caption of cluster name for a clustering model. We can use the following query to update the content:

```
Update MyClusteringModel.Content
Set NodeCaption = 'Important Customers'
Where NodeId = '000102'
```

It is also possible to clear the contents of a mining model just as it is possible to delete all the rows in a table. The following statement removes all the contents of the `MemberCard_Prediction` model. The model then becomes untrained.

```
Delete from MemberCard_Prediction.content
```

The Mining_Functions Schema Rowset

Some prediction functions, such as `Predict` and `PredictHistogram`, are supported by all data mining algorithms, while other prediction functions are algorithm-specific. For example, `Cluster()` is supported only by cluster type of algorithms. In Microsoft Data Mining Provider, two algorithms support the

Cluster() function: the Microsoft Clustering algorithm and the Microsoft Sequence Clustering algorithm.

The Mining_Functions schema rowset is used to describe the list of prediction functions supported by each mining algorithm. (See Table 2.16.)

Table 2.16   Mining_Functions Schema Rowsets

COLUMN NAME	TYPE INDICATOR	DESCRIPTION
SERVICE_NAME	DBTYPE_WSTR	The name of the algorithm or service.
FUNCTION_NAME	DBTYPE_WSTR	The name of the function.
RETURNS_TABLE	DBTYPE_BOOL	The return value can be either table or scalar. If this attribute is set True, it returns a table.
DESCRIPTION	DBTYPE_WSTR	Description of the function.

The Model_PMML Schema Rowset

The Model_PMML schema rowset is a schema rowset used to store the XML representation of the content of each model. The format of the XML string follows the PMML standard. The most important column in this schema rowset is Model PMML, which is the PMML document about the model content.

Table 2.17 lists a few main columns in Model_PMML schema rowset:

Table 2.17   Model_PMML Schema Rowset

COLUMN NAME	TYPE INDICATOR	DESCRIPTION
MODEL_NAME	DBTYPE_WSTR	Model name. This column cannot contain NULL.
MODEL_TYPE	DBTYPE_WSTR	Model type, a provider-specific string – can be NULL.
MODEL_GUID	DBTYPE_GUID	GUID that uniquely identifies the model. Providers that do not use GUIDs to identify tables should return NULL in this column.
MODEL_PMML	DBTYPE_WSTR	An XML representation of the model's content with PMML format.
SIZE	DMTYPE_UI4	Number of bytes of the XML string size.

The following query returns the PMML string of the `MemberCard_Prediction` model:

```
Select * from MemberCard_Prediction.PMML
```

You can also create a new model from a PMML string by using the `Create` statement as follows:

```
CREATE MINING MODEL <mining model name> FROM PMML <xml string>
```

Understanding Extensions for Mining Structures

After DMX 1.0, a new and important data mining concept, *Mining Structure*, is introduced. In this section, you will learn about the mining structure concept, the DMX extensions related to mining structure object, and the mining structure schema rowsets.

The Mining Structure

In a real-life data mining project, you always build multiple models on the same dataset, so you can compare them for accuracy. The mining structure is an abstraction of the source data and mining model. A mining structure contains the data type and content definition of all the columns. However, it does not contain the column usage definition, that is, `input`, `predict_only` and `predict`. Multiple mining models can be created based on the same mining structure, using all columns or a subset of columns of the structure. These mining models can use different algorithms and columns.

Processing a mining structure includes tokenizing the source data and building marginal statistical models.

Depending on the implementation, a mining structure may or may not cache the training data. When the mining structure caches the training dataset, you can issue the drill through queries against its mining models.

> **NOTE** With the introduction of mining structures, training a mining model consists of two phases: processing the mining structure (if it is not processed) and processing the mining model. After a mining structure is processed, multiple associated mining models can be processed in parallel.

DMX Extensions on Mining Structure

With the introduction of mining structure, there are a few new query statements added in DMX.

The following statement creates a mining structure with seven columns:

```
Create mining Structure Customer
(
CustomerId   long key,
Gender       text   discrete,
Age          long   continuous,
Profession   text   discrete,
Income       long   continuous,
HouseOwner   text   discrete,
MemberCard   text   discrete
)
```

After a mining structure is created, you can create mining models based on the mining structure using the `Alter` statement. You need to specify the column usage (the default is input), and the associated algorithm and its parameter settings.

```
ALTER Mining Structure Customer
ADD MINING MODEL MemberCard_DT(
      CustomerId,
      Gender,
      Age,
      Profession,
      MemberCard PREDICT
)
USING Microsoft_Decision_Trees(Minimum_Support = 10)
```

If all your mining columns are for input, and you want to use all the columns in the mining structure, then you don't need to specify the columns in the `Alter` statement. The following statement creates a clustering model using all the mining structure columns as input.

```
ALTER MINING STRUCTURE Customer
ADD MINING MODEL CustomerClustering
USING Microsoft_Clustering (Cluster_Count = 8)
```

After creating a mining structure, you can process it using the `Insert into` statement. The `Insert into` statement is exactly the same as the `Insert into` statement in the mining models you learned earlier in this chapter.

```
Insert into Customer
( CustomerId, Gender, Age, Profession, MemberCard)
OpenRowset('sqloledb', 'myserver';'mylogin';'mypwd',
'Select CustomerId, gender, age, profession, membercard From customers')
```

NOTE Microsoft data mining provider allows the mining structure and mining model to share the same name. If there is a mining model that has the same name as a mining structure, you need to specify the object type in the statement: `Insert into Mining Structure Customer . . . . Insert into` **in a mining structure will process the mining structure as well as all the associated mining models.**

A mining structure may cache training cases. You can remove the cache by using the following statement:

```
Delete from mining structure Customer.cases
```

The following statement deletes the content of a mining structure and returns it to an unprocessed state:

```
Delete from mining structure Customer
```

To remove a mining structure, you can use:

```
Drop mining structure Customer
```

If a mining structure is removed, all the associated mining models are dropped as well.

NOTE You can always use the mining model creation statement without creating a mining structure first. In this case, the Microsoft data mining provide automatically creates a mining structure for you.

You can also use `Insert into` statement for a mining model, which causes both the mining structure and mining model to be processed. However, if the model contains sibling models in the same structure, you will get a processing error.

Mining Structure Schema Rowsets

Because mining structure is a major data mining object, we need to add new schema rowsets that allow client applications to discover the list of mining structures and their attributes dynamically. Table 2.18 contains a list of important columns in the Mining Structure schema rowsets.

Table 2.18 Important Columns in the Mining Structure Schema Rowsets

COLUMN NAME	TYPE INDICATOR	DESCRIPTION
STRUCTURE_NAME	DBTYPE_WSTR	Structure name. This column cannot contain NULL.
DESCRIPTION	DBTYPE_WSTR	Human-readable description of the structure. Null if there is no description associated with the column.
CREATION_ STATEMENT	DBTYPE_WSTR	Optional. The statement used to create the original data mining model.
IS_POPULATED	DBTYPE_BOOL	VARIANT_TRUE if the structure is populated; VARIANT_FALSE if the structure is not populated.

Summary

In this chapter, you learned the basic concepts about OLE DB for Data Mining, including definitions of case, nested case, nested rowsets, and mining models. You learned four types of DMX queries: model creation, model training, model prediction, and content query. We also explained the set of typical prediction functions and their usages. These prediction functions return very useful information for your predictions.

This chapter also explained the schema rowsets in OLE DB for Data Mining. These schema rowsets store metadata for mining services, models, columns, and contents. Schema rowsets are global tables. User applications can dynamically discover data mining–related objects by querying schema rowsets. Content schema rowsets is the most important one. It stores the patterns of a mining model. These schema rowsets allow you to display mining patterns graphically.

The last part of the chapter explained the concept of mining structures, and associated DMX statements.

DMX is similar to SQL and simple to use. By now, you should be able to write prediction queries to query mining models.

Using SQL Server Data Mining

This chapter will review the Analysis Services toolset and provide techniques to effectively create and analyze mining models. Before reading this chapter, you should be familiar with the model-building concepts introduced in Chapter 2. In particular, you should understand the concept of a mining model, mining model columns, and case and nested tables.

This chapter is designed to help novice users get started and provide experienced users with techniques that will help them get the most out of the toolset. This is not meant to be a substitute or a replacement for the excellent documentation and tutorials found in the product documentation. Rather, it describes and applies the general tools provided with Analysis Services specifically for data mining purposes.

Throughout this chapter, we will be describing features of Analysis Services through the user interface and providing step-by-step instructions for creating a set of mining models for illustrative purposes. Feel free to deviate from these instructions and explore the concepts introduced in the chapter. If you stray too far, starting over is not difficult, or you can always pick up the completed project from this book's companion Web site for examination.

We will be using the MovieClick database to exemplify tool usage. This database is described in Appendix A.

In this chapter, we will cover:

- Using the Business Intelligence Development Studio
- Understanding Immediate mode and Offline mode
- Creating and modifying data source, data source views, and data mining objects
- Exploring data and evaluating models

Introducing the Business Intelligence Development Studio

Most of your time using SQL Server Data Mining will be spent in the Business Intelligence Development Studio (BI Dev Studio). This environment is integrated into the Microsoft Visual Studio (VS) shell to provide a complete development experience for business intelligence operations. Working inside Visual Studio, a data mining project becomes part of a collection of projects known as a "solution." Additional projects required for your application can be grouped together into this cohesive solution. For example, a database administrator (DBA) might create an Integration Services project to pull the data out of your OLTP system and transform it into a form suitable for data mining. An analyst could create an Analysis Services project containing models that explored and examined the transaction data. Finally, a developer could create a Web service and a Web site, embedding these models in an end-user application and commercializable service. All of these projects can be contained inside a single solution encompassing the entire body of the collaborative work. Furthermore, all aspects of the work can be captured with complete version histories in the source control system.

Understanding the User Interface

The BI Dev Studio is designed mainly for developers, with an unstructured approach to solution implementation, which is very different from traditional data mining tools. This approach, along with the added complexity from the fully featured development environment, can be daunting to those familiar with other data mining toolsets. However, once you get past the initial shock of dealing with the myriad of options and windows inherent in Visual Studio, creating and analyzing models is fairly simple. The first step in familiarizing yourself with the BI Dev Studio is understanding which of the various parts of the user interface are interesting and for what they are used. Figure 3.1 shows a typical window layout for the BI Dev Studio with elements of interest demarked.

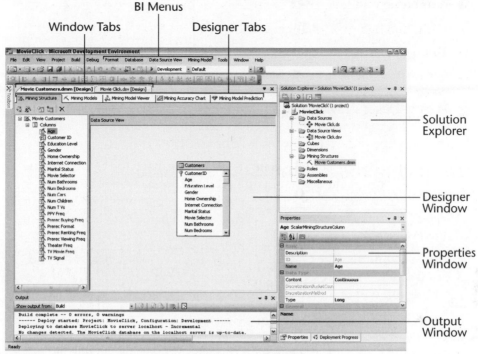

Figure 3.1 Business Intelligence Development Studio

The most important parts of the BI Dev Studio are:

- **Solution Explorer:** Solution Explorer is where you manage your solution and projects. All objects are created and managed in this window. To add objects to your project, you right-click the project name and select Add New Item, or right-click on a particular folder and select New. Doing so will launch a dialog or wizard, allowing you to create the specified object.

- **Window tabs:** The Window tabs allow you to quickly switch between designer windows. A tab will be displayed for each object or file that is currently open. If more objects are open than can appear in the tab area, additional windows can be accessed using the down area to the right of the tabs.

- **Designer window:** The Designer window is where you edit and analyze your objects. Creating a new object or double-clicking on an object in Solution Explorer will open that object's specific designer, allowing you to modify and interact with the object.

- **Designer tabs:** Many objects have different aspects that can be edited or interacted with. These aspects are indicated by tabs within the Designer window.

- **Properties window:** The Properties window is a context-sensitive window that displays properties for the currently selected item. This is a general concept in Visual Studio and applies to any type of operation performed within the studio. For example, selecting an object in Solution Explorer causes properties of that object, such as object ID, filename, and so forth, to be displayed. Selecting a column in the Data Mining Designer window causes column properties, such as name and data type, to be displayed. When an item that has no properties is selected, the property window will be empty.

- **BI menus:** The area on the main menu bar between the Debug menu and the Tools menu is where you will find context-sensitive menus specific to Analysis Services objects. For instance, opening the Data Source View (DSV) Editor will cause Format and Data Source View menus to appear in that area.

- **Output window:** The Output window displays messages when you build and deploy projects. If there are errors in your project, this is where you will find their descriptions.

TIP To make the environment more suitable for your data mining use, you can reorganize the workspace as you see fit. Clicking and dragging the title bar of any window displays floating icons that will help you float or dock the window. You can even stack these windows on top of each other, causing selectable tabs to appear beneath the windows.

As you experiment with different options in the studio, additional windows may appear. You can always close the windows you are no longer interested in — don't worry, if you need them, they are always available from the View menu. If you want the windows to be readily available, but are running short on screen space, you can click the push pin icon on the window's title bar and the window will slide out of sight when not in use.

Offline Mode and Immediate Mode

BI Dev Studio works in two operating modes. Which mode you use is sometimes based on personal preference and sometimes on necessity. Each mode has its advantages and drawbacks, and it is important to understand the differences between them when working with the product.

Immediate Mode

Working in Immediate mode is generally a more natural experience for data mining users. When you work in Immediate mode, you are connected directly and continually to an Analysis Services server. When you open an object, such as a mining structure, you are opening the object from the server as you would expect. When you change the object and save it, the object is immediately changed on the server. In Immediate mode, your BI Dev Studio project is a link to a database on your server. In Solution Explorer, you see all objects that are currently in that database. If you close and reopen this project, you automatically reconnect to the database. If objects on the database have changed since the last time you opened the project, those changes are present when you open it again.

Although this mode is very intuitive and easy to understand, you should take some factors into consideration during use. Most importantly, it is truly *immediate*. If you have a working model in production and you modify and save that model, it is instantly changed and becomes unprocessed, causing any queries against that model to fail. Additionally, other users can modify objects while you have them open. You see a warning when you try to save an object if it has been modified. Saving then overwrites any changes that other users have made. Changes to objects on the server are reflected in your project only when you close and reopen the object. New or deleted objects in the database are reflected only when you close and reopen the project itself.

One huge advantage that Immediate mode has over Offline mode has to do with security. Working in Immediate mode allows you to work within the confines of a single database, allowing users with Database Administrator permissions to create and modify objects. For reasons described in the next section, using Offline mode requires the user to be a server administrator.

Getting Started in Immediate Mode

To get started in the BI Dev Studio with Immediate mode, follow these steps:

1. Launch the BI Dev Studio.
2. From the File menu, select Open/Analysis Services Database; the dialog in Figure 3.2 will appear.
3. Enter the server name and database name to which you want to connect.
4. Click OK.

You can also create new databases on servers where you have server administrator permissions by selecting Create new database and specifying the server and database names.

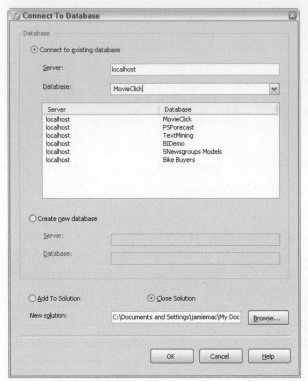

Figure 3.2   Dialog box to connect to database in Immediate mode

Offline Mode

When working in Offline mode, your project contains files that are stored on your client machine. As you make modifications to objects in this environment, the changes are stored in XML format on your hard drive. The models and other objects are not created on the server until you decide to deploy them to the destination server of your choosing. This provides you as the data mining developer/analyst with the ability to design and test your models on a test server before deploying them to a live server. Also these files can be checked into a source control system to track changes in the object metadata over time and to share among a development team. You can view and edit the source code of these files by right-clicking an object in Solution Explorer and selecting View Code.

When you deploy a project, the BI Dev Studio validates the objects in your project, creates a deployment script, and sends that script to the server. The unit of deployment is the entire project, representing an entire Analysis Services database. The tools are smart enough to deploy incremental changes while you are working on a project. However, if you deploy the project to a server that has a database of the same name as the one in your project settings, or if the project is deployed from a different machine, the deployment will completely overwrite the database. Luckily, you will be warned before this situation occurs. Also, because a database is created upon deployment, you must be a server administrator to deploy a project from offline mode to the server.

Getting Started in Offline Mode

To get started in the BI Dev Studio with Offline mode, follow the following steps:

1. Launch the BI Dev Studio.

2. Select New/Project from the File menu. The New Project dialog box appears as shown in Figure 3.3.

3. Open the Other Languages node in the Project Types pane if it is not already open.

4. Select Business Intelligence Projects.

5. Select Analysis Services Project from the Templates pane.

6. Give your project a name, and click OK.

7. Select Build/Deploy to deploy your project to the server, creating your database.

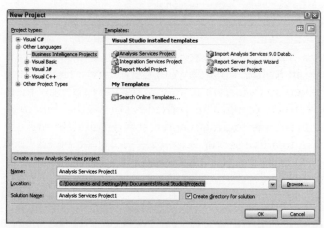

Figure 3.3 New Project dialog

By default, the project will be deployed to the localhost server, that is, the server on the same machine as your tools. To change the target server, select Project/Properties to launch the Configuration Property Management dialog box. In this dialog box, you can create different deployment configurations and specify the target server and database name for each potential configuration, as illustrated in Figure 3.4.

The other important properties to note for deployment are the Processing Option and Deployment mode. By default, deployment automatically processes any objects that have been created or invalidated by the project changes. The Processing Option property controls this behavior. Again, by default, only the incremental changes from the tools are deployed to the server. This can result in errors if the database has been changed from another client or if a database with the same name already exists on the server. The Deployment Mode property controls this behavior.

TIP You can set a property to change the default deployment server that is set every time you create a new offline project. To do so, go to the Options dialog box by selecting Options on the Tools menu. Drill down to Business Intelligence Designers/Analysis Services Designers/General and set the Default Target Server property to the server instance of your choice. This setting affects only new projects, so you still have to manually change any projects previously created.

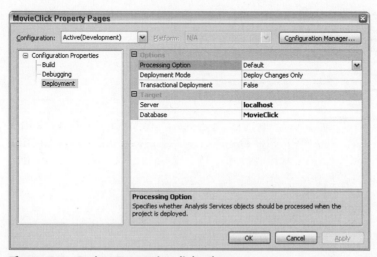

Figure 3.4   Project Properties dialog box

Switching Project Modes

You may find yourself in one mode and need to be in the other, for example when making a quick update to a deployed project from a different machine, or when you want to save the object metadata of an operational database to source control. Luckily, it is easy and painless to make the switch. The easiest is to switch from Offline mode to Immediate mode. You simply go to the File menu, select Open/Analysis Services Database, and select the database you previously deployed. To go the other way, that is, to switch from Immediate mode to Offline mode, you create a new project and select Import Analysis Services 9.0 Database, as shown in Figure 3.3. This launches a wizard where you can specify the server and source database name and then extract the metadata into a new project. Note that you still need to set the deployment options to indicate the target server and database name as necessary.

> **TIP** You can tell if you are in Immediate or Offline mode by looking at the
> name of the project in the Solution Explorer. If you are in Immediate mode,
> the project name will be followed by the server instance name in parenthesis.
> Additionally, all window tabs will have the text (Online) after the object name.

Creating Data Mining Objects

After you open your database or project, the operations performed inside an Analysis Services project are similar regardless of the operational mode you chose. To perform data mining, you need to indicate and describe your source data and then create mining structures and models.

Setting Up Your Data Sources

Two objects in Analysis Services act as interfaces to your data, the Data Source and the data source view (DSV). The Data Source is essentially a connection string indicating data location, whereas the DSV is an abstraction layer that enables you to modify the way you look at data sources, or even define a schema and switch the actual source at a later time. In this section, we talk about how to set up these objects for use in data mining.

Data Source

A data source is a rather simple object. It consists of nothing more than a connection string, plus some additional information indicating how to connect. However two aspects of data sources can easily trip you up and cause general frustration if you don't understand them. Both issues will manifest by allowing you to create objects on the client that will fail to work properly when deployed.

The first issue is *data location*. Unlike most data mining products, SQL Server Data Mining is a server based solution. This means that when you set up your data sources, the data source has to be accessible not only to the client where you used the tools to build the model, but also to the server where the model will be processed. For example, if you built your model based on an Access database in C:\My Documents\Northwind.mdb, your model would fail to process unless the file was located on the same place on the server. Even if the file happened to be present, this would be a bad thing, as you would have no way of knowing if such a file actually contained the same data or even the same schema as your local version. In general, when mining on local data, you should move the data to a SQL Server database using SQL Server Integration Services (SSIS) before building your models.

The second issue is *security*. It is important to understand the user credentials that are used to access data from Analysis Services. When you set up your connection, you generally choose to use *integrated security*, that is, use account credentials to access the data, or *simple security*, using a specified username and password. Microsoft recommends always using integrated security if supported by the source database. Regardless of the method the source database supports, a data source object contains additional information telling Analysis Services exactly which security credentials to use, or *impersonate*, when connecting to the database. A data source object can be created with four different impersonation options:

1. Impersonate Current User
   This method in general is the most secure for data sources accessed through query statements. It causes Analysis Services to use the current user credentials to access the remote data. However, in many implementations, Analysis Services has to delegate credentials to the source database machine. For delegation to work correctly it must be configured by your domain administrators. Consult the Windows Server documentation regarding Kerberos for more information on this topic. This method cannot be used in data sources that are used for processing Analysis Services objects, because it can result in different data being accessed, depending on who processes an object.

2. Impersonate Account
   When Impersonate Current User isn't an option, Impersonate Account is the second best choice. Impersonate Account allows you to specify the account credentials that will be used to access the data source. The credentials, consisting of a username and password, are stored with

Analysis Services, and all access to that data uses those credentials. This method is the most secure if delegation is not an option.

3. Impersonate Service Account
   Impersonate Service Account causes all data access to occur under the account which Analysis Services itself is running. This method exists mainly for testing purposes and is discouraged for production use. In general, Analysis Services should be running under an account with the most limited privileges as possible.

4. Default
   Default causes different credentials to be used, depending on how the data source is accessed. If accessed for processing, the service account credentials will be used to access data. If accessed for querying, the current user credentials will be used, if possible.

Creating the MovieClick Data Source

To create a data source to the MovieClick database:

1. Download the MovieClick database and install it as described in Appendix A.

2. Right-click the Data Sources folder in the Solution or Object Explorer and select New Data *Source* to launch the Data Source Wizard.

3. Skip the introductory page and click the New Connection button on the second page to launch the Data Link dialog box.

4. Enter the Server name where you installed the database, specify your security settings, and select the MovieClick database.

5. Click OK to exit the Data Link dialog box; click Next to advance the wizard to the Impersonation Information page.

6. Enter the username and password you want Analysis Services to use to access the MovieClick database and click Finish to close the wizard.

Using the Data Source View

The data source view (DSV) is an abstract client-side view of your data. This is where your modeling begins. The DSV is where you select, organize, explore, and, in a sense, manipulate the data in the source. In essence, the DSV tells Analysis Services how you want to see the data on the source. Since the object exists on your Analysis Services server and not your relational source, you can perform such manipulations even if you only have read access to the relational server.

When creating a DSV for data mining purposes, the most important table to identify is your case table. This is the table that contains the cases you want to analyze. Additionally, you need to bring in any related tables, such as nested or lookup tables, which provide additional information about your cases.

Creating the MovieClick Data Source View

To create a DSV from the MovieClick data source:

1. Right-click the Data Source Views folder in the Solution or Object Explorer and select New Data Source View to launch the Data Source View Wizard.

2. Skip the introductory page and the MovieClick data source on the Select Data Source wizard page will be selected; click Next to continue

3. The Name Matching page performs no function for the data source as imported, so click Next to continue. This page appears only when relationships are not specified in the source database and allows you to choose how to automatically create relationships based on the key columns of the tables. Since the MovieClick database, as imported, has neither relationships nor keys, the algorithm it uses does not work.

4. On the Select Tables and Views wizard page click the >> button to move all tables from the Available Objects list to the Included objects list.

5. Click Next and then Finish to exit the DSV Wizard and display the DSV Designer.

6. Drag a relationship to the CustomerID column in the Customers table from the CustomerID table in each of the other tables. After each connection you can right-click in the designer and select Arrange Tables to make the tables easier to see. When finished, your DSV should look like Figure 3.5.

The DSV Designer initially displays a diagram of the tables in your data source and the relationships between them. If you already know your data, and it is in the proper shape for mining, you can begin creating your mining models at this point. However, if this is not true, which is generally the case, you can use the DSV Designer to explore the data and alter it to the shape you need for your models. Initially, you can simply annotate the tables and columns in your schema to make them easier to understand and more supportable. You can add descriptions to these objects and even change the names to be something more readable and understandable. For example, if you had a table named NWSFYO3 you could rename it to Fiscal Year 03 Northwest Sales or rename column 014 to Quantity. You do this by selecting the object and typing the description and the friendly name in the Properties window. Additionally, any relationships between tables that were not specified in the source database can be indicated here simply by dragging from the foreign key column in one table to the primary key column in another. All of these modifications occur only in the DSV and do not affect your original data in any way.

> **NOTE** If the relationship between a case table and a nested table does not exist in the database, you must specify it in the DSV or you will not be able add the nested table to your model.

On top of annotating your schema, the DSV allows you to create named calculations, Named Queries, and views and interactively explore your data using pivot charts.

Working with Named Calculations

Named calculations are additional virtual columns on the tables in your DSV. This allows you to mine derived information in your data without having to change your source data. A named calculation consists of name, a SQL expression containing the calculation, and an optional description.

The calculation can be any valid SQL expression. If you are not a SQL expert, here are some types of expressions that are useful in many data mining projects.

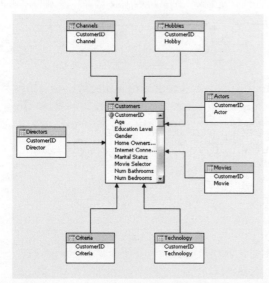

Figure 3.5   Completed MovieClick data source view

Arithmetic Operations

Standard SQL supports +, -, * , /, and % (modulo). For example you could create a *Profit* named calculation with the following formula:

```
[Sales Price] - [Item Cost]
```

Mathematical Functions

Mathematical functions are useful, especially when data in a column does not follow a uniform distribution. The SQL functions ABS, LOG, SIGN, and SQRT are particularly useful. Here are two examples:

- To flatten out an exponentially increasing variable:

  ```
  LOG([Sales Quantity])
  ```

- To create a flag for over/under budget quarters:

  ```
  SIGN([Actual Expenses] - [Budgeted Expenses])
  ```

Compositing Expressions

Often, the hypothesis you want to test depends on a variable that is a combination of two of the variables you already have. For example, it may not be interesting that a person is married or has children, but the combination of the two may provide valuable information. A composite expression for this situation could look like this:

```
[Marital Status] + ' ' + [Has Children]
```

CASE Expressions

CASE expressions are an extremely flexible way to create meaningful variables for data mining. The CASE expression allows you to assign results based on the evaluation of one or more conditions. Useful applications of CASE are to change value labels, manually discretize columns, reduce the number of valid states, and convert an attribute from a nested table to the case level.

- To change value labels:

  ```
  CASE [Category]
      WHEN 1    THEN 'Food'
      WHEN 2    THEN 'Beverage'
      WHEN 3    THEN 'Goods'
  END CASE
  ```

■ To manually discretize a column:

```
CASE
    WHEN [Age] < 20 THEN 'Under 20'
    WHEN [Age] <= 30 THEN 'Between 20 and 30'
    WHEN [Age] <= 40 THEN 'Between 30 and 40'
    ELSE 'Over 40'
END
```

■ To reduce the number of valid states:

```
CASE [Marital Status]
    WHEN 'Married'        THEN [Marital Status]
    WHEN 'Never Married' THEN [Marital Status]
    ELSE 'Other'
END
```

■ To convert an attribute from a nested table to a case table:

```
CASE
    WHEN EXISTS
            (SELECT [Movie] FROM [Movies]
                WHERE [Movie]='Star Wars' AND
                        [Movies].[CustomerID]=[Customers].[CustomerID])
            THEN 'True'
    ELSE 'False'
END
```

This would be done, for instance, when you wanted to convert a nested attribute to a case-level attribute. Note that if you still want to use the nested table in the model, you will have to use a named query to filter the attribute from the nested table, as described in the next section.

Creating a Named Calculation on the Customers Table

To create a named calculation to discretize and reduce the number of states in the Num Bedrooms column:

1. Right-click the Customers table and select Create a named calculation.

2. Enter the calculation name Bedrooms and optionally enter a description.

3. Enter the following expression:

```
CASE
    WHEN [Num Bedrooms] = 1  THEN 'One'
    WHEN [Num Bedrooms] <= 3 THEN 'Two or Three'
    WHEN [Num Bedrooms] >= 4 THEN 'Four or more'
    ELSE 'None'
END
```

Upon closing the dialog box, the DSV Designer will validate your expression and return any applicable errors. Once you have successfully created your calculation you can see the results by right-clicking the table and selecting Explore Data.

Working with Named Queries

As a named calculation is a virtual column on a DSV table, a named query is nothing but a virtual view on your data source. Again, this allows you to change the data you are mining without making any changes to your original data. Even when modifications to the source are possible, creating Named Queries directly in your DSV is quick and easy and allows you to maintain these views alongside the models where they are used instead of polluting your databases with single-use objects.

The Named Query editor provides a standard query builder user interface to assist in creating queries which is very useful for complicated joins. Note that Named Queries can only be built upon database tables and not other DSV objects.

Typical queries that are useful for data mining are filtering, joins, and sampling.

- To filter rows based on column values:

```
SELECT * FROM [Movies] WHERE [Movie] != 'Star Wars'
```

- To filter out unpopular items from a nested table:

```
SELECT [CustomerID], [Movie] FROM [Movies]
WHERE [Movie] IN
    (SELECT DISTINCT
        [Movie]
    FROM [Movies] GROUP BY [Movie]
        HAVING COUNT([Movie]) > 20)
```

- To join information from a foreign table:

```
SELECT
    Customers.*, Education.[Education Level]
FROM Customers JOIN Education
ON Customers.[Education Id] = Education.[Education Id]
```

- To sample rows from a SQL Server database:

```
SELECT * FROM CUSTOMERS
    TABLESAMPLE (30 PERCENT)
    REPEATABLE (1)
```

NOTE Analysis Services issues several queries to the named query, so when using TABLESAMPLE, it is necessary to use the REPEATABLE clause to guarantee Analysis Services retrieves the same rows each time. Also, since there is no efficient method for querying the complement of a sample, this method is useful for reducing the data size, but not for splitting data into training and testing sets. For that operation you should use SQL Server Integration Services (SSIS)

Creating a Named Query Based on the Customers Table

We want to create a named query based on the Customers table in the DSV that contains only homeowners. Since this table contains a named calculation, we have to manually add the calculation into the query.

1. Double-click the Bedrooms Named Calculation in the Customers table to open the Named Calculation dialog and copy the SQL text.

2. Right-click in the DSV Designer, and select New Named Query.

3. Enter the query name Homeowners, and optionally enter a description.

4. Click the Add Table button, select the Customers table, and close the Add Table dialog box.

5. Select the * (All Customers) check box on the Customers table.

6. To add the calculated column:

   a. Enter a comma after Customers.* in the query window, and paste the contents of the clipboard into the second row of the Column column.

   b. Type as Bedrooms after the pasted text.

   c. The query will expand to replace Customers.* with the list of all the table columns.

7. To filter on homeowners:

   a. In the grid control, find the row containing [Home Ownership] in the Column column.

   b. Clear the checkmark in the second row of the Output column.

   c. Enter ='Own' in the criteria column

8. Your final query should look like Figure 3.6. Click OK to close the dialog box.

Your named query can now be explored from the context menu using Explore Data, like any other DSV table.

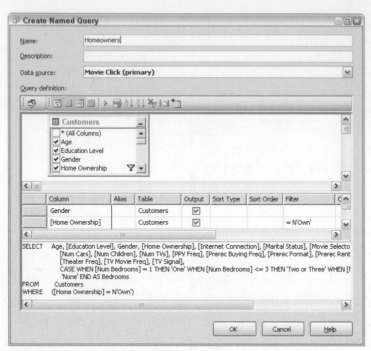

Figure 3.6 Homeowners named query

Organizing the DSV

When a named query is created, any relationships that the original table had are not carried over to the new table. This means that to use those relationships, you have to recreate them by dragging from the foreign key to the primary key for each table relationship. When you complete the plethora of crossing relationships in your DSV, it will be very difficult to read and comprehend, as in Figure 3.7.

You can remedy this problem by using DSV diagrams. The DSV Designer allows you to create any number of diagrams allowing you to select a subset of DSV tables and arrange them as you see fit. To create these diagrams, you click the New Diagram button, name the diagram, and drag tables from the list on the left to it. You can also add tables to the view by right-clicking a table already in the view and selecting Show Related Tables. After adding tables, you can clean up your arrangement by right-clicking in the design area and selecting Arrange Tables.

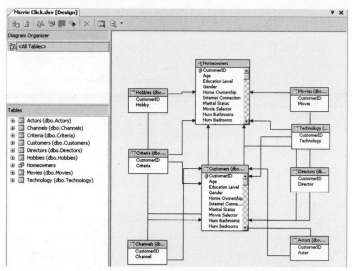

Figure 3.7   DSV with many relationships in the DSV Designer

NOTE Named queries and named calculations rely on the processing power of your relational server. The additional resources required to process the generated queries will have an impact on the initial processing time of your mining models. If this increase becomes too severe, and you will be frequently repeating these queries, you should consider materializing these views on the relational server.

Exploring Data

Part of any data mining project is learning about and understanding the nature of your data. By leveraging controls from Office Web Components (OWC), the DSV Designer provides the functionality to explore your data in four different views. By right-clicking a DSV table and selecting Explore Data, you can view your data as a table, pivot table, simple charts, and a pivot chart. By default, the Explore Data component will sample 5,000 points of your data. The option buttons in the upper left of the Explore Data window allow you to change this setting to a maximum of 20,000 points, due to a limitation of the OWC controls.

The tabular views allow you to do a simple exploration of your data. Clever use of the pivot table will allow you to get a better understanding of the data by arranging, slicing, and aggregating your data in different ways. For example, by exploring a pivot chart on the Customers table, you can find the average Age and its standard deviation by using the Bedrooms column we created previously. (See Figure 3.8.) This is possible because we are exploring the DSV table and not the actual source table as it is in the data. We can explore Named Queries in the DSV in precisely the same manner.

The graphical exploration offers a page of simple column, pie, and bar charts plus a pivot chart view. Using the simple charts you can see histograms and pies of various attributes side by side. If your data is continuous, the chart divides the continuous range into 10 buckets. The pivot chart, on the contrary, provides a wealth of graphing controls to analyze your data, from your standard line, bar, scatter, column, and pie charts, to more exotic types such as doughnut and radar charts, as shown in Figure 3.9.

The pivot table and chart have many configuration options to help you analyze your data in different ways. Many of these are available through the context-sensitive Command and Options dialog box, from the Context menu, or from embedded toolbars. Virtually every aspect of the tables and charts can be modified, either by graphically selecting the object or by using the selection box on the General tab of the dialog. Describing the full feature set of the OWC could easily fill another book and mastering the OWC controls for best value will take some practice, but with experience you will be able to manipulate the controls to find exactly the right view for you. Additionally, the pivot table and chart are linked, so you can switch back and forth, make edits, and see how the change affected the other view.

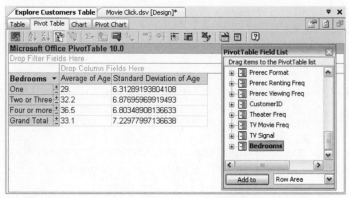

Figure 3.8 Exploring data with the pivot chart

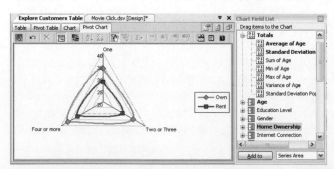

Figure 3.9 Radar chart showing Age by Bedrooms and Home Ownership

One additional feature of the pivot chart that is important for data exploration is graphical named query generation. By clicking the Named Query button on the toolbar, you can use elements of the chart to define a named query. For instance you could select only those homeowners with one bedroom and renters with four or more on the chart and add them to the query. This named query becomes like any other and can be used as a source for exploring data.

> **TIP** Although the Explore Data window looks like other document windows, it is, in fact, a tool window like the Solution Explorer and Properties windows. By right-clicking the Window tab you can change the Explore Data window into a floating or dockable window. You can also open up many Explore Data windows on different DSV tables to display charts and tables side by side.

Creating and Editing Models

Once you have organized, modified, selected, and understand the data you want to analyze, you can start to create data mining objects. The first step is to run the Data Mining Wizard. After completing it, you can refine the results in the Data Mining Designer.

Structures and Models

SQL Server Analysis Services has two major objects that deal with data mining: *mining structures* and *mining models*.

A mining structure defines the domain of a mining problem, whereas a mining model is the application of a mining algorithm to the structure in a mining structure. A mining structure contains a list of *structure columns* that have data and content types, bindings to the data source, plus some optional flags that control how the data is modeled. Additionally, a mining structure contains a list of mining models that use the columns from the structure.

The definition of a mining model contains an algorithm with its associated parameters, plus a list of columns from the mining structure. Each model in a structure can use a different algorithm or the same algorithm with different parameters, and/or a different subset of the columns in the structure. For each column in the model, you can assign how it is to be used in that model and algorithm-specific modeling flags. This feature allows you to easily test different hypotheses on the same data set.

Using the Data Mining Wizard

The Data Mining Wizard creates two objects for you: the mining structure that describes the columns and training data you will use for mining, and a mining model, which takes those columns, applies an algorithm, and defines the usage of each column for that algorithm. The wizard wraps the creation of these two objects into one simple set of steps.

The steps of the wizard are to select your algorithm, select the source tables and specify how they are used, select the columns from those tables and specify how they are used, name the model, and you're done. At that point, you can process and analyze the results of your model without further adieu. Analysis Services makes it that simple to get started. The wizard also allows you to create models from multidimensional, that is, OLAP, sources. This topic is covered in Chapter 11, so we will focus only on relational sources for the time being.

Using the wizard is simple because it performs several steps automatically, based on the input you provide. As a data miner, it is important that you understand these steps and how and when decisions that impact your model are made.

On the first page in the wizard, you choose whether you are creating a model from a relational or multidimensional source, as shown in Figure 3.10. Although in the end a model created from one source appears identical to those created from another, the creation process is slightly different, so there are different wizard paths for each option. Also, a particular mining algorithm may not support creating models from OLAP sources, so this question is asked first.

The next page asks you which algorithm to use to create your initial mining model. The list of algorithms is determined by the capabilities of your target server and may contain more or less than the list of algorithms covered in this book. The reasons for and process by which this occurs are described in Chapter 13. If you cannot connect to a server at the time the wizard is run, you get the default list of algorithms provided with SQL Server Data Mining, as shown in Figure 3.11. Choosing which algorithm you are going to use is dependant on the business problem you are trying to solve. The application of each algorithm is described in its respective chapter.

On the next two pages, you indicate the data you will be mining. You choose the DSV containing the tables, then you specify the actual tables themselves. When choosing the tables, you have to specify whether each table is the *case* table or if it is a *nested* table, as shown in Figure 3.12. As described in Chapter 2, the case table is the case that contains the entities you want to analyze, and a nested table contains additional, usually transactional, information about each case.

TIP Sometimes determining which table is the *case* table can be a bit confusing. For example, if you want to analyze how products are purchased together, you may naïvely choose products as the case table. However, you are actually analyzing the groups of those products that were purchased by a single customer. In this case, the *customer* becomes the case with the transaction table containing the product purchases as a nested table.

When you have only a transaction table, the table can be used as both the case table and the nested table by specifying the transaction ID as the case-level key and the other columns as columns in the nested table.

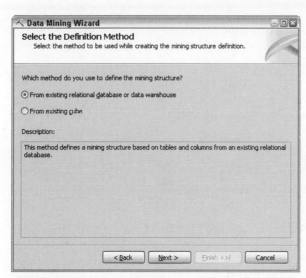

Figure 3.10   Select Method screen of the Data Mining Wizard

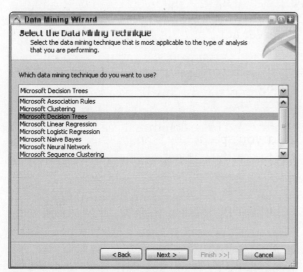

Figure 3.11   Select Data Mining Technique page of the Data Mining Wizard

Figure 3.12   Specifying table types in the Data Mining Wizard

On the next two pages, you indicate which columns you are using plus how you want the mining algorithms to interpret each one. First, you specify which columns are used in the model, plus whether they are *key*, *input*, and/or *predictable*. Then you specify the data and content types for each of the columns.

You must specify a key for the case table and each nested table in your model, as shown in Figure 3.13. Remember that the key of a nested table in DMX *is not* the foreign key that relates the nested table to the case table, rather it is the key in the context that you have it nested. The wizard enforces this relationship by not presenting the foreign key as a choice and warning the user if a key is not specified. For example, a nested table representing a customer's shopping cart comes from a table that may have a row ID as a key, plus transaction ID, product name, quantity, and price. The nested table in our model would only have the product, quantity, and price columns, because the row ID isn't of interest in our model, and the transaction ID is the foreign key to the case table. In this reduced context, you can see that the quantity and price relate to the *product*, which becomes the key of the nested table. Sequence clustering and time series models have special rules regarding the specification of keys. See Chapters 8 and 10, respectively, for specific details.

> **TIP**   One thing to consider when determining the correct column to be a nested key is that data mining finds patterns by examining similarities and differences between cases. If you chose a column as a nested key such that the values in that column would only show up in a single case, the data mining algorithms would find no patterns relative to that column. This logic summarily dismisses the use of transaction IDs or row IDs as nested keys.

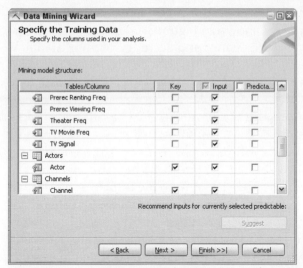

Figure 3.13   Indicating column usages in the Data Mining Wizard, showing the specification of nested keys

Which columns you specify as input and which as predictable depends on your business problem, the hypothesis you are trying to test, and the algorithm you chose. In general, specifying a column as Input indicates that the algorithm will use that column to determine the columns marked as Predictable, or an output. The exact way that each algorithm uses this information varies somewhat, so you should familiarize yourself with the specific semantics detailed in each algorithm chapter. One fact that remains constant among all algorithms is that if you want to be able to select a column from the model in a PREDICTION JOIN statement, the column must be predictable. To predict a nested table, check the box in the Predict column next to its key.

> **TIP**   If you have many columns in your table, it can be difficult to know which to choose as inputs. You can always use all the columns, but this involves additional processing power and, depending on the algorithm, may make your model difficult to interpret.
>
> The Suggest button on the Specify Column Usage page of the wizard performs a quick entropy-based analysis to indicate which columns are likely to provide information toward a selected output, thereby reducing the number of columns in your final model. Note that this feature only considers case-level columns in its analysis and is not a guarantee that the selected columns will impact or that the nonselected columns will not impact your target variable.

Next, you are presented with the list of columns you have chosen and their respective data and content types, as shown in Figure 3.14. Indicating the correct content type is crucial to the performance and accuracy of your model. If you had a field such as Income marked as DISCRETE, for instance, the algorithm would assume that each possible income value was a distinct category and would likely spend extra processing power to learn absolutely nothing. On the flip side, if you had a categorical column where the categories were indicated by integers (for example, 1–Blue, 2–Yellow, 3–Red, 4–Green, and so on) marked as CONTINUOUS, the algorithm would assume that it could compare them and measure distances between points, in this case creating the bizarre logic that Green(4) – Red(3) = Blue(1)! Luckily, the Data Mining Wizard has the ability to automatically detect whether a numeric column is categorical (discrete) or continuous. Clicking the Detect button on this page causes the wizard to sample and analyze the source data and choose an appropriate content type. If a continuous type is determined and your selected algorithm does not support continuous columns, the content type will be specified as DISCRETIZED. You can set discretization parameters in the designer, as specified in the next section. Before moving on with the wizard, you should verify that the content types were assigned correctly and modify any that were not.

The final page of the wizard, shown in Figure 3.15, allows you to specify the names of the structure and model and enable the drill-through feature if it is supported by the algorithm. When completed, the wizard creates a mining structure containing a mining model and launches the Data Mining Designer.

Figure 3.14 Specifying content and data types in the Data Mining Wizard

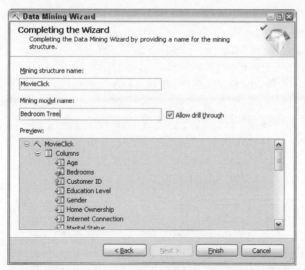

Figure 3.15   Naming objects in the Data Mining Wizard

Creating the MovieClick Mining Structure and Model

We will use the Mining Model Wizard to create a mining structure and model to predict the number of bedrooms for customers who own their homes, based on all of the information we know about them.

1. Right-click the Mining Models folder in the Solution Explorer or the Object Explorer, and choose New Mining Model.

2. Skip the description page and go to the Select the Definition Method page. As we are building our model from relational data, leave the default option selected and click Next.

3. On the Select the Data Mining Technique page, you can view the list of available algorithms if you are connected to your server. Leave Microsoft Decision Trees selected, and click Next.

4. On the Select Data Source View page, you are presented with the single DSV in this project or database. Click Next to continue.

5. On the Specify Table Types page, we need to indicate our case and nested tables. Since we only want to analyze homeowners, click the check box in the Case column next to the Homeowners named query. We want to add all of the nested tables, so click the check box in the Nested column next to the Actors, Channels, Criteria, Directors, Hobbies, Movies, and Technology tables. Click Next to continue.

6. On the Specify the Training Data page, we indicate which columns we are going to use in our model and how they are to be used. Since the key column for the Homeowners table was indicated in the DSV, it is already selected as the key of the model. We are predicting Bedrooms, so click the check box in the Predictable column next to the named calculation Bedrooms.

7. We want all other case-level columns to be inputs except for Num Bedrooms from which Bedrooms is derived. Check the check box in the Input column next to all case columns except Customer Id and Num Bedrooms. Note — you can use the SHIFT key to check multiple columns at the same time.

8. For each nested table, we need to indicate the nested key. The wizard automatically filters out the foreign key column, so each nested table is left with a single column. Click the check box in the Key column for each column in each nested table. Check the input column as well. Click Next to continue.

9. On the Specify Columns' Content and Data Type page, click the Detect button to automatically assign the correct content types. Click Next to continue.

10. On the completion page of the wizard, type MovieClick as the name of the structure and Movie Trees as the name of the model, then check the Allow Drill through box and click Finish to end the wizard.

Upon completing the wizard, the Data Mining Designer opens to the Mining Structure Editor.

Using the Data Mining Designer

The Data Mining Designer is where most of the work with your models will take place. It contains the facilities for editing, browsing, querying, and comparing models distributed in five panes, the Mining Structure pane, the Mining Models pane, the Mining Model Viewer pane, the Mining Accuracy Chart pane, and the Mining Model Prediction pane. In this section, we will focus on editing only, with the Mining Structure and Mining Models panes, leaving the other functionality for the "Using Your Models" section of this chapter.

Working with the Mining Structure Editor

The Mining Structure Editor allows you to add and remove columns to and from your mining structure and also set the properties of each mining structure column. You need to use the Structure Editor to perform modeling operations that are not possible in the Mining Model Wizard. Even if the Wizard-generated structure suits your needs, it is a good idea to inspect your mining structure after running the wizard to be sure that it contains everything you want.

The three components of the Mining Structure Editor are the structure tree, the DSV view, and the Properties window, as shown in Figure 3.16. Clicking columns in the structure tree or the DSV will cause their properties to show in the Properties window. Dragging columns from the DSV to the structure tree will add the column to the mining model. Right-clicking almost any item produces a menu providing a list of actions to be performed on that item. You can browse your data and explore your DSV. Note that to edit the DSV you must return to the DSV Designer.

The editor allows you to perform certain operations that are not available using the wizard. You cannot perform the following modeling operations in the wizard:

- **Set discretization properties:** The Mining Model Wizard will automatically set the content type of continuous columns to DISCRETIZED if the selected algorithm does not support continuous attributes. However, you may want to be able to specify the discretization method or the number of buckets that the attribute will be divided into.

  To set these values, click the column you want to modify, and set the DiscretizationMethod and DiscretizationBuckets properties in the Properties window. The various discretization methods that are available are described in Chapter 2.

- **Add a column to the structure multiple times:** Since a structure may contain multiple models, you may find that you want to model a specific column in different ways to see how it impacts the results. For example, you may want to compare how Age influences the results when it's treated as a continuous value or when it's discretized into three, five, or seven buckets. You can add a column multiple times to the model simply by dragging the source column from the DSV to the structure tree. Each column will be given an incremental name, which you can change in the Properties window.

- **Create hierarchies among your attributes:** In Chapter 2, we described the RELATED TO construct in DMX that allows you to create hierarchies. In the Structure Editor, you can use the Classified Column property of a structure column to perform the same functionality. For example, to create a Product Category-Product Name hierarchy, set the Classified Column property of the Product Category column to Product Name.

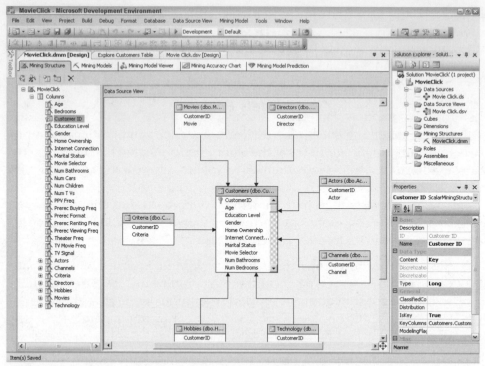

Figure 3.16　Mining Structure Editor in the Data Mining Designer

- **Add a column that has its values looked up in another table:** If your data is normalized, it is likely that the table you want to mine contains foreign keys to lookup tables instead of the actual data labels you want to appear in the model. Using the Structure Editor, you can add these columns directly to your model. To add such a column, right-click the table that has the foreign key and select Show Related Tables. The table that contains the primary key will appear in the DSV area of the Structure Editor. If the relationship is not specified in the DSV, you will have to return to the DSV editor and add it. From this new table, drag the column that contains the data name you want to use in your model to the structure tree.

For example, assume that you were mining a Purchases table that had a Product Id column and another table Products that related Product Id to Product Name. To create a structure that used the Product Name column you would right-click the Purchases table and select Show Related Tables to introduce the Products table. Then you would click and drag the Product Name column to your structure.

TIP The easiest way to add a nested table to a mining structure is to drag the key of the nested table to the structure tree. When you drop the key, the editor will automatically create a nested table with the key you specified.

Working with the Mining Models Editor

The Mining Models Editor is where you can create multiple models on the structure. You use the editor to set the algorithm and algorithm parameters for each model, as well as to select which columns are used in each model, how they are used, and setting algorithm-specific modeling flags on each column.

The editor consists of a table showing the models and their columns and again the Properties window, as shown in Figure 3.17. This configuration allows you to quickly see how each column is used in each model and set properties appropriately.

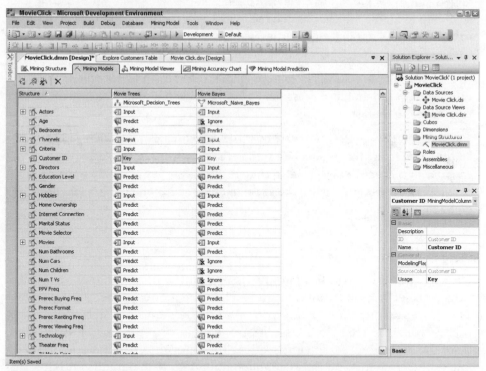

Figure 3.17   Mining Models Editor in the SQL BI Development Studio

Setting Column Properties

Setting the usage of each column involves selecting the column and choosing whether you want this column to be used as Input, Predict, PredictOnly, or Ignore. Selecting Input is analogous to selecting the Input column in the Mining Model Wizard. Selecting PredictOnly is analogous to selecting the Predictable column in the wizard. Generally this usage implies that this column will not be used as input for other predictable targets; however, you should check the chapters on each algorithm for the exact semantics. Selecting Predict is analogous to selecting both the Input and Predictable columns in the wizard and implies that the column will be treated both as an input for other targets and as a target in and of itself. Again, the exact semantics should be checked for each algorithm. Setting a column to Ignore creates a model that simply does not contain the specified column. Additional, model-specific properties for each column can be set in the Properties window.

TIP You can multiple select columns by using the Shift and Ctrl keys. This allows you to set properties on many columns at the same time. Since setting a column to Ignore removes it from the model, you can set Ignore only in the column grid and not in the Properties window. Also, you cannot change the usage of any ignored columns in the Properties window.

To change multiple columns to or from Ignore, select them in the column grid using Shift or Ctrl and then press the F2 key to show the combo box where you can make the change.

You can also change the properties of structure columns in the Mining Models Editor by selecting the column and setting the properties in the Properties window. In this editor, you can also change the properties of multiple structure columns simultaneously, using the same multiple selection methods you used on mining columns.

Setting Model Properties

To edit and set the algorithm parameters, select the mining model itself. You do this by selecting the column header so that the model properties are shown in the Properties window. Here, you can set the name and algorithm used, annotate your model with a description, enable drill-through if supported, and set the algorithm parameters. Setting the algorithm parameters brings up a dialog box showing you the available parameters with defaults and descriptions, as shown in Figure 3.18. See the chapter on each individual algorithm for detailed discussions of each parameter.

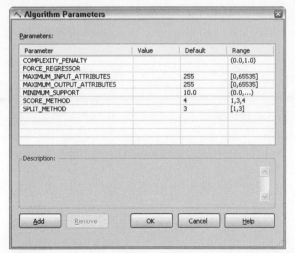

Figure 3.18   Algorithm Parameters Dialog for Microsoft_Decision_Trees

TIP   An easier way to set algorithm parameters is to right-click the column header for the desired algorithm and select Set Algorithm Parameters.

Creating Additional Models

To create multiple models on the same structure, simply select the New Mining Model item in the Mining Model menu. You are prompted to enter a name and select the algorithm, and the editor creates a new mining model in the structure. The new model you create maintains the settings of the model that you selected when you chose the creation operation. The new model will use the same inputs, have the same targets, and use any additional settings that are compatible with the new algorithm you selected.

Creating and Modifying Additional Models

We are going to set all of the case-level columns of the MovieClick model to be predictable, then we will create a new model in the same structure, using the Microsoft Naive Bayes algorithm

1. Switch to the Mining Models Editor by clicking the Mining Models icon in the View column of the Data Mining Designer.

2. Click the row for the Age column in the Movie Trees model column to select the table cell.

3. While holding down the Shift key, click the row for the Bedrooms column in the Movie Trees model. Now the usage for both Age and Bedrooms should be selected.

4. Press the F2 key to bring up a drop-down box where you can select the type of usage.

5. Change the usage to Predict. All the selected columns' usage will change.

6. Use Ctrl, Shift, and F2 to select the remaining case-level columns and change their usage to Predict.

7. Select New Mining Model from the Mining Model menu.

8. In the dialog that appears, type Movie Bayes for the name and select Microsoft Naive Bayes as the algorithm. Click OK.

9. A warning appears that the Age, Num Bathrooms, Num Children, and Num TVs columns contain a content type not supported by the new algorithm and asks if you want to continue. Click Yes, and the new model will be created with those columns set to Ignore.

At this point, you have a mining structure containing two models. The new model has all of the same columns set to Predict as the first, with the exception of the columns that had a content type not supported by the selected algorithm, which were set to Ignore.

Processing

In Chapter 2, we described how to train a model using an INSERT INTO statement. Using the tools to train models on the server is called *processing*. Analysis Services. Data Mining has the ability to process all the models in a structure in parallel on a single data read. It does this by creating a compressed cache of the data that is used to train each of the models in the structure. This functionality requires several processing options to control exactly what is processed when, and how to clean up after you're done. The mechanism is described in more detail in Chapter 13.

NOTE Before processing a newly created or edited structure or model, you must first send the object to the server. In immediate mode, simply saving your work deploys the object. However, in offline mode, you must first deploy the project. To do so select Deploy Solution from the Build menu. When you use the default settings, deploying the project will also cause any objects in the project to be processed.

Mining Models and Structures can have three states in regard to processing: processed, partially processed, and unprocessed. A processed object is completely finished and ready to go. Partially processed is an ambiguous state that indicates that part of the object is processed and other parts are not. This may be acceptable for your circumstances — for example, you may have a mining structure with several mining models. At the current time, you may only want to process one of the models within — the structure would then be partially processed. Unprocessed implies that the object contains absolutely no data whatsoever.

The processing options for Mining Structures and Mining Models are as follows:

- **Process Full:** Process Full causes the object to be completely reprocessed from the source data. When this option is sent to a mining structure, the structure is processed and then each model within is processed in parallel. When sent to a model, the source data is only read if the structure has not been processed.

- **Process Default:** Processing an object with Process Default causes the server to do whatever it takes to bring the object to a fully processed state. For example, if the object is already processed, the server will perform no action or if you edit a model within a structure and send Process Default to the structure, the server will process that one model without rereading the source data.

- **Unprocess:** Unprocess causes the object to be completely unprocessed, dropping all data associated with that object. Sending this command to a structure causes any caches to be cleared and contained models to be unprocessed.

- **Process Structure:** Process Structure is only valid on a mining structure and causes the structure to read and cache the source data without processing the contained models. Executing subsequent Process Full and Process Default commands on the models will process information from this cache.

- **Process Clear Structure:** Using this option on a structure causes the structure to drop any cached source data while leaving the contained models processed. This greatly reduces the disk footprint of your mining structure at the cost of having to reread the data on the next process command. Additionally, drill-through functionality on any contained models will be disabled until the models are reprocessed.

Processing the MovieClick Mining Structure

Here, we will process the MovieClick Mining Structure.

In Immediate mode:

1. Save your structure by clicking the Save button on the toolbar.
2. Select Process Mining Structure and All Models from the Mining Model menu, or click the Process button on the Designer toolbar.
3. Click Run in the processing dialog.

In Offline mode:

1. Select the Deploy option from the Build menu. By default, deploying the solution will process all objects.
2. If the default has changed, deploy the solution and follow the instructions for Immediate mode.

At this point, the Processing Progress dialog will appear, providing status information for the processing operation. When the process is complete, you can view details about each step, including the processing time.

Using Your Models

Once you have created and processed your models, you need to be able to explore, query, and compare them so that you can understand and apply the information they provide.

Understanding the Model Viewers

Each algorithm provided with Analysis Services for data mining has its own associated viewers. Detailed descriptions of how you can use each viewer to interpret the models you create are described in each algorithm chapter. However, the viewers have some common functionality that is better described outside the context of a specific algorithm.

The data mining Viewer pane provides a drop-down control that allows you to select which model you want to view. When you select a model, it is loaded into an algorithm-specific viewer. All of the viewers provided allow you to view multiple aspects of your models, which are indicated by tabs on the top of the viewer.

The actual views come in two basic types — diagrams and tables. Each diagram view has the basic zoom and size to fit buttons on their embedded toolbars. Copying a bitmap of the entire diagram or just the displayed portion is supported through the toolbar or the pop-up menu that appears when you click the right mouse button. Additionally, there are some special mouse handling abilities available for all diagram views. Rolling the mouse wheel will cause the diagram to zoom in and out, and pressing the mouse wheel like a button will bring up a mini-navigator, as shown in Figure 3.19; this will allow you to quickly and easily move to any portion of your view.

Tabular views support a variety of features. Every tabular view supports Copy functionality that copies the table contents in HTML format so that they can be pasted into Word, Excel, FrontPage, or any other application that supports HTML. Headers in many views contain informative tooltips and can be clicked to sort the view by the information in that column. Columns can be resized by dragging the edges between column headers. Some views also support the rearranging of columns by dragging and dropping column headers.

You can also view the rowset form of any model by setting the Viewer control to Microsoft Mining Content Viewer. This is the raw data form of the model content. The Viewer control is also used if you install custom visualizations provided by third parties for the algorithms.

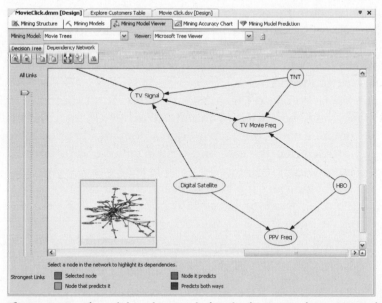

Figure 3.19 The mini-navigator window in the Dependency Network view

TIP If you don't like the colors the viewers use to display graphs, you can always change them. Selecting the Options item from the Tools menu brings up the Visual Studio Options Dialog. Drilling down in the tree control to Business Intelligence Designers/Analysis Services Designers/Data Mining Viewers provides a panel where you can customize the color of pretty much any aspect of any data mining chart.

Changing the color will not affect currently open visualizations. Close the mining viewer and reopen it, or switch to a different model, to notice the change.

Many viewers show statistics about the currently selected item in the Mining Legend. The Mining Legend is a dockable window that automatically appears when a viewer requiring it is displayed.

Using the Mining Accuracy Chart

The Mining Accuracy Chart pane provides tools to help gauge the quality and accuracy of the models you create. The accuracy chart performs predictions against your model and compares the result to data for which you already know the answer. The profit chart performs the same task, but allows you to specify some cost and revenue information to determine the exact point of maximum return. The classification matrix (also known as a confusion matrix) shows you exactly how many times the algorithm predicts results correctly, and what it predicts when it is wrong. In practice, it is a better to hold some data aside when you train your models, to use for testing. Using the same data for testing that you trained your models with may make the model seem to perform better than it actually does.

To use the accuracy chart, you need to select source tables from your DSV or other data sources and bind them to your mining structure. If the columns from the tables have the same name, this step is done automatically upon table selection. Once you have selected the case and nested tables and performed the binding, you can optionally filter the cases — this can be done when you have a specific column that indicates if a case is for training or testing, or simply to verify how the model performs for certain populations: for example, does the model perform differently for customers over 40? Last, you choose which target you are testing and, optionally, the value you are testing for. By default, the accuracy chart selects the same column and value for each model in the structure. However, you can also test different columns at the same time. This is useful, for instance, if you have different discretizations in different models; you might want to see how well predicting Age with five buckets compares to doing the same with seven buckets.

The type of chart you receive depends on whether the target you chose is continuous or discrete, and whether or not you chose a target value to predict.

The latter case is the most common, so we will explain that first. When you select a discrete target and specify a target value, you receive a standard lift chart. A standard lift chart always contains a single line for each model you have selected, plus two additional lines, an ideal line and a random line. The coordinates at each point along the line indicate what percentage of the target audience you would capture if you used that model against the specified percentage of the audience.

For example, in Figure 3.9 the top line shows that an ideal model would capture 100% of the target using 36% of the data. This simply implies that 36% of the data indicates the desired target — there is no magic here. The bottom line is the random line. The random line is always a 45-degree line across the chart. This indicates that if you were to randomly guess the result for each case, you would capture 50% of the target using 50% of the data — again, no magic here. The other lines on the chart represent your mining models. Hopefully, all your models will be above the random line. When you see a model's line hovering around the random guess line, this means that there wasn't sufficient information in the training data to learn patterns about the target. In the model in Figure 3.20, both models are about equal, and we can get about 90% of our target using only 50% of our data. In other words, if we had $5,000 to hold a mailing campaign, each mailing cost $10, and we had 1,000 customers on our list, we could get 90% of all the possible respondents using the model, whereas we would only get 50% if we randomly sent the mailings. Note that this does not mean that 90% of the people we send to will respond. We have already determined that only 36% of the population matches the target. Using the model, we will get 90% of that 36%, or 32.4% of the total population to respond. Randomly guessing would net us only 18% of the total.

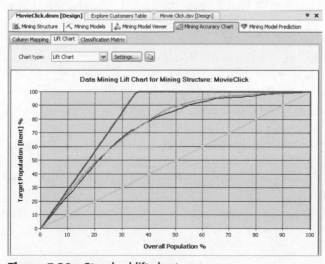

Figure 3.20 Standard lift chart

By changing the chart type to Profit Chart, you get a much better idea about the quality of the model. This chart prompts you to enter the initial cost, cost per item, and revenue per successful return, and plots a chart of the profits you will receive, using the models you've created. This can help you decide which model to use and how many people to send mail to. For example, from the chart in Figure 3.21, you can tell that if you only had enough money to mail to less than 25% of the population, you should go with the Movie Bayes model. If you had enough to go up to about 37%, the Movie Trees model would be your best bet. Most importantly, it tells you that regardless of how much money you can spend, you will maximize your profits by sending mail to about 50% of the population, using the Movie Bayes model. Additionally, it tells you how to determine the people to send to. Clicking on the chart causes a vertical line to appear with statistics about each line at the point displayed in the Mining Legend. In this case, the model says that sending a mailing to everyone with a propensity to buy of 10.51% or better using the Movie Bayes model will maximize your profit.

Another type of accuracy chart is produced when you select a discrete target variable and you do not specify which value of the target you are looking for. In this case, you get a modified lift chart that looks a bit like an upside-down standard chart. This chart shows the overall performance of the model across all possible target states. In this version, a line coordinate indicates how many guesses you would have gotten correct had you used that model. The ideal line here is at a 45-degree angle, indicating that if you had used 50% of the data, you would have been correct about 50% of the population, or if you had used 100% of the data, you would have been correct all the time. The random guess line is based on the most likely state discovered in the training set. For example, if you were predicting gender and 57% of your training data was female, you could presume that you would get the best results by guessing female for every case. The random guess line will end at the percentage of the target that was equal to the most likely state in the training set. That is, for our gender example, if the testing set had the same distribution as our training set, the line would end at 57%, but if only 30% of the testing set was female, the line would end at 30%.

The Classification Matrix tab shows you how many times a model made a correct prediction and what answers were given when the answers were wrong. This can be important in cases where there is a cost associated with each wrong decision. For example, if you were to predict which class of member card to assign to a customer based on his or her creditworthiness, it would be less costly to misclassify someone who should have received a bronze card as a normal card than it would to issue that person a platinum card. This view simply shows you a matrix per model, illustrating counts of each pairwise combination of actual value and predicted values.

The last type of accuracy chart is strictly for continuous values. This chart is a scatter plot, comparing actual values versus predicted values for each case. In a perfect model, each point would end up on a perfect 45-degree angle, indicating that the predicted values exactly matched the actuals. On any other model, the closer the points fall to the 45-degree line, the better.

Figure 3.22 shows a scatter accuracy plot. You can see that this model performed well for most cases, with only one point that was significantly off. The scatter accuracy plot is automatically displayed instead of the lift chart when a continuous target is selected.

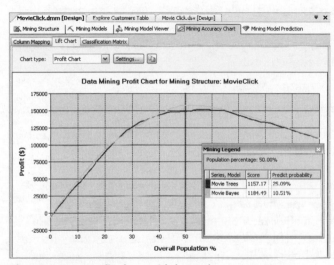

Figure 3.21   Profit chart with legend

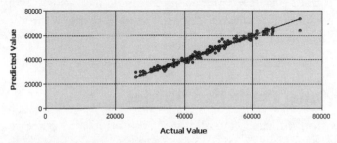

Figure 3.22   Scatter accuracy plot

Creating a Lift Chart on MovieClick

Here, we will create a lift chart targeting those customers who go to the theater weekly.

1. Switch to the Mining Accuracy Chart pane by clicking the Mining Accuracy Chart icon.

2. Click Select case table on the Select Input Tables window in the Column Mapping pane.

3. Select the Homeowners table in the dialog box that appears, and click OK.

NOTE In practice, you should select a table that has data held out from training. The source table is being used only to exemplify use of the control.

4. In the lower part of the pane, choose the column Theater Freq in the Predictable Column Name column.

5. In the Predict Value column, choose Weekly.

6. Click the Lift Chart tab on the top of the pane to switch to the Chart view.

At this point a query is sent to the server and a chart similar to that in Figure 3.20 is displayed.

NOTE You may find cases where a model provides significant lift, yet rarely or possibly never classifies your specified target correctly. This is because the standard lift chart doesn't actually care if the model predicts correctly. The lift chart sorts the predictions by the highest probability that the prediction hits the target. If the maximum probability for the target in the model is 25%, then the model may never actually predict the target. The plot of the lift chart consists of the number of targeted cases that were captured by that ordering. Since the result of the lift and profit chart is simply a probability threshold indicating where you should stop considering customers, it doesn't actually matter if the final prediction was actually correct.

Using the Mining Model Prediction Builder

The Mining Model Prediction Builder pane allows you to build and edit prediction queries, view the results, and save the results back to a table. The Query Builder has three views, Design View, Query View, and Results View, which you select using the View button on the toolbar.

The Design View for building queries is similar to those in other products such as Access, so if you are familiar with them, you should feel right at home.

The process of selecting input tables is the same as in the Mining Accuracy Chart. The only difference is that you also have to indicate which model from the structure you are using as well. After doing so, you need to build your query. You do so by dragging and dropping columns from the model or input tables to the grid below. In addition to dragging and dropping columns, the grid control allows you to manually specify output columns by clicking in empty cells and selecting from drop-down controls that appear or typing as appropriate.

NOTE You can drag only columns that are predictable from the model. These columns are marked with a diamond in the Query Builder.

When selecting a prediction function, the drop-down list in the Field column contains all of the functions that are allowed on the algorithm used by the selected model. You specify the function parameters in the Criteria/Argument column, which will contain a description of what type of parameters you can use.

The Query View shows you the query generated by the builder. You can copy and paste this query into your applications if needed or edit it here as necessary. This view is very handy for modifying queries to use constructs that aren't supported by the query builder, such as `SELECT TOP n <column> FROM <model> ORDER BY PredictProbability(<column>)` to retrieve the respondents above the threshold you determined using the accuracy charts. Note that the edits you make to the query are not reflected in Design View, so switching back to that view will override your changes.

Switching to the Results View executes your query and displays the results in a table. You can copy the results to other applications or click the Save Query Result button to export the results to a database table.

TIP You can export your results to a table and add this table to your DSV to perform iterative data mining.

Executing a Query on the MovieClick Model

We will execute a query that will return the predicted frequency that a customer goes to movies at theaters, along with the probability that the customer would have done so on a monthly basis.

1. Switch to the query builder by choosing the Mining Query Builder icon in the Data Mining designer.
2. Click Select case table on the Select Input Tables window in the top pane of the view.

3. Select the Homeowners table in the dialog box that appears, and click OK.

4. Drag the Customer ID column from the Homeowners table, and drop it on the grid.

5. Drag the Theater Freq column from the mining model, and drop it on the grid.

6. In the Source column of the last row, select Prediction Function.

7. In the Field column of that row, select PredictProbability.

8. In the Alias column of that row, type ProbMonthly.

9. Drag the Theater Freq column from the mining model, and drop it into the Criteria/Argument column of that row.

10. Edit the Criteria/Argument column of that row, and add 'Monthly' to the end of the text already there.

11. Switch to the Query view using the drop-down button on the Query Builder toolbar to view the query and see how much typing you saved.

12. Switch to the Results view to execute the query and see the results.

The query is executed on a separate thread and the results are streamed to the client. This means that the user interface is still active while the query is running, so you can cancel it or perform any other user interface task while it runs. When it is complete, you can copy the results or save them to a database.

Creating Data Mining Reports

Another way to access data mining query results and to distribute those results is to use SQL Server Reporting Services. Reporting Services provides a mechanism for creating custom reports containing text and graphics that can be distributed via HTML, email, or in print or Microsoft Office documents. Web-based reports can be made interactive by adding report parameters that modify the report contents. Reporting Services has options to run reports periodically and cache the results to expedite report retrieval, and you can even specify queries to control report distribution. The product documentation has extensive details on Reporting Services functionality, and there are several books on how to create and manage reports, so I will only discuss how data mining features are integrated.

To use Reporting Services with data mining, you simply create a Reporting Services project with the BI Dev Studio and specify an Analysis Services database as your data source. Depending on the contents of the database, you will be presented with either an OLAP or Data Mining query builder as in Figure 3.23. You can always switch between the two modes by clicking the Switch

Command Type button indicated in the figure. The Set Parameters button allows you to create parameters that can be set by Reporting Services. The Switch Query Mode button allows you to switch between Design mode and SQL mode so that you can create queries not supported by the Query Builder.

TIP You can create reports from user defined functions using the `CALL` syntax. To do this, you must be in the DMX Query Builder and switch to the SQL mode where you can directly type in your `CALL` statement.

When creating a report from a data mining query, you have all of the functionality of Reporting Services to work with. For example, DMX does not support grouping operations, but Reporting Services does. You can use the grouping functionality of Reporting Services against the query described in Figure 3.23 to create a report that is the equivalent of the classification matrix described previously. Figure 3.24 shows the result of such a report.

Figure 3.23   Data Mining Report Designer indicating important controls

Home Ownership Matrix		
Home Ownership	Predicted Home Ownership	Count
Own	Own	1850
Own	Rent	212
Rent	Own	272
Rent	Rent	853

Figure 3.24   Classification matrix report

Using SQL Server Management Studio

Management Studio in SQL Server 2005 is an environment familiar to DBA's — it replaces Enterprise Manager and Query Analyzer from SQL Server 2000, which are the tools of the trade for many administrators. In SQL Server 2005, this environment has been expanded to cover all SQL Server technologies. One user interface can manage relational databases, OLAP cube, data mining models, Reporting Services, and more. The tasks that can be performed in the Management Studio that are pertinent to data mining are:

- Server maintenance
- Database creation and maintenance
- Browse models
- Build queries using Prediction Builder
- Build queries using Query Editor
- Process models and structures
- Assign object permissions
- Backup and restore databases

To perform operations on an Analysis Services database in SQL Manager, you must have Database Administrator permissions on the database you are modifying. You do not need to be an administrator of the entire server.

NOTE If you want to set up a database for a nonserver administrator to create mining models, a user with server administrator privileges needs to create a new database in SQL Management Studio and make the nonserver administrator a database administrator for that database. The user will then use BI Dev Studio in immediate mode to create and edit mining models.

Understanding the Management Studio User Interface

The Management Studio interface has the same look and feel as the BI Dev Studio. Windows, menus, and toolbars all work the same way in both studios, so you can customize your layout in the Management Studio just as you can in the BI Dev Studio. The tool windows of most interest to data mining are the Registered Servers (Server Explorer) window, Object Explorer, and Template Explorer, as shown in Figure 3.25. The Server Explorer window allows quick access to a number of servers you interact with regularly. To access Analysis Services servers, you need to click the cube icon in the embedded toolbar, as shown in Figure 3.25. The Object Explorer window is where you will perform most of your work and is described in more detail in the next section. The Template Explorer is hidden by default and must be selecting from the View menu. The Template Explorer contains a set of syntax templates to make it easier to create queries. As in the Server Explorer, you need to select the indicated cube icon to access the templates specific to Analysis Services.

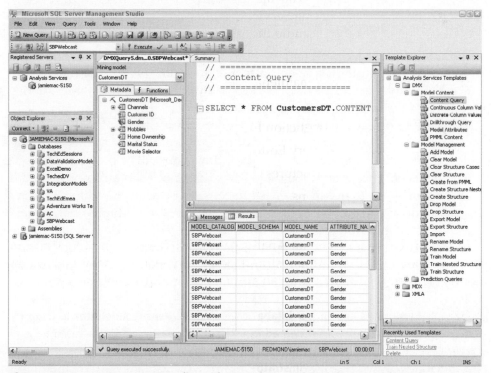

Figure 3.25 Management Studio with Template Explorer shown and Analysis Services Icons indicated

Using the Object Explorer

The Object Explorer is where the majority of data mining management operations will occur. Most operations can be performed by expanding the tree structure to the object of interest and then right-clicking the object and selecting the desired operation. The most common operations you will perform here are processing, security management, and backing up and restoring databases. Security management is described in Chapter 13, and backing up and restoring are well documented in the product documentation. Looking at the object properties from this interface will provide you with creation date and last processing date.

From the Object Explorer, you can also create XML for Analysis (XMLA) scripts that will create, alter, or delete the specified object. Selecting Script Mining Model as Create from the context menu will create an XMLA script to the clipboard, a file, or a Query Editor window. Using XMLA is a quick and convenient way to create objects that differ only slightly by scripting them, changing the object identifiers, and making other edits. XMLA is described in more detail in Chapter 13.

Using the Query Editor

The Query Editor is designed for advanced users with a solid understanding of DMX syntax. The editor is a freeform text editor with IntelliSense that allows you to type and execute ad hoc queries. You can then execute these queries directly from the interface and examine the results.

There are two ways to create a DMX query: you can click theNew DMX Query button on the toolbar, or you can open a template from the Template Explorer. When you create a new query window, you will be prompted to connect to a server. The Connection dialog box does not ask you to provide the database name you to which you wish to connect, so after the editor window opens, you need to select the target database in the SQL Editor toolbar. At this point, you can start authoring your queries. In the editor, you have all of the standard Visual Studio editing features, such as search and replace, bookmarking, keyword color coding, and IntelliSense. You can use IntelliSense by beginning to type a keyword and pressing Ctrl+Space to show a menu of likely matches. You can have many DMX queries in the same file. To indicate which query to execute, simply select it before pressing the Execute button or pressing F5.

Although the level of flexibility provided by the Query Editor demands quite a bit of DMX knowledge from the user, there are ways to jumpstart the query authoring process to make it easier. The first is to use the Template Explorer, which provides many syntax examples from which to choose. The other is to use the Query Builder described earlier in this chapter. You can launch the

Query Builder by right-clicking on a mining model and selecting the Query Builder from the model's context menu. Once you have built enough of your query to get started, you can simply switch to SQL view and copy the text into a Query Editor window. This automatically creates any source data queries for prediction join statements and frees you from writing lengthy On clauses.

TIP You can also drag Template Explorer items into existing query windows to add the template contents to your current query.

Summary

In this chapter, you learned about the breadth of tools available for data mining. The BI Dev Studio, with its wizards and editors, is where you will perform most of your data mining by creating and examining models either attached to a server or in an offline project. In this environment, you complete a data mining project by creating a data source, a data source view, and finally a mining structure with its contained mining models. All of these objects are fully editable through a combination of custom designers and the property grid. In addition, you can use the Data Mining Designer to view models with a variety of custom viewers and to test models with a variety of accuracy charts.

SQL Management Studio is where models are managed throughout their lifetime. This environment provides tools for security, processing, backing up and restoring databases, and other management functions. The viewers, accuracy charts, and Prediction Builder that are available in the BI Dev Studio are available here as well. Additionally, there is the free-form Query Editor with a query template library that you can leverage to create ad hoc DMX queries.

These two tools create the user interface suite for Analysis Services.

Microsoft Naïve Bayes

Picture a newborn witnessing his first sunset. Being new to this world, he doesn't know if the sun will rise again. Making a guess he gives the chance of a sunrise even odds and places in a bag a black marble, representing no sunrise, and a white marble, representing a sunrise. As each day passes, the child places in the bag a marble based on the evidence he witnesses — in this case, a white marble for each sunrise. Over time, the black marble becomes lost in a sea of white and the child can say with near certainty that the sun will rise each day.

This was the example posed by Reverend Thomas Bayes in his 1763 paper establishing the methodology that is now one of the fundamental principals of modern machine learning.

In this chapter, you will learn about:

- The principles of the Naïve Bayes algorithm
- How to tune the Naïve Bayes algorithm using parameters
- Creating Naïve Bayes models using DMX
- How to interpret Naïve Bayes results

Introducing the Naïve Bayes Algorithm

The Naïve Bayes algorithm enables you to quickly create models that provide predictive abilities and also provide a new method of exploring and understanding your data. Thinking about the metaphor from the chapter introduction, it is easy to see how Bayes' technique can be applied to predictive analysis. Bayes' paper provides a systematic method for learning based on evidence. The algorithm learns the "evidence" by counting the correlations between the variable you are interested in and all other variables. For example, if you are trying to determine whether a congressperson is Republican or Democrat based on her voting history, your evidence would be the counts of how congress members from each party voted on each issue. The algorithm would then use these counts to form a prediction based on the voting history of the congressperson you were interested in.

Alternatively, you may really be more interested in learning about what issues differentiate the parties. The counts taken by the Naïve Bayes algorithm can be used to explore the relationships among the various attributes in your model. For example, Figure 4.1 shows the top issues that distinguish Democrats from Republicans in the House of Representatives.

Understanding Naïve Bayes Principles

The mathematical method proposed by Bayes uses a combination of conditional and unconditional probabilities. At first glance, the formula may seem a bit daunting, but when you break it down into its principal components, it's really quite easy to understand.

Let's use the congressional records as an example to build up Bayes' rule. First, suppose that you had to simply guess the party affiliation of a congressperson during the 2002 congressional sessions without any additional information. Given that there were more Republicans in the House than Democrats that year (51% to 49% in fact), your best guess would be to choose Republican, because it is the most likely choice. In data mining terms, this unconditional probability is called the *prior* probability of a hypothesis and can be written P(H). In this case P(Republican) = 51% and P(Democrat) = 49%.

Additionally, you could increase the likelihood of your guess being correct if you knew the overall voting records of the House members and those of your representative. Table 4.1 shows the votes by party for selected issues in 2002, and Table 4.2 shows how the representative in question voted.

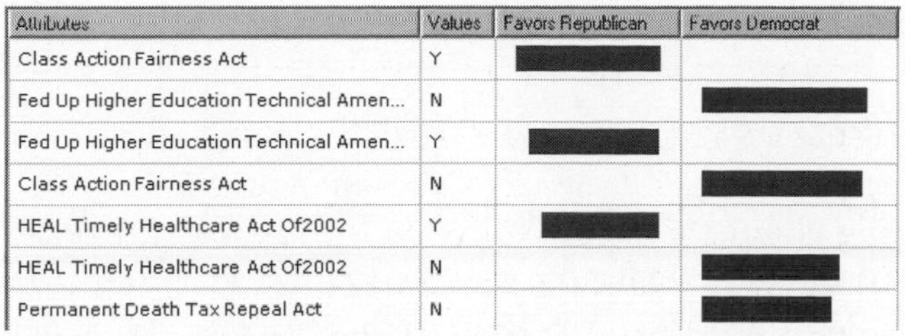

Attributes	Values	Favors Republican	Favors Democrat
Class Action Fairness Act	Y	███████████	
Fed Up Higher Education Technical Amen...	N		█████████████
Fed Up Higher Education Technical Amen...	Y	██████	
Class Action Fairness Act	N		█████████████
HEAL Timely Healthcare Act Of2002	Y	████████	
HEAL Timely Healthcare Act Of2002	N		███████████
Permanent Death Tax Repeal Act	N		████████████

Figure 4.1 Distinguishing congressional parties by their 2002 voting records

Table 4.1 Voting Data by Party Affiliation

	DEATH TAX		HOMELAND SECURITY		HELP AMERICA VOTE		CHILD ABDUCTION		PARTY	
	D	R	D	R	D	R	D	R	D	R
YEAH	41	214	87	211	184	172	178	210	211	223
NAY	166	4	114	6	11	36	23	1		
YEAH	20%	98%	43%	97%	94%	83%	89%	99.5%	49%	51%
NAY	80%	2%	57%	3%	6%	17%	11%	0.5%		

Table 4.2 Target Representative

DEATH TAX	HOMELAND SECURITY	HELP AMERICA VOTE	CHILD ABDUCTION	PARTY
YEAH	NAY	YEAH	YEAH	?

The numbers in Figure 4.1 represent the counts of votes broken down by party affiliation — your target variable. For example, 41 Democrats voted Yeah for the Death Tax Repeal Act and 166 voted Nay. This gives you the percentages in the lower part of the graph: 41/(41 + 166) = 20% Yeah and 166 / (41 + 166) = 80% Nay. The final column of the table provides you with the counts and percentages of Democrats and Republicans overall.

The Naïve part of Naïve Bayes tells you to treat all of your attributes as *independent* of each other with respect to the target variable. This may be a faulty assumption, but it allows you to multiply your probabilities to determine the likelihood of each state. For your representative represented in Table 4.2, the likelihood calculation that this person is a Democrat would be:

Likelihood of (D) = 0.2 * 0.57 * 0.94 * 0.89 * 0.49 = 0.0467

Likewise the calculation for Republican would be:

Likelihood of (R) = 0.98* 0.03 * 0.83 * 0.995 * 0.51 = 0.0124

You can instantly see that the representative is almost four times as likely to be a Democrat as a Republican based on this voting behavior. You can convert these likelihoods to probabilities by normalizing them to sum to 1.

$$P(D) = \frac{0.0467}{0.0467 + 0.0124} = 79\%$$
$$P(R) = \frac{0.0124}{0.0467 + 0.0124} = 21\%$$

Bayes' Rule states that if you have a hypothesis H and evidence about that hypothesis E, then you can calculate the probility of H using the following formula:

$$P(H|E) = \frac{P(E|H) \times P(H)}{P(E)}$$

This simply states that the probability of your hypothesis given the evidence is equal to the probability of the evidence given the hypothesis multiplied by the probability of the hypothesis and then normalized. While that seems like a mouthful, let's apply this to our congressional example.

First, you tackle the probability of the hypothesis given the evidence; in this case, this would be the probability that the representative is a Democrat given that she voted Yeah on the Death Tax Repeal, Help America Vote, and Child Abduction Acts, and Nay on the Homeland Security Act. To determine this probability, you need to compute the probability of the evidence, given that your hypothesis is true. This is simply a lookup from the counts presented in Table 4.1. That is, your evidence states that the representative voted Yeah on the Help America Vote Act and your hypothesis is that the representative is a Democrat. From the table, you see that the probability of this piece of evidence is 94%. The probability of *all* the evidence given the hypothesis is simply the product of the probabilities of each individual piece. Next, you multiply by the overall probability, the prior probability, of your hypothesis — in this case 49%.

Last, you divide by the probability of the evidence; however, in practice this isn't necessary. Since you will test all possible hypotheses, both Democrat and Republican, this factor is eliminated when you normalize the results.

USING BAYESIAN PRIORS

Using the methodology discussed here can have some undesirable side effects if there is no evidence for an event in the training data. For example, if no Democrat voted Yeah on the Death Tax Act, there would be 0% probability that your sample case could be a Democrat, regardless of the other votes. Similarly, if no Republican had voted Nay on Homeland Security, there would be 0% probability that our sample case could be a Republican.

To resolve this problem, you consider all available values to be possible. When calculating the likelihoods of each state, you add a nonzero amount to each count; this amount is called a *prior* and indicates the prior belief of each possible output. In practice, you simply add one to each count. This provides you with a value that loses significance as the amount of evidence grows, but guarantees that you never run into the 0% issue.

Naïve Bayes Parameters

The implementation of Naïve Bayes is fairly straightforward and therefore isn't heavily parameterized. The parameters that exist ensure that the algorithm is completed in a reasonable amount of time by default. As the algorithm considers all pairwise attribute combinations, the time and memory usage to process the data is related to the total number of input values multiplied by the total number of output values. The algorithm in general does a good job of choosing which inputs and outputs are considered when the parameters are applied, and each of them can be turned off to force the algorithm to consider them all.

- The MAXIMUM_INPUT_ATTRIBUTES parameter determines the number of attributes that will be considered as inputs for training. If there is more than this number of inputs, the algorithm will select the most important inputs and ignore the rest. Setting this parameter to 0 causes the algorithm to consider all attributes.

  The default value is 255.

- The MAXIMUM_OUTPUT_ATTRIBUTES parameter determines the number of attributes that will be considered as outputs for training. If there is more than this number of outputs, the algorithm will select the most important outputs, generally the most popular, and ignore the rest. Setting this parameter to 0 causes the algorithm to consider all attributes.

  The default value is 255.

- MAXIMUM_STATES controls how many states of an attributes are considered. If an attribute has more than this number of states, only the most popular states will be used. States that are not selected will be considered to be missing data. This parameter is useful when an attribute has a high cardinality, such as zip code. As with the other parameters, setting this parameter to 0 will allow the algorithm to consider all states.

  The default value is 100.

- The MINIUMUM_DEPENDENCY_PROBABILITY is a measure from 0 to 1 of how likely it is that an input attribute is predictive of an output. Using the voting records as an example, assume that 100% of the congresspersons that voted Yeah on issue A also voted Yeah on issue B. If only 25% of Congress actually voted Yeah on B, then issue A provides information. However, if most everyone voted for B, then the preceding fact is simply superfluous because no information is gained.

  Setting the MINUMUM_DEPENDENCY_PROBABILITY parameter does not impact model training or prediction; rather it allows you to reduce the amount of content returned by the server from content queries. Setting this value to 0.5 returns only those inputs that are more likely than random to be correlated with the outputs. If you browse a model and do not find any information, try lowering this value until correlations are observed. The default value is 0.5.

Algorithm Parameters

The Naïve Bayes algorithm in conjunction with the viewers provided in SQL Server Analysis Services 2005 provides a very effective way to explore your data. Since the processing phase of the algorithm merely counts the first-order correlations between the inputs and the outputs, you really don't have to worry about picking the "correct" inputs, and you can simply throw anything you've got at it. This does not hold true when using the algorithm for predictive purposes. When building a predictive model with Naïve Bayes, you must take care that the input attributes are relatively independent. For example, if input A and input B always have the same value, this would have the effect of multiplying the weight of input A by two, which is something you generally want to avoid. Because of this behavior, it is particularly important to evaluate to accuracy of your model with holdout data using the lift chart as described in Chapter 3. Typically, although Naïve Bayes can be a powerful predictor, many people use more sophisticated algorithms such as decision trees or neural networks for prediction when available.

Exploring a Naïve Bayes model will tell you how your attributes are related to each other in ways that aren't easily discovered when using other methods. Using the previous example of congressional voting records, you can easily see what the most important votes are for each party. You can see how votes on a particular act are distributed across party lines. You can even see how votes on an act are distributed across the votes of every other act and how they are related to each other.

This ability to explore the relationships between attributes can be applied to many problems. What are the differences between my satisfied and unsatisfied customers? What factors are related to defects in my production line? What differentiates weekly and monthly movie renters? This ability can be combined with the concept of nested tables to provide a further realm of insights. What's the difference between people who bought the movie *Fargo* and those who didn't? How are all my products related? Naïve Bayes provides quick and understandable answers to all of these questions.

TIP A good way to start mining your data is to create a Naïve Bayes model and check both input and predictable on all nonkey columns. The resultant model will give you a better understanding of your data and help you build better subsequent models.

DMX

Because Naïve Bayes is a rather simple algorithm, issuing DMX commands to Naïve Bayes models is completely standard. The only issue to keep in mind is that the Microsoft_Naive_Bayes implementation supports only discrete attributes, so any continuous input or output columns must be discretized to be consumed by the algorithm. Creating a Naïve Bayes model with continuous columns will result in an error.

Given the exploratory nature of the Naïve Bayes algorithm, it is often useful to create ad hoc data mining models on arbitrary sets of data. For instance to create the voting model described previously, you would issue a statement such as:

```
CREATE MINING MODEL VotingRecords
(
    [ID]    LONG  KEY,
    [Party] TEXT  DISCRETE PREDICT,
    [Campaign Finance Overhaul]     TEXT  DISCRETE,
    [Unemployment and Tax Benefits] TEXT  DISCRETE,
    [Fiscal 2003 Budget Resolution] TEXT  DISCRETE,
    ...
) USING Microsoft_Naive_Bayes
```

You would then train the model with a standard INSERT INTO statement. If all the columns in the source table are the same as those in the model and in the same order as the model, you can simplify the INSERT INTO statement by not specifying any column names, like this:

```
INSERT INTO VotingRecords
    OPENQUERY([Voting Records], 'SELECT * FROM VotingRecords')
```

At this point you can use the model for prediction or browsing. For predicting, you use a standard SELECT statement with a PREDICTION JOIN clause. For example, the following statement uses parameters to predict party affiliation based on the Food Stamps and Nuclear Waste issues:

```
SELECT Predict(Party) FROM VotingRecords
    NATURAL PREDICTION JOIN
    (SELECT @FoodStamps AS [Food Stamps],
            @NuclearWaste AS [Nuclear Waste]) as t
```

The result will be based on the values specified in the parameters.

Understanding Naïve Bayes Content

Naïve Bayes content is laid out in four levels. The first level is simply the model itself. The children of the model are the output nodes. Each output node has for its children the entire set of input attributes with a dependency probability higher than the MINIMUM_DEPENDENCY_PROBABILITY parameter. Finally, each input node has a child for each state the input can take, with the distributions of the output attribute states. This arrangement is displayed in Figure 4.2.

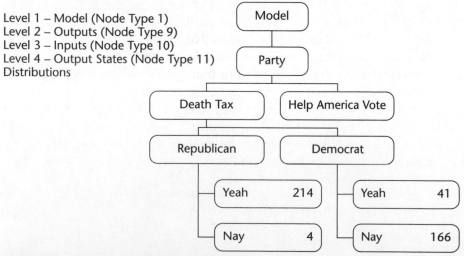

Level 1 – Model (Node Type 1)
Level 2 – Outputs (Node Type 9)
Level 3 – Inputs (Node Type 10)
Level 4 – Output States (Node Type 11)
Distributions

Figure 4.2 Naïve Bayes content hierarchy

Fortunately for many content-browsing purposes, there are user-defined functions that can condense the Naïve Bayes content into a somewhat more useful form. The Attribute Characteristics View and the Attribute Discrimination View described later in this chapter both receive their data through built-in user-defined functions that you can use as well.

GetPredictableAttributes returns the list of predictable attributes for a specified model along with the NODE_ID for each attribute.

```
CALL GetPredictableAttributes('Voting Records')
```

After you have the list of attributes, you can call GetAttribute-Characteristics to return a table describing the characteristics of a value of an attribute. This function takes the attribute's node ID, the value of interest, a value type flag, and a threshold value along with the model name and returns an ordered list of attributes and values that correlate with the selected attribute value along with the strength of the correlation. The value type flag tells the function if the value you are specifying is a value from the model or the intrinsic "missing" value. Setting the value type to 1 indicates that the value of interest is a known state of the attribute — for example, Yes or No. Setting it to 0 indicates that the value is the intrinsic "missing" value, which occurs when the attribute does not appear in a case, when it is NULL, or when the specific value is removed from the model by feature selection. The threshold indicates the minimum correlation strength returned by the function and is used to limit the number of returned rows. A call to get the characteristics of Democrats from the Voting Records model would look like this:

```
CALL GetAttributeCharacteristics('Voting Records', '10000000i',
     'Democrat', 1, 0.0005)
```

A similar function, GetAttributeDiscrimination, takes two values of an attribute and returns an ordered list of attributes along with the strength with which they differentiate the two values. Negative strength numbers indicate that the attribute value pair on the row favors the first specified value, while positive strength numbers indicate that the second value is favored. Similar to GetAttributeCharacteristics, a value type has to be specified for each value; however, an additional value, 2, can be specified to indicate that you want to compare a value against all other possible values. For example, a query to compare Democrats against all other possible parties would look like this:

```
CALL GetAttributeDiscrimination('Voting Records', '10000000i',
     'Democrat', 1, 'All other states', 2, 0.0005)
```

To compare Democrats and Republicans, you would issue the following query:

```
CALL GetAttributeDiscrimination('Voting Records', '10000000i',
    'Democrat', 1, 'Republican', 1, 0.0005)
```

NOTE You can issue all of these queries using the DMX query editor in SQL Server Management Studio. Training the model requires that a Data Source object representing the Voting Records database described in Appendix A be created using the BI Development Studio.

Exploring a Naïve Bayes Model

When exploring a Naïve Bayes model, it is easier to think of the process as simply exploring your data. Since the Naïve Bayes algorithm does not perform any kind of advanced analysis on your data, the views into the model really are simply a new way of looking at the data you always had.

The Naïve Bayes viewer contains four views. SQL Server Data Mining provides four different views on Naïve Bayes models that help provide insight into your data. The viewer is accessed through either the BI Development Studio or SQL Management Studio by right-clicking on the model and selecting "Browse." The views are:

- Dependency Net
- Attribute Profiles
- Attribute Characteristics
- Attribute Discrimination

Dependency Net

The first tab of the Naïve Bayes viewer is the dependency net. The dependency net (see Figure 4.3) provides a quick display of how all of the attributes in your model are related. Each node in the graph represents an attribute, whereas each edge represents a relationship. If a node has an outgoing edge, as indicated by the arrow, it is predictive of the attribute in the node at the end of the edge. Likewise, if a node has an incoming edge, it is predicted by the other node. Edges can also be bidirectional, indicating that the attributes in the corresponding nodes predict and are predicted by each other.

You can easily hone in on the attributes that interest you by using the Find Node feature. Clicking the Find Node button provides a list of all attributes in the graph or hidden. Selecting a node from the list will cause the node to become selected in the graph. Selected nodes are highlighted and all connected nodes are highlighted with a color representing their relationship with the selection. Figure 4.3 shows a portion of the dependency net for the Congressional Voting model with the Party node selected. From this view, it is easy to see the relationships that Party has with the other attributes in the model.

In addition to displaying the relationships and their directions, the dependency net can also tell you the strength of those relationships. Moving the slider from top to bottom will filter out the weaker links, leaving the strong relationships.

NOTE You will not see all of the possible relationships in your model unless all columns are checked both predictable and input in the Mining Model Wizard or marked Predict in the Mining Model Editor. Additionally, some links may be missing if you raise the MINIMUM_NODE_SCORE parameter.

Attribute Profiles

The second tab, the Attribute Profile viewer, provides you with an exhaustive report of how each input attribute corresponds to each output attribute one attribute at a time. At the top of the Attribute Profile viewer, you select which output to look at, and the rest of the view shows how all of the input attributes correlated to the states of the output attribute.

Figure 4.4 shows the attribute profiles for the party attribute. You can see that the Abortion Non-Discrimination Act vote was approximately even, with Republicans voting Yeah and Democrats Nay. At the same time, you can see the almost unanimous support for the Child Abduction Prevention Act.

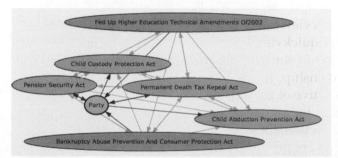

Figure 4.3   Naïve Bayes Dependency Net viewer with the Party node selected

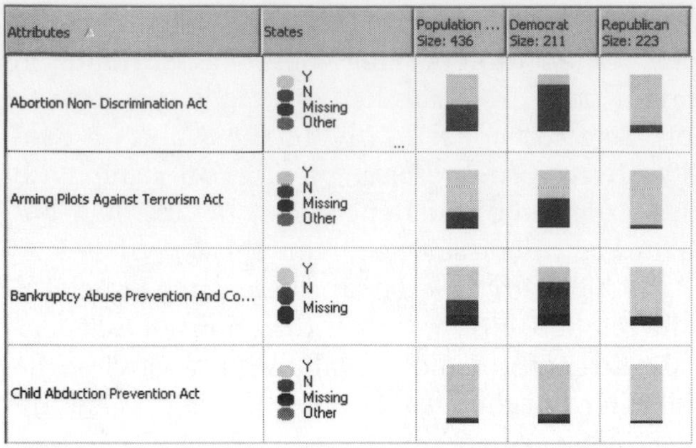

Attributes △	States	Population ... Size: 436	Democrat Size: 211	Republican Size: 223
Abortion Non- Discrimination Act	Y N Missing Other			
Arming Pilots Against Terrorism Act	Y N Missing Other			
Bankruptcy Abuse Prevention And Co...	Y N Missing			
Child Abduction Prevention Act	Y N Missing Other			

Figure 4.4   Attribute profiles for the party attribute

You can also use this view to organize your data to be presented the way you see fit. You can rearrange columns by clicking and dragging on their headers, or you can even remove a column altogether by right-clicking the column header and selecting Hide Column. Additionally, if the alphabetical order doesn't suit you, simply click the header for the attribute state you are interested in, and the row ordering changes based on how important that attribute is in predicting that state.

Attribute Characteristics

The third tab allows you to select an output attribute and value and shows you a description of the cases where that attribute and value occur. Essentially, this provides answers to the question "what are people who _____ like?" For example, Figure 4.5 shows the characteristics of Democrats. You can see that these representatives in general voted No on the health care, class action, and rental purchase acts, but voted Yes on the Child Abduction Act.

When viewing the attribute characteristics, there are two issues you should keep in mind. First, an attribute characteristic does not imply predictive power. For instance, if most representatives voted for the Child Abduction Prevention Act, then it is likely to characterize Republicans as well as Democrats. Second, inputs that fall below the minimum node score set in the algorithm parameters are not displayed.

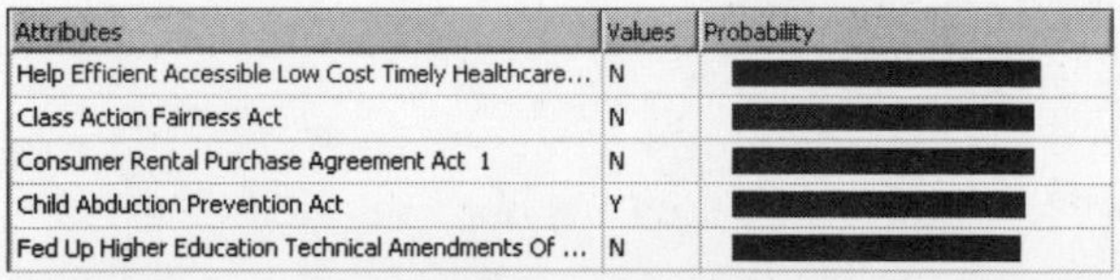

Attributes	Values	Probability
Help Efficient Accessible Low Cost Timely Healthcare...	N	
Class Action Fairness Act	N	
Consumer Rental Purchase Agreement Act 1	N	
Child Abduction Prevention Act	Y	
Fed Up Higher Education Technical Amendments Of ...	N	

Figure 4.5   Characteristics of attributes, values, and probability

Attribute Discrimination

The last tab, Attribute Discrimination, provides the answers to the most interesting question — what is the difference between A and B? With this viewer, you choose the attribute you are interested in and select the states you want to compare, and the viewer displays a modified tornado chart indicating which factors favor each state.

Figure 4.6 shows the results distinguishing Republicans and Democrats. Republicans tended to vote for most issues, while Democrats voted against them. When reading this view, you also need to take care in your interpretation. It is *not* implied that no Democrats voted for the Death Tax Repeal Act, rather that these factors favor one group over the other.

TIP You can determine the unique characteristics of a group by comparing a state to "all other states." This will give you a view of what seperates that particular group from the rest of the crowd.

When interpreting this view, you have to be careful to consider the support level of the attribute before making judgments. Figure 4.7 shows the discrimination between Independents and all other congresspersons. Looking at this figure, you could say that a strong differentiator between Independents and Democrats is the support for the Low Cost Healthcare Act. Unfortunately, you would be wrong. When examining the Mining Legend for that issue, you see that there are actually only two Independents in your data set. Obviously, it is not prudent to make conclusions based on such limited support.

NOTE If the Mining Legend is not visible, you can display it by right-clicking on the view and selecting "Show Legend."

Attributes	Values	Favors Republican ▽	Favors Democrat
Class Action Fairness Act	Y	■■■■■■■■	
Fed Up Higher Education Technical ...	N		■■■■■
Fed Up Higher Education Technical ...	Y	■■■■■■	
Class Action Fairness Act	N		■■■■
Help Efficient Accessible Low Cost T...	Y	■■■■■	
Help Efficient Accessible Low Cost T...	N		■■■■■
Premanent Death Tax Repeal Act	N		■■■■■■
Pension Security Act	N		■■■■■■
Premanent Death Tax Repeal Act	Y	■■■■	

Figure 4.6 Distinguishing between Republicans and Democrats

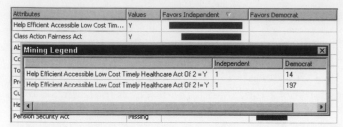

Figure 4.7 Discrimination between Independents and Congresspersons

Summary

Naïve Bayes is a machine implementation of Bayes Rule created by the Reverend Thomas Bayes in the eighteenth century, which has become the foundation for many machine-learning and data mining methods. It is a quick, approachable data mining algorithm that you can use to perform predictions and do advanced exploration of your data. The visualizations provided for Naïve Bayes are easy to understand by a wide audience and are particularly suitable for inclusion in reports.

Microsoft
Decision Trees

Put yourself in the place of a loan officer at a bank. A young couple walks into request a loan. Young, you think — not a good sign. You talk to them. They're married and that's a plus. He's worked the same job for three years. Job stability is another good sign. A look at their credit reports shows they've missed three payments in the last 12 months — a big negative. From your experience, you've created a tree in your mind that allows you to determine how you rank each loan application. The question remains, does this couple get the loan? Let's see how decision trees can help to solve this puzzle.

In this chapter you will learn about:

- The principles of the Microsoft Decision Trees Algorithm
- Using the Microsoft Decision Trees algorithm
- Interpreting the tree model content

Introducing Decision Trees

The decision tree is probably the most popular data mining technique. The most common data mining task for a decision tree is classification; for example, to identify the credit risk for each customer of a bank or to find those customers who are likely to be online buyers.

The principle idea of a decision tree is to split your data recursively into subsets so that each subset contains more or less homogeneous states of your target variable (predictable attribute). At each split in the tree, all input attributes are evaluated for their impact on the predictable attribute. When this recursive process is completed, a decision tree is formed.

There are a few advantages of using decision trees over using other data mining algorithms, for example, decision trees are quick to build and easy to interpret. Each path from the root to a leaf forms a *rule*. Prediction based on decision trees is efficient. You can imagine the prediction process as dropping a ball through a pachinko machine; as the ball hits each pin, it falls to the left or the right. Finally, it lands and you can see the score of the slot in which it landed. An input case for a prediction falls through the tree, coming to rest at a leaf, based on the split conditions associated with tree nodes. When the case lands on a leaf node, the predicted value of this case is based on the statistics stored at the node.

There are different methods for growing a tree. For example, you can use a variety of formulas to determine how to split the tree. The shape of the tree can also vary: a tree can be a binary shape or a bushy shape (a tree node that contains multiple children). As for the depth of the tree, there are also different techniques to control the tree growth; for example you can grow the tree as deeply as possible and then prune it back, or stop growing it proactively when some predetermined condition is met.

ID3 is a well-known decision tree proposed by Ross Quinlan of the University of Sydney, Australia. ID3 tree was later enhanced to be C4.5. C4.5 can handle numeric attributes, missing values, and noisy data.

Some decision trees can perform regression tasks, for example, to predict continuous variables such as temperature and humidity. The Classification and Regression Tree (CART) proposed by Professor Briemann is a popular decision tree algorithm for classification and regression.

Microsoft Decision Trees is a hybrid decision tree algorithm developed by Microsoft research. It supports classification and regression tasks. One of the unique features of Microsoft Decision Trees is that it can also be applied for association analysis. We will explain this later in the chapter.

There are a couple of reasons to name this tree algorithm Microsoft Decision Trees instead of Microsoft Decision Tree. First, based on the parameter settings, the resulting trees can be very different in terms of node splits and tree shapes. These are in fact different decision tree algorithms. Second, a tree model may contain multiple trees, sometimes even hundreds of trees. These trees can be visually linked through dependency network for further analysis.

Decision Tree Principles

In this section, we will have a closer look at the principles of the Microsoft Decision Trees algorithm.

Basic Concepts of Tree Growth

The basic idea of decision tree algorithm is fairy straightforward. We will describe the algorithm by going through an example based on the college plan data shown in the Chapter 1. The table contains 3,000 students with information about their IQ, gender, parents' income, and parental encouragement. The predictable attribute is College Plan, a binary column indicating if the student is planning to attend college.

The first step of the tree algorithm is to build a correlation count table as displayed in the top part of Figure 5.1. Each column in the correlation count table is an attribute/value pair of input attributes. Each row is a state value of predictable attribute. The cells in the table are the counts of correlations of input attribute values and predictable states. From the table, you can see that there are 400 high-IQ students, 300 of them are associated with College Plan = Yes, while 100 of them associated with College Plan = No. The bottom part of Figure 5.1 contains four bar charts graphically displaying the information in the correlation count table. The light bars represent College Plan = Yes, while the dark bars represent the College Plan = No.

The decision tree algorithm will first pick an attribute to split at the root level. The selection criteria that the subsets after the split should be very different in terms of the predictable attribute value. From the four bar charts in the figure, you can identify that Parental Encouragement is the most significant attribute. If Parental Encouragement = True, the light bar is longer. If Parental Encouragement = False, the dark bar is much longer. You can also see from the last bar chart that the Gender doesn't contain useful information related to College Plan in the overall dataset. Whether the Gender = Male or Female, the College Plan distributions are the same.

Although we can easily pick the best attribute to split by examining these bar charts, the decision tree algorithm can't view these charts. However, we can measure the information contained in these bar charts by using some formal criteria (math formulas). Well-known criteria are *entropy* (or *information value*) and *Bayesian score*. We discussed the details of Bayesian score in Chapter 4. Here we explain the concept of entropy.

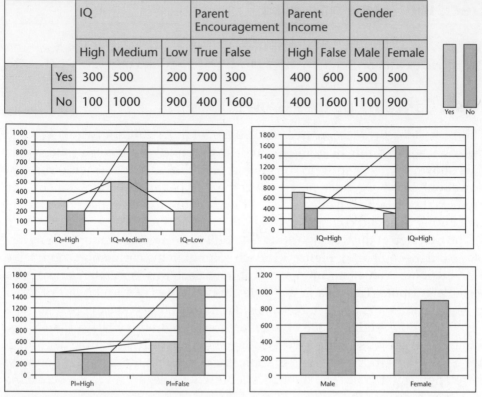

		IQ			Parent Encouragement		Parent Income		Gender	
		High	Medium	Low	True	False	High	False	Male	Female
	Yes	300	500	200	700	300	400	600	500	500
	No	100	1000	900	400	1600	400	1600	1100	900

Figure 5.1   Select the best attribute to split

We need to find a math formula to measure the purity of a dataset on a given attribute (predictable attribute). This formula needs to satisfy the following properties:

- In a dataset, if all the cases with College Plan = Yes (or No), the information is zero, thus the formula returns zero.

- In a dataset, if the number of cases of College Plan = Yes and the number of cases of College Plan = No are the same, the information reaches the maximum, thus the formula returns the maximum value.

- Predictable attributes may have multiple states. For example, in a bank loan analysis scenario, the predictable attribute CreditRisk has three states: High, Medium, and Low. In this case, we have two choices for decision making. We can make the decision in a single step to each individual state, or we can make the decision in two steps: the first stage is to consider CreditRisk = High or Not High, and the second stage is to consider CreditRisk = Medium or Low. The amount of information in both cases should be the equivalent.

Magically, the following formula satisfies all the three properties:

```
Entropy (p₁, p₂,...,pₙ) = -p₁log₂p₁ -p₂log₂p₂... -pₙlog₂pₙ
Where p₁, p₂,...,Pₙ are the probability of each state on the predictable
attribute, p₁+ p₂...+Pₙ= 1.
```

In our example, there are only two predictable states: Yes and No, $n = 2$. Using the preceding formula, we can calculate the entropies of the splits on the four input attributes:

- Split on Parental Encouragement

    ```
    Entropy(700, 400) + Entropy(300, 1600) = 0.946 +0.629 = 1.571
    ```

- Split on IQ

    ```
    Entropy(300, 100) + Entropy(500, 1000) + Entropy(200, 900) =0.814 +
    0.918 + 0.684 = 2.416
    ```

- Split on Parents' Income

    ```
    Entropy(400,400) + Entropy(600,1600)  = 1.0 + 0.845 = 1.845
    ```

- Split on Gender

    ```
    Entropy(500, 1100) + Entropy(500, 900)  =0.896 + 0.941 = 1.837
    ```

Based on these calculations, we find the subsets after the splits on Parental Encouragement have the lowest entropy. Thus the most significant attribute to split at the root level is Parental Encouragement. Once the data is split into two subsets, the algorithm repeats the same process on each leaf node to grow the tree. Figure 5.2 displays the new correlation count table on the subset where Parental Encouragement = True.

Working with Many States in a Variable

For classification trees, a reasonable number of states of an input variable would be less than 100. However, in real dataset, this is not always the case. Some attributes may have thousands of states, for example, the zip code. Some decision tree algorithms simply ignore these attributes. However, these attributes can contain useful information. Customers living in certain zip codes may have a higher credit risk than customers living in others.

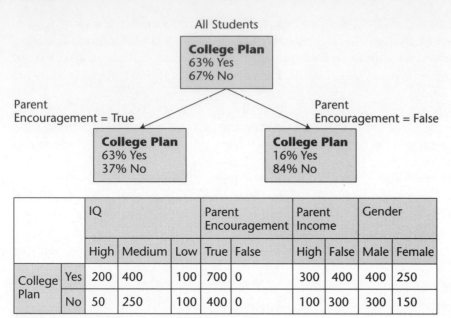

Figure 5.2   Continuing to grow the tree

There are different techniques to resolve this issue, for example, grouping those similar states to reduce the total number of states. The grouping method is accurate; however, it is very time-consuming, because the algorithm has to repeat it at each split. Microsoft Decision Trees algorithm deals with this issue through dynamic grouping. At each split, the algorithm considers only 100 states, with 99 of the most popular states plus one state representing all the others. After each split, the popular states can be different across subsets. Of course, this is based on a heuristic assumption that more popular states have a larger impact on the prediction than less popular states do.

Alternatively, you can solve this problem before processing the model. You can visualize the impact of these states by using data visualizing tools such as bar charts during the data exploration stage and then manually group those similar states. Most of those less important states can be grouped into one single value.

> **TIP** For discrete predictable attributes, the recommended number of states is less than 10. If you have too many states in the predictable attributes, you should consider grouping some states.

Avoiding Overtraining

As explained in the previous sections, the decision tree algorithm grows the tree recursively. Sometimes, it can end up with a fairly large tree. These trees have many levels and branches, and thus contain many rules.

However, the size of the tree has no direct relation to the quality of prediction. As a matter of fact, when the tree becomes too deep, it tends to memorize the training cases instead of generalizing rules. Such a model does a great job of classifying the training dataset. However, it has bad prediction accuracy for the new dataset. This problem is called *overtraining* or *overfitting*.

There are many ways to deal with the overtraining issue. Some decision tree algorithms contain two processing steps: growing and pruning. During the growing step you develop the tree, and in the pruning step you cut tree nodes and braches making the rules more generally applicable.

Microsoft Decision Trees doesn't offer the pruning step. The tree growth is controlled in two ways: by use of the Bayesian score, which can avoid splitting when there is not enough data to justify a split, and with a parameter named `Complexity_Penalty` with values from 0 to 1. If this parameter value is set high, more restrictions are imposed during the tree growth, thus the tree size is smaller.

Incorporating Prior Knowledge

In many cases, we do have prior information about events. For example, when flipping a coin, we know that we are most likely to seeing 5 heads in 10 flips. This sort of prior information can be integrated with the training dataset to make sure the model is more objective. Microsoft Decision Trees algorithm adds priors (counts) at each tree node for each state of the predictable attribute. The predicted probability is calculated with priors added.

Suppose that we build a decision tree about the presidential election without prior (knowledge). The tree is trained with the candidates' demographic information in historical elections. As there is no female president in U.S. history, the decision tree will give a female candidate a 0% probability to win the election. With prior knowledge integrated in the decision tree, the predicted probability will no longer be 0, although still very low.

Feature Selection

Data mining algorithms are very sensitive to the number of attributes you include. Too many attributes requires extensive CPU and memory resources for processing. Also, not all the attributes are equally important in terms of the prediction accuracy. Feature selection is a process that selects a subset of attributes so that the processing time can be substantially reduced but with no or limited sacrifices on the model accuracy.

The basic idea of feature selection is quite simple. You use some statistical functions, such as the Bayesian score or entropy, to calculate the impact of each input attribute related to the predictable attribute, and then select the most significant attributes for the model.

Feature selection is applied not only to input attributes, but also to output (predictable) attributes. Some models may have lots of predictable attributes. For example, if a model contains a nested table, and the nested table is predictable, all the nested keys are modeled as predictable attributes. In the case of the market basket model of a retail store, the nested table key is often the product. There could be thousands of products in a store. The algorithm can't deal with so many trees in the model efficiently; thus, a feature selection technique is applied to speed up model building. For those output attributes that are filtered out, the prediction is based on marginal statistics.

A feature selection component is used internally by all Microsoft data mining algorithms. Users don't need to invoke this process explicitly. Different algorithms have different feature selection criteria. Two algorithm parameters control the feature selection thresholds: `Maximum_Input_Attributes` and `Maximum_Output_Attributes`.

Using Continuous Inputs

Continuous, in contrast with discrete, is one of the content types for numeric attributes. Continuous attributes must be numeric; however, numeric attributes can be modeled as discrete, for example, zip code. Continuous variables can be used as input for classification tree. Suppose that the Parent Income column in the College Plan dataset contains continuous numbers instead of High and Low as in the previous example. We cannot use the same approach we would use for discrete attributes to measure the tree split score. There are simply too many different states. Also, the split condition should recognize the ordered nature of a continuous variable (for example, by using less than and greater than operators).

Different proposals support continuous inputs in decision trees. Microsoft Decision Trees deals with continuous inputs in a unique way. It first bins the continuous input into n buckets based on the equal range; n is a system parameter with default value of 99. Then the algorithm starts the merge process between neighbor buckets based on the same measurement we use for a discrete attribute such as Entropy. If merging two buckets can increase the split score, these two buckets are combined. This process is calculated recursively. At the end, we have a set of buckets with an optimized split score. This score is then compared with other discrete or continuous input attributes, and the attribute with the best score will be selected for the split.

Regression

Regression is similar to classification. The only difference is that regression predicts continuous attributes. Although the basic task of a decision tree algorithm is classification, it can be used for regression as well. A well-known

MICROSOFT LINEAR REGRESSION ALGORITHM

To make the linear regression feature of the Microsoft Decision Trees algorithm more visible, SQL Server Analysis Services 2005 added a new algorithm: Microsoft Linear Regression. It is actually based on the Microsoft Decision Trees algorithm. The linear regression algorithm doesn't split the data. The regression formula is based on the entire dataset.

regression tree algorithm is CART. The Microsoft Decision Trees algorithm adds the support for regression in SQL Server 2005.

There is at least one regressor in a regression model. A *regressor* is a continuous input attribute that is used to model the continuous predictable attribute in a linear way. For example, suppose IQ is the continuous predictable attribute and Parent Income is the regressor. The classic linear regression formula is the following:

```
IQ = a + b*Parent Income + e
```

The residual e represents the noise, with a mean of zero. The coefficients *a(intercept)* and *b(slope)* are determined by the condition that the sum of the square residuals is as small as possible.

In each node of the tree viewer, the regression formula is displayed in the following form:

```
IQ = a + b*(Parent Income - m)
```

a is the value when input variable Parent Income is at its mean *m*.

In many cases, a regression model has multiple regressors.

Microsoft Regression Trees contains a linear regression formula at each leaf node. Using a regression tree has its advantages over simple linear regression in that a tree can represent both linear and nonlinear relationships. For example, if the relation between IQ and Parent Income is very different for male students and female students, the regression tree will have a split on the gender and return two different formulas: one for each gender. When there is no tree split, the regression tree reverts to a linear regression.

Association Analysis with Microsoft Decision Trees

One of the unique features of Microsoft Decision Trees is that it can be used for association analysis. A mining model may contain a forest of trees. If a model contains a nested table and the nested table is predictable, all the nested keys are considered to be predictable attributes. The Microsoft Decision Trees algorithm builds trees for each of them, more precisely, for each nested key that is selected feature.

Figure 5.3 illustrates a set of trees to predict movie relationships. The top-left tree predicts the popularity *Stargate*. The dark bar in the histogram represents the probability of a viewer not liking *Stargate*, while the white bar represents the probability of a viewer liking *Stargate*. The first split is on the *Star Wars* attribute. If a person likes *Star Wars*, he or she is much likelier to like *Stargate*. The second split, shows that a person who likes *Star Trek* also has a high probability of liking *Stargate*.

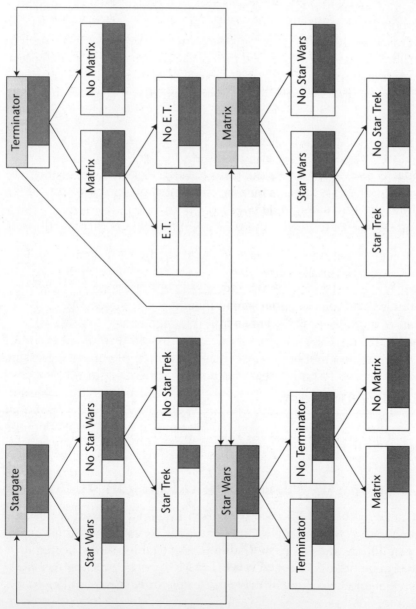

Figure 5.3 Association using Microsoft Decision Trees

There are multiple trees in the model. From each tree, we can find a set of movies that is correlated with the predictable movie. For example, based on the *Stargate* tree, we can say that fans of *Star Wars* and *Star Trek* are likely to enjoy *Stargate* with certain weights (calculated based on the probability gain). Based on the *Terminator* tree, we can predict that *Matrix* and *ET* fans will also like *Terminator*. By going over the entire forest of trees, we can derive all the relationships among the movies. These relationships are, in fact, association rules and can be used for making associated predictions. For example, if a person likes *Star Wars*, we can recommend *Stargate* and *Matrix* to him.

Using Microsoft Decision Trees for association analysis is very interesting; associated items are displayed in the tree form and dependency network form. However, there are also limitations to this association task. Because it builds a decision tree for each item, this may take time and resources when there are lots of items. The default maximum number of trees is 255. If there are more than 255 items, the algorithm uses feature selection techniques to select the important features.

TIP The Microsoft Decision Trees algorithm does association analysis by combining all the trees and deriving the correlations among the tree roots. It is best when the number of items for associative analysis is limited; otherwise, the algorithm has to build large number of trees. This is time- and resource-consuming.

The other issue is that Microsoft Decision Trees doesn't return itemsets and rules as an association algorithm does. The user has to figure out the relationship using a content viewer. Our recommendation is to build models with both the decision tree and association algorithms. You may find complementary information. If you have a large number of items, you should use an association algorithm.

Algorithm Parameters

There are a number of parameters for Microsoft Decision Trees. These parameters are used to control the tree growth, tree shape, and the input/output attribute settings. By adjusting these parameter settings, you can fine-tune the model accuracy. The following is the list of decision tree algorithm parameters.

- Complexity_Penalty is used to control the tree growth. It is a floating number with range [0,1]. When its value is set close to 0, there is a lower penalty for the tree growth after model training; thus, you may see a large tree. When its value is set to close 1, the tree growth is penalized, and the final tree is relatively small. Generally speaking, large trees tend to have overtraining issues, whereas small tree may miss some patterns. The recommended way to tune the model is to try multiple trees with different settings and then use a lift chart to verify the model's accuracy on testing data in order to pick the best one. The default setting is related to the number of input attributes. If there are fewer than 10 input attributes, the value is set to 0.5; if there are more than 100 attributes, the value is set to 0.99. If you have between 10 and 100 input attributes, the value is set to 0.9.

- `Minimum_Support` is used to specify the minimum size of each leaf node in the tree. For example, if this value is set to 20, any tree split that can produce a child node containing less than 20 cases is not accepted. The default value for `Minimum_Support` `Minimum_Leaf_Cases` is 10. Usually, if the training dataset contains lots of cases, you will need to raise the value of this parameter to avoid oversplitting (overtraining).

- `Score_Method` is a parameter of Integer type. It is used to specify the method for measuring a tree split score during the tree growth. We have discussed the concept of entropy in this chapter. To use an entropy score for tree growth, you need to set `Score_Method = 1`. There are a few other score methods supported by Microsoft Decision Trees: Bayesian K2, 3 (BK2) and Bayesian Dirichlet Equivalent with Uniform prior, 4 (BDEU). BK2 adds a constant for each state of the predictable attribute in a tree node, regardless the node level of the tree. BDEU adds weighted support to each predictable state based on the node level. The weight of the root node is higher than that of the leaf node; thus, the assigned prior (knowledge) is larger. The default value for Score_Method is 4, which is a BDEU method. `Score_Method = 2(orthogonal)` is no longer supported in SQL Server 2005.

- `Split_Method` is a parameter with integer type. It is used to specify the tree shape, for example, whether the tree shape is binary or bushy. `Split_Method = 1` means the tree is split only in a binary way. For example, Education is an attribute with three states: high school, undergraduate, and graduate. If the tree split is set to be binary, the algorithm may split the tree into two nodes with the criteria "`Education = Undergraduate?`" If the tree split is set to be complete (`Split_Method = 2`), the split on the Education attribute produces three nodes, one corresponding to each educational state. When `Split_Method` is set to 3 (the default setting), the decision tree will automatically choose the better of the first two methods to create the split.

- `Maximum_Input_Attribute` is a threshold parameter of feature selection. When the number of input attributes is greater than this parameter value, feature selection is invoked implicitly to select the most significant input attributes.

- `Maximum_Output_Attribute` is a threshold parameter of feature selection. When the number of predictable attributes is greater than this parameter value, feature selection is invoked implicitly to select the most significant attributes. A tree is built for each of the selected attributes.

- `Force_Regressor` is a parameter for regression trees. It forces the regression and uses the specified attribute as the regressor. Suppose that you have a model to predict Income using Age, IQ, and other attributes. If you specify `Force_Regressor = {Age, IQ}`, you get regression formulas using Age and IQ for each leaf node of the tree.

Using Decision Trees

In this section, you will learn how to use the Microsoft Decision Trees algorithm, including how to perform model interpretation and DMX queries.

DMX Queries

Microsoft Decision Trees can be used for three different data mining tasks: classification, regression, and association. It is a very unique and powerful algorithm. In this section, we will build three different models using DMX to illustrate these usages.

Classification Model

The first model, shown in the following code, predicts College Plans based on Gender, IQ, Parents' Income, and Parental Encouragement. The DMX for the model creation is the following:

```
Create mining model CollegePlan
(    StudentId  long Key,
     Gender text discrete,
     ParentIncome long discrete,
     IQ long continuous,
     ParentEncouragement text discrete,
     CollegePlans text discrete predict
)
Using Microsoft_Decision_Trees (Complexity_Penalty=0.5)
```

After the model is created, we can process the model. To train the model, we need a training dataset. The training dataset can be stored in any data source as long as you have a right OLE DB driver. This feature is called *in-place mining*. The following training statement uses data stored in an Access table:

```
INSERT INTO CollegePlan
(StudentId, Gender, Iq, ParentEncouragement, ParentIncome,
CollegePlans)
OPENROWSET('Microsoft.Jet.OLEDB.4.0',
 'Data Source=C:\data\CollegePlan.mdb;',
 'select StudentId, Gender, IQ, ParentEncouragement, ParentIncome,
CollegePlans from CollegePlans')
```

After training, we can browse the model using a content query:

```
Select * from CollegePlan.Content
```

This query returns the model's content in a tabular format. In the case of the decision tree model, each row in the query result represents a node in the decision tree. Each row contains a column with data type Chapter, which is a nested table storing the statistics (node distribution). You can write your own decision tree viewer based on the results of this query.

Now, we will apply the model to predict the College Plans for new students through the following query:

```
SELECT T1.StudentID, CollegePlan.CollegePlans,
PredictProbability(CollegePlans) as Proba
FROM CollegePlan
    PREDICTION JOIN
    OPENROWSET('Microsoft.Jet.OLEDB.4.0', 'Data
Source=C:\data\CollegePlan.mdb',
    'SELECT StudentID, Gender, IQ, ParentEncouragement, ParentIncome
        FROM NewStudents') AS T1
ON CollegePlan.ParentIncome = T1.ParentIncome AND
    CollegePlan.IQ = T1.IQ AND
    CollegePlan.Gender = T1.Gender AND
    CollegePlan.ParentEncouragement = T1.ParentEncouragement
```

This query returns three columns: StudentID, CollegePlans, and Proba.

As explained in Chapter 2, a data mining query result may contain nested tables and sometimes even multiple levels of nesting. The following query returns the histogram of College Plans' predictions in the form of a nested table:

```
SELECT T1.StudentID,
        PredictHistogram(CollegePlans) as CollegePlans
FROM CollegePlan
    PREDICTION JOIN
    OPENROWSET('Microsoft.Jet.OLEDB.4.0', 'Data
Source=C:\data\CollegePlan.mdb',
    'SELECT StudentID, Gender, IQ, ParentEncouragement, ParentIncome
        FROM NewStudents') AS T1
```

```
ON CollegePlan.ParentIncome = T1.ParentIncome AND
CollegePlan.IQ = T1.IQ AND
CollegePlan.Gender = T1.Gender AND
   CollegePlan.ParentEncouragement = T1.ParentEncouragement
```

The result of the query is displayed in Table 5.1. The Histogram column embeds a nested table. Besides College Plans, there is a set of predefined columns in the nested table, including $Support, $Probability, $AdjustedProbability, and so on. Each row represents a state of the College Plan, and the last row represents the missing state.

Table 5.1   Query Results

STUDENTID	COLLEGEPLANS				
1	CollegePlans	$Support	$Probability	$Adjusted Probability	....
	Yes	1175	0.91665	0.00052	
	No	106	0.08301	0.00593	
	Missing	0	0.00034	0.00034	
2	CollegePlans	$Support	$Probability	$Adjusted Probability	....
	Yes	327	0.81992	0.00047	
	No	71	0.17893	0.01280	
	Missing	0	0.00115	0.00115	
3	...				

Regression Model

Regression predicts continuous variables using regression formulas. The regressor must have a continuous content type. Normally, a regression formula contains one or more regressors. When there is no regressor in the formula, the result tree contains a constant in each leaf node.

The following predicts Parents' Income using IQ, Gender, Parental Encouragement, and College Plans. IQ is used as a regressor.

```
Create mining model ParentIncomePrediction
( StudentId  Text Key,
    Gender text discrete,
    IQ long regressor continuous ,
```

```
        ParentEncouragement long continuous,
        CollegePlans text discrete predict,
        ParentIncome long continuous predict
)
Using Microsoft_Decision_Trees
```

The training statement is independent of the algorithm and the column usage settings. It mainly specifies the binding of input columns and the mining model columns. The `ParentIncomePrediction` training statement is the same as in the College Plans model given in the previous example.

After training, we can query the content schema rowset of the model. The overall content structure of a regression model is similar to a classification model, with each node representing a tree node. The difference is in the nested distribution table. For the regression model, each row in the distribution table represents a coefficient for the regressor or the intercept.

The following query predicts the Parents' Income for new students. It also returns the standard deviation for each prediction. The smaller the deviation, the more accuracy the prediction has.

```
SELECT T1.StudentID, ParentIncomePrediction.ParentIncome,
       PredictStdev(ParentIncome) as deviation
FROM ParentIncomePrediction
  PREDICTION JOIN
  OPENROWSET('Microsoft.Jet.OLEDB.4.0',
'Data Source=C:\data\CollegePlan.mdb',
  'SELECT StudentID, Gender, IQ, ParentEncouragement, CollegePlans
    FROM NewStudents') AS T1
ON ParentIncomePrediction.CollegePlans = T1.CollegePlans AND
  ParentIncomePrediction.IQ = T1.IQ AND
  ParentIncomePrediction.Gender = T1.Gender AND
  ParentIncomePrediction.ParentEncouragement = T1.ParentEncouragement
```

We can also apply the `PredictHistogram` function on the continuous column; it returns two rows in the nested table: the predicted mean value and the missing state, and each is associated with a probability. If the probability of missing state is over 50%, the predicted value for Parents' Income is missing.

```
SELECT T1.StudentID, PredictHistogram(ParentIncome) as Histogram
FROM CollegePlan
    PREDICTION JOIN ...
```

The previous query returns the results shown in Table 5.2.

Table 5.2 Query Result

STUDENTID	HISTOGRAM					
1	Parents' Income	$Support	$Probability	$Adjusted Probability	$Variance	$Stdev
33679	4336	0.99977	0	225949017	15031.6	
Missing	0	0.00023	0.00023	0	0	
1	Parents' Income	$Support	$Probability	$Adjusted Probability	$Variance	$Stdev
49082	2672	0.99962	0	225151659	15005.1	
Missing	0	0.00037	0.00037	0	0	
...						

Association Model

As explained in the previous section, we can use Microsoft Decision Trees for association tasks. The model builds a set of trees for each predictable attribute and calculates the relationship among these trees.

The association model usually contains a nested table, and the nested key is the attribute to use for the association analysis. It is also possible to have only a case table for an association model, with each column representing one item. However, when there are large amount of items, it is difficult to store this information in a single table because most databases have limitations the on number of columns a table can contain. The following is an example of an association model built on the movie dataset:

```
Create mining model MovieAssociation
(
CustomerID long key,
Gender      text      discrete,
MaritalStatus text      discrete,
Movies table Predict (
     MovieName text key
 )
)
Using Microsoft_Decision_Trees
```

This query analyzes the associations among all movies together with customer's gender and marital status. It builds a decision tree for each movie up to 255 trees. Each movie is considered an attribute with binary states: existing or missing. Trees may have splits on movie name, gender, and marital status.

Because the model contains a nested table, the training statement involves the Shape provider.

```
Insert into MovieAssociation
( CustomerId, Gender, MaritalStatus,
Movies (SKIP, MovieName))
OPENROWSET('MSDataShape', 'data provider=Microsoft.Jet.OLEDB.4.0; data
source=C:\data\moviesurvey.mdb' ,
 'SHAPE { select CustomerId, Gender, MaritalStatus From Customer Order
by CustomerID}
 APPEND ({select CustomerId, MovieName from Movies order by CustomerID}
 RELATE CustomerID to CustomerID) AS Movies' )
```

Suppose that there is a married male customer who likes the movie *Terminator*. The following singleton query returns the other five movies this customer is most likely to find appealing:

```
SELECT
  CustomerID,
  Predict(MovieAssociation.Movies,5) as Recommendation
From
  MovieAssociation
NATURAL PREDICTION JOIN
(SELECT '101' as CustomerID, 'Female' AS Gender,
 'Married' AS MaritalStatus,
 (SELECT 'Terminator' AS [ovie) AS Movies) AS t
```

The result of the query is shown in Table 5.3, with Recommendation as a nested table containing the five movies to recommend.

Table 5.3 The Five Recommended Movies

CUSTOMERID	RECOMMENDATION
101	*A Beautiful Mind* *Lord of the Rings: The Fellowship of the Ring* *Princess Bride, The* *Star Wars* *Apollo 13*
...	

Model Content

You have already seen the content of Microsoft Decision Trees in Chapter 2, when we discussed mining model content schema rowsets. Figure 5.4 displays the layout of a tree model. The top level is the model node. The children of the model node are a set of tree root nodes. If a tree model contains a single tree, there is only one node in the second level. The nodes of the other levels are either intermediate nodes or leaf nodes of the tree. The probabilities of each predictable attribute state (or regression coefficients in the case of a regression model) are stored in the distribution rowsets, as shown in Figure 5.4.

Interpreting the Model

Each Microsoft data mining algorithm in SQL Server 2005 is associated with a content viewer. The viewer is specifically designed to display the patterns discovered by the associated algorithm.

Figure 5.5 is a screenshot of Microsoft Decision Tree Viewer, displaying the classification tree model of CollegePlans. The tree is laid out horizontally with the root node on the left side. Each node contains a histogram bar with different colors, representing various states. In this case, there are two colors in the histogram bar. The dark color represents College Plan = Yes, and the white color represents College Plan = No. The bottom part of the screen is a dockable window, displaying the node legend of the selected node. The decision tree patterns are very easy to interpret. Each path from the root to a given node forms a rule. In the figure, the selected node represents the node path: Parent Encouragement = Encouraged and IQ >= 110 and Parent Income >= 49632.238 and Gender = Male. From the Node Legend window, you can see that there are 537 cases classified to this node, and probability of College Plan = Yes in this node is 88.54%.

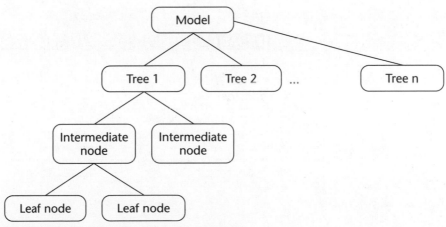

Figure 5.4   Content for decision tree model

NOTE You may notice the probability of the missing state in Figure 5.5 is 0.01%, though no one among 437 students classified in this node has a missing state. This is becase a prior is considered when calculating the probability for each state. Usually, this favors those states with low supports.

There are a number of buttons and drop-down lists on the toolbar, including buttons for Zoom in, Zoom out, and Zoom to fit. The Tree drop-down list is used for making tree selections. Remember, a model may contain a set of trees. The left bar in this drop-down list is a handy indication, telling us the size of the associated tree. The Histograms combo box allows users to specify the number of states (colors) to display in the histogram bar of each tree node. For example, if a predictable attribute has 10 states, you can use this drop-down list to display the most important five states. The other states are all grouped and shown in gray.

You may want to find the nodes representing the highest probability of College Plan = Yes. You can do so by looking at the histogram bar of each node. But when there are many states of the predictable attribute, it is not obvious which are the desired nodes. The Background drop-down list is very useful for this purpose. It controls the background color of the tree nodes. By default, the tree node background color represents the number of cases classified in each node. The darker a node is, the more cases it contains. You can also pick a particular state of the predictable attribute in this drop-down list — for example, College Plan = Yes. In this case, the background color represents the probability for the selected state. If a node is a dark color, it has high probability associated with the given state.

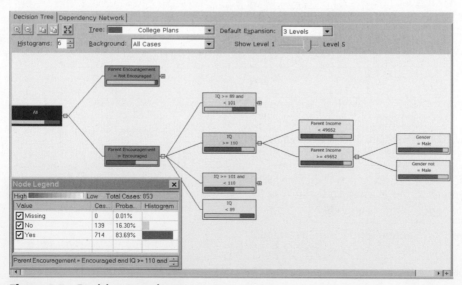

Figure 5.5   Decision tree viewer

TIP Take a closer look at the node labeled `Parent Income >=49652`, it splits on the `Gender` attribute. But its two children have very similar probability distributions. This split doesn't give additional information. This is a case of over split. To avoid this, you may raise the value of Complecity_Penalty.

All Microsoft data mining viewers in SQL Server 2005 have multiple tabs, which display the patterns at different angles. Figure 5.6 is the Dependency Network tab for decision tree algorithms. The dependency network displays the relationships among attributes derived from decision tree model's content. Each node in the figure represents one attribute, and each edge represents the relationship between two nodes. An edge has a direction, pointing from the input attribute (node) to the predictable attribute (node). An edge can be bidirectional, which means two nodes can predict each other. In the figure, Parental Encouragement, IQ, Parents' Income, and Gender can all predict College Plans. An edge has a weight; the weight is associated with the slider at the left side. The heavier the weight, the stronger the predictor is. The weight is derived from the tree's statistics, mainly based on the split score. In this example, if we move the slider down, we can see that the most important attribute for predicting College Plans is Parental Encouragement, and the weakest one is Gender.

The Dependency Network viewer can be very useful when there are lots of predictable attributes, for example, a model with a predictable nested table. In this case, each node in the dependency network represents a tree root. You can think this graph as bird's-eye view over a forest. It provides extremely useful information for exploratory data analysis.

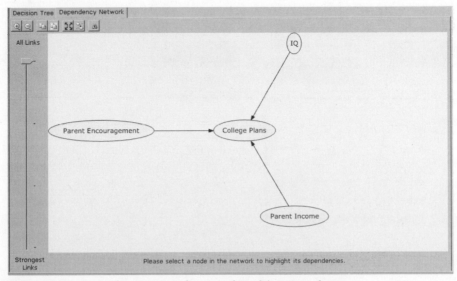

Figure 5.6 Dependency network pane of Decision Tree viewer

TIP In most cases, not all the input attributes are used for splitting a tree. The unselected attributes generally have less impact on the predictable attribute has. They are not displayed in the dependency network.

But be careful. In some cases, important attributes don't appear in the tree split. For example, suppose that a tree predicts HouseOwnership. Education and Income are two attributes that have a major impact on HouseOwnership. These two attributes are highly correlated. For example, higher education is always associated with high income. When the tree splits on one attribute, it is almost equivalent to splitting on the other. After the split on Income, Education is not an important attribute in subtrees. As a consequence, there is no tree split based on Education. Thus Education is not displayed in the dependency network, even though it is a good predictor for HouseOwnership. This is a weakness of decision trees. We recommend building an additional model using Naïve Bayes, which doesn't have this shortcoming.

Figure 5.7 displays a regression tree model predicting Parents' Income. The regressor is IQ. The overall view of the regression tree is similar to that of a classification tree. However, the tree nodes are different. There is no histogram bar in a regression tree. Instead, it contains a diamond bar representing the distribution of predictable variables (continuous values). The diamond represents the value distribution of the given node. The diamond is centered on the mean of the predictable attribute of those cases that are classified in the current node. The width of the diamond is twice the standard deviation. If the diamond is thin, the prediction on this node is more precise.

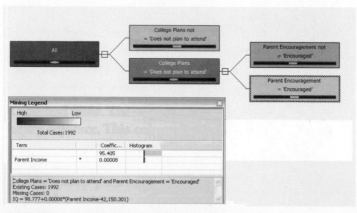

Figure 5.7 Visualizing a regression tree

As explained previously, each node of a regression tree model contains a regression formula. For example, the selected node in Figure 5.7 contains the following regression formula:

$$IQ = 98.777+0.00008*(Parent\ Income-42,150.301)$$

Summary

The decision tree is a very popular data mining algorithm. Microsoft Decision Trees can be used for three different data mining tasks: classification, regression, and association.

In this chapter, you were given an overview of the decision tree and the principles of the Microsoft Decision Tree algorithm. By now, you should know the concept of entropy, which is one of the popular tree splitting scores. You also know how to use the set of parameters to tune the accuracy of a tree model. For example, `Complexity_Penalty` is a parameter you can use frequently to avoid overtraining or undertraining.

You've learned how to build mining models, using the decision tree algorithm, for three types of data mining tasks using DMX query. You also learned the prediction queries for three different types of tree models.

The last part of the chapter taught you how to interpret a tree model, using the Decision Tree viewer. Viewing a tree is not as simple as it seemed to be; you've learned how to identify whether a tree is overtrained and how to determine the importance of each input attribute (predictor).

Microsoft Time Series

Suppose that you are a retail store manager. You want to know the sales forecast for the next few weeks for each product category, each subcategory, and each individual item. This information can help you optimize your inventory. You don't want to have items out of stock when there is a strong customer demand, nor do you like to overstock items. When holidays approach, the sales of certain items may peek. For example, Easter triggers the sale of Easter eggs, chocolate, jelly beans, and so on. You want to know when and how much to order of each of these products.

The Microsoft Time Series Algorithm is designed to resolve this kind of puzzle. Let's have a closer look at this data mining technique in this chapter.

In this chapter, you will learn about:

- The principles of the Microsoft Time Series algorithm
- Setting the algorithm parameters
- DMX queries related to time series
- Interpreting a Microsoft Time Series model

Introducing the Microsoft Time Series Algorithm

A *time series* consists of a series of data collected over successive increments of time or some other indicator of sequence. Our world is not stationary; many variables change their values over time. A sequence of values of a variable over the time forms a time series. For example, the daily closing price of Microsoft stock is a time series (see Figure 6.1), the monthly store sales of Pepsi form a time series, and the quarterly revenue of a company is a time series. Often in a time series, a value at a given time is correlated to the values at preceding times. For example, the closing price of Microsoft stock on May 10th is strongly related to its closing price on May 9th and May 8th.

Generally speaking, the time increments in a time series can be discrete or continuous. We consider only time series types in which the time increments are discrete. In addition, the observed values in a time series may be discrete or continuous. The stock value, store sales, and company revenue examples have continuous observations. A time series of weather forecasts with values of sunny, cloudy, or rainy has discrete observations. In most forecasting literature, people use *time series* to refer to the case in which observations are continuous and use *sequence* to refer to the case in which observations are discrete.

The main purpose of collecting time series data is to forecast, or make predictions about, future values. In the manufacturing example, a factory needs to forecast the demands of its customers in the coming months for production planning. A Web site needs to know the growth of its user traffic in order to choose the right hardware. Retail stores want to predict product sales to optimize their storage. Forecasting is a very common data mining task. Any CRM or ERP applications can benefit from time series forecasting feature.

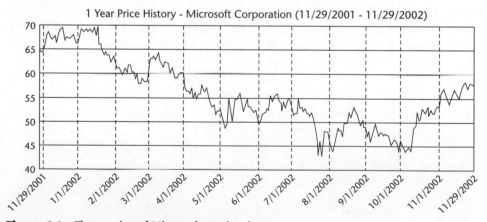

Figure 6.1 Time series of Microsoft stock value

Introducing the Principles of The Microsoft Time Series Algorithm

The Microsoft Time Series algorithm is a novel forecasting algorithm. It is a hybrid of the autoregression and decision tree techniques. We also name this algorithm as ART (AutoRegression Tree). In this section, you take a closer look of the principles underlying this algorithm.

Autoregression

Autoregression is a popular technique for dealing with time series. An autoregressive process is one in which the value of x and time $t(xt)$ is a function of the values of x at previous time, for example:

$$X_t = f\left(X_{t-1}, X_{t-2}, X_{t-3}, X_{t-n}\right) + \varepsilon_t$$

where xt is the time series under investigation, and n is the order of autoregression, which is generally much less than the length of the series. The last term, epsilon, represents the noise.

One of the key steps of ART is to transform single cases of a time series into multiple cases internally. The process is illustrated in Figure 6.2. The left table in the figure contains two time series (two cases) of a month's milk and bread sales. The right table is the transformed data. There are seven columns in the table: the first one is the case ID. The second column shows milk sales at the t-2 time slot; the third column shows milk sales at the t-1 time slot; the fourth column shows milk sales at the t time slot. The last three columns contain similar information about bread sales. Each row in the right table represents a case. Milk($t0$) and Bread($t0$) are the two predictable columns. Because our decision trees support regression, we can use this technique to predict these two columns. Milk(t-1), Milk(t-2), Bread(t-1), and Bread(t-2) are considered to be regressors. In the Microsoft Time Series algorithm, the case transform uses the previous eight time slots by default.

One of the advantages of case transformation is that all time series within the same mining model are converted to columns in the same table. While using decision tree techniques to predict Milk ($t0$), all columns other than Milk or Bread are considered to be input columns. If there is strong correlation between Bread and Milk sales, this correlation will show up in the function f.

The goal of a time series algorithm is to find the function f.

If f is a linear function, we have

$$X_t = a_1 X_{t-1} + a_2 X_{t-2} + a_3 X_{t-3} + \ldots + a_n X_{t-n} + \varepsilon_t$$

where ai are the autoregression coefficients.

Case Transform

Month	Milk	Bread
Jan-2005	5000	4500
Feb-2005	5200	4600
Mar-2005	5240	5130
Apr-2005	6390	6280
May-2005	6750	6160
Jun-2005	6280	6560
July-2005	7680	7200
...		

Case Id	Milk (t-2)	Milk (t-1)	Milk (t0)	Bread (t-2)	Bread (t-1)	Bread (t0)
1	5000	5200	5240	4500	4560	5130
2	5200	5240	6390	4560	5130	6280
3	5240	6390	6750	5130	6280	6120
4	6390	6750	6280	6280	6120	6560
5	6750	6280	7680	6120	6560	7200
...						

Figure 6.2 Case transformation

This model, often referred to simply as autoregression, or AR, was first proposed and solved by Yule in 1927. Verbally, the current term of the series can be estimated by the linear weighted sum of previous terms in the series. The weights are the autoregression coefficients.

There are a number of ways to solve for the autoregression coefficients. The most popular method is to fit these autoregressive coefficients by minimizing the mean-squared difference between the modeled time series $Xnmodel$ and the observed time series Xn. The minimization process results in a system of linear equations for the coefficients an, known as the Yule-Walker equations as listed in the following. These equations enable us to compute the AR coefficients given the covariance matrix shown in Figure 6.3.

$$
\begin{bmatrix}
1 & r_1 & r_2 & r_3 & r_4 & \cdots & r_{n-1} \\
r_1 & 1 & r_1 & r_2 & r_3 & \cdots & r_{n-2} \\
r_2 & r_1 & 1 & r_1 & r_2 & \cdots & r_{n-3} \\
\cdot & \cdot & \cdot & \cdot & \cdot & \cdot & \cdot \\
\cdot & \cdot & \cdot & \cdot & \cdot & \cdot & \cdot \\
\cdot & \cdot & \cdot & \cdot & \cdot & \cdot & \cdot \\
r_{n-1} & r_{n-2} & r_{n-3} & r_{n-4} & r_{n-5} & \cdots & 1
\end{bmatrix}
\begin{bmatrix}
a_1 \\ a_2 \\ a_3 \\ \cdot \\ \cdot \\ \cdot \\ a_n
\end{bmatrix}
=
\begin{bmatrix}
r_1 \\ r_2 \\ r_3 \\ \cdot \\ \cdot \\ \cdot \\ r_n
\end{bmatrix}
$$

Figure 6.3 The covariance matrix where r_d is the autocorrelation coefficient at delay d.

Using Multiple Time Series

In terms of DMX, a time series is a single case. The weekly sales amount of Pepsi during the past year forms a single case of a time series, although there are 52 data points. A mining model may contain multiple time series. For example, a model can contains all the time series of beverage products, including Pepsi, beer, juice, milk, and so on. Series are not always independent. The sales of Pepsi and juice may be strongly correlated. The Microsoft Time Series algorithm recognizes cross-series correlations when they exist. This is one of the unique features of this algorithm.

Autoregression Trees

Microsoft Time Series algorithm is an autoregressive model in which the function f corresponds to a regression tree. As mentioned earlier, in research publications the name of this algorithm is AutoRegression Trees (ART). ART was developed by three researchers from Microsoft Research: Chris Meek, David Maxwell Chickering, and David Heckerman, in 2001.

In ART, the function f is represented by a regression tree. Figure 6.4 displays a regression tree built using the time series data in Figure 6.2. The first tree split is on bread sales two months before. If bread sales were more than 110 two months ago, there is another tree split on milk sales of previous month. In the case of previous month, milk sales were less than 120, and the regression formula for milk is $3.02 + 0.72 * Bread(t\text{-}1) + 0.31 * Milk(t\text{-}1)$.

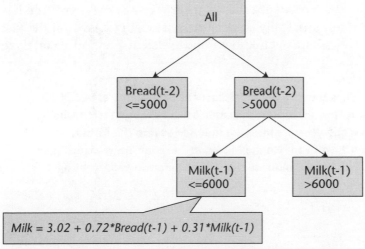

Figure 6.4   Regression tree on time series data

Seasonality

Most time series have seasonal patterns. For example, the sales in retail stores peak in December, or the last quarter of the year. The average temperature in summer months is higher than in winter months. In Pacific Northeast region, the quantities of monthly rainfall from November to March are the highest in the year.

There are many techniques for dealing with seasonality. Most time series algorithms decompose the series and treat seasonality independently. ART solves this problem in a straightforward way. During the case transformation step, ART adds historical data points based on the seasonality parameter `Periodicity_Hint` in addition to the pervious eight time slices. In our example of monthly sales, the period of seasonality is presumably 12, because there are 12 months in the year. Given a periodicity of 12, ART includes observations for Milk(t-12), Milk(t-24), Milk(t-36), . . . ,Milk(t – 8 * 12), Bread(t-12), Bread(t-24), Bread(t-36) . . ., Bread(t – 8 * 12) in the table. If there are strong yearly patterns in the data, the regression tree will use these observations in splits and in the regression formulas at the tree nodes.

A series may contain multiple periodicity hints. For example, the monthly revenue of a company follows the yearly periodicity (12) as well as quarterly periodicity (3), because the last month of the fiscal quarter may record stronger revenues than other months. When there are multiple periodicities, ART adds more columns in the transformed case table based on the seasonality.

Note that `Periodicity_Hint` is just that — a hint. If a hint is given, and it turns out that there is no strong seasonality effect within that period, the algorithm will discard the dependence.

If you don't specify the periodicity, the Microsoft Time Series algorithm has a built-in feature that automatically detects the seasonality based on the fast Fourier transform, which is a well-known and efficient method to analyze frequencies.

NOTE After the case is transformed and seasonal data points are collected, the core part of the ART processing is the same as using a regression tree. In other words, if you manually transform the time series into the format displayed in Figure 6.2, you can use the Microsoft Decision Trees algorithm to do the forecasting. You should indicate that all the columns representing previous time slices are regressors.

Making Historical Predictions

After a time series model is processed, it can perform forecasting as well as historical prediction. In DMX, there is a predefined prediction function call `PredictTimeSeries`. For example, `PredictTimeSeries(Bread, 5)` returns a nested table of five rows, representing the bread sales in the next five months.

However, you should trust the results only if you know how well the algorithm predicted results in the past. You can determine the reliability of previous results by using the same prediction function with negative numbers as parameters, for example, `PredictTimeSeries(Bread, -10, -5)` returns the historical prediction of the past 5 to 10 months worth of Bread sales. Because the current model is trained with all the historical data points, its predictive accuracy appears to be better than it actually is. If you really want to see how the time series algorithm predicts on historical data points, you should use these two parameters: `Historical_Model_Count` and `Historical_Model_Gap`. `Historical_Model_Count` specifies the number of historical models to build, while `Historical_Model_Gap` specifies the time increments in which historical models are to be built. Figure 6.5 displays a setting of four historical models, with the gap equal to 30. When the mining model is processed, it contains five models. The first one ends at `Time` -120, and the last one ends at `Now`. When predicting the value at time –100, it uses the first model implicitly. When predicting the value at time –70, it uses the second model implicitly. However, from the user's point of view, there is only one time series model.

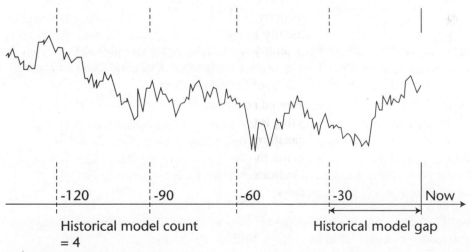

Figure 6.5   Historical models

Caching Predictions

Each time series is considered to be a single case. Time series prediction, then, can be thought of as extending the single case. Thus the semantics of time series prediction is different from that of other algorithms, such as decision trees, that learn from multiple cases. The way to predict non-time-series models is to apply the patterns learned from training cases to the unknown cases using the prediction join query. You don't use a prediction join with a time series model because there is no new case to join with. The time series prediction syntax is a simple Select statement from a trained model.

Because the time series prediction is on the training case itself, the prediction's result remains the same at a given time slot. Because of this property, you can cache the prediction result right after model processing. This reduces the response time during the query execution.

Understanding the Algorithm Parameters

The following list describes the algorithm parameters available to you:

- **Minimum_Support:** Used to specify the minimum case number of each leaf node. For example, if this value is set to 20, any tree split that may produces a child node containing less than 20 cases is not accepted. The default value for Minimum_Support is 10. If the training dataset contains lots of cases, you may need to raise the value of this parameter to avoid oversplitting (overtraining). This is the same parameter that is used in the Microsoft Decision Trees algorithm.

> **NOTE** You have just learned that one time series forms a single case. Minimum_Support doesn't really restrict the number of original case in a leaf node, rather it resticts the transformed cases (see Figure 6.2).

- **Complexity_Penalty:** Used to control the tree's growth, this is a floating number within [0,1]. While its value is set close to 0, there is a lower penalty for the tree growth, thus after model training, you may see a very large tree. This parameter also exists in the Microsoft Decision Trees algorithm.
- **Historical_Model_Count:** Used with the Integer type. It defines the number of historical models to build.
- **Historical_Model_Gap:** Used with the Integer type. This parameter is associated with Historical_Model_Count. It specifies the number of time slices between historical models.

- **Periodicity_Hint:** Provides a hint to the algorithm about seasonality information in the data. `Periodicity_Hint` is used with the String type. The format is: `{n [, n]}`, where the part in the square brackets is optional and can be repeated, and *n* is any positive number or floating-point number. When the month revenue of a given company follows yearly and quarterly patterns, the setting for `Periodicity_Hint` should be `{3, 12}`.

TIP `Periodicity_Hint` **is an important parameter. The algorithm is sensitive to this, since it adds additional data points for model training. In most cases, you should know the periodicity of your data. You can also use a chart to plot the time series, which can help you to identify the sesonality. Note that providing more hints typically increases accuracy, but also increases training time.**

- **Auto_Detect_Periodicity:** A floating number with value between 0 and 1. It is used to detect periodicity. Setting its value closer to 1 favors the discovery of many near periodic patterns and the automatic generation of periodicity hints. Dealing with a large number of periodicity hints will likely lead to significantly longer model training times. If the value is closer to 0, periodicity is detected only for strongly periodic data.

- **Maximum_Series_Value:** Specifies the upper constraint for any time series prediction. Predicted values will never be greater than this constraint.

- **Minimum_Series_Value:** Specifies the lower constraint for any time series prediction. Predicted values will never be greater than this constraint.

- **Minimum_Support:** Specifies the minimum number of time slices required to generate a split in each time series tree.

- **Missing_Value_Substitution:** Specifies the method used to fill the gaps in historical data. By default, irregular gaps or ragged edges in data are not allowed. The methods available to fill in irregular gaps or edges are: by Previous value, by Mean value, or by specific numerical constant.

Using Microsoft Time Series

You have learned the principles of Microsoft Time Series algorithm in the previous section. Now, we will create a few time series models for forecasting.

DMX Queries

There are a couple of popular formats for storing time series data in a relational table. Figure 6.6 displays the two table schemas. In Figure 6.6a, each column represents a time series. In Figure 6.6b, the column Product contains the name of each series, and the sales column stores the sales amount, which is the value of the time series. Each format has its pros and cons. Table a is more compact with fewer rows. However, when there are many series to model, for example, thousands of different products, Table a becomes unscalable. Table b contains only three columns and is scalable to the number of series. The disadvantages of Table b are: first, the table contains many rows; second, the prediction queries require adding a Where clause in order to predict a particular series.

The following statements create two time series models, using the two tables in Figure 6.6.

```
Create Mining Model MilkBreadTSa (
     Month date key time,
     Milk long continuous predict,
     Bread long continuous Predict
) Using Microsoft_Time_Series
```

```
Create Mining Model MilkBreadTSb (
    Month date key time,
    Product text key,
    Sales     long continuous Predict
) Using Microsoft_Time_Series
```

Month	Milk	Bread
Jan-2005	5000	4500
Feb-2005	5200	4560
Mar-2005	5240	5130
Apr-2005	6390	6280
May-2005	6750	6120
Jun-2005	6280	6560
July-2005	7680	7200
...		

(a)

Month	Product	Sales
Jan-2005	Milk	5000
Jan-2005	Bread	4500
Feb-2005	Milk	5200
Feb-2005	Bread	4560
Mar-2005	Milk	5240
Mar-2005	Bread	5130
Apr-2005	Milk	6390
...		

(b)

Figure 6.6 Input table formats for time series

USING NESTED TABLES IN INPUT FORMATS

There are actually two other input formats for time series. Both of these formats require nested tables.

The first one has two tables: a single column case table that contains a list of products and a nested table as displayed in Figure 6.5b. The creation statement of this format is:

```
CREATE MINING MODEL MilkBreadTSc
(
 Product text key,
 Series table
 (
   TimeID long key time,
   Sales double continuous predict
  )
) USING Microsoft_Time_Series
```

The second format also has two tables: a single row case table that contains a single row and a nested table with four columns (caseid, timeid, milk and bread). The creation statement is the following:

```
CREATE MINING MODEL MilkBreadTSd
(
   CaseId text key,
   Series   table
   (
      TimeID   long key time,
      Milk double continuous predict,
      Bread double continuous predict
   )
) USING Microsoft_Time_Series
```

These two formats semantically map well with the nested table concepts defined in DMX; however, we recommend that you use the two formats of MilkBreadTSa and MilkBreadTSb due to their simpicity.

A time series model must have one and only one Key Time column, which represents the key in the time dimension. Usually, the data type of the Key Time column is Date. It can also be an Integer type.

There are two key columns inMilkBreadTSb model: One is the Date column, and the other is the Product. Each value in the Product column is a case key that represents the name of a time series.

As we said before, the training statement is algorithm independent. The training statements for these two models follow:

```
Insert into MilkBreadTSa (Month, Milk, Bread)
OPENROWSET('Microsoft.Jet.OLEDB.4.0', 'Data
Source=C:\data\MilkBreadTS.mdb;',
'SELECT Month, Milk, Bread From ProductSales_A')
```

```
Insert into MilkBreadTSb (Month, Product, Sales)
OPENROWSET('Microsoft.Jet.OLEDB.4.0', 'Data
Source=C:\data\MilkBreadTS.mdb;',
'SELECT Month, Product, Sales From ProductSales_B')
```

Because each time series is a single case, prediction on a time series model doesn't join with new cases. The predicted value is directly derived from the training case. The prediction function for time series is PredictTimeSeries. The following is an example of prediction:

```
SELECT PredictTimeSeries(Bread, 5) As BreadSales
FROM MilkBreadTSa
```

This query forecasts bread sales over the next five months based on Milk-BreadTSa model. PredictTimeSeries returns a single row with a nested table column BreadSales. There are five rows in the nested table, as displayed in Table 6.1. The nested table has two columns: $Time and Bread.

Table 6.1 Bread Sales over the Next Five Months Based on the MilkBreadTSa Model

BREADSALES	
BreadSales	
$Time	Bread
6/1/2005	21010
7/1/2005	22200
8/1/2005	26210
9/1/2005	22830
10/1/2005	23280

The following is a similar query based on the MilkBreadTSb model:

```
SELECT Product, PredictTimeSeries(Sales, 5) As productSales
FROM MilkBreadTSb
```

The result of this query contains two rows: one for each product. Each row contains a nested table, ProductSales, with five rows. The nested table contains the forecasted value over five months. There are two columns: $Time and Sales. The result is displayed in Table 6.2.

Table 6.2 Bread and Milk Sales Forecast

PRODUCT	PRODUCTSALES	
Bread	ProdcutSales	
	$Time	Sales
	6/1/2005	21010
	7/1/2005	22200
	8/1/2005	26210
	9/1/2005	22830
	10/1/2005	23280
Milk	ProductSales	
	$Time	Sales
	6/1/2005	22680
	7/1/2005	23490
	8/1/2005	27870
	9/1/2005	25950
	10/1/2005	26800

If you are interested in only bread sales in this example, you can add a Where clause in the prediction query: Where Product = 'Bread'.

The PredictTimeSeries function doesn't always return nested tables. If there is no argument about the predicting range, it returns the predicted value of the next time unit in scalar format. The following query returns a flat row of BreadSales:

```
SELECT PredictTimeSeries(Bread) As BreadSales
FROM MilkBreadTSa
```

As mentioned briefly in the Chapter 3, the Predict function supports polymorphism. You can replace PredictTimeSeries with Predict, and get the same query results. The Predict function will invoke the PredictTimeSeries function during the query processing.

You can also use the following queries by directly selecting the predictable columns in the model. In this case, Bread is equivalent to Predict (Bread), and Sales is equivalent to Predict (Sales). These queries return the time series values at the next time unit.

```
Select Bread
From MilkBreadTSa

Select Product, Sales
From  MilkBreadTSb
```

You can specify the time range for `PredictTimeSeries`, as in the following two examples:

```
SELECT PredictTimeSeries(Bread, -5, 5)
FROM ProductForecast_A
```

```
SELECT PredictTimeSeries(Sales, -5, 5)
FROM ProductForecast_B
Where Product = 'Bread'
```

The negative value of the parameter represents the prediction over the past. These two queries return the prediction result from the past five time units to the next five time units. If the time series model contains historical models, the historical predictions are based on these historical models.

You can also get the time series training data from the following query:

```
Select * from ProductForecast_A.Cases
Select * from ProductForecast_B.Cases
```

Model Content

The content of time series model is similar to the content of the decision tree model, after all, ART is a tree-based algorithm. A model contains one or more trees. Each tree has one or more nodes. Each nonleaf node contains a linear regression formula. The values of coefficients and intercepts for the linear regression are stored in the distribution rowsets of each content node.

Interpreting the Model

The Time Series viewer contains two tabs: the Tree tab and the Chart tab. The Tree tab displays the tree layout and regression formula of the model. The Chart tab displays the time series data and the future predicted values graphically. We will discuss the Time Series viewer using a model built on sales of milk and bread.

Figure 6.7 displays the Tree tab of Time Series viewer. The tree predicts monthly milk sales. The tree has only one split, which is based on the previous month's milk sales.

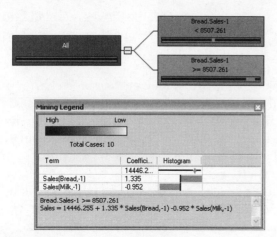

Figure 6.7 Time series Tree tab

The selected node indicates whether the previous month's milk sales were above 8507.261; the next month's milk sales can be forecasted using the following regression formula:

```
Milk Sales = 14446.255 + 1.335 * Sales(Bread,-1) -0.952 * Sales(Milk,-1)
```

NOTE Besides previous month's milk sales, the regression formula also uses the previous month's bread sales to predict the next month's milk sales. This is because the model finds there is strong regression relationship between the milk sales and bread sales series. If you don't want the cross-prediction behavior, you can make the series attribute (`Sales`) `predict_only` in the mining model.

Each leaf node has a distribution bar with a diamond. The diamond position and width reflects the mean and standard deviation, respectively, of the data at the given node.

The Node Legend window displays the residual standard deviation of the data and the correlation coefficients. The width of the diamond corresponds to residual (or conditional) standard deviation of the predicted variable given the regressor. Note that the square (the width of bar in node legend multiplied by the width of bar in node) corresponds to the familiar R-squared measure of linear regression.

The bars in the Node Legend window correspond to the correlation coefficients. The length of each bar is proportional to the distance that the predicted variable moves when the corresponding regressor variable moves one standard deviation. If the direction of the bar is to the right, it means that the regressor and predicted variables are positively correlated. If the direction of the bar is to the left, they are negatively correlated.

Figure 6.8 displays the Chart tab of Time Series viewer. The blue chart represents the monthly milk sales. There is a vertical line in the figure; the left side of the line represents the historical series value, and the right side of the line represents the future predictions. The predicted values are indicated using a dotted line. You can use the Prediction Step combo to specify the number of future steps to be displayed in the chart.

Users can also view the prediction's deviation in the Charts tab by checking the Show Deviations check box. Figure 6.9 shows the two charts with deviation on the predicted value. Usually, the further in the future, the larger the prediction's deviation is.

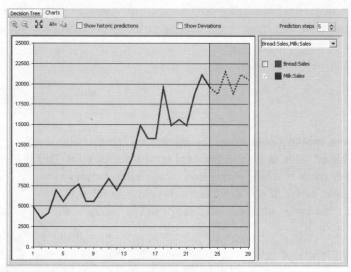

Figure 6.8 Time series Chart view tab

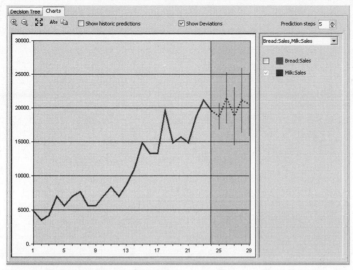

Figure 6.9 Prediction deviation

Summary

In this chapter, you learned the basics of the Microsoft Time Series algorithm, which is also called ART. It is a hybrid algorithm of autoregression and decision tree algorithms. You learned how to build time series models on different input data formats. The prediction in time series is different from that in other algorithms because a time series doesn't have new cases to prediction join with. This chapter has shown you DMX examples for a new prediction function: `PredictTimeSeries`. The result of the prediction is often stored in a nested table.

You also learned how to interpret the result of a time series model using the Microsoft Time Series viewer and how to set the appropriate value of parameters to tune a model.

Time series analysis covers a broad range of business problems. Now you should be able to build a few time series models to forecast your own business predictions.

Microsoft Clustering

Imagine yourself as a child sitting on the floor with a bag of marbles. You undo the leather strap and let the marbles spill out onto the floor. Instantly, you notice that you have lots of different colors: red, blue, yellow, green. You separate the marbles by color until you have four groups, then you notice that some of the marbles are regulars, some are shooters, and some are peewees. You decide that the peewees can stay with the regular marbles, but the shooters belong in a separate group, since only one will be used per player. You look at the organization and are happy with your groups. You have just performed a clustering operation.

You look at the clusters again and see that not only do you have solid-color marbles, but also cat's-eyes, starbursts, crystals, steelies, and genuine agates. Some of your marbles are in perfect condition, while others are scuffed. Some are so chipped that they don't roll straight. Now you are confused. Do you keep your simple groupings based on size and color, or do you add additional factors of style, material, and condition? Most likely, you just go ahead and play marbles.

Clustering is a simple, natural, and even automatic human operation when dealing with a small set of attributes. However, as the number of attributes grows addressing the problem of clustering becomes increasingly difficult and eventually impossible for the human mind to handle. It is possible for people with particular domain expertise and a deep understanding of the data to create clusters in up to five or six dimensions, but modern data sets typically contain dozens, if not hundreds, of dimensions, leaving us with the impossible task of creating groupings where we can't even conceive of the possible relationships between the attributes.

In this chapter, you will learn about:

- The principles of the Microsoft Clustering algorithm
- Using the Microsoft Clustering algorithm
- Interpreting the model content

Introducing the Microsoft Clustering Algorithm

The Microsoft Clustering algorithm finds natural groupings inside your data when these groupings are not obvious. Another way to put this is to say that it finds the *hidden variable* that accurately classifies your data. For example, you may be part of a large group of people picking up bags at the baggage claim. You notice that a significant percentage of the travelers are wearing shorts and sporting tans, whereas the rest are bundled up in sweaters and coats. You deduce a hidden variable — that one group returned from a tropical clime, and the other group arrived from some cold, wet place.

This capacity for determining the common thread that holds people together makes clustering a popular data mining technique for marketing. You could use clustering to learn more about your customers to target your message to specific groups. For example, a movie retailer may find a group of customers that purchases family movies on a regular basis and another that purchases documentaries less frequently. Sending monthly coupons for Disney films to the latter group obviously wouldn't be a wise choice. The ability to define and identify your market segments gives you a powerful tool to drive your business.

Identifying natural groups in your data frees you from simply analyzing your business based on the existing organization. Otherwise, you are limited to the groups that you can imagine, which may not have any bearing on how your customers contribute to your business. Do I sell more family favorites or documentaries? Does more profit come from the Northwest or Southeast region? Are renters better for my business than buyers are? There is an almost limitless number of ways to group your data, and very few (if any) will provide any deep insight into your business. The organization hidden inside your data is a powerful tool for business analysis. A retailer who knows the groups her customers fall into can track sales to those groups on a regular basis.

Figure 7.1 shows revenue for the movie retailer by region — a typical method of organizing and analyzing sales data. This view shows a healthy growth in business and how each region contributes to that growth. Not all regions are equal, and there are slight differences in the growth for each region. However, there is not much *actionable* information here — what can you do to increase the overall revenue of your company?

Figure 7.2 shows revenue divided by clusters automatically found in the retailer's data. You still see the same growth in the company overall, but now you have a completely different breakdown of that information. The retailer has done an excellent job of catering to the Frequent Viewers customers, but revenue has decreased in the Family Buyers and Single Moviegoers segments. Breaking down your revenue this way gives you the actionable information you need to affect our business. Where are those Family Buyers going? How can you get them back? Do you worry about the Single Moviegoers, or do you sacrifice that business to focus on segments that contribute more to the bottom line? Clustering finds the hidden dimension that is unique to your data and your data alone — that provides information in a way that is impossible to achieve with the predefined organizational methods typically employed to examine your data.

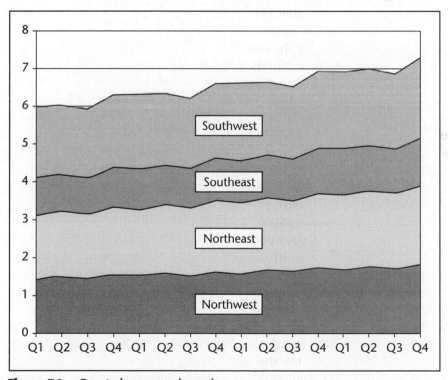

Figure 7.1   Quarterly revenue by region

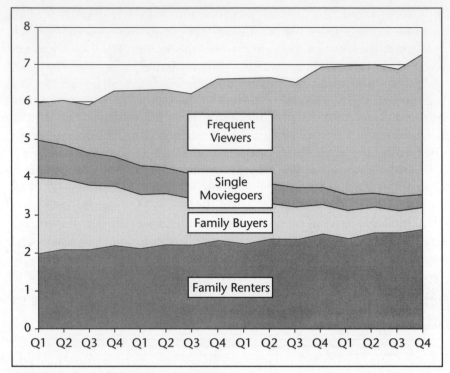

Figure 7.2 Quarterly revenue by cluster

Introducing the Principles of Clustering

Clustering relies on guessing and lying. You guess about the organization of data and create a set of clusters, arbitrarily deciding the set of attributes and values that belong in each cluster. Then you lie to yourself and assert that your guess is correct. Now that you've created this model of the world, you can take each case from your training data and assign it to clusters as fits that model. You can adjust your model of the world by looking at how well it fit the data of the world; you move the clusters. Again, you lie and say that you believe this new model correctly describes the world, and again you take the world's data and throw it at the model. This time, not all of the same cases fall into the same clusters. You repeat this process of updating your guess and assuming it's true until it either becomes true — cases no longer switch clusters — or you don't believe that you are going to get a better solution.

Figure 7.3 demonstrates this procedure in one dimension. The top chart shows the point distribution along the x-axis along with an initial guess. In this case, we chose clusters evenly spaced across the range of data with similar distributions. We consider the cluster borders to be the midpoints between the cluster centers. Based on this model, you can assign each data point to a cluster, and subsequently set the cluster centers to the mean of the data in each cluster. The second chart shows the new cluster centers and borders after performing this operation. Repeat this operation until the data stops moving between clusters, when the model has *converged*, or until you decide that the model will simply not improve with further iterations.

In practice, clusters are initialized randomly along all of the dimensions of the data. The clustering methodology is very sensitive to the starting points and can converge at local solutions that may not be an optimal global solution. For this reason, you initialize several candidate models and train them simultaneously. When the models have converged or when you have otherwise finished, you pick the best model from the candidates.

Hard versus Soft Clustering

One of the most important differentiators in a clustering algorithm is how the algorithm decides how to assign cases to clusters. The Microsoft Clustering algorithm allows two distinct methods of cluster assignment: *K-means* and *expectation maximization* (EM).

The K-means algorithm assigns cluster membership by means of distance. As shown in Figure 7.3, an object belongs to the cluster whose center is closest to it, measured using simple Euclidean distance. After all, the objects have been assigned to clusters, the center of the cluster is moved to the mean of all assigned objects, thus the name *K-means* — *K* being the typical denomination for the number of clusters to look for. This technique is considered *hard clustering* because each object is assigned one and exactly one cluster. The clusters are disjoint and do not overlap.

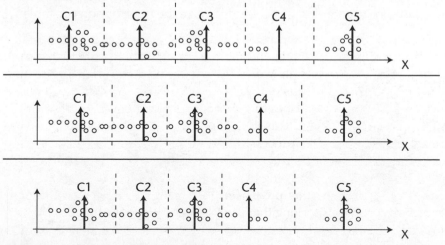

Figure 7.3 Basic clustering procedure

The EM algorithm uses a probabilistic measure, rather than a strict distance measure, to determine which objects belong to which clusters. Instead of choosing a point for each dimension and computing a distance, the EM algorithm considers a bell curve for each dimension, with a mean and standard deviation. As a point falls within the bell curve, it is assigned to a cluster with a certain probability. Because the curves for various clusters can and do overlap, any point can belong to multiple clusters, with an assigned probability for each. This technique is considered *soft clustering* because it allows for clusters to overlap with indistinct edges. This method permits the clustering algorithm to find nondisjoint clusters, such as dense regions, as illustrated in Figure 7.4.

The dot size in Figure 7.4 refers to the probability that each dot is in its respective cluster. Note that the dot sizes are uniform in the K-means diagram, whereas they are reduced in size near the cluster borders in the EM diagram. These diagrams were created with the two-dimensional cluster test.xls spreadsheet included at wiley.com/tang/Chapter7.

Discrete Clustering

So far, we've described how clustering works in terms of numerical values. These values are easy to compare and relate, computing distances and whatnot, but what happens when the objects you're trying to cluster do not have attributes that can be easily compared? A marble's size could potentially be represented by its diameter, but what value would you assign to a marble's material or color?

Luckily, the clustering techniques here can also handle discrete variables. Just as you assign random points along each dimension for continuous attributes, you assign random distributions for each discrete attribute. For instance, if you had an equal number of red, blue, green, and yellow marbles, your global distribution for each color would be 25%. As you initialize each cluster, you assume a random distribution that could look like the distributions in Table 7.1

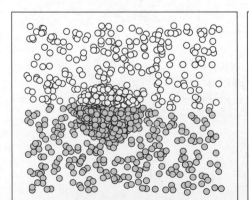 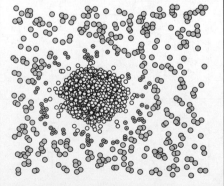

Figure 7.4   Clustering of dense region using (left) K-means and (right) EM

Table 7.1 Discrete Cluster Initializations

COLOR	CLUSTER 1	CLUSTER 2	CLUSTER 3	CLUSTER 4
Red	5%	70%	35%	0%
Blue	15%	5%	45%	30%
Green	50%	25%	0%	25%
Yellow	30%	0%	20%	45%

For EM clustering, you can pick a marble — say green — and can say that it is in cluster 2 with 25% likelihood. As you determine all the probabilities across all the discrete attributes of a case, you can compute the probability that it exists in each cluster and assign its values accordingly to each cluster of which it could be a member.

K-means clustering, being distance-based, does not fit as naturally in this model of probabilistic measures and traditionally isn't used for clustering discrete attributes. K-means can still be applied if you can infer some sort of distance from the cluster. The Microsoft Clustering implementation measures the distance from a value to a cluster as one minus the probability of that value in the cluster. For example, a green marble in cluster 2 would be $(1 - .25) = .75$ "color" units away from cluster 2. This distance factors into the distance calculation as would any continuous value.

Discrete clustering is used not only for multivalued attributes such as the color of an object but also to cluster attributes that appear in nested tables. In our movie store, we could cluster our customers not only by their demographics and movie watching behavior but also by the actual movies they watched. For such attributes, the clustering algorithm treats each movie as having two possible values — existing and missing — and considers those values in a manner similar to other discrete attributes.

Scalable Clustering

One of the problems in clustering data is that to determine the appropriate segmentation requires multiple iterations over the training dataset. In small datasets this is not a problem, because iterating over data in memory is very fast. After the data grows to the point where it can no longer fit into memory, the performance of clustering degrades to the point where it is no longer feasible to continue computing. In this case, you have a scalable framework for clustering that allows you to efficiently cluster datasets regardless of the size of the data.

The principle of the scalable framework is that particular data points that are unlikely to change clusters can be compressed out of the data you are iterating over, providing room to load more data. This way the entire data stream is loaded once, one chunk at a time. Additionally, it is possible for the model to converge at each chunk of data, completing the clustering operation without even seeing all of the data.

The basic outline of the scalable framework implemented in Microsoft Clustering is:

1. Initialize a set of candidate models to random initialization points.

2. Collect a sample of the source data to fill the memory buffer.

3. For each model perform the following scalable steps:

   a. Perform a clustering iteration as described in "Introducing the Principles of Clustering."

   b. Add information gathered from previous scalable steps.

   c. Reinitialize any clusters that disappear or merge.

Repeat until convergence occurs or you have completed sufficient iterations.

4. If models have converged since the last scalable step or you have run out of data, you are finished — choose the best model from the candidates.

5. Select and remove data from buffer, adding sufficient statistics to each model.

6. Repeat from step 2.

Clustering Prediction

Clustering algorithms can also be used to predict values as well as provide natural groupings. While this seems like a natural and obvious application, traditionally, clustering hasn't been used for such purposes. The Microsoft Clustering algorithm employs two tricks to accomplish this. First, it considers missing values to be uninformative. For example, if I have a new marble and I don't know the color, I won't use the fact that the color value is missing to determine which cluster the marble belongs to. Rather, the algorithm will only use the information for which it knows the values.

Once the cluster membership has been determined, the second trick is to simply read off the values from the cluster. For example, if this hypothetical marble had been found to be in cluster 2 from Table 7.1, I would say that it is

70% likely to be a red marble. Of course, with soft (EM) clustering, you would generally find that this marble didn't belong to a single cluster but rather to a set of clusters with a particular probability for each. In this case, you create a composite result based on the contribution of each member cluster and present that as the result.

Algorithm Parameters

You can tune the behavior of the clustering algorithm by tweaking the various parameters of the algorithm. The defaults handle most situations, but under certain circumstances you may find that you get better results by manipulating one or more of these knobs.

- The `Clustering_Method` indicates which algorithm is used to determine cluster membership. The vanilla versions of each algorithm eschew the scalable framework described previously and operate only on one sample of the data. The possible values for this parameter are:

  1 — Scalable EM (default)

  2 — Vanilla (non-scalable) EM

  3 — Scalable K-means

  4 — Vanilla (non-scalable) K-means

- `Cluster_Count` is the "K" in K-means — it would also be the "K." in EM, if EM had a K. `Cluster_Count` indicates to the algorithm how many clusters to find. Set this parameter to a number that makes sense for your business problem. If you can comprehend eight clusters, set it to eight and see what you find. In practice, the more attributes you have, the more clusters you need to describe your data correctly. If you have too many attributes, you may want to organize your data ahead of time so that the number is reduced. Using the movie retailer as an example, instead of clustering by the individual movies that your customers watched, you could cluster by the genres of those movies. This technique substantially reduces the attribute cardinality and creates much more meaningful models.

  Setting `Cluster_Count` to 0 will cause the algorithm to perform a heuristic to guess the correct number of clusters in the data.

  The default value is 10.

- Minimum_Support controls when a cluster is considered "empty" and it is discarded and reinitialized. Usually, you will not need to modify this parameter, except in certain cases when business rules apply. For example, for privacy reasons you may not want to create clusters smaller than 10 people. Note that this number is used internally only, and due to the nature of soft clustering you may have clusters reporting membership lower than this amount after training. Setting this number too high can create bad results.

  The default value is 1.

- Modelling_Cardinality controls how many candidate models are generated during clustering. Reducing this value will increase performance, at the potential cost of reducing accuracy.

  The default value is 10.

- Stopping_Tolerance is used by the algorithm to determine when a model has converged. It represents the maximum number of cases that can change membership before you consider a model to have converged. This value is checked at each iteration of the internal clustering loop, plus at the outer scalable step as well. Increasing this number will cause the algorithm to converge more quickly, resulting in fuzzier clusters, while decreasing it will result in tighter clusters. (See Figure 7.5.) If you have a small data set or very distinct clusters, you can set this value to 1.

  The default value is 10.

- Sample_Size indicates the number of cases used in each step of the scalable framework. When using the vanilla versions of the algorithm, Sample_Size indicates the total number of cases seen. Reducing this value can cause the algorithm to converge early without seeing all of the data, especially when coupled with a large Stopping_Tolerance. This can be useful for creating a quick clustering on a large dataset.

  Setting this value to 0 will cause the algorithm to use all available memory on the server. Note that due to the nature of the scalable framework, this can cause the algorithm to produce slightly different results with different memory configurations.

  The default value is 50,000.

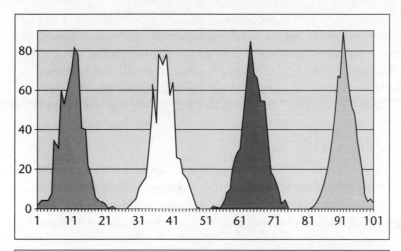
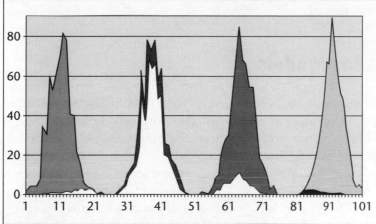

Figure 7.5   One-dimensional EM clustering (top) stopping tolerance = 1 (bottom) stopping tolerance = 10.

■ Cluster_Seed is the random number seed used to initialize the clusters. This parameter is provided to allow you to test the sensitivity of your data to the initialization point. If your models stay relatively stable when changing this value, you can be sure that the segmentation of your data is correct.

The default value is 0.

- `Maximum_Input_Attributes` controls how many of the attributes considered for clustering are allowed before automatic feature selection is invoked. If there are more than this number of attributes in your data set, feature selection will choose the most popular attributes from the set. The unselected attributes are ignored during clustering. This limit exists because the number of attributes has a significant impact on performance.

  The default value is 255.

- `Maximum_States` controls how many states one particular attribute can have. If an attribute contains more than this number of states, the most popular states are chosen and the others are considered an "other" state. This limit exists due to the impact of high cardinality attributes on performance and memory.

  The default value is 100.

Using Clustering Models

Clustering models are great models to throw your data at just to see what comes out the other side. However, as with all data mining techniques, you get the best answers when you ask your questions the right way. Do you want to group your salespeople by total sales, or by the ratio of sales in each category? Is it important that your clustering model understand income as a continuous value, or do you need to break it down into categories first? The clustering algorithm is very flexible in that it supports all data and content types specified in OLE DB for Data Mining, but you still need to take care to provide the data to the algorithm in the form that is most likely to solve your problem.

For example, if a large company issues an annual employee satisfaction survey to determine an Organizational Health Index (OHI). The results are a percentage for each category, for example 65% for the set of compensation questions. You could simply cluster over all of these results for all of your employees, but could you understand the results? Is 65% in compensation a good response, a bad response, or neutral? In this case, you could transform your data into buckets of High, Medium, and Low by considering High to be higher than half of a standard deviation above the average response and Low to be lower than the same amount below the same amount. Now, when you examine resultant clusters, the results will be easier to read; it's easy to pick out the cluster of people who love their jobs but want to get paid more. You can increase the buckets to the granularity you wish to explore. This kind of transformation can be done in the Data Source view, or using Data Transformation Services as described in Chapter 12.

The Clustering algorithm has some special behavior associated with the column usage flag on the mining model. When you set the column usage to `Input` or `Predict`, the algorithm acts as described; the difference, of course, being that the predictable columns are selectable from the model during predictions and the input columns are not. When you set the column usage to `Predict Only`, the column is treated specially. `Predict Only` columns in the clustering algorithm are not used during the clustering phase of the model training. When the model is completely trained, the algorithm takes another run over the training data and assigns the values of these attributes based on how the training cases fall into the clusters. When using the previous OHI example, to ensure that the company complies with federal guidelines regarding workforce diversity, it may be important to determine the distribution of gender and race among the clusters. When creating the clusters, you only want to consider the answers to the survey, but at the end of the day you need to know that there is the same ratio of men to women in that group of happy, underpaid employees as there is in the rest of the company.

Clustering as an Analytical Step

Clustering is also used as a step in a larger analytical project. By segmenting your data into groups of self-similarity, you can create better supplemental models to answer deeper questions. Surely, the decline in revenue among Family Buyers has occurred for a different reason than the decline among Single Moviegoers. By analyzing the data along the lines of these clusters, you are able to more tightly focus on the exact reasons for the revenue loss. Perhaps you want to create a tree model to predict whether a customer will give you repeat business within a month. Creating a model on all of your customers will provide valuable information, but it will be a model that is generalized to the entire data set. (See Figure 7.6.) By training the tree models on only the areas that clustering has demonstrated are where the revenue has declined, you can focus on where the problem lies.

DMX

Clustering supports all content and data types and predictions, so all of the DMX language that is not specific to other algorithms can be used to query cluster models. The following sections discuss the functionality particular to the clustering algorithm.

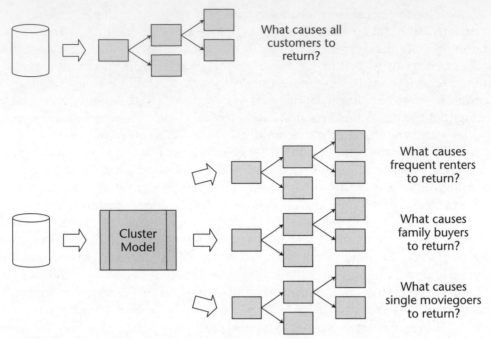

Figure 7.6 Clustering as a preprocessing step for decision trees

Cluster

The Cluster function returns the cluster that is most likely to contain a particular case. For example, to retrieve all cases from an input set that belong to the Family Buyers cluster, you would use the following syntax:

```
SELECT t.* FROM CustomerClusters
    NATURAL PREDICTION JOIN <Input Set> AS t
    WHERE Cluster()='Family Buyers'
```

The Cluster function can also be used as a column reference for functions that take such references as parameters. $Cluster can be used as a synonym for Cluster().

ClusterProbability

ClusterProbability returns the probability that a case belongs to a particular cluster. Calling ClusterProbability without specifying a parameter returns the probability of the primary cluster. The following query returns the cluster ID for each case and the probability that the case is in that cluster:

```
SELECT t.id, Cluster(), ClusterProbability()
     FROM CustomerClusters
     NATURAL PREDICTION JOIN <Input Set> AS t
```

This query returns the probability that each case is in the Family Buyers cluster:

```
SELECT t.id, ClusterProbability('Family Buyers')
     FROM CustomerClusters
     NATURAL PREDICTION JOIN <Input Set> AS t
```

PredictHistogram

PredictHistogram is not specific to the clustering algorithm, but when specified using the Cluster function as the column reference, it can be used to return a histogram of the likelihood of the input case existing in each of the model's clusters. This query returns a table with a nested table containing the top three likely clusters for each case, along with associated statistics:

```
SELECT t.id, TopCount(PredictHistogram(Cluster()),(Probability),3)
     FROM CustomerClusters
     NATURAL PREDICTION JOIN <Input Set> AS t
```

CaseLikelihood

CaseLikelihood returns a measure from 0 to 1 that indicates how likely an input case is to exist considering the model learned by the algorithm. This measure is very good for use in anomaly detection because it quickly and easily tells you if new data is similar to any data seen before. This function operates in two modes: normalized and nonnormalized.

In the nonnormalized mode, the value of the measure is the raw probability of the case, that is, the product of the probabilities of each of the attributes in the case. For instance, if the probability of Home Ownership = Yes is 40% and the probability of Occupation = Craftsmen is 10%, then the probability of the case is 40% × 10% = 4%.

Nonnormalized likelihoods can be useful, but due to the nature of the probabilities, as you increase the number of attributes in a case, the probability of the case becomes correspondingly smaller. Additionally, as a user, you cannot understand whether a 4% probability for a certain combination of attributes is a good thing or a bad thing. The normalized likelihood divides the probability of the case as provided by the model by the probability computed without the model, using raw statistics. This provides a lift number that is normalized between 0 and 1 using the formula $(lift)/(lift + 1)$. This is interpreted to mean that cases with likelihood values greater than 0.5 have positive lift and are more likely than random to occur, and that values less than 0.5 have negative lift and are less likely than random to occur.

For continuous attributes, the probability distribution is used for this computation.

The following query returns the normalized case likelihood for each case in the input set:

```
SELECT t.id, CaseLikelihood()
    FROM CustomerClusters
    NATURAL PREDICTION JOIN <Input Set> AS t
```

This query returns the nonnormalized case likelihood for each case in the input set:

```
SELECT t.id, CaseLikelihood(NONNORMALIZED)
    FROM CustomerClusters
    NATURAL PREDICTION JOIN <Input Set> AS t
```

Model Content

The content of a clustering model is easy to understand. The content contains:

- One row for the model, indicated by node type DM_NODE_TYPE_ MODEL (1).

- One row for each cluster, indicated by node type DM_NODE_TYPE_ CLUSTER (5).

Each row contains general information about the node plus the distributions of all attributes contained in the node that row represents. The model node contains the global distributions, and the cluster nodes contain the distributions particular to those individual clusters.

The first row of the model contains a score for the model in the MSOLAP_NODE_SCORE column of the model content. This score is the average case likelihood for each of the training cases. This score represents how well the model describes the training data.

This query returns the model score:

```
SELECT TOP 1 MSOLAP_NODE_SCORE FROM CustomerClusters.CONTENT
```

Each cluster row contains the cluster caption and an algorithm-generated textual description of the clusters. This query retrieves the caption and description for each cluster.

```
SELECT NODE_CAPTION, NODE_DESCRIPTION FROM CustomerClusters.CONTENT
    WHERE NODE_TYPE=5
```

The cluster captions can also be set through DMX. The default caption for clusters simply assigns a numeric value. This query changes the caption for cluster 2 of the model:

```
UPDATE CustomerClusters.CONTENT SET NODE_CAPTION='Family Buyers'
    WHERE NODE_UNIQUE_NAME='002'
```

Understanding Your Cluster Models

Clustering is very good at taking data with scores of attributes and distilling them down into a handful of groupings. Comprehending what the resultant groups mean can be quite a challenge. This is particularly difficult because each cluster cannot be considered in isolation; rather a cluster can only be understood in relation to all other clusters.

The naming convention used by the clustering algorithm is simply the word Cluster followed by a cluster index. When presenting your model to others, or even referring to it for your own personal use, you will need to choose appropriate labels for each cluster. With models built on dozens or even hundreds of attributes, a short label seems like a tall promise. The most effective labels come from your personal understanding of the business problem you are trying to solve combined with the patterns uncovered by the clustering engine.

SQL Server Analysis Server provides a viewer that contains four tabbed cluster views that help you to build this understanding. Alone, each view does not provide enough insight to accomplish this task. When used together, you can apply the following strategy, which is effective in understanding and labeling your clusters. The viewer is accessed through either the BI Development Studio or SQL Management Studio by right-clicking on the model and selecting Browse.

1. Get a high-level overview of your clusters.
2. Pick a cluster, and determine how it is different than the general population.
3. Determine how that cluster is different from nearby clusters.
4. Verify that your assertions about the cluster are true.
5. Label the cluster.
6. Repeat for all remaining clusters.

The following sections will review these steps in detail.

Get a High-Level Overview

The first views provide a high-level overview of clusters: the Cluster Profiles view and the Cluster Diagram view. At first glance, Cluster Profiles provide too much information, and Cluster Diagram provides too little, but together they provide the topology of your cluster model.

The Cluster Profiles view, accessed through the second tab of the Cluster Viewer, contains a column for each cluster in your model and a row for each attribute. This set up makes it easy to see interesting differences across the cluster space. Using this view, you can choose an attribute of interest and visibly scan horizontally to see its distribution across all clusters. When an item catches your interest, you can look at neighboring cells or other cells of the same cluster to learn more about what that cluster means.

Figure 7.7 shows a portion of the Cluster Profiles view on the Customer Clustering model. Cluster 21 clearly contains people who are older than the average customer, who like the Arts & Entertainment and American Movie Classics channels. In contrast, Cluster 25 contains younger customers, who like Cinemax. Cluster 10 looks similar to Cluster 21, but is a tad younger and is not quite as much into the classics.

TIP You can drag clusters by their headers for easy, side-by-side comparison.

The Cluster Profiles view displays everything in your model in a manner that is easy to see. Binary and continuous attributes are particularly easy to discern, as are discrete attributes with a small number of states. Exploring your clusters through the cluster profiles is a good way to find a starting point for further exploration.

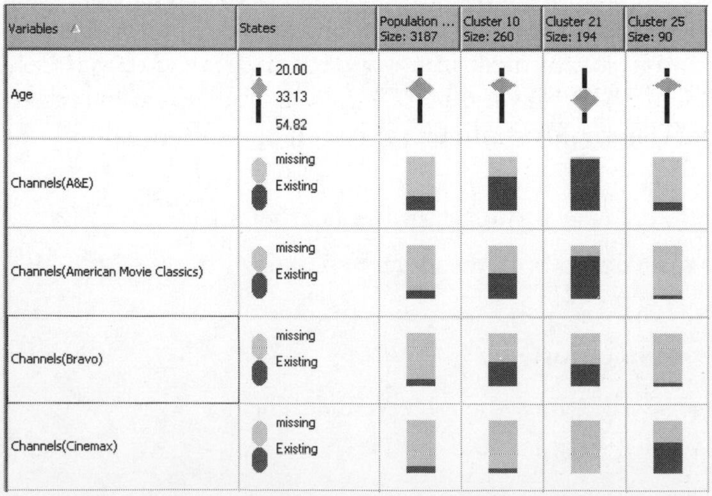

Figure 7.7 Continuous and binary attributes in the Cluster Profile viewer

After exploring the minute details of the model, you can move to the other extreme. The Cluster Diagram view, the first and default tab of the Cluster viewer, represents each cluster as a single node. These nodes are scattered across a field and allowed to group based on similarities. The resultant view is a diagram indicating which clusters are similar or dissimilar and the relative strength of these similarities.

Using this view, it is easy to expand on the exploration you began in the Cluster Profile viewer. Using the shading feature of the view, it is easy to ask some more targeted questions about your model. You can ask, "In which clusters will I find customers who like the Arts & Entertainment channel?" or "Where are my customers between 20 and 25 years of age?" Furthermore, you can determine which clusters are very similar by moving the link slider down to remove weak links, leaving only the strongest links (see Figure 7.8).

Continue to explore the Cluster Profiles and Diagram views until you feel comfortable with the overall layout of your model.

Pick a Cluster and Determine How It Is Different

Choose a cluster for further analysis. At this point, it really isn't important which cluster you choose. One method for picking a cluster is to determine which clusters have the strongest link and choose one of them, or to pick a cluster that seems far removed from the rest. Or you may simply have found an interesting cluster during your initial exploration.

The first thing to do is to look at the third tab of the Cluster viewer, the Cluster Characteristics view. This view describes the characteristics of the cluster cases by displaying attributes in decreasing probability. Figure 7.9 shows the top characteristics for cluster 21. The members of this cluster are married homeowners with more than one car. They own DVD and VHS players and watch a variety of cable movie channels. It may seem like this is enough information to choose an adequate label for the cluster. However, how do you know that this information is the most important? It may be true that customers in this group own DVD players, but all of your customers may own DVD players, which makes that fact uninteresting.

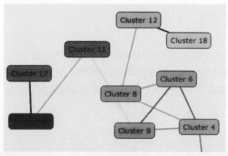

Figure 7.8 Cluster diagram showing strong (dark) links between clusters

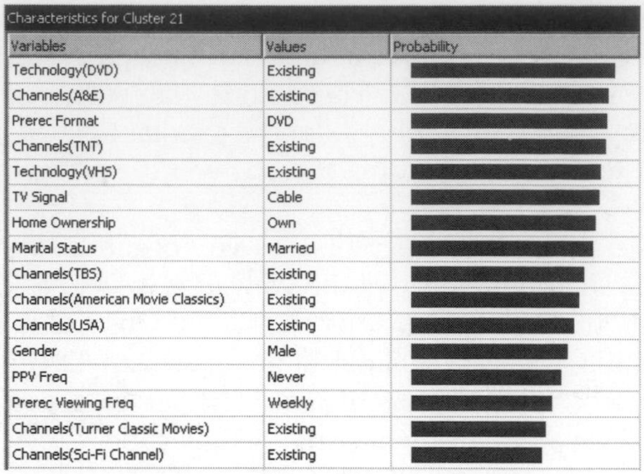

Variables	Values	Probability
Technology(DVD)	Existing	
Channels(A&E)	Existing	
Prerec Format	DVD	
Channels(TNT)	Existing	
Technology(VHS)	Existing	
TV Signal	Cable	
Home Ownership	Own	
Marital Status	Married	
Channels(TBS)	Existing	
Channels(American Movie Classics)	Existing	
Channels(USA)	Existing	
Gender	Male	
PPV Freq	Never	
Prerec Viewing Freq	Weekly	
Channels(Turner Classic Movies)	Existing	
Channels(Sci-Fi Channel)	Existing	

Characteristics for Cluster 21

Figure 7.9   Cluster characteristics

You determine what is important about the cluster by comparing it to everything outside the cluster. Figure 7.10 compares cluster 21 and its complement. Here you see that DVD or VHS ownership aren't quite so important for describing the cluster, but the preference for classic movie channels are. You also can infer that members of this cluster have children and are either married or have been in the past. Your picture of who the customers of cluster 21 are is becoming clear.

Determine How a Cluster Is Different from Nearby Clusters

You may now have enough information to accurately label this cluster. However, this cluster may be very similar to other clusters and any labeling you do at this point may also apply to those. Therefore, you must use due diligence and compare your chosen cluster to its nearest neighbors. To accomplish this, go to the Cluster Diagram view and determine which clusters are close to the cluster of interest. If no links to the cluster are very strong, it is probably safe to stop. For any clusters that are close, you need to switch back to the Cluster Characteristics view to compare those clusters one by one. Through this process you will refine your view of your chosen cluster. For example, comparing cluster 11 to cluster 17 indicates that the most important differences involve marital status and housing.

NOTE The bars of the Cluster Discrimination view indicate which cluster the attribute *favors*. It does not imply either that the opposing cluster does not contain the attribute or that the attribute is particularly common in a cluster.

| Discrimination scores for Cluster 21 and Complement of Cluster 21 | | | |
Variables	Values	Favors Cluster 21	Favors Complement of Clus...
Channels(American Movie Classics)	Existing	████████	
Channels(A&E)	Existing	████████	
Channels(Turner Classic Movies)	Existing	███████	
Channels(TNT)	Existing	█████	
Channels(TBS)	Existing	█████	
Channels(USA)	Existing	████	
Channels(Sci-Fi Channel)	Existing	███	
Marital Status	Never Married		███
Channels(Bravo)	Existing	██	
Education Level	Associate's Degree	██	
Channels(Lifetime Movie Network)	Existing	██	
Marital Status	Married	██	

Figure 7.10   Cluster discrimination versus complement

Verify That Your Assertions Are True

At this point, you probably have a pretty good idea about the members of your chosen cluster. Switching back to the Cluster Characteristics view allows you to ensure that none of the other viewers mislead you about the cluster. This can happen particularly when refining your cluster understanding by comparing it to neighboring clusters. The difference between the clusters that appeared important may be caused by an attribute that is uncommon in both, but simply less uncommon in one.

Label the Cluster

Labeling the cluster is a simple technique of switching to the cluster diagram, right-clicking the cluster node, and selecting Rename Cluster. The model label has an important impact on the understanding and future use of your model. What are the important attributes to express? This depends on your business knowledge of the data you are clustering and on which attributes are interesting to the intended audience of the model. Cluster 21 could be Classic Movie Watchers or Married, No Premium Channels, or any number of other monikers, depending on how you want to display your model and how you want others to perceive it.

The project containing the model used in this example is located on the Web site www.wiley.com/go/tang/Chapter7.

Summary

Clustering is a powerful tool that groups your data by similarity. It can be used for understanding your data and is an essential part of any data analysis. The clustering operation determines the variables that ties and separates your data allowing for insights impossible or impractical to achieve with other methods. Once clustered, the results can be used for marketing campaigns, anomaly detection, trending, or further analysis.

In this chapter, you learned how the clustering algorithm works, how to apply it, and how to tune it using algorithm parameters. Additionally, you learned how to extract information about the clusters through accessing the clustering content or determining cluster membership of new data through DMX queries. Finally, you learned a strategy for leveraging the four views provided in the Cluster viewer to create a holistic business understanding of the clusters generated by the model.

Microsoft Sequence Clustering

You are a marketing manager of a popular online retailer site. You sell various categories of products, including books, magazines, electronics, cookware, office products, and so on. Every day, thousands of Web customers come to your site, navigating among different domains of your portal. In a physical shop, you can visually identify those departments and products that attract most customers and the customer interactions on various products. In a virtual store, you don't see your customers. However, you still want to learn more about your customers to provide them with better services. You want to find out how your customers are using your site and the list of products in which they have shown interest. You also want to know the natural groups among these customers, based on their navigation patterns. For example, one group of customers shops all sorts of products from your Web site, while others visit only certain categories of books and magazines. This information not only gives you a clear picture of your customer's behaviors in your virtual shop but also allows you to provide personalized shopping guidance to each customer, based on his or her profile. In this chapter, you will learn how to analyze navigation sequences and organize sequences into natural groups based on their similarities, using the Microsoft Sequence Clustering algorithm.

In this chapter, you will learn about:

- The principles of the Microsoft Sequence Clustering Algorithm
- Using the Microsoft Sequence Clustering Algorithm
- Interpreting the model's content

Introducing the Microsoft Sequence Clustering Algorithm

As the name suggests, the Microsoft Sequence Clustering algorithm is a hybrid of sequence and clustering techniques. It is designed to analyze a population of cases that contains sequence data and group those cases into more or less homogeneous segments based on the similarity of those sequences.

A *sequence* is a series of discrete events (states). Usually the number of discrete states in a sequence is finite. Sequence data is ubiquitous in the real world. Lots of information is encoded in sequence form. For example, a DNA sequence is a series of four discrete states: A (adenosine), G (guanine), C (cytosine), and T (thymidine). The list of courses a student takes at a university forms a sequence. The series of URL clicks of a Web user is a sequence. In a shopping basket example, if we don't care about the order of the product purchases, the business problem of market basket analysis is an association task. If we do care about the order of the product purchases, the purchase data forms a sequence, and this problem is a sequence task.

Figure 8.1 displays a weather forecast sequence.

Microsoft Sequence Clustering Algorithm Principles

Before learning about the inner workings of the algorithm, you need to know a new concept: the Markov chain.

As stated previously, sequence clustering works by merging two technologies, clustering and sequence analysis. While the clustering is similar to that in Chapter 6, the sequence analysis is something new — a Markov Chain model.

What Is a Markov Chain?

Andrei Markov was a famous Russia mathematician born in 1856. He was a professor at Saint Petersburg University and is remembered in particular for his study of Markov chains, which are sequences of random variables in which the future variable is determined by the present variable but is independent of the way in which the present state arose from its predecessors.

Showers   Partly Cloudy   Partly Cloudy   Light Rain   Mostly Sunny

Figure 8.1   A weather sequence

Figure 8.2 illustrates an example of a Markov chain of the DNA sequence. A Markov chain contains a set of states. Most states emit events; other states like Begin and End are silent.

A Markov chain also contains a matrix of transition probabilities. The transitions emanating from a given state define a distribution over the possible next states. $P\,(x_i = G \mid x_{i-1} = A) = 0.15$ means given the current state A, the probability of next state being G is 0.15.

The Microsoft Sequence Clustering algorithm models sequence events based on the Markov Chain model.

Order of a Markov Chain

One of the important properties of a Markov chain is the order. In a Markov chain, the order n specifies the probability of a state depending on the previous n states. The most common Markov chain is 1st order, which means the probability of each state xi depends only on the state of $xi.1$. We can build high-order Markov chains using more "memory" to remember the previous n states.

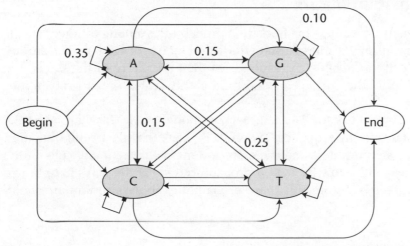

Transition probabilities:
$P(x_i = G \mid x_{i-1} = A) = 0.15$
$P(x_i = C \mid x_{i-1} = A) = 0.15$
$P(x_i = T \mid x_{i-1} = A) = 0.25$
$P(x_i = A \mid x_{i-1} = A) = 0.35$
$P(x_i = End \mid x_{i-1} = A) = 0.10$

Figure 8.2   Markov Chain model

An *nth*-order Markov chain over *k* states is equivalent to a first order Markov chain over *kn* states. For example, a 2nd- order Markov model for DNA can be treated as a 1st-order Markov model over the following states: AA, AC, AG, AT, CA, CC, CG,CT, GA, GC, GG, GT, TA, TC, TG, and TT. The total number of states is 4^2. The higher the order of a Markov chain, the more memory and time required for the processing.

Based on the Markov chain, for any given length *L* sequence x {x_1, x_2, x_3,...,xL}, we can calculate the probability of a sequence as follows:

```
P(x) = P(xL . xL-1, . . . , x1)
     = P(xL| xL-1, . . . , x1) P (xL-1|xL-2, . . . , x1) . . . P(x1)
```

In the case of a 1st-order Markov chain, the probability of each *xi* depends only on xi_{-1}, the preceding formula is equivalent to the following:

```
P(x) = P(xL . xL-1, . . . , x1)
     = P(xL|xL-1) P(xL-1|xL-2) . . . P(x2|x1) P(x1)
```

State Transition Matrix

A Markov chain remembers the transition probabilities among different states. Figure 8.3 graphically displays a state transition matrix of a 1st- order Markov chain. Each cell in the table corresponds to the probability of the transition. The probability in the grid is encoded by the gray scale; higher probabilities are brighter.

The transition matrix for 1-order Markov model is *M**M*, where *M* is the number of states in the sequence. When *M* is large, the size of the transition matrix can be significant. When there are too many states, many cells in the matrix are dark with a low transition probability. One of the ways to optimize the matrix storage is to store only those probabilities above a certain threshold.

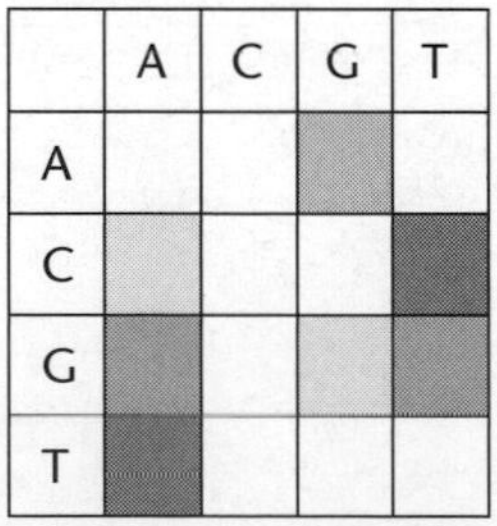

Figure 8.3 State transition matrix

UNDERSTANDING THE HIDDEN MARKOV MODEL

Some of you may have heard the term Hidden Markov model (HMM). The difference between an HMM and a normal Markov Chain model is that the state sequence of the model is hidden. We only know the observed sequence of outputs. There are five attributes of a HMM: the set of states, the output alphabet $\{O_1, O_2, \ldots OT\}$, the probabilities of initial states at t_0, the state transition probabilities, and the output probabilities of each given state.

For example, we have n biased coins (the coins are the states of the HMM), the output alphabet is $\{H, T\}$. We know the transition probabilities among these coins and the output probabilities of H and T for each coin. We also know the initial probabilities of the coins to flip. But we don't know exactly which coin is used to produce the output at each step, because the state sequence is hidden from us. Based on the sequence of observed outputs, we can figure out the following questions:

- What is the probability of observed outputs $O_1, O_2, \ldots OT$ given the model, for example $P(O_1, O_2, \ldots OT|model)$?

- At each step, what state is most likely given the model and outputs? That is, find the sequence $q_1, q_2, \ldots qT$ such that $P(q_1, q_2, \ldots qT \mid O_1, O_2, \ldots OT, model)$ is maximized.

- Given an HMM structure and observed data, find the model parameters that maximize $P(O_1, O_2, \ldots OT|model)$.

HMM is used in many applications from voice recognition to DNA analysis. The Microsoft Sequence Cluster algorithm is based on an observable Markov chain, not on HMM.

Clustering with a Markov Chain

The Microsoft Sequence Clustering algorithm learns a mixture of Markov chains, where each mixture component corresponds to a particular cluster. To understand what a mixture model is, it is useful to understand how a mixture model generates data. A single case is generated from a mixture model as follows. First, a particular component (cluster) is randomly selected using a probability distribution over the clusters. Second, depending on which cluster is selected, a sequence is generated from the Markov chain corresponding to that cluster (each cluster or component corresponds to a different Markov chain).

Given data, the Microsoft Sequence Clustering algorithm learns the parameters of the mixture model — the mixture weights (the probability distribution over the clusters) and the parameters of each Markov chain. Note that the algorithm never sees the cluster identities of any case.

As we explained in the Chapter 6, expectation and maximization (EM) is an iterative algorithm that finds parameters corresponding to a local optima for a model — parameters that locally maximize the likelihood of the data. The overall process of the clustering algorithm is:

1. Initialize the model parameters somehow (e.g., at random)
2. Given a current model parameters, each case is assigned to each of the K clusters with some probability. This is the E step.
3. Revaluate the model parameters based on the weighed assignment of each case. This is the M step.
4. Check whether the model has converged. If not, go to step 2 for a new iteration.

We explained the method to calculate the probability and likelihood of scalar attribute in each cluster in Chapter 6. For the sequence attribute, the model parameters have the sequence state transition matrix for each cluster. For a given sequence x, we know its probability in a given cluster C is calculated using the following formula:

$$P(x|C) = P(xL|xL_{-1}) P(xL_{-1}|xL_{-2}) \ldots P(x_2|x_1) P(x_1)$$

where $P(xj|xi)$ is the transition probability of state i to j in cluster C.

We can then use Bayes rule to calculate the cluster membership probabilities of x in cluster C:

$$P = \left(x_i = G | x_{i-1} = A\right) = 0.15$$

Where $P(C)$ is the marginal probability of cluster C, for example the weight of cluster C over the whole population.

The Microsoft Sequence Clustering lgorithm supports both sequence and nonsequence attributes. Nonsequence attributes can be scalar attributes or nested attributes, as explained in the previous chapter. Sequence data is stored in a nested table. The sequence nested table must contain a column modeled as the *key sequence*. This column is the key of the sequence. The sequence key can be of any data type that can be sorted, such as date, integer, and string. In some cases, your data may have multiple sequence attributes. For example, you may want to group your customers by a sequence of Web pages that he or she visited, and a sequence of products that he or she bought. However, multiple sequences in a single model are not supported in SQL Server 2005.

It is possible to build a sequence model without any sequence data. In this case, the model becomes a simple clustering model. Nonsequence and sequence attributes are assumed to be mutually independent given cluster identity.

What's the cost of processing a clustering a Markov chain? Supposing that the number of clusters in the model is K, the number of cases is N, the average length of each sequence is L, and the number of states in the sequence is M, the cost of each iteration is $O(KNL + LM^2)$. The first part $O(KNL)$ is the cost to assign each sequence to a cluster with a membership probability, and the second part $O(LM^2)$ is the cost to calculate the transition matrix after each iteration. In many applications such as a DNA sequence, M is relatively small. This complexity can be reduced to $O(KNL)$, which means the total runtime of the algorithm scales linearly in both N and K.

Cluster Decomposition

The number of natural groups in a sequence clustering model is different from that in a normal clustering model. In normal clustering, people tend to build the clustering model with $k < 10$. When the number of clusters is too large, it is difficult to interpret the final results. If a really large number of distinct groups exist, people usually build clustering models in multiple steps, and in each step, they break the population into a handful groups.

In the sequence clustering model, when the number of states in the sequence is large, there could be many distinct clusters. For example, in a Web navigation scenario, there may be over 60 URL categories in a portal site. The first group of Web customers mainly navigates among news, the second group of customers focuses on music and movies, and the third group of customers is interested in front pages and weather. While clustering these customers, we usually get a larger number of clusters, compared to the nonsequence cluster model. It is relatively easy to interpret these models based on their sequences of states.

One step during the sequence clustering algorithm processing is *cluster decomposition*. If a user specifies a small number of clusters, and there are different types of sequences in a cluster, the algorithm will decompose the cluster into multiple clusters. For example, if a cluster contains two sets of sequences — Movie ⇨ Music ⇨ Download and New ⇨ News ⇨ Weather — the algorithm breaks it into two clusters at the final stage of the model processing.

Algorithm Parameters

There are a few parameters for the Microsoft Sequence Clustering algorithm. These parameters are used to control the cluster count, sequence states, and so on. By adjusting these parameter settings, we can fine-tune the model's accuracy. The following is the list of the algorithm parameters:

- Cluster_Count: The definition of Cluster_Count in the Microsoft Sequence Clustering algorithm is same as in the Microsoft Clustering algorithm. It defines the number of clusters a model contains. Setting this value to 0 will cause the algorithm to automatically choose the best number of clusters for predictive purpose. The default value for Cluster_Count is 0.

- Minimum_Support: The definition of Minimum_Support in the Microsoft Sequence Clustering algorithm is the same as in the Microsoft Clustering algorithm. It is an integer. It specifies the minimum number of cases in each cluster to avoid having clusters with too few cases. The default value is 10.

- Maximum_States: The definition of Maximum_States is the same as in the Microsoft Clustering algorithm. This parameter specifies the maximum number of states of a clustering algorithm attribute. This parameter is integer type. The default value is 100; attributes with more than 100 states invoke feature selection.

- Maximum_Sequence_States: Maximum_Sequence_States defines the maximum number of states in the sequence attribute. It is integer type, with default value 64. Users can overwrite this value. If the sequence data has more states than Maximum_Sequence_States, feature selection is invoked, and the selection is based on the popularity of the states in the marginal model.

TIP Suppose that there is a total of *m* distinct sequence states. Each cluster content contains an *M*M* matrix. The processing time is proportional to M^2. If *M* is large, it may take long time to process the model. Our recommendation is to make *M* no more than 100. If there are too many states, for example, hundreds of pages on your Web site, you can reduce *M* by grouping Web pages into categories.

Using the Sequence Clustering Algorithm

The Sequence Clustering algorithm can be applied in many areas such as click stream analysis, customer purchase analysis, bioinformatics, and so on. In this section, you learn about creating DMX queries for the Sequence Clustering algorithm and how to interpret the model using the Sequence Clustering viewer.

DMX Queries

Figure 8.4 displays two tables: Customer and ClickPath. The Customer table contains customer profiles about Web usage on a portal site. ClickPath is a transaction table. It contains three columns: CustomerGuid, URLCategory, and SequenceID. CustomerGuid is the foreign key to the Customer table. SequenceID is a numeric column that stores the Web click sequence number 1, 2, 3 . . . *n*. URLCategory is the state of the sequence. The sequence is the series of Web clicks on the URLCategory in this model, such as News ⇨ News ⇨ Sports ⇨ News ⇨ Weather. A sequence may have various lengths because some customers stay longer and visit various URL categories.

The following statement creates a mining model using the Microsoft Sequence Clustering algorithm. Sequence data must be stored in a nested table. The Microsoft Sequence Clustering algorithm doesn't support multiple sequence tables in a model; neither supports more than one nonkey attribute in the sequence table.

```
Create mining model WebSequence (
    CustoemrGuiId text key,
    GeoLocation   text discrete,
    ClickPath table Predict (
            SequenceID long key Sequence,
         URLCategory text,
    )
)

Using Microsoft_SequenceClustering_Algorithm
```

The nested table — ClickPath — or the nonkey attribute in the nested table — URLCategory — may be specified as predictable. In this case, when the model is processed, you see customer segments based on their Web clicks and geolocations. You can also use the model to predict the next *n* sequence states for a given customer.

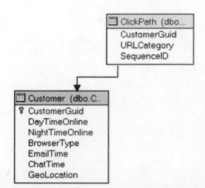

Figure 8.4 Customer and ClickPath tables

The following `Insert into` statement trains the sequence model:

```
Insert into WebSequence
( CustomerGuid, GeoLocation,
  ClickPath (SequenceID, URLCategorty)
)
OPENROWSET('MSDataShape',
      'data provider=Microsoft.Jet.OLEDB.4.0; data
source=C:\data\webclick.mdb',
 'SHAPE {
       Select CustomerGuid, GeoLocation from Customer
       }
       Append (
      {Select CustomerGuid, SequenceID, URLCategory from ClickPath}
       Relate CustomerGuid To CustomerGuid
    ) As ClickPath'
)
```

Similarly to the Microsoft Clustering algorithm, the Microsoft Sequence Clustering algorithm supports prediction. For cluster membership prediction, we can use the `Cluster()` function, which returns the cluster ID for each case.

The following query returns the cluster ID for each input case:

```
SELECT   t.CustomerGuid,  Cluster()
From WebSequence PREDICTION JOIN
SHAPE {
  OPENROWSET('SQLOLEDB.1',
    'Integrated Security=SSPI; Initial Catalog=Sequence;Data
Source=localhost ',
    'SELECT  CustomerGuid, GeoLocation
   FROM Customer ORDER BY CustomerGuid')}
  APPEND ({
  OPENROWSET('SQLOLEDB.1',
    'Integrated Security=SSPI;Persist Security Info=False;Initial
Catalog=Sequence;Data Source=localhost ',
    'SELECT SequenceID, CustomerGuid, URLCategory
   FROM ClickPath ORDER BY CustomerGuid')}
   RELATE CustomerGuid TO CustomerGuid)
   AS ClickPath AS t
ON
  WebSequence.CustomerGuid = t.CustomerGuid AND
  WebSequence.GeoLocation = t.GeoLocation AND
  WebSequence.ClickPath.URLCategory = t.ClickPath.URLCategory AND
 WebSequence.Click Path.SequenceID = t.ClickPath.SequenceID
```

The previous query returns a table of two columns: CustomerGuid and the predicted cluster number for each case.

NOTE The Select **query shown here uses the** Shape **provider from Analysis Services instead of the standard Microsoft Data Access Component (MDAC)** Shape **provider. The syntaxes of these two Shape providers are slightly different. The** Shape **provider of Analysis Services put the** Shape **command outside two** Openrowset **statements. It requires that both input rowsets be sorted on the same join key and in the same order. The Analysis Services** Shape **essentially does a merge operation and is much more scalable.**

Because the nested table ClickPath is predictable, it is possible to use the Sequence Clustering algorithm to predict the subsequent states of a given sequence. There is a new prediction function called PredictSequence, which has the following syntax:

```
PredictSequence(ClickPath) (Returns the next state predicted sequence
state for a given sequence. The result is in a table form.)
PredictSequence(ClickPath, 3) (Returns the next three predicted sequence
states for a given sequence. The result is in a table form.)
```

When the prediction returns a number of consequence steps, the probability of Pn is always less than $Pn_{-1,}$ where n is the step number. The formula to calculate of Pn is the following:

```
Pn = Pn - 1*P(Sn|Sn - 1)
```

where P(Sn|Sn - 1) is the probability from state Sn - 1 to Sn in the closest cluster for the case.

The following query predicts the next three steps for each customer.

```
Select CustomerId, PredictSequence(ClickPath, 2) as Sequences
From WebSequence Prediction Join ...
```

It returns the results shown in Table 8.1. The predicted sequence states are stored in a nested table. There are three columns in the nested table. $Sequence is the generated column. It is an integer indicating the future steps, with ordinal numbers 1, 2, 3 . . . . "1" means the next step. The Sequence ID has the same data type as the sequence column. If the sequence key is date type, it returns the consequent dates. The Microsoft Sequence Clustering algorithm doesn't fill this column. The last column URLCategory is the predicted state of the sequence.

Table 8.1 Prediction Query Result with Sequences

CUSTOMERGUID	SEQUENCES		
1	$Sequence	SequenceID	URLCategory
	1		Sport
	2		Sport
2	$Sequence	SequenceID	URLCategory
	1		Front Page
	2		Weather
3	$Sequence	SequenceID	URLCategory
	1		Hotel
	2		Flight
...			

You can also use a subselect statement on the nested table produced by `PredictSequence`. For example:

```
Select CustomerGuid, (Select $Sequence, URLCategory
                From PredictSequence(ClickPath, 2)) as Sequences
From WebSequence Predict Join ...
...
```

To get the probability of each predicted sequence state, you can use the `PredictProbability` function:

```
Select CustomerGuid, (Select $Sequence, URLCategory,
                    PredictProbability(URLCategory)
                From PredictSequence(ClickPath, 2)) as Sequences
From WebSequence Predict Join ...
...
```

Sometimes, you want to have a histogram of the probability for each sequence state at each step. You can use the `PredictHistogram` function on the sequence state column. For example:

```
Select CustomerGuid, (Select $Sequence,
                    PredictHistogram(URLCategory)as Histogram
                From PredictSequence(ClickPath, 2)) as Sequences
From WebSequence Predict Join ...
...
```

This result of this query contains two levels of nesting: one level is generated by PredictSequence, and another level is generated by Predict-Histogram. The result format is displayed in Table 8.2:

Table 8.2 Query Result with PredictHistogram Function

CUSTOMER GUID	SEQUENCES				
1	$Sequence	Histogram			
	1	URLCategory	$Support	$Probability	...
		Front page	80	0.80	
		News	15	0.03	
		Sport	3	0.15	
		...			
	2	URLCategory	$Support	$Probability	...
		Front page	55	0.55	
		News	35	0.35	
		Sport	5	0.05	
		...			
...					

In a Web click scenario, you know your Web visitor's navigation sequence within a session, and you may want to predict his or her next few possible clicks in real time so that you can provide a personalized guide for the visitor. The click path is not yet recorded in database. In this case, you can use single-ton query to make your prediction:

```
Select
  PredictSequence(ClickPath,3)
From
  [WebSequence]
Natural Prediction Join
(Select (Select 1 As SequenceID,
  'Baseball' As URLCategory
  Union Select 2 As SequenceID,
  'Business' As URLCategory) As ClickPath) As t
```

Model Content

The content of a sequence clustering model is laid out in four levels, as illustrated in Figure 8.5. The root node represents the model. The second level is the cluster level; each node except the last one represents a cluster discovered by the algorithm. The last node in the second level is a transition matrix, which represents the state transition probabilities of the overall population. The transition matrix has a set of children; each represents a row in the transition matrix. Due to content size, the matrix stores only those items with a probability greater than 0. Each cluster node also has a transition matrix as its child, which represents the transition probability of the given cluster. Therefore, there are four levels in the content of a sequence clustering model.

Interpreting the Model

Once the sequence clustering model is defined and processed, you can browse the content of the model using the Sequence Clustering viewer. The Sequence Clustering viewer contains five tabs: Cluster Diagram, Cluster Profile, Cluster Characteristics, Cluster Discrimination, and Cluster Transition. The overall design of this viewer is very similar to that of the Clustering viewer, except for the Sequence Transition tab, which graphically displays the transition matrix for each cluster.

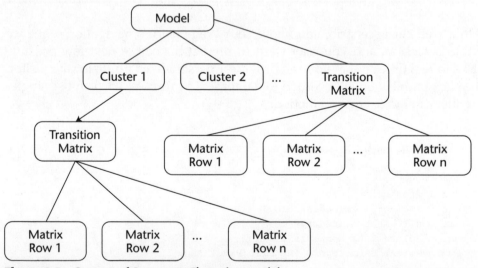

Figure 8.5 Content of Sequence Clustering model

Figure 8.6 displays the Cluster Diagram pane. This tab is the same as in the Clustering viewer. Clusters are layouts based on relationships. Similar clusters (clusters with similar probability distributions, such as clusters 1, 5, and 7 in the figure) are closer to each other. The default node background represents the size of the cluster. For example, Cluster 5 is a large cluster and Cluster 9 is much smaller. You can also use the node color-coding to represent other attribute values, including a sequence state, for example, Weather. The clusters representing those with high probabilities of clicking on the Weather page are highlighted with a darker color.

Figure 8.7 displays the cluster profile. Each column represents a cluster. Each row represents an attribute. The URLCategory row represents the sequence attribute. Each cell in this row contains a histogram of sequences. Each line in the histogram represents a sample case in this cluster, and a line is composed of a series of sequence states. Each sequence cell displays about 20 cases. These are the sample sequences from the training cases.

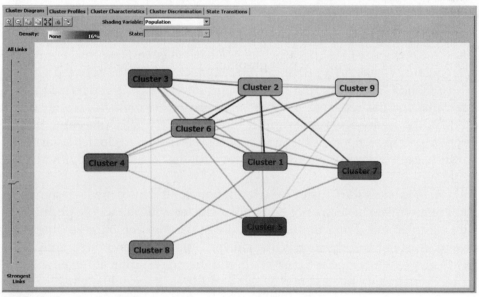

Figure 8.6   Cluster diagram

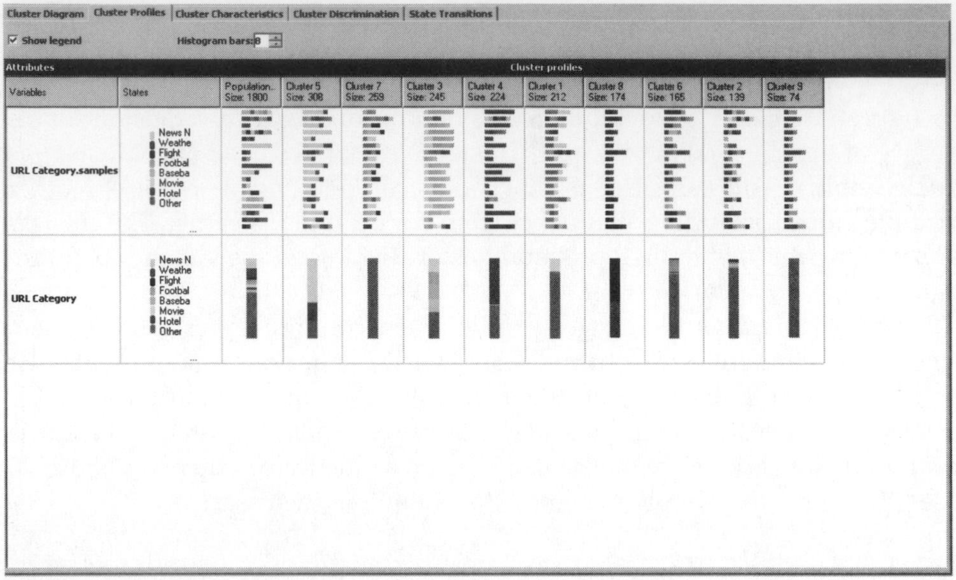

Figure 8.7 Cluster profile

Figure 8.8 displays the characteristics of each cluster. Each row represents the frequency (probability) of an attribute/value pair in the selected cluster. Each sequence state (including the Start and End events) is considered a distinct value for the sequence attribute. The list of attribute values is sorted based on the frequency. For example, the most likely attribute value in 1 is Start ⇨ Music, which means that most of the Web visitors in cluster 1 start with the Music page. Movie is another popular URL that cluster 1 individuals like to visit.

Figure 8.9 shows the Cluster Discrimination pane. This pane is designed to compare any two clusters, or to compare a cluster with the whole population or its complement. From the figure, you can see that the biggest difference between cluster 1 and cluster 8 is that cluster 1 customers end their navigation at a Music site while cluster 8 customers end their navigation at the Flight site. Cluster 5 customers like to go to Music and Movie sites, while cluster 8 customers like to visit Flight and Hotel URLs.

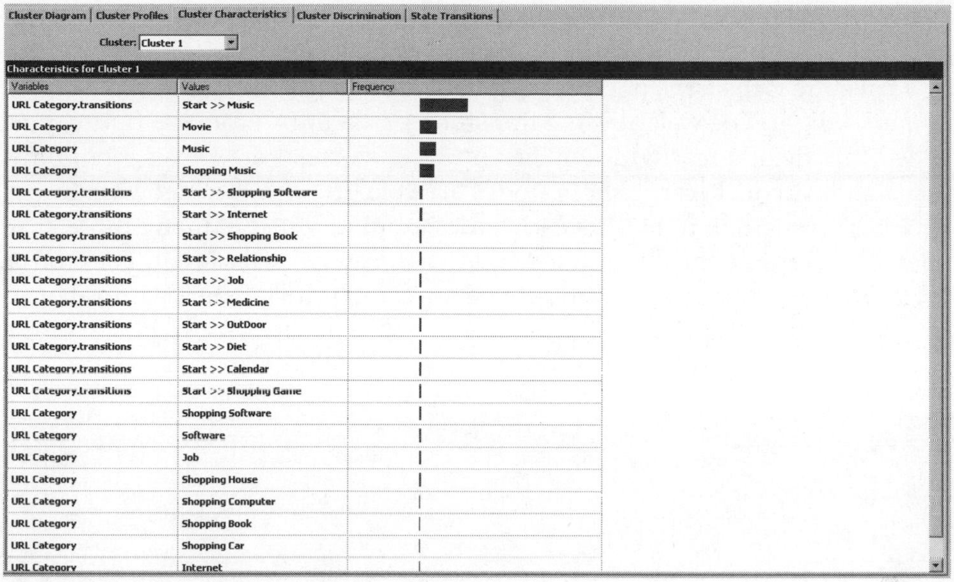

Figure 8.8   Cluster characteristics

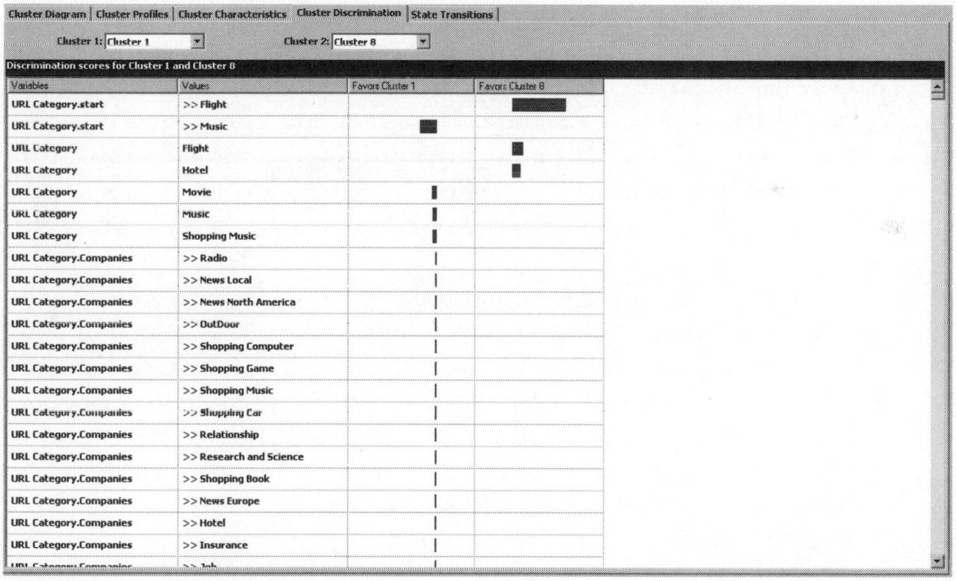

Figure 8.9   Cluster Discrimination

Figure 8.10 shows the Cluster Transition pane. It is designed to display the sequence navigation patterns of each cluster. Each node is a sequence state, and each edge is the transition between these two states. Each edge has a direction and weight. The weight is the transition probability. From the figure, you can see that the main activities of customers in cluster 1 are Music, Shopping Music, and Movie, because those nodes are colored with the highest density. There is a strong link from Music toward Shopping Music. Among those customers who are in the Shopping Music URL category, 64% will click on a Movie site next. About 45% of the customers in the cluster start with a Music page in the portal site.

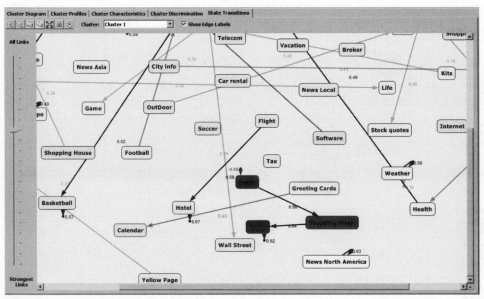

Figure 8.10 Cluster transitions

Summary

In this chapter, you have learned the basic concepts of the Markov model and its application on sequence data. You also learned the principles of clustering based on sequenced attributes and nonsequenced attribute.

Lots of information in real life can be modeled as sequences, including weather, Web clicks, purchases, and so on. This chapter taught you how to build clustering models on these sequence data. PredictSequence is a new DMX function introduced to predict the consequent states of a sequence attribute. You have learned the syntax and query result format of this function.

The Sequence Clustering viewer is a very powerful tool to help you explore the Sequence Clustering model. The State Transition tab of the viewer provides you with an easy way to understand the state transition matrix of each cluster.

Microsoft Association Rules

Beep . . . beep . . . Good afternoon, sir. Did you find everything you need? . . . beep . . . beep . . . bacon, eggs . . . beep . . . coffee, sugar . . . beep . . . milk, cookies . . . ketchup, mustard, hot dogs . . . beep . . . cake mix . . . Did you forget the frosting? I thought so! Service to aisle nine, could you bring over a can of frosting? . . . Would you like any help out today, sir?

Every purchase a customer makes builds patterns about how products are purchased together. You can use these patterns to learn more about your customers' shopping behaviors to help you optimize product layout and to cross-promote the right products to the right customers.

The process of finding these patterns, called market basket analysis, is accomplished using the Microsoft Association Rules algorithm, described in this chapter.

In this chapter, you will learn about:

- The principles of the Microsoft Association Rules
- Using Microsoft Association Rules
- Interpreting your model

Introducing Microsoft Association Rules

Put yourself in the role of a supermarket manager. One of your many responsibilities is to ensure that you sell the highest volume of product. Your goal is to sell more and be more profitable than your peers managing other stores in the chain are. Understanding the purchasing patterns of your customers is the first step toward reaching this goal.

By using the Association Rules algorithm to perform market basket analysis on your customers' transactions, you can learn which products are commonly purchased together and how likely a particular product is to be purchased along with another. For example, you might find that 5% of your customers have bought ketchup, pickles, and hot dogs together, and that 75% of those customers that bought ketchup and hot dogs also bought pickles. Now that you have this information you can take action. You could change the product layout to increase sales. You can use the insight to manage stock levels. You can determine whether baskets containing pickles, hot dogs, and ketchup are more or less profitable than those without. If more profitable, you could run a special to encourage this kind of shopping.

Additionally, you may want to learn more about the customers who shop at your store. With your courtesy cards and video club cards, you have collected several bits of information. You may learn that while 15% of your female customers have video cards overall, 75% of those customers rent their homes and live close to the store. While it is possible to derive such patterns from standard SQL queries, you would have to write hundreds or thousands of queries to explore all the possible combinations. This type of data exploration is made easy with the association algorithm.

Association Algorithm Principles

The association algorithm is nothing more than a correlation counting engine. The Microsoft Association Algorithm belongs to the a priori association family, which is a very popular and efficient algorithm for finding frequent *itemsets* (common attribute value sets). There are two steps in the association algorithm, as illustrated in Figure 9.1. The first step of the algorithm, a calculation-intensive phase, is to find frequent itemsets. The second step is to generate association rules based on frequent itemsets. This step requires much less time than the first step does.

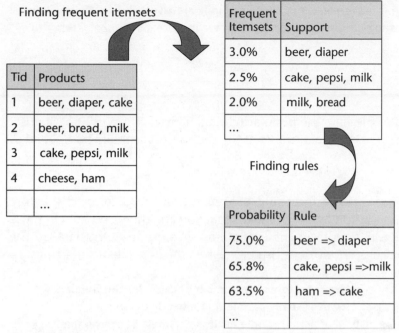

Figure 9.1   The two-step process of the association algorithm

Understanding Basic Association Algorithm Concepts

Before going to the algorithm principles, this section introduces a few basic association algorithm concepts. The following sections define the terms and concepts you will need to understand before implementing the algorithm principles:

Itemset

An *itemset* is a set of items. Each item is an attribute value. In the market basket example, an itemset contains a set of products such, as cake, Pepsi, and milk. In the customer demographic exploration example, an itemset contains a set of attribute values such as {Gender = 'Male', Education = 'Bachelor'}. Each itemset has a size, which is the number of items contained in the itemset. The size of itemset {Cake, Pepsi, Milk} is 3.

Frequent itemsets are those itemsets that are relatively popular in the dataset. The popularity threshold for an itemset is defined using *support*, which is covered in the next section.

NOTE To be more precise, cake, Pepsi, and milk are all attributes. Their values are binary: existing or missing. For simplicity, we use {Cake, Pepsi, Milk} to denote {Cake= Existing, Pepsi = Existing, and Milk = Existing}.

Support

Support is used to measure the popularity of an itemset. Support of an itemset {A, B} is made up of the total number of transactions that contain both *A* and *B*.

```
Support ({A, B}) = NumberofTransactions(A, B)
```

`Minimum_Support` is a threshold parameter you need to specify before processing an association model. It means that you are interested only in those itemsets and rules that represent at least minimum support of the dataset. The parameter `Minimum_Support` is used to restrict the itemset, but not rules.

NOTE `Minimum_Support` **represents the number of cases for the frequency threshold of itemset. However, many people find it handy to have a percentage value instead of actual counts for this parameter. For example,** `Minimum_Support=0.03` **means that the threshold for frequency is 3%. In Microsoft Association Rules, if a user specifies this parameter with an integer number, the algorithm considers the actual case count to be the threshold. If a user inputs a float number (less than 1.0) for this parameter, the algorithm considers it the percentage threshold.**

Probability (Confidence)

Probability is a property of an association rule. The probability of a rule A=>B is calculated using the support of itemset {A, B} divided by the support of {A}. This probability is also called *confidence* in the data mining research community. It is defined as follows:

```
Probability (A => B) = Probability (B|A) = Support (A, B)/ Support (A)
```

`Minimum_Probability` is a threshold parameter you need to specify before running the algorithm. It means that the user is interested in only those rules that have a high probability rather than a minimum probability. `Minimum_Probablity` has no impact on itemsets, but it does impact rules.

NOTE Even though we don't talk about the probability of an itemset. You can get it using the following formula:

```
Probability ({A, B}) = NumberofTransactions (A, B)/
TotalNumberofTransactions
```

Importance

Importance is also called the interesting score or the lift in some literature. Importance can be used to measure itemsets and rules.

The importance of an itemset is defined using the following formula:

```
Importance ({A,B}) = Probability (A, B)/(Probability (A)* Probability
(B))
```

If importance = 1, A and B are independent items. It means that the purchase of product A and purchase of product B are two independent events. If importance < 1, A and B are negatively correlated. This means if a customer buys A, it is unlikely he will also buy B. If importance > 1, A and B are positively correlated. This means if a customer buys A, it is very likely he also buys B.

For rules, the importance is calculated using the following formula:

```
Importance (A => B) = log (p(B|A)/p(B|not A))
```

An importance of 0 means that there is no association between A and B. A positive importance score means that the probability of B goes up when A is true. A negative importance score means that the probability of B goes down when A is true.

Table 9.1 gives the correlation counts of donut and muffin derived from a purchase database. Each cell value represents the number of transactions. For example, 15 out of 100 transactions include a customer purchasing both donuts and muffins.

Table 9.1 Correlation Count for Donut and Muffin

	DONUT	NOT DONUT	TOTAL
Muffin	15	5	20
Not muffin	75	5	80
Total	90	10	100

In the following, we will use the previous definitions to calculate the support, probability, and importance of related itemsets and rules for donut and muffin:

```
Support({Donut}) = 90
Support({Muffin}) = 20
Support ({Donut, Muffin}) = 15
Probability({Donut}) = 90/100 = 0.9
Probability({Muffin}) = 20/100 = 0.2
Probability({Donut, Muffin}) = 15/100 = 0.15

Probability(Donut|Muffin) = 15/20 = 0.75
Probability(Muffin|Donut) = 15/90 = 0.167

Importance({Donut, Muffin}) = 0.15/(0.2*0.9) = 0.833

Importance (Muffin=>Donut) = ln(Probability(Donut|Muffin)
/Probability(Donut|Not Muffin))= ln(0.8) = -0.223


Importance(Donut=>Muffin) = ln(Probability(Muffin|Donut)
/Probability(Muffin| Not Donut)) = ln(0.33) = -1.100
```

From the importance of the itemset {Donut, Muffin}, we can see that Donut and Muffin are negatively correlated; it is rather unlikely for someone who buys a donut to also buy a muffin.

Finding Frequent Itemsets

Finding frequent itemsets is the core part of the using the association algorithm. First, you need to specify the frequency threshold using the Minimum_Support parameter, for example, Minimum_Support = 2%. This means you are interested in analyzing only those items that appear in at least 2% of all shopping baskets.

The algorithm finds all frequent itemsets with size = 1 in the first iteration (those popular products with support greater than Minimum_Support). The algorithm does this by scanning the dataset and counting the support of each individual item. The second iteration finds those frequent itemsets of size = 2. Before starting the second iteration, the algorithm generates a set of candidate itemsets of size 2 based on the result of first iteration (frequent itemsets of size 1). Again, the algorithm scans the dataset and counts the supports for each generated candidate itemset. At the end of the iteration, it selects those candidates with support less than Minimum_Support to get the list of frequent itemsets with size equal to 2.

The algorithm repeats the same procedure to find frequent itemsets with size 3, 4, 5 . . . until no more itemsets meet the Minimum_Support criteria.

Figure 9.2 illustrates the process of identifying frequent itemsets. The Minimum_Support is set to 250/1000. At the first iteration, cheese and cake are filtered out. At the second iteration, the candidate {diaper, milk} is disqualified. At the third iteration, the candidate {beer, diaper, bread} has enough support; whereas the candidate {beer, milk, bread} is filtered out.

The following pseudocode is the main procedure for generating frequent itemsets:

```
F: result set of all frequent itemsets
F[k]: set of frequent itemsets of size k
C[k]: set of candidate itemsets of size k
SetOfItemsets generateFrequentItemsets(Integer minimumSupport){
  F[1] = {frequent items};
  for (k =1, F[k] <>0; k++) {
     C[k+1] = generateCandidates(k, F[k]);
     for each transaction t in databases {
         For each candidate c in C[k+1] {
            if t contains c then c.count++
        }
  } //Scan the dataset.
     for each candidate c in C[k+1] {
        //Select the qualified candidates
        if c.count >=Minimum_Support F[k+1] = F[k+1] U {c}
     }
  }
  //Union all frequent itemsets of different size
  while k>=1 do {
     F = F U F[k];
     k--;
  }
  return F;
}
```

Once you have your frequent itemsets, generateCandidates is a function that returns all the candidate itemsets with size = $k + 1$. One important property of a frequent itemset is that every subset of a frequent itemset must be a frequent itemset. For example, if {beer, diaper, bread} is a frequent itemset, {beer}, {diaper}, {bread}, {beer, diaper}, {beer, bread}, and {diaper, bread} must also be frequent itemsets.

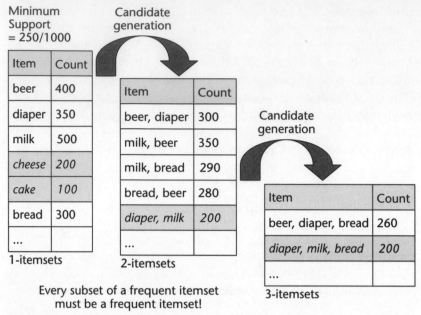

Figure 9.2   Finding frequent itemsets

The following SQL join statement can be used to generate candidate itemsets Ck+1 from frequent itemsets Fk.

```
Insert into Ck+1
Select x1.a1, x1.a2, ..., x1.ak, x2.ak
From Fk as x1, Fk as X2
Where
    //match the itemset prefixes of size k-1
                                               x1.a1 = x2.a1 And
    x1.a2 = x2.a2 And
    ...
    x1.ak-1 = x2.ak-1 And
//avoid duplicates
    x1.ak < x2.ak
```

This SQL statement generates those candidate itemsets with prefixes of itemsets size *k*. However, it doesn't guarantee that all the subsets of candidate itemsets are frequent itemsets. So, we need to prune those candidates containing infrequent subsets by using the following procedure:

```
Boolean hasInfrequentSubset(Itemset c, SetofItemsets F) {
    For each (k-1) subset s of c {
```

```
      If s not in F then return true;
   }
 return false;
}
```

Candidate itemsets generation and counting their correlation are time-consuming. In some cases, it can generate a huge number of candidate sets. For example, suppose that there are 10,000 products (a medium-sized supermarket). If the minimum support is low enough, the algorithm will generate over 10^7 candidate 2 itemsets. Many optimization techniques are available in this phase; for example, Microsoft Association Rules stores the itemsets in a tree data structure to save space.

Some association algorithms generate frequent itemsets without candidate generation.

NOTE The best known algorithm is FP-Tree proposed by Professor JiaWei Han and implemented in DBMiner's OLE DB for DM provider. Detailed descriptions of these improvements are beyond the scope of this book. We list several references at the end of the book for readers who are interested in learning more about association.

TIP Association algorithm processing is very sensitive to the `Minimum_Support` parameter. When its value is set too low (less than 1%), the processing time and required memory become exponential. This is due to the large number of qualified frequent itemsets and frequent itemset candidates.

For large datasets with lots of distinct items, we recommend you avoid setting this parameter too small.

The number of items is also critical to the performance of the processing. When there are too many unique items, consider grouping them into categories. For example, your store may have a dozen different JellyBeans, you may group these JellyBeans to a single JellyBeans category. This can greatly reduce the total number of items and thus reduce the model processing time.

Generating Association Rules

The next step in the association algorithm process is to generate association rules. We're looking for rules of the form: cake $\geq$ milk, and we're interested in rules that have a high correlation. To generate this rules we need the count for the { cake, milk } itemset as well as the counts for cake and milk (the 1-itemsets). In general you need the itemsets to the left of the arrow, the left hand side along with the itemset including all items in the rule.

As rules are generated from the itemset, each item in the rule automatically satisfies the minimum support condition. The following procedure generates all the qualified association rules:

```
For each frequent itemset f, generate all the subset x and its complimentary set
y = f - x
If Support(f)/Support(x) > Minimum_Probability, then x => y is a qualified
association rule with probability =  Support(f)/Support(x)
```

The following property can be used to accelerate the rule-generation process:

```
If a, b, c => d has probability lower than the minimum probability, rule
a, b => c, d doesn't have enough probability neither.
```

NOTE The Microsoft Association Rules algorithm doesn't generate multiple items on the right side of the rule. However, if you want to have multiple recommendations, you can use a prediction query against an association model, which can return multiple items.

Prediction

In an association model, if a column is used for input, its values can be used only in frequent itemsets and on the left side of association rules. If a column is used to make predictions, the column's states can be used in frequent itemsets and on the left and right sides of the association rules. If a column is predict_only, its states can appear in frequent itemsets and on the right side of rules.

Many association algorithms in commercial data mining packages stop at finding itemsets and rules; the Microsoft Association Algorithm can perform predictions using these rules. The results of the predictions are usually a set of items to recommend.

You can build an association model not only based on shopping baskets but also based on customer demographics. For example, you can include gender, marital status, and home ownership as case-level attributes in the mining structure and include the shopping basket as a nested table in the same structure. In this case, you analyze the shopping patterns not only based on the relationship of itemsets but also based on the demographics. For example, you may find a rule that predicts that 65% of male customers who purchase beer also purchase diapers in the same transaction, and 20% of female customers who purchase diapers also purchase wine.

These rules can be applied for prediction. For a male customer, you may recommend a list of wines. If a male customer has already bought beer in the shopping cart, you may recommend both wine and diapers.

However, not every itemset is associated with a rule. For example, there is no rule that has the itemset {beer, diaper, bread, milk} on the left side. What would the recommendation list be for a customer who bought beer, diapers, bread, and milk? Here is the method the Microsoft Association algorithm uses to execute associative prediction:

1. Given a list of items, find all rules with the left side matching the given items or any subsets of the given items. Apply those rules to get the list of recommendations.

2. If there is no appropriate rule or there are too few recommended items, apply marginal statistics to predict and return the *n* most popular items.

3. Sort the items from steps 1 and 2 based on probability.

TIP The number of qualified association rules is based on the parameter Minimum_Probability **(of course, each item in a rule must be a frequent item). For example, when** Minimum_Probability **is set to 30%, this means 30% of customers who purchase A also purchase B, A => B, and this is a qualified rule. Rule generation is a relatively fast process, and you may lower the probability to have more rules. In a sparse dataset like the shopping transaction table, you may set** Minimum_Probability **to 5–10% and get reasonable rules. In a dense dataset like a customer demographic table, you need to raise this parameter to 40–50%; otherwise, you may get contradictory rules. For example, High IQ => Gender = Male and High IQ => Gender = Female.**

Algorithm Parameters

As indicated in previous sections, the association algorithm is very sensitive to the algorithm parameter settings. The following is the list of parameters for the Microsoft Association Rules algorithms.

- Minimum_Support is a threshold parameter. It defines the minimum support requirement items must meet to qualify as a frequent itemset. Its value is within the range of 0 to 1. The default value is 0.03. If this value is set too low — for example, 0.001 — the algorithm may take much longer to process and require much more memory.

  If Minimum_Support is set to more than 1, it is considered to be the threshold for number of cases instead of percentage.

- `Maximum_Support` is a threshold parameter. It defines the maximum support threshold of frequent itemset. Its value is within the range of 0 to 1. The default value is 0.03. This parameter can be used to filter out those items that are too frequent.

   If `Maximum_Support` is set to more than 1, it is considered to be the threshold for the number of cases instead of a percentage.

- `Minimum_Probability` is a threshold parameter. It defines the minimum probability for an association rule. Its value is within the range of 0 to 1. The default value is 0.4.

- `Minimum_Importance` is a threshold parameter for association rules. Rules with importance less than `Minimum_Importance` are filtered out.

- `Maximum_Itemset_Size` specifies the maximum size of an itemset. The default value is 0, which means that there is no size limit on the itemset. Reducing the maximum itemset size reduces the processing time as the algorithm can save further iterations over the dataset when the candidate itemset size reaches this limit.

- `Minimum_Itemset_Size` specifies the minimum size of the itemset. The default value is 0. Sometimes you don't care about the large number of smaller itemsets. For example, you may be interested only in itemsets with size > 4.

   Reducing `Minimum_Itemset_Size` will not reduce the processing time because the algorithm has to start with itemset size 1 and increase the size step by step.

- `Maximum_Itemset_Count` defines the maximum number of itemsets. If not specified, the algorithm generates all itemsets based on `Minimum_Support`. This parameter avoids generating a large number of itemsets. When there are too many itemsets, the algorithm will keep only the top *n* itemsets based on importance score of itemset.

- `Optimized_Prediction_Count` is used to set the number of recommended items asked by prediction query. By default, the algorithm uses rules with length 2 for prediction. You may increase this number to have better prediction qualities.

Using the Association Algorithm

Now you have learned the principles of the Microsoft Association algorithm and the list of tuning parameters. In this section, you are going to build a few association models using this algorithm.

DMX Queries

Suppose that you have two tables: Customer and Purchase. The Customer table contains customer demographic information. It includes attributes such as gender, age, marital status, profession, and so on. The Purchase table is a transaction table containing the list of movies each customer purchased in the store. There are two columns in the Purchase table: Customer_ID and Movie_Name. In this section, you build an association model to analyze the relationships among movies and demographics.

The following statement creates a model about associative analysis using Gender, Marital_Status, and the purchased movies:

```
Create Mining Model MovieAssociation (
    Customer_Id long key,
    Gender text discrete predict,
    Marital_Status text discrete predict,
    MoviePurchase table predict (
        Movie_Name text key
    )
)
Using Microsoft_Association_Rules(Minimum_Support - 0.02,
    Minimum_Probability = 0.40)
```

Although most market basket models contain nested tables, it is possible to use an association algorithm to analyze only the case table for advanced data exploration. The following is a model to analyze the Customer table. The purpose of the model is not market basket analysis; rather it helps you explore the dataset and find common attribute value sets. The association algorithm doesn't accept continuous attributes because it is a counting engine that counts the correlations among discrete attribute states. You need to make the continuous attributes in the mining model discrete, as shown here:

```
Create Mining Model CustomerExploration (
    Customer_Id long key,
    Gender text discrete predict,
    Marital_Status text discrete predict,
    Education text discrete predict,
    Home_Ownership text discrete predict
  )
Using Microsoft_Association_Rules(Minimum_Support = 0.05,
        Minimum_Probability = 0.75)
```

As you already know, a model training statement mainly depends on the model structure, not on the algorithm on which the model is based. The following is the training statement for the MovieAssociation model:

```
Insert into MovieAssociation ( Customer_Id, Gender, Marital_Status,
MoviePurchase(Customer_Id, Movie_Name) )
OPENROWSET('MSDataShape', 'data
provider=SQLOLEDB;Server=myserver;UID=myloging; PWD=mypass' ,
 'Shape
   { Select Customer_Id, Gender, Marital_Status From Customers }
Append (
   { Select Customer_Id, Movie_Name From Purchases }
  Relate Customer_Id to Customer_Id ) as MoviePurchase')
```

After the model is processed, you can issue queries to retrieve itemsets and rules from the content. You do this by filtering the content on the node types for itemsets and rules, which are 7 and 8, respectively:

```
//retrieving all the frequent itemsets
Select Node_Description from MovieAssociation.Content
Where Node_Type = 7

//retrieving all the rules
Select Node_Description from MovieAssociation.Content
Where Node_Type = 8
```

If you have only customer demographic information and you would like to give movie recommendations based on Gender, Maritual_Status and Age, you can use the following prediction query:

```
Select t.CustomerID, Predict(MoviePurchase, 5) as Recommendation
From   MovieAssociation
Natural Prediction Join
  OPENROWSET('MSDataShape', 'data provider=SQLOLEDB;
Server=myserver;UID=myloging; PWD=mypass' ,
 'Select CustomerID, Gender, Marital_Status, Age from  NewCustomer') as
 t
```

Predict(MoviePurchase, 5) returns the top five movies in a table column based on the probability. This kind of prediction is called an *associative* prediction.

Sometimes, you not only know the customer demographics, but also know a few movies a customer has already purchased. You can use the following prediction query to give more accurate recommendations:

```
Select t.CustomerID, Predict(MoviesPurchase, 5) as Recommendation
From   MovieAssociation
PREDICTION JOIN
  Shape {
  OPENROWSET('SQLOLEDB',
'Integrated Security=SSPI; Data Source=localhost;Initial Catalog=
MovieSurvey',
'Select CustomerID, Gender, Marital_Status, Age
     From Customer Order By CustomerID')}
  Append ({
  OPENROWSET('SQLOLEDB',
    'Integrated Security=SSPI; Data Source=localhost; Initial Catalog =
MovieSurvey',
    'Select CustomerID, Movie
    From Movies Order By CustomerID')}
  Relate CustomerID to CustomerID)
  As MoviePurchase As t
On
    MovieAssociation.Gender = t.Gender
And  MovieAssociation.Marital_Status = t.Marital_Status
And  MovieAssociation.MoviesPurchas.Movie_Name = t.MoviePurchase.Movie
```

Model Content

The content of an association model is displayed in Figure 9.3. There are three levels. The top level has a single node that represents the model. The second level contains nodes representing qualified itemsets with their associated supports. The Distribution rowsets of the itemset nodes contain detailed information about the itemsets, with each row representing an individual item. The third level contains nodes that represent qualified rules. The parent of the rule node is the itemset that represents the left side item of a rule. The right side of a rule always has a single item, which is stored in the Distribution rowsets.

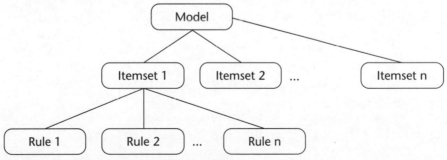

Figure 9.3 Content of association model

Interpreting the Model

After the association model is processed, you can browse the contents of the model using the Association viewer. The Association viewer contains three tabs: Itemsets, Rules, and Dependency Net.

The Itemsets tab (shown in Figure 9.4) displays the frequent itemsets discovered by the association algorithm. The main part of the screen is a grid showing the list of frequent itemsets and their supports and sizes. Sometimes, if `Minimum_Support` is set too low, there can be lots of itemsets. Some drop-down lists are available to enable you to filter these itemsets based on support and itemset size. You can also use the Filter itemset to filter the itemsets. For example, you could select those itemsets that contain `Gender=Male`.

The Rules tab (shown in Figure 9.5) displays the qualified association rules. The main part of the tab is the rule grid. It displays all the qualified rules, their probabilities, and their importance scores. The importance score is designed to measure the usefulness of a rule. The higher the importance score, the better the quality of the rule is. Similar to the Itemsets tab, the Rules tab contains some drop-down lists and text files for filtering rules. For example, you can select all the rules that contains `Gender=Male` on the right side.

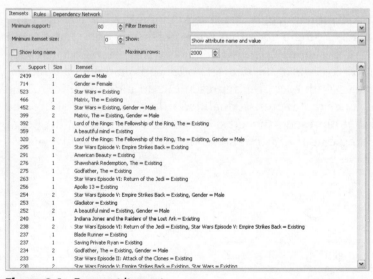

Figure 9.4 Frequent itemsets

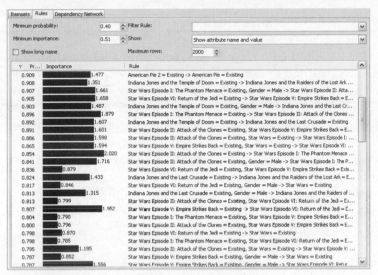

Figure 9.5 Association rules

The third tab of the association is Dependency Net viewer (shown in Figure 9.6). Each node in the viewer represents an item, for example, StarWars = Existing or Gender = Male. Each edge represents a pairwise association rule. The slider is associated with the importance score. By default, it displays up to 60 nodes. You may add hidden nodes to the graph using the Search button in the toolbar. You can also filer out the weak edges using the slider. If you want to have more nodes and edges in the dependency net, you can lower the value of `Minimum_Probability` and reprocess the model.

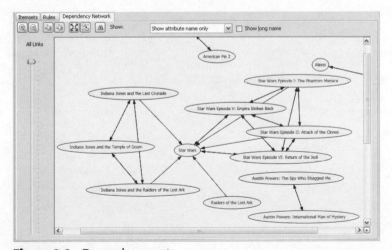

Figure 9.6 Dependency net

Summary

In this chapter, we gave you an overview of Microsoft Association algorithm and its main usages. You learned the set of key terms of association algorithm including itemset, rule, support, probability, and importance. The chapter also taught you the principles of association algorithm processing. There are two steps in this algorithm: identifying frequent itemsets and generating rules. Rules can be used for prediction.

You also learned the DMX queries to use with the association model. These queries generate recommendations based on probabilities or adjusted probabilities. The results of these queries can be used in cross-selling applications.

By now, you should be able to do market basket analysis and advanced data exploration using the Microsoft Association algorithm.

Microsoft Neural Network

Suppose that you are a data miner working for the marketing department of a real estate company. You want to understand the factors that impact home ownership from your customers' demographic data. You have built mining models to predict home ownership based on age, income, gender, and marital status. You have tried decision trees and Naïve Bayes, but the results from the lift chart don't show great predictive accuracy. You wonder if there are other methods that can get better results. In this chapter, you learn the principles of the neural network algorithm and how to apply the Microsoft Neural Network to solve data mining classification and regression tasks.

In this chapter you learn about:

- The principles of the Microsoft Neural Network
- Using Microsoft Neural Networks
- Interpreting your model

Introducing the Principles of the Microsoft Neural Network Algorithm

The origin of the neural network can be traced to 1940s when two researchers, Warren McCulloch and Walter Pits, tried to build a model to simulate how biological neurons work. Though the focus of this research was on the anatomy of the brain, it turns out that this model introduced a new approach for solving technical problems outside neurobiology.

During the 1960s and 1970s, with the advance of computer technology, researchers implemented some prototypes of the models based on the work of McCulloch. In 1982, John Hopfield invented *backpropagation*, a method to adjust the weights of a neural network in backward direction based on the learning error, as is explained later in this chapter.

Since 1980s, the theories of neural networks have matured, and the computing power of modern computers has enabled the processing of large neural networks within a reasonable time frame. Neural network technologies are applied to more and more commercial applications, for example, voice and handwriting recognition, fraud detection of credit card transactions, and customer churn analysis.

Neural networks mainly address the classification and regression tasks of data mining. Like decision trees, neural networks can find nonlinear relationships among input attributes and predictable attributes. Neural networks, however, find smooth rather than discontinuous nonlinearities. On the negative side, it usually takes longer to learn to use a neural network than it does to use decision trees and Naïve Bayes. Another drawback of neural networks is the difficulty in interpreting results. A neural network model contains no more than a set of weights for the network. It is difficult to see the relationships in the model and why they are valid.

Neural networks support discrete and continuous outputs. When the outputs are continuous, the task is regression. In fact, classic regression techniques, such as logistic regression, can be represented as special cases of neural networks.

Although typically used for classification and regression, feed-forward neural networks can also be applied to segmentation, when used with a bottleneck configuration (small hidden layer).

What Is Neural Network?

What is a feed-forward neural network? Neural networks are more sophisticated than decision trees and Naive Bayes are. Figure 10.1 displays a couple of examples. A neural network contains a set of nodes (neurons) and edges that form a network. There are three types of nodes: input, hidden, and output. Each edge links two nodes with an associated weight. The direction of an edge represents the data flow during the prediction process. Each node is a unit of processing. Input nodes form the first layer of the network. In most neural networks, each input node is mapped to one input attribute such as age, gender or income. The original value of an input attribute needs to be massaged to a floating number in the same scale (often between –1 to 1) before processing.

Hidden nodes are the nodes in the intermediate layers. A hidden node receives input from nodes in the input layers or precedent hidden layer. It combines all the input based on the weight of associated edges, processes some calculations, and emits a result value of the processing to the following layer.

Output nodes usually represent the predictable attributes. A neural network may have multiple output attributes, as displayed in Figure 10.1b. It is possible to separate the output nodes to several different networks. But in most cases, it reduces the processing time when they are combined as these networks can share the common cost of scanning the source data. The result of the output node is often a floating number between 0 and 1.

The prediction for neural network is straightforward, the attribute values of an input case are normalized and mapped to the neurons of the input layer. Then each hidden layer node processes the inputs and triggers an output for the layers that follow. At the end, the output neurons start to process and generate an output value. This value is then mapped to the original scale (in terms of continuous attribute) or original category (in terms of discrete attribute). While processing a neural network is time-consuming, making predictions against a trained neural network is rather efficient.

As displayed in Figure 10.1, the topologies of the neural networks may vary. Figure 10.1a shows a very simple network. It has one output attribute without a hidden layer. All the input neurons connect to the output neuron directly. Such a neural network is exactly same as logistic regression.

Figure 10.1b is a network with three layers: input, hidden and output. There are three neurons in the hidden layer. Each neuron of the hidden layer is fully connected to the input of the precedent layer. The hidden layer is a very important aspect of neural network. It enables the network to learn nonlinear relationships.

Non-feed-forward networks have directed cycles in their topology or "architecture." That is, while following the direction of edges in a neural network, you can return to the same node. The Microsoft Neural Network is a feed-forward network.

After the topology of a neural network is configured, that is, the number of hidden nodes is specified, the training process involves finding the best set of weights for the edges in the network. This is a time-consuming task. Initially, the weights are randomly assigned. During each training iteration, the network processes the training cases to generate predictions on the output layer based on the current network configurations. It then calculates the error for the outputs. Based on these errors, it adjusts the weights of network using backward propagation. We will go over the details of the neural network learning process in the following sections.

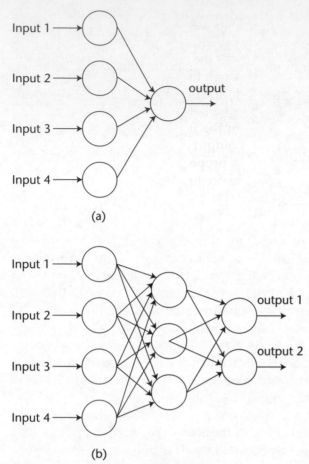

(a)

(b)

Figure 10.1 Example of neural network

Combination and Activation

Each neuron in the neural network is a basic processing unit. A neuron has a number of inputs and one output. It combines all the input values (combination), does certain calculations, and then triggers an output value (activation). The process is very similar to the biological neuron.

Figure 10.2 displays the structure of a neuron. It contains two functions: a combination of inputs and a calculation of outputs. The combination function combines the input values into a single value. There are different ways to combine inputs. The most popular method is the weighted sum, meaning that the sum of each input value is multiplied by its associated weight. Other combination functions include mean, max logical OR, and logical AND of the input values. The Microsoft Neural Network uses the weighted sum approach. The output of combination is then passed through the activation function.

Similar to the way that a biological neuron works, when using the activation function, small changes of the input value sometimes trigger large output changes, and sometimes large changes of the input value have insignificant impact on the output. In particular, the output is sensitive to the input only when the input is in its midrange. This property enhances the neural network's ability to learn as it introduces the nonlinearity into the network. Several math functions satisfy this property. The most well-known functions are sigmoid (logistic) and tanh. These are nonlinear functions and result in nonlinear behavior. The definitions of sigmoid and tanh are:

```
sigmoid: O = 1/(1+eᵃ)
tanh: O = (eᵃ - e⁻ᵃ)/(eᵃ + e⁻ᵃ)
```

where a is the input value and o is the output value.

Figure 10.3 displays the distribution of the sigmoid and tanh functions. The x-axis is the input value and the y-axis represents the output it triggers. The output value of sigmoid function is between 0 and 1, whereas the output value for tanh is between –1 and 1. When the input value is close to 0, the output is very sensitive to slight changes in the input. When the absolute value of the input gets larger, the output becomes less sensitive.

Microsoft Neural Network uses tanh as the activation function in the hidden nodes. For output nodes, it uses the sigmoid function.

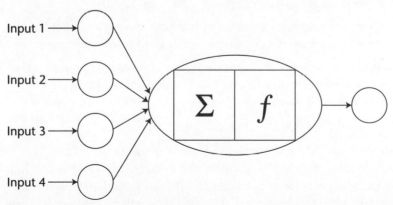

Figure 10.2 A basic processing unit

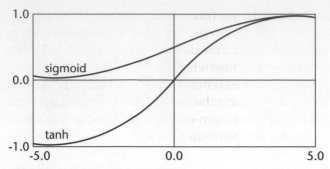

Figure 10.3   Activation function

Backpropagation, Error Function, and Conjugate Gradient

The core part of processing a neural network is backpropagation. The training of neural network is an iterative process. At each iteration, the algorithm compares the output values with the actual known values to get the errors for each output neuron. The weights pointing to the output neurons are modified based on the error calculations. These modifications are then propagated from the output layer through the hidden layers down to the input layer. All the weights in the neural network are adjusted accordingly.

The core process of neural network training is described in the following steps:

1. The algorithm randomly assigns values for all the weights in the network at the initial stage (usually ranging from –1.0 to 1.0).

2. For each training example (or each set of training examples), it calculates the outputs based on the current weights in the network.

3. The output errors are calculated, and the backpropagation process calculates the errors for each output and hidden neuron in the network. The weights in the network are updated.

4. Repeat step 2 until the condition is satisfied.

Some neural networks update the weights after examining each case. This is called *case[online] updating*. Other neural networks update the weights until all the sample cases are analyzed. This is called *epoch[batch] updating*. One interaction through the training dataset is called an epoch. The Microsoft Neural Network uses epoch updating because it is more robust for regression models.

The neural network needs a measure to indicate the quality of the training. This measure is the error function (also called a *loss* function). The whole purpose of neural network training is to minimize the training error.

There are many different choices for error functions, for example, the squared residual (the square of the delta between predicted value and actual value) or binary threshold for binary classification (if the delta between output and actual value is less than 0.5, then the error is 0; otherwise, it is 1).

The following formula gives one of the common methods for calculating the error for neurons at the output layer using the derivative of the logistic function. (The Microsoft Neural Network uses sum-of-squares error for continuous attribute and cross-entropy for discrete attribute):

$$Err_i = O_i(1 - O_i)(T_i - O_i)$$

In this case, Oi is the output of the output neuron unit i, and Ti is the actual value for this output neuron based on the training sample.

The error calculation of hidden neuron is based on the errors of the neurons in the following layers and the associated weights. The following is the formula:

$$Err_i = O_i(1 - O_i)\sum_j Err_j w_{ij}$$

Here, Oi is the output of the hidden neuron unit i, which has j outputs to the following layer. $Errj$ is the error of neuron unit j, wij is the weight between these two neurons.

Once the error of each neuron is calculated, the next step is to adjust the weights in the network accordingly, using the following method.

$$w_{ij} = w_{ij} + l*Err_j*O_i$$

Here l is a value ranging from 0 and 1.

The variable l is called learning rate. If the value of l is smaller, the changes on the weights are smaller after each iteration, thus the learning rate is slow. The value of l usually decreases during the training process. At the initial stage of training, l is large, which allows the neural network to move quickly towards the optimum solution. Afterward it decreases, so you can fine-tune the network to search for the best solution.

Many neural networks apply a method called the *conjugate gradient* in the process of adjusting the weight after each iteration. Conjugate gradient method is an algorithm for finding the nearest local minimum. The gradient method uses derivative (gradient) to find the next direction. Conjugate takes into account the previous direction when it calculate the next direction so that it could avoid zig-zag problem, meaning taking short-cut.

Because the search space for the best set of weights is huge, with many local optimal points, researchers apply different nonlinear optimization methods to guide the training process. There are many optimization algorithms, such as genetic algorithms, simulated annealing, iterative improvement, and so on.

A Simple Example of Processing a Neural Network

The best way to explain the neural network training process is to go through a simple case of updating an example. In this example, we use weighted sum as the combination function, and the sigmoid as the activation function. Figure 10.4 shows the topology of a simple neural network with six neurons. The initial weights of the edges are displayed in the figure.

This example has three input nodes and one output node, which mapped to the four attributes of a sample case. Suppose that the sample case is (1, 1, 0, 1), the last digit is the output.

The first step is to calculate the outputs of each hidden and output neuron as shown in Table 10.1.

Table 10.1 Calculation of Outputs for Hidden and Output Neurons

NEURON	INPUT	OUTPUT
4	$0.2 + 0.2 + 0 = 0.4$	$1/(1 + e^{0.4}) = 0.401$
5	$0.1 - 0.4 + 0 = -0.3$	$1/(1 + e^{-0.3}) = 0.574$
6	$-0.3*0.401 + (-0.1)* 0.574 = -0.694$	$1/(1 + e^{-0.694}) = 0.667$

We get the output value of neuron 6 which is 0.667. The actual value is given by the sample as 1. We can thus calculate the error of the output neuron. Using the backpropagation method, we can derive all the errors for all the output and hidden neurons as listed in Table 10.2.

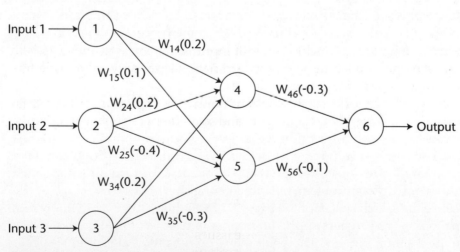

Figure 10.4 An example of neural network training

Table 10.2 Calculation of Errors for Hidden and Output Neurons

NEURON	ERROR
6	0.667*(1 − 0.667)*(1 − 0.667)= 0.074
5	0.574*(1 − 0.574)*0.074*(−0.3) = −0.005
4	0.401*(1 − 0.401)*0.074*(−0.1)= −0.002

The sample neural network uses the case updating method. Once the error is calculated, we can adjust the weights accordingly. Table 10.3 gives the new set of weights after the first training case. The step size is a constant, with a value of 0.8.

Table 10.3 Calculation of New Weights

WEIGHT	NEW WEIGHT
W_{46}	−0.3 + 0.8* 0.074*0.401 = −0.276
W_{56}	−0.1 + 0.8* 0.074*0.574 = −0.066
W_{14}	0.2 + 0.8*(−0.002)*1 = 0.198
W_{15}	0.1 + 0.8*(−0.005)*1 = 0.096
W_{24}	0.2 + 0.8*(−0.002)*1 = 0.198
W_{25}	−0.4 + 0.8*(−0.005)*1= −0.404
W_{34}	0.2 + 0.8*(−0.002)*0 = 0.2
W_{35}	−0.3 + 0.8*(−0.005)*0 = −0.3

Normalization and Mapping

The neural network requires the value of input variables to be normalized in the same scale of value; otherwise, those variables with large value scale will dominate the training process.

There are a dozen different methods to normalize continuous input attributes, including z-score, z-axis, log score, and so on. The simplest method is the following:

$$V = (A - A_{min}) / (A_{max} - A_{min})$$

where A is the value of the attribute, Amin is its minimum value, and Amax its maximum value.

However, this simple method has some issues. For example, if extreme minimum or maximum values exist in the distribution, the normalized result will be skewed. Suppose that the attribute you want to normalize is income, and the majority of the households have income less than $200,000. If there is a household with over $1,000,000 income, the majority of the families will be mapped to the first 10–20% of the range. In this case, the log score is a better solution because it maps all the values to the log space first to reduce the scale issue.

For discrete variables, the easiest method is to map it to equal space points from 0 to 1. For example, there are five states for Education: partial high school, high school, undergraduate, graduate, and Ph.D. These values can be mapped to 0, 0.25, 0.50, 0.75, and 1.0, respectively.

Working with the Microsoft Neural Network, you would use the following method for input attribute normalization:

$$V = \frac{(x - \mu)}{\delta}$$

Where for continuous input, μ is mean and δ is the standard deviation; for discrete input, $\mu = p$ (probability of a state), and $\delta^2 = p * (1 - p)$

The relationship between the attribute and neurons is 1 to n. An attribute is mapped to n neurons. The Microsoft Neural Network maps a continuous attribute to two nodes: one representing the value and the other representing the missing state. It maps a discrete attribute into $n + 1$ nodes, n being the number of distinct states and 1 representing the missing state. If the attribute is binary with two states — Missing or Existing — it is modeled as a single node.

Figure 10.5 shows an example of input normalization and mapping. The top table is the training input data. The bottom table displays the data after normalization and mapping process. You can see from the figure that the four input columns (not counting the ID) are mapped to 10 input neurons. If Gender, Income, and IQ are the input attributes, and Plan is the predictable attribute, there are seven input neurons and three output neurons.

ID	Gender	Income	Age	Owner
1	Male	46500	33	No
2	Male	39600	40	No
3	Male	63400	34	Yes
4	Female	40400	43	No

ID	Gender			Income		Age		Owner		
	-	M	F	-	val	-	val	-	Y	N
1	0	0.58	-0.58	0	-.09	0	-.91	0	0	1
2	0	0.58	-0.58	0	-.71	0	.56	0	0	1
3	0	0.58	-0.58	0	1.44	0	-.77	0	1	0
4	0	-1.73	1.73	0	-.64	0	1.12	0	0	1

Figure 10.5 Input normalization and mapping

Topology of the Network

The topology of the neural network needs to be fixed before processing. The number of input and output neurons is fixed with a training dataset. The options are mainly related to the configuration of the hidden layers, such as number of hidden layers and the number of hidden neurons at each hidden layer.

A neural network could have any number of hidden layers. The capacity of a network is a complicated function of the number of nodes and number of layers. So, multiple hidden layers may increase the learning capacity. It will also increase the processing time. The other drawback is potentially overtraining. With too many hidden layers and hidden nodes, the network tends to remember the training cases instead of generalizing the patterns (similar to the oversplit issue in decision trees). It has been proven that in most cases, one hidden layer is sufficient. The Microsoft Neural Network doesn't allow more than one hidden layer.

The number of neurons in the hidden layer is also very important. Using too few will starve the network of the resources it needs to solve the problem. Using too many will increase the training time. Researchers propose a rough guideline for choosing the number of hidden neurons: $c*sqrt(m*n)$, where n is the number of input neurons, m is the number of output neurons, and c is a constant. The optimal number varies from problem to problem: you should experiment with the number of nodes. In the Microsoft Neural Network, the default value for c is 4.

Similar to other Microsoft algorithms, a mining model based on the Microsoft Neural Network can have multiple predictable attributes. This results in multiple sub-neural-networks. For example, if there are two predict attributes — Age and Home Ownership — you have to create two separate neural networks, one to predict each predictable attribute. However, if these two attributes are predict_only, they can share the same network.

Each input attribute will be mapped to multiple input neurons. Sometimes, this can result in a large number of input neurons if there are many discrete attributes with many distinct values. By default, the total number of output neurons per subnetwork is limited to 500 in the Microsoft Neural Network algorithm. It will build multiple neural networks in case the number of output neurons is over 500.

When there are lots of input attributes, the Microsoft Neural Network algorithm invokes the feature selection process. The feature selection process selects the most important 255 input attributes.

TIP   Having multiple predictable attributes results in multiple neural networks. This causes performance issues during the processing. We recommend that you use only one predictable attribute in your neural network model.

Training the Ending Condition

The training process of neural network is iterative. Depending on the complicity of patterns in the sample dataset, it may take hundreds or even thousands of iterations through the data. What is the stop condition for a neural network? The following is a list of possible stop criteria:

- **Sufficient accuracy on a holdout set:** The misclassification rate is below a given threshold.

- **Maximum iteration:** The training process has reached the high limit of the number of iterations.

- **Convergence of the weights:** The change on the weights after each iteration falls below a threshold.

- **Time out:** The number of iteration exceeds the limit.

The Microsoft Neural Network uses the first three conditions as the stop criteria. The training stops when any of the top three conditions is satisfied.

Introducing the Algorithm Parameters

The following is a list of parameters for Microsoft Neural Network algorithm.

- `Maximum_Input_Attributes` is a threshold parameter for feature selection. When the number of input attributes is greater than this parameter setting, feature selection is invoked implicitly to pick the most significant attributes.

- `Maximum_Output_Attributes` is a threshold parameter of feature selection. When the number of predictable attributes is greater than this parameter setting, feature selection is invoked implicitly to select the most significant attributes.

- `Maximum_States` specifies the maximum number of attribute states that the algorithm supports. If the number of states that an attribute has is greater than the maximum number of states, the algorithm uses the attribute's most popular states and treats the remaining states as missing.

- `Holdout_Percentage` is specifies the percentage of holdout data. The holdout data is used to validate the accuracy during the training. The default value is 0.1.

- `Holdout_Seed` is an integer for specifying the seed for selecting the holdout dataset.

> **MICROSOFT LOGISTIC REGRESSION ALGORITHM**
>
> **Microsoft Logistic Regression algorithm is based on Microsoft Neural Network algorithm implementation, by setting the parameter** Hidden_Node_Ratio **to** 0. **If you use Microsoft Neural Network to build a model without hidden layer, you get exactly the same result as using Microsoft Logistic Regression. The reason it is packaged as a separate algorithm is mainly for the discoverability issue for the users.**

- Hidden_Node_Ratio is used to configure the number of hidden nodes. The unit of hidden node number is $sqrt(m^*n)$, where n is the number of input neurons and m is the number of output neurons. If Hidden_Node_Ratio is equal to 2, the number of hidden node is equal to $2 * sqrt(m^*n)$. By default, Hidden_Node_ratio is equal to 4.
- Sample_Size is the upper limit of the number of cases used for training. The default value is 10000.

DMX Queries

The Microsoft Neural Network supports all the tasks that Microsoft Decision Trees can do, including classification, regression and association. The first two tasks are the most common ones for the neural network, while the association task may be too time- and resource-consuming; hence, using the neural network is generally not recommended. The support of association task of Neural Network was removed after beta 2. The DMX statements for decision trees and neural networks are the same in terms of model creation, training, and prediction. The only differences are the algorithm name and parameter settings.

The following is a model creation statement to predict HouseOwnership using the Microsoft Neural Network algorithm:

```
Create Mining Model HouseOwnershipPrediction(
     Customer_Id long key,
     Gender text discrete,
     Marital_Status text discrete,
     Income long continuous,
     Age long continuous,
     Education text discrete,
     HouseOwnership text discrete predict
)
Using Microsoft_Neural_Network
```

For regression-type models, you don't need to specify columns with regressor content type as you do in the Microsoft Decision Trees algorithm. All the input values are mapped to numbers and used as regressors; regression is a built-in feature of neural networks.

```
Create Mining Model IncomePrediction(
     Customer_Id long key,
     Gender text discrete,
     Marital_Status text discrete,
     Age long continuous,
     Education text discrete,
     HouseOwnership text discrete,
     Income long continuous predict
)
Using Microsoft_Neural_Network
```

You can also include a nested table in a neural network algorithm. For example, the following model predicts Income based on the customer demographic data as well as the items in the customer's shopping cart:

```
Create Mining Model IncomePrediction(
     Customer_Id long key,
     Gender text discrete,
     Marital_Status text discrete,
     Age long continuous,
     Education text discrete,
     HouseOwnership text discrete predict,
     Income long continuous predict,
     Purchase table (
        ProductName text key
     )
)
Using Microsoft_Neural_Network
```

As you have already learned, the training statement is independent of the algorithm type. The following is the training statement for HouseOwnershipPrediction model:

```
Insert Into HouseOwnershipPrediction
(Customer_Id, Gender, Marital_Status, Income, Age, Education,
HouseOwnership)
Openrowset('Microsoft.Jet.OLEDB.4.0', 'Data
Source=C:\data\Customer.mdb;', 'Select Customer_Id, Gender,
Marital_Status, Income, Age, Education, HouseOwnership From Customer'
)
```

Once a model is trained, you can execute prediction queries against it. There are no prediction functions specifically for neural network. You can use those algorithms independent of prediction functions such as `Predict` and `PredictProbability`.

The following query returns three columns, the `customer id`, the predicted `Houseownership` and the probability of the prediction.

```
SELECT T1.Customer_ID, HouseOwnershipPrediction.HouseOwnership,
PredictProbability(HouseOwnership)
FROM HouseOwnershipPrediction
    PREDICTION JOIN
    OPENROWSET('Microsoft.Jet.OLEDB.4.0', 'Data
Source=C:\data\Customer.mdb;',
    'SELECT Customer_Id, Gender, Marital_Status, Income, Age, Education
From Customer') As T1
ON HouseOwnershipPrediction.Gender = T1.Gender AND
HouseOwnershipPrediction.Marital_Status = T1.Marital_Status AND
HouseOwnershipPrediction.Age = T1.Age AND
HouseOwnershipPrediction. Education = T1. Education AND
HouseOwnershipPrediction.Income = T1.Income
```

Model Content

A neural network model has one or more subnets. The model content describes the topologies of these subnets. It also stores the weights of each edge of the neural network.

Figure 10.6 displays the layout of the neural network model's content. The root node contains a set of child nodes with one special child representing the input layer node. Each input neuron in a neural network is a child of the input layer node.

Apart from the input layer node and marginal statistics node, the root node contains a set of subnet nodes. Each subnet node represents a neural network associated with one or more predictable attributes. If the model contains only one predictable attribute, there is only one subnet in the content.

Each subnet has two children: one for the hidden layer and one for the output layer. Each hidden node is a child of the hidden layer. It has incoming edges from input nodes. These input node IDs, and their associated weights are stored in the hidden node distribution rowsets. Each row in the distribution rowsets stores one weight. For example, to represent the weight of the edge from input node i (Gender = Male) to the hidden node h, there is a row in the distribution rowsets of h where Attribute name = i and Attribute Value = weight ih. Each output node is a child of the output layer. It has incoming edges from hidden nodes. These hidden node IDs and their associated weights are stored in the output node distribution rowsets.

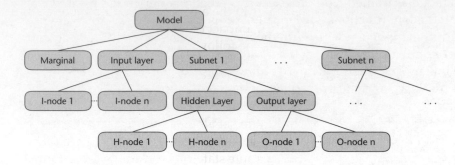

Figure 10.6   Content of the Neural Network model

The marginal statistics node contains the marginal distributions of all the attributes in the model. For discrete attributes, it lists the support for each state. For continuous attributes, it lists the mean and standard deviations.

Interpreting the Model

After your neural network model is processed, you can browse its contents using the Neural Network viewer. The Neural Network viewer is different from other Microsoft data mining content viewers in the sense that it is mainly prediction-based. It does not display the information derived from the model content schema rowsets, and there is no graphical display of the layout of the trained neural network. The main purpose of the viewer is to display the impact of attribute/value pairs (AV) related to the predictable attribute.

Figure 10.7 is a snapshot of the Neural Network viewer. This is a single-tab viewer with three parts. The top-left part is the input grid, where you can specify the values of input attributes. When no input is specified in this grid, the viewer displays the information of all the input AVs related to the predictable states. The top-right part is for the output selection. You can select any two states of a predictable attribute using the drop-down list. For the continuous attribute, the drop-down list provides five ranges based on the mean and standard deviation.

The main part of the screen is the grid that displays the impact of attribute/value pairs related to the predictable states. For example, in Figure 10.8 you can say the most important AV that favors owning a house is the age range between 38 and 54, and the most important AV that favors renting a house is age range between 11 and 28.

The Neural Network viewer is similar to the attribute discrimination tab of the Naïve Bayes viewer. It evaluates the impact of each AV related to the predictable states, and then sorts based on the following score:

Score = P(AV |Predictable_State_1)/ P(AV|Predictable_State_2)

The neural network can quickly calculate P(Predictable_State|AV). The method used to get this probability to set all the other input attributes as missing, and the AV as the only input neuron; the neural network then calculates the probability of a predictable attribute state. Since we have the marginal states of P(Predictable State 1), P(Predictable State 2), and P(AV). We can derive P(AV | Predictable State 1) using the Bayes rule.

P(AV | Predictable State 1) = P(Predictable State 1 |AV) * P(AV) / P(Predictable State 1)

NOTE The scores shown in the bars' tooltip are slightly different from the scores described here. The scores are applied to the log scale, and also normalized based on all the AV scores. The grid displays only the top 50 AVs and their scores.

Also note that Microsoft Neural Network doesn't return the score of P(Predictable_State|AV), **instead, it returns the** *score* P(Predictable_State|(AV, all other states missing))**).**

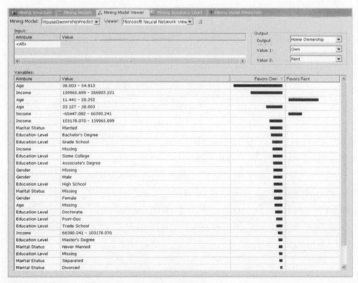

Figure 10.7 Neural Network viewer

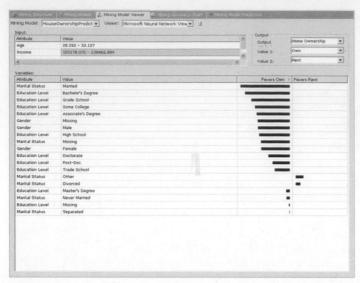

Figure 10.8 Specifying input attributes in the Neural Network viewer

You can also specify multiple AVs as input. For example, in Figure 10.8, the user specifies the Age to be [28.252, 33.127], and income to be [103178.070 – 139965.000]. In this case, the viewer displays the impacts of AVs of other attributes related to Houseownership, given the two other input AV pairs. The neural network calculates P(Predictable_State|AV) by fixing the neuron for Age to be in [28.252, 33.127], and the neuron for income to be [103178.070 – 139965.000]. The rest of the calculation is the same as we described previously.

Summary

In this chapter, we gave you an overview of the Microsoft Neural Network algorithm and its main uses: classification and regression. You have learned the basic concepts of a neural network and how its training process works. We explained the advantages and disadvantages of neural network versus other algorithms. This is a nonlinear algorithm that is able to discover complex patterns that decision trees and Naïve Bayes may miss. We recommend that you start with the decision tree algorithm because it is simpler to interpret the patterns than it is to interpret the output from the Microsoft Neural Network; try a neural network only when the accuracy of other algorithms is not satisfactory.

You should now be able to build mining models using the Microsoft Neural Network algorithm.

Mining OLAP Cubes

You may have already heard of or even have experience with Online Analytical Processing (OLAP). E. F. Codd, the originator of the relational data model, wrote a white paper in 1994 that introduced the term *Online Analytical Processing* into the lexicon of database users. OLAP is the current term for systems that were formerly called decision-support systems (DSS) or multiple dimensional databases.

OLAP plays an important role in today's business intelligence (BI) market. An OLAP database contains a number of cubes, similar to the way a relational database contains a number of tables. A cube has a set of well-defined dimensions and measures. Each dimension has one or more hierarchies. For example, a typical sales cube of a supermarket contains dimensions such as Customer, Product, Time, and Store. The Customer dimension contains a geographic hierarchy Country-State-City. The cube also contains measures such as Unit Sales, Store Sales, Profit, and Cost.

OLAP and data mining are two complementary technologies for BI. Large cubes often have millions of members in some dimensions, and fact tables can contain billions of transaction records. Finding useful information in such a large cube is challenging. There is definitely a requirement to apply data mining techniques to dig for patterns from these cubes.

In this chapter, you will learn about:

- The principles of OLAP
- The relationship between OLAP and data mining
- How to apply data mining on OLAP cubes

We will present a few sample models demonstrating some popular scenarios. You will learn how to create OLAP mining models both through SQL Server 2005 UI tools and through programming using Analysis Services Management Object Model (AMO).

Introducing OLAP

OLAP is used for decision support systems to analyze aggregated information for sales, finance, budget, and many other types of applications; while Online Transaction Processing (OLTP) is mainly used to record transactions of daily operations such as updating an account balance for a bank transaction.

OLTP database schema are not organized in a manner that can easily provide the summarized information required by managers at different levels of an organization. Managers need aggregated data from which they can view reports and analyze the trends. They need to know the key indications that affect their business success in order to make critical decisions. They need to find how their enterprise's workload is affected by seasonal and yearly trends so that they can plan and optimize resources.

The OLTP system is not designed for this kind of decision-support query for two reasons. The first is performance. Getting the summarized information requires querying a large amount of transaction data with joins among many different dimension tables. These queries may take hours for a relational database system to compute; meanwhile, the OLTP system has heavy operational duties. The second reason is the schema. The database schema in the OLTP system is not designed to answer decision-support questions. Extensive numbers of joins among OLTP tables are required to generate the reports the managers need.

An OLAP cube is built for decision-support queries. A cube is a multidimensional database. A typical cube contains a set of well-defined dimensions such as Customer, Product, Store, and Time. Each dimension contains many members. For example, each product and each product category is a member of the Product dimension. Dimension members are organized in hierarchies. For example, the hierarchy in the product dimension is All Products ⇨ Category ⇨ SubCategory ⇨ Product Name. You can query aggregated values on different levels of a hierarchy.

A cube has a set of measures such as Store Sales and Unit Sales. Measures come from a transaction table (fact table), where details of each transaction are stored. These measures are preaggregated (or partially preaggregated) based on the dimension hierarchies. For example, the store sales of beverage products in 2005 in all the stores in Washington state is calculated during the cube-processing stage. When a user queries this information, the result can be retrieved very fast thanks to the precalculation and the multidimensional index structure.

In summary, OLAP is about aggregating measures based on dimension hierarchies and storing these precalculated aggregations in a special data structure. With the help of preaggregations and special indexes, you can query aggregated data and get decision-support query results back in real time, which had to be done in batches and offline mode traditionally.

Microsoft OLAP Services was initially introduced in SQL Server 7.0 and largely enhanced in SQL Server 2000 and SQL Server 2005. In this section, we go over the key OLAP concepts, using the FoodMart Sales cube as an example. The Sales cube contains sales data of an imaginary supermarket chain FoodMart that specializes in food products. The data is shipped as an Analysis Services sample database since SQL Server 7.0.

For more detailed technical documents about OLAP, you can refer to SQL Server Books Online and OLAP-specific books.

Understanding Star and Snowflake Schema

A star schema is a database schema with a star shape. The heart of the schema is the fact table, which records the details of each transaction. The fact table contains a large amount of records, and it is the largest table in the database. Surrounding the fact table are a set of dimension tables, which describes the properties of each dimension. Figure 11.1 shows the star schema of the Food-Mart retail store database. Sales_fact is the fact table that contains every sales transaction from all the FoodMart stores. Product, Customer, Time_by_day, Store, and Promotion are all dimension tables. The fact table is fully normalized. It links to the dimension tables through foreign keys. In addition to foreign keys, a fact table contains a set of numeric columns, which are the measures. A star schema is a typical schema in a database warehouse.

Sometimes a dimension table is partially normalized. For example, in the customer table there is an Education attribute, which contains the educational level of a customer, such as Bachelors, Masters, and so on. To normalize this attribute, you can create a separate Education table that contains two columns: Education_id and Description. The Education attribute in the customer table is changed to Education_id, which is a foreign key from Education table. Education becomes a lookup table for the Education_id attribute of Customer table. Similarly, you can create more lookup tables for other attributes in the dimension table. We call the snowflake shape formed by these relationships a schema. Star schemas can be considered special kinds of snowflake schemas, where there is no lookup table. Both star schema and snowflake schema are popular schemas in data warehouse design.

Understanding Dimension and Hierarchy

Each cube contains a number of dimensions. The Sales cube in FoodMart contains five dimensions: Product, Customer, Time, Store, and Promotion. A dimension has dimension members. Each dimension member is a uniquely identifiable unit within a dimension. For example, each customer is identified by `Customer_id` in the Customer dimension. `Customer_id` is the dimension key. A dimension may contain a large number of members. For example, the FoodMart supermarket may have millions of customers.

A dimension member has a set of attributes. In the Customer dimension, a member has attributes such as gender, education, state, city, country, and so on. Each column in the dimension table could be a member attribute.

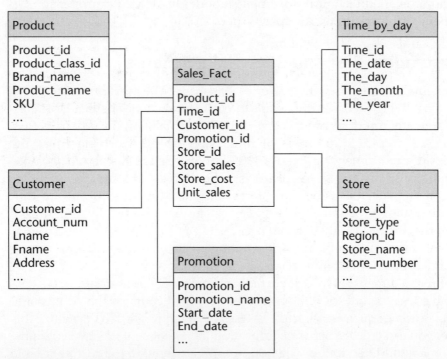

Figure 11.1   Star Schema of the FoodMart database

Attributes may contain relationships among them. For example, a country has a number of states; a state has a number of cities. These relationships form hierarchies, as displayed in Figure 11.2.

Each hierarchy has a name. The hierarchy in Figure 11.2 is named Geo in the Customer dimension. Country, State, City, and Name are the levels of the hierarchy. USA is a member in the Country level. CA, ID, and WA are members in the State level. The lowest level in the Geo hierarchy is Name. Each customer is a member in the Name level. Hierarchy is a very important concept in OLAP. The hierarchy level is the basic unit of aggregation. Users can query aggregated data at different levels of the hierarchy, for example, to obtain the total beverage sales in Washington state.

The Geo hierarchy is a natural hierarchy; the relationships among levels exist naturally. You can also define an attribute hierarchy without having a natural relationship. For example, you can build a hierarchy Gender ⇨ Education ⇨ Name. Based on this hierarchy, the customers are separated first by their gender, then by their educational level. You can query aggregated data about store sales of male customer with bachelor's degree based on this hierarchy.

Analysis Services allows each dimension to have multiple hierarchies.

Understanding Measures and Measure Groups

Measures are the numeric values to be aggregated by the cube. They are based on the numeric columns of the fact table. There are three measure columns in Sales_Fact: Store_Sales, Unit_Sales, and Store_Cost. Measures are the numeric data of primary interest to end users browsing a cube. Each measure specifies an aggregate function that determines how values in the measure's source column are aggregated. This function also determines how measured values for sibling members are aggregated to produce a value for their parent. The aggregation functions include Sum, Min, Max, Average, Distinct Count, and so on.

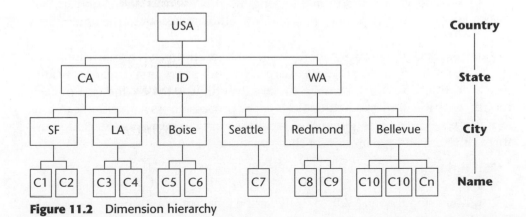

Figure 11.2 Dimension hierarchy

A cube contains a special type of dimension that contains a member for each measure. This dimension is called the *Measure dimension*. The Measure dimension doesn't contain hierarchies. It is always flat with one level. While browsing the cube, you can slice by a member in the Measures dimension to display values for the selected measure; you can also place the Measures dimension on an axis to view all the measures of the cube.

The fact table stores the value of each measure of each individual transaction. Before SQL Server 2005, each cube could have only one fact table. In SQL Server 2005, a cube can actually have multiple fact tables. For example, a cube can store both the information about sales and about inventory, with one sales fact table and one inventory fact table. Due to this enhancement, the fact table is renamed to the measure group. A cube may have multiple measure groups.

Understanding Cube Processing and Storage

A cube contains a set of dimensions and measures. There are two steps to processing a cube: dimension processing (if a dimension hasn't been processed previously) and cube processing. Dimension processing reads dimension data from underlying dimension tables, builds the dimension structure, creates hierarchies, and assigns members to proper levels of the hierarchy. After all the dimensions are processed, cube processing can be started.

The main task of cube processing is to precalculated aggregations based on the dimension hierarchies. When there are many dimensions and each dimension contains several levels and many members, the total number of aggregations could be exponential. One of the challenges of cube processing is to choose the optimal number of aggregations to precalculate. Other aggregated values can be derived from those precalculated measures efficiently. For example, if the monthly Store_Sales values are preaggregated, quarterly and yearly Store_Sales values can be derived easily.

Both dimension processing and cube processing have the options of *full processing* and *incremental processing*. During the processing stage, Analysis Services also builds bitmap indexes that allow efficient access to the aggregated cells.

Analysis Services allows cube to be separated into different partitions. For example, for the FoodMart Sales cube, each month's fact data can be separated into a partition. Partitions can be processed individually. By the end of each month, only the newest partition needs to be processed. As a partition can contain huge amount of aggregations, Analysis Services provides the following three different storage modes for these partitions:

Multidimensional OLAP (MOLAP): The data of a partition is stored in the special format of Analysis Services, which allows efficient retrieval of multidimensional data. MOLAP is by far the most common storage format.

Relational OLAP (ROLAP): All data is stored in RDBMS. Additional tables are created to store precalculated aggregations. ROLAP has the advantage of scalability as compared to the MOLAP structure. However, the performance of ROLAP is less than optimal.

Hybrid OLAP (HOLAP): The HOLAP partition stores the fact table in RDBMS while all the aggregations are stored in the special format of Analysis Services, just like MOLAP. When your query requires aggregated data, Analysis Services can return these aggregations efficiently because they are stored in its special format. When your query requires atomic-level facts, Analysis Services generates SQL to query the fact table in RDBMS.

Using Proactive Caching

The OLAP server is an efficient counting engine that calculates all the aggregations based on the dimension definitions. A cube can be considered simply as a cache that stores precalculated aggregations. MOLAP is the most popular storage mode as it has a special structure that is optimized for search. MOLAP has good performance, but it requires the cube to be processed. This is in conflict with the real-time concept. A ROLAP cube, on the other hand, directly queries the relational data source. It lets users immediately browse the most recent changes in a data source, but it can have significantly poorer performance than MOLAP storage has.

You may have applications in which your users need to see recent data, but you want the performance advantages of MOLAP storage. The proactive caching feature introduced in Analysis Services 2005 can provide a balance between the enhanced performance of MOLAP storage and the immediacy of ROLAP storage.

With proactive caching, queries against an OLAP object are made against either ROLAP storage or MOLAP storage, depending on whether recent changes have occurred to the data. The query engine directs queries against source data in MOLAP storage until changes occur in the data source. After changes occur in a data source, cached MOLAP objects are dropped and querying switches to ROLAP storage while the MOLAP objects are rebuilt in cache. After the MOLAP objects are rebuilt and processed, queries are switched again to the MOLAP storage. The cache refresh can occur extremely quickly for a small partition.

Caching may also be used without dropping the current MOLAP objects. Queries then continue against the MOLAP objects while data is read into and processed in a new cache. This method provides better performance but may result in queries returning old data while the new cache is being built.

Proactive caching features simplify the process of managing data obsolescence. If a transaction occurs on the source database, such as the addition of a new dimension member or new fact transaction, the existing cache becomes obsolete. The proactive caching settings determine how frequently the multidimensional cache is rebuilt, whether the outdated MOLAP storage is queried while the cache is rebuilt, and whether the cache is rebuilt on a schedule or based on changes in the database.

Querying a Cube

Once a cube is processed, you can query the cube to retrieve aggregated information. OLE DB for OLAP has defined a query language for querying OLAP cubes. The language is called MDX, which stands for MultiDimensional Expressions. MDX is similar to SQL in the sense that it follows the `Select . . . From . . . Where` framework. But MDX is not an extension of SQL and its syntax is much more complicated than standard SQL's syntax is. SQL only deals with two-dimensional data, while MDX allows for querying data with almost any number of dimensions. In SQL, the `Select` clause is used to define the column layout for a query, and the `Where` clause is used to define the row layout. However, in MDX the `Select` clause can be used to define several axis dimensions, while the `Where` clause is used to restrict multidimensional data to a specific dimension or member. MDX has also defined hundreds of functions, which helps users specify dimension navigations and calculations. The detailed syntax of MDX can be found in SQL Server Books online. The following is a simple example of MDX query to retrieve the total Unit Sales and Store Sales of beverage products:

```
Select
    {Measures.[Unit Sales], Measures.[Store Sales]} on columns,
     {Store.[Store Name].members} on rows
From Sales
Where Product.[All Products].Drink.Beverages
```

The result of this MDX query is shown in Table 11.1.

Table 11.1 Results of MDX Query to Retrieve Beverage Product Sales

	UNIT SALES	STORE SALES
Store 1	2085	4018.15
Store 2	3898	8002.32
Store 3	3985	8123.68

Performing Calculations

A cube stores aggregated information. The aggregated values are based on the measures in the measure group. The most common arithmetic operator is sum. However, other type of arithmetic functions may be applied on measures as well, for example, min, max, count, average, and so on.

A cube may also contain *calculated measures*, measures that are derived from other basic measures. For example, you can create a calculated measure Profit based on Store Sales and Store Cost using the following MDX expression:

```
Profit = [Store Sales] - [Store Cost]
```

From the user's point of view, Profit is just another measure similar to Store Sales and Store Cost. Calculated measures are evaluated during the query time, while other measures are aggregated during the cube processing stage.

Apart from calculated measures, you can also create calculated members for dimensions. Actually since a measure is a special kind of dimension, a calculated measure is a special type of calculated member. For example, the following query creates two calculated members 1st Half Sales and 2nd Half Sales in the time dimensions, and asks for the store sales for these two calculated members.

```
WITH
    MEMBER [Time].[1st Half Sales] AS 'Sum({[Time].[Q1], [Time].[Q2]})'
    MEMBER [Time].[2nd Half Sales] AS 'Sum({[Time].[Q3], [Time].[Q4]})'
SELECT
     {[Time].[1st Half Sales], [Time].[2nd Half Sales]} ON COLUMNS
FROM Sales
WHERE [Measures].[Store Sales]
```

A cell in a cube can also contain calculations. These cells are called *calculated cells*. With a calculated cell, you can define a MDX formula that can be used to supply a new value for each cell in a specific group of cells. These cells are evaluated during the query time by the MDX formula engine. For example, you can define the next year's new sales quota for the NorthWest region (a subcube) is the actual value multiplied by 120%. In AS 2005, the calculated cell feature is enhanced to use MDX Script. Users can use MDX statements to write calculation scripts and can even debug the calculations step by step.

Browsing a Cube

There a dozen OLAP client tools available in the market that allow the interactive querying of OLAP cubes and the generation of dynamic reports. These tools include three Microsoft Office family products which are Excel, Office Web Components (OWC), and Microsoft Data Analyzer, as well as many third-party OLAP client tools such as ProClarity and Panorama. These products provide more sophisticated browsers for visualizing the cube data either in numeric format or graphic format. Users can easily slice and dice the cube to generate reports with these tools. The following are a couple of screenshots using Excel to browse the Sales cube. Figure 11.3 analyzes store sales for females and males.

Figure 11.4 analyzes product sales during a Sale Days promotion.

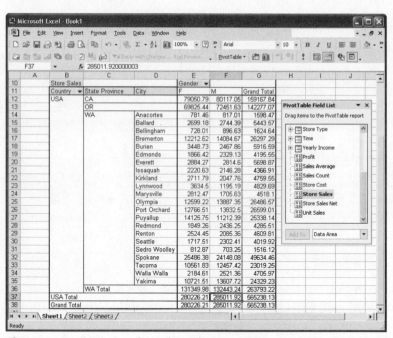

Figure 11.3 Browsing the Sales cube to analyze store sales for female and male customers

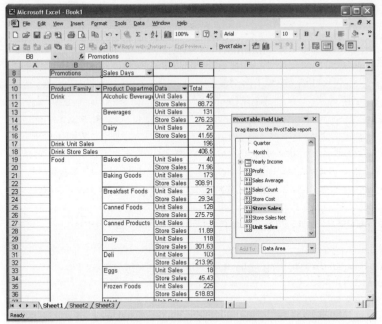

Figure 11.4   Browsing the Sales cube to analyze product sales during a Sale Days promotion

Understanding Unified Dimension Modeling

Unified Dimension Modeling (UDM) is a new concept introduced in AS 2005. Your data is stored in various data sources, for example, heterogeneous relational databases, text files, Excel, and OLAP cubes. Because the data models for relational and multidimensional data are different, you have to use different APIs to access these data types. UDM is designed to address this issue. It provides a bridge between the user and the data source and allows the user to define a single metadata model for dimensions and facts from various sources. Here are some key benefits of UDM:

- **Provides a standard model for all BI applications:** There are various types of BI components for enterprise applications, for example, data warehouse, OLAP, data mining, reporting, and so on. UDM provides a standard model that all these BI technologies can understand, and they all benefit from its richness. This reduces the number of data models in an enterprise. Figure 11.5 shows an example of UDM. The left side presents the contents of the UDM, including a few of measures and a set of dimensions. The right side shows those elements included in the current query.

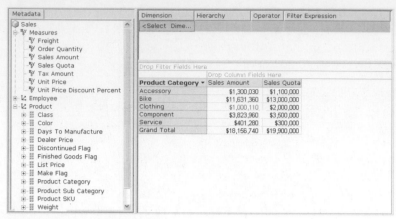

Figure 11.5 A simple UDM

- **Provides a rich data-modeling tool:** Dimensions contain hierarchies. For example, the Product dimension contains a hierarchy All Product ⇨ Product Category ⇨ Product SubCategory ⇨ Product SKU. You can perform analysis based on such hierarchies, first seeing totals by category, and then drilling down to subcategory and subsequently to the lowest SKU level. UDM allows the definition of such hierarchies. Each hierarchy is simply a sequence of attributes that can then be used in queries to ease such drill-down/drill-up scenarios. A dimension may contain multiple hierarchies. For example, the Time dimension contains two hierarchies: fiscal time and calendar time. Figure 11.6 shows an example of dimension modeling. The warehouse dimension contains a set of attributes and four hierarchies. The source table for this dimension has two tables: warehouse and warehouse class.

- **Provides high query performance:** A UDM may contain one or more cubes. In most cases, cube aggregations are preprocessed. This allows user queries to be executed rapidly.

- **Provide advanced analytics:** UDM not only provides simple aggregations, it also allows you to define advanced calculations based on the powerful MDX and DMX. In many cases, you want know more than just aggregations, for example, you want to know the three-month moving average for each time period, the year on year growth in each period, the sales and inventory forecast, and so on. With MDX and DMX, you can perform sophistic calculations on UDM.

- **Supports closing the loop:** UDM not only enables you to visualize information, it also allows you to act on the data. From the aggregated values, you can drill through the source data and make changes. In addition, it is possible to update summary numbers. For example, consider a budgeting scenario. While eventually the budgeted amount might be known down to a detailed level (for example, by team and account), on the way to that, values might only be known at a more summarized level (by department and account type).

Figure 11.7 shows the overall architecture of UDM. Consumer applications, most often BI applications, can access the Analysis Services UDM via the XML for Analysis protocol. The XML for Analysis commands embed the DMX, MDX, or SQL queries. UDM gets these queries, and depending on the query type and data the UDM contains, it executes the query directly against itself or forwards it to other sources such as an RDBMS or text files. The result is mapped back in an XML rowset format to client application. In this way, various client applications can use the same API to query the same data model and get back either relational or multidimensional query results.

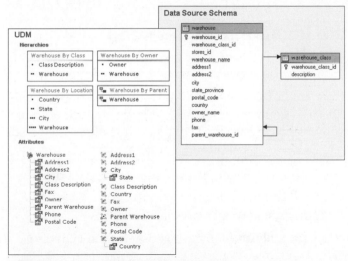

Figure 11.6 UDM dimension example

IS UDM JUST A CUBE?

Is UDM a cube? The answer is no. UDM is a broader concept than cube. UDM is more about dimension modeling than aggregation. It integretes both relational and mutlidimensional technologies. You can think of a UDM as a combination of cubes and dimensions. You can create a UDM without actually building a cube. In this case, UDM will forward queries to the relational source during the query time, though the performance may not as fast as having a cube served as aggregation cache. It is also possible for a UDM to contain multiple cubes, though in most cases a UDM contains a single cube, which has one or more measure groups.

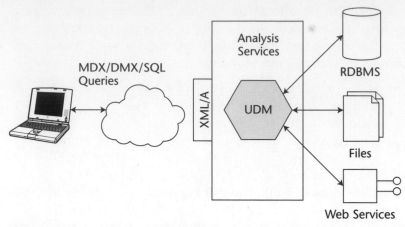

Figure 11.7   Architecture of UDM

Understanding the Relationship Between OLAP and Data Mining

Both OLAP and data mining are important analytical technologies in the business intelligence family. OLAP is good at aggregating of large amount of transaction data based on the dimension definitions. The typical questions answered by OLAP are:

- What is the total sales amount of beverage products in the past three months in the Northwest region?
- What are the top 10 products sold in all stores last month?
- What are the store sales for male and female customers, respectively?
- What is the daily sales difference during a promotional period versus a normal period?

The core technique of OLAP is aggregation calculation. An OLAP server is a special kind of database server that deals with multidimensional data. It has most of the challenges that RDBMS has, including indexing, querying, persistence, data caching, and so forth. However, due to its multidimensional nature, an OLAP server can't just simply apply relational technology without major enhancements. For example, OLAP indexing requires indexes based on multidimensional coordinates. It uses a specially designed data structure based on a bitmap index. MDX is more complicated than SQL is. It has many predefined functions for dimension navigation.

Data mining is good at finding the hidden patterns of a dataset by analyzing correlations among attribute values. As explained in Chapter 1, there are two kinds of data mining techniques: supervised and unsupervised. Supervised data mining requires the user to specify a target attribute and a set of input attributes. The typical supervised data mining algorithms include decision trees, Naïve Bayes, and neural networks. An unsupervised data mining technique doesn't have to have a predictable attribute. Clustering is a good example of unsupervised data mining. It groups heterogeneous data points into subgroups so that data points in each subgroup are more or less homogeneous.

The following are typical questions answered by data mining:

- What is the profile of customers who like to buy the newest model digital cameras?

- What are the products to recommend to this particular customer?

- What's the estimated sales amount for digital cameras in the next three months?

- How should I segment the customer base?

While most of OLAP techniques come from the database family, data mining techniques come from three academic fields: statistics, machine learning, and database technology.

One of the fundamental processes of data mining is to analyze correlations among attributes and their values. Statisticians have been working on this issue for centuries. These are many profound statistical theories that we can still apply today. Most data mining algorithms use more or less statistical techniques, such as Naïve Bayes and clustering.

Machine learning has introduced many new concepts for information discovery. Some of these can be applied to data mining. The most common ones are decision trees and neural networks. Other algorithms such as genetic algorithms and fuzzy logic are also included in some data mining packages.

While traditional statisticians don't pay too much attention to data volume, the database community knows how to deal with large amounts of data. For example, many popular association algorithms for analyzing product associations of large transaction tables were proposed by database researchers.

Data Mining Benefits of OLAP for Aggregated Data

Both OLAP and data mining are key members of the business intelligence technology family. They are complementary and can benefit from each other's characteristics to provide deep analysis. OLAP can help data mining tasks with the data transformation step thanks to its data aggregation engine. In many cases, patterns can be found only in aggregated data. It is difficult to discover patterns directly from the fact table. For example, analyzing the sales of snow tires at the city level can be challenging for many data mining algorithms, because there are too many cities. However, when data is aggregated to the state level, these algorithms may easily discover the pattern such as "the most important factor of sales of snow tires is region; people in Northeast are more likely to purchase snow tires."

TIP A large retail customer asked us to do a data mining project. They gave us a fact table with tens of millions of transactions from the past few years. Their dimension tables contained thousands of items and hundreds of stores. The business problem was to forecast weekly sales for each item at each store. With a relational database, it took about 1 hour for the computer to pull out related sales information about an item (imagine that there are thousands of items!). Using a cube, it took about three seconds to get the same information. If you have large amount of transaction data and your mining model requires aggregated data, you should consider using OLAP technologies for data transformation.

OLAP Needs Data Mining for Pattern Discovery

A cube is a well-structured database. There are often millions of members in a dimension and tens of millions of aggregated values in a cube. Like any relational database, a cube contains hidden patterns such as sales trends, product associations, customer segments, and so on. An OLAP cube needs data mining techniques to discover the inside information. The following is a list of typical business questions about OLAP cubes that require DM techniques:

- **Market basket analysis about products:** Market basket analysis of product associations is a frequent marketing problem. Store managers want to know which products sell together in order to do promotional cross-selling.

- **Customer segmentation:** Store managers also like to group customers into segments using customer demographic information as well as aggregated measures, for example, monthly spending at the store. Segmentation can be done on dimensions other than the customer. For example, the marketing department of a retail chain may want to cluster its stores based on store attributes and sales.

- **Customer classification:** Based on the customer attributes in the customer dimension and measures, it is possible to build a classification type mining model to analyze the customer information. For example, a store manager might want to know the profile of customers who are interested in applying for a golden membership card.

- **Sales trend analysis:** Based on historical product sales, a store manager might like to know projected future sales amounts. For example, what are the potential sales of all beverages in all stores in Washington state next month?

- **Target promotion:** Suppose that a store ordered a product — for example, a new kind of beer. The store manager wants to know which customers are most interested in buying this product. He can apply data mining techniques to discover the profile of customers who are interested in buying beer and send mailings to those people with similar profiles.

OLAP Mining versus Relational Mining

The fundamentals of OLAP mining and relational mining are the same. The OLAP mining model and relational mining model use the same set of data mining algorithms. The only difference is the mining column's binding. Instead of being bound to table columns, the mining columns are bound to dimension attributes, measures, and measure groups.

Because the OLAP cube contains precalculated aggregations, attributes bound to measures can be accessed very efficiently. This information can be derived from relational tables as well; however, this requires extra data transformation steps. In addition to aggregated data, dimensions contain hierarchies in a cube, which define relationships among attributes. This hierarchy information can be used during data mining processing for attribute roll-up.

In SQL Server 2000, mining models built on OLAP cubes used to have different structures and metadata than those built on relational tables. In SQL Server 2005, there is no difference between OLAP mining models and relational mining models. In this chapter, we use *OLAP mining model* to refer those mining models built upon OLAP cubes and *relational mining model* to refer those mining models built upon relational data tables.

The OLAP mining model often contains nested tables. The case table of an OLAP mining model is always one of the dimensions and nested tables always come from one of the fact tables using a another dimension attribute as the nested key.

Probably the best way to understand the OLAP mining model is to think in a relational way. Figure 11.8 provides a relational view of an OLAP mining model. The model analyzes customer segmentation based on customer profiles such as age, gender, the list of products they purchased and the associated quantity. Some mining model attributes come directly from relational tables (dimension tables) such as gender and age. Some attributes come from nested tables (the fact table) such as quantity (aggregated value of unit sales). Product Name is an attribute that comes indirectly from the Sales_fact table, by joining the Product dimension table through the lookup key (Product_id).

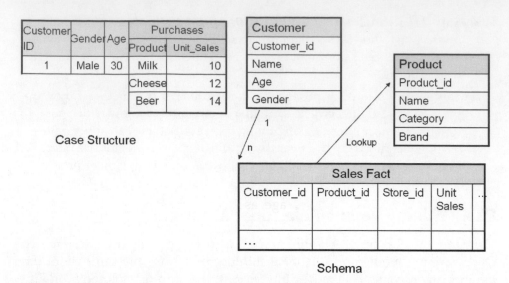

Figure 11.8 Relational view of an OLAP mining model

Building OLAP Mining Models Using Wizards and Editors

You have just learned about the basic concepts of OLAP, the relationship of OLAP and data mining, and a few business problems for which data mining techniques can be applied to OLAP cubes. In this section, you build a few typical mining models on a cube. The best tools for creating OLAP mining models are the Data Mining Wizard (DMW) and the Data Mining Editor. Note that you can only build an OLAP mining model based on a cube located in the same Analysis Services database.

Using the Data Mining Wizard

The Data Mining Wizard is a handy and powerful tool to help you build data mining models. There are two branches in the DMW based on the types of the data source, the relational branch and the multidimensional branch. In Chapter 2 we showed you how to build mining models using DMW on relational tables. Now, you will use the other half of the wizard to build a few OLAP mining models. The source cube is the Sales cube of FoodMart database, as described in the previous sections of the chapter.

Building the Customer Segmentation Model

The first model to build is about customer segmentation. You want to group customers based on their demographics (Occupation, Marital Status, Member Card, and so forth) as well as the total Store Sales for the segmentation. The demographics are dimension attributes, and Store Sales is a measure that contains the aggregated value of each transaction for each customer. In this model, the case 'table' is the Customer dimension and there is no nested table.

To invoke DMW, you simply use the context menu by right-clicking the Mining Model folder in the Solution Explorer window of BI Development Studio. Since the source data is a cube, you select the From existing cube option in the Select the Definition Method page, as illustrated in Figure 11.9.

After selecting the cube as data source, you also select Microsoft Clustering algorithm as the mining technique for this model.

The next step is to specify the case key. For the OLAP mining model, a case key is a dimension attribute, and the dimension that contains the case key is the Case dimension. The case key may or may not be a dimension key. For example, you can select Last Name as case key. You can even choose Gender as case key, ; as a result, you will have only two cases for the training data, Male and Female. In this example, as because you want to segment all customers, you choose Customer, the dimension key, as the case key (see Figure 11.10).

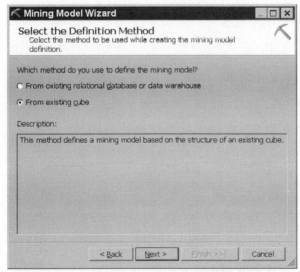

Figure 11.9   Select From existing cube as data source

Figure 11.10 Select the case key

After specifying the case key, the DMW asks you to select case-level attributes from a set of related attributes and measures, as displayed in Figure 11.11. In this case, you select `Member Card`, `Marital Status`, `Yearly Income`, `Occupation`, `Num Car Owned`, `Num Children At Home`, and a measure, `Store Cost`. Because a clustering algorithm doesn't require a predictable attribute, you specify all the selected columns as input in the Specify Mining Column Usage Wizard page.

By now, you have defined the mining model. All you need to do is name the model at the last page of the wizard and process the model.

CHOOSING DIMENSION PROPERTIES

In this example, you use the dimension key Customer as the case key. Since all the dimension properties have a 1-*n* relationship with the dimension key, you can choose any other properties as case-level attributes for the mining model.

It is possible for you to choose dimension properties other than dimension key as the case key, for example, City. In this case, your model will cluster cities based on the attributes you specified in the model. Most attributes in the Customer dimension, such as Gender and Occupation, don't have a 1-*n* relationship with City. It doesn't make sense to select these attributes to cluster City. However, if there is an attribute hierarchy, such as Country ⇨ State ⇨ City ⇨ Customer, you can select Country and State as input attributes to the cluster City. Country and State are both at a higher level in the hierarchy than the case key City is, and they have 1-*n* relationships to City. So, the wizard allows you to select Country and State after you specify City as the case key.

Figure 11.11   Select case-level attributes

NOTE You may have noticed that the number of training cases of an OLAP mining model is not exactly the same as the number of cases of a relational mining model built directly on the dimension table. This is because there is always an additional member, called Unknown, in an OLAP dimension. This also affects the prediction probability slightly.

Creating a Market Basket Model

Market basket analysis is a popular data mining task. In this example, you will do some market basket analysis of customer purchases in Washington state based on Sales cube. The algorithm to use for this task is Microsoft Association Rules.

Before starting to build the model, you need to define the basket and item. Since the model is for analyzing customer purchase behavior, the unit of a basket is a customer. A customer buys a set of products, and the purchase details are modeled as a nested table (as you learned in Chapter 9). In an OLAP mining model, a case table is mapped to a case dimension, and a nested table is mapped to a measured group dimension. The dimension, which serves as lookup table for the measure group, is called a nested dimension. In this example, the case dimension is the Customer dimension and the nested dimension is Product.

You use DMW to define the model. Similarly to the Customer Segmentation model in previous example, you choose Customer as the Case dimension and Customer attribute as the case key. You don't select any attribute other than the case key in the case level (You may select properties in the Customer dimension if needed). After selecting the case key, the mining structure is displayed in Figure 11.12.

Now, you add the nested table by clicking the Add Nested Table button shown in Figure 11.12. A pop-up wizard appears, as displayed in Figure 11.13. This pop-up wizard is used to add nested tables for the mining structure. In this example, your nested dimension is Product, and the nested key is the dimension key Product. You can also choose non-dimension-key attributes such as Brand to be the nested key; in this case, you would analyze the relationship among product brands, not individual products.

TIP If you are mining a cube with several measure groups, make sure that you select the key attribute from the appropriate measure group containing the relation you want. For instance, if `Product` appeared in a Sales measure group and an Inventory measure group, you would want to choose the nested key from the Product dimension in the Sales measure group to analyze sales.

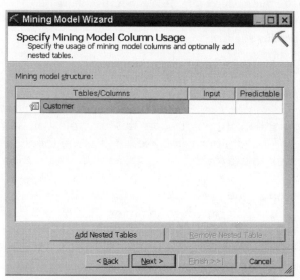

Figure 11.12   Specify mining model column usage

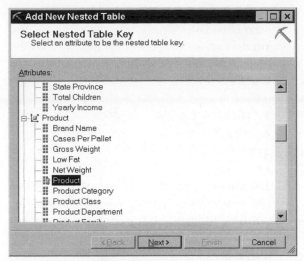

Figure 11.13 Adding the nested table key

Since this model is purely for analyzing the relationships among products, you don't need to include any other attributes in the nested table, neither do you need to add other nested tables. The mining structure is displayed in Figure 11.14. The nested table is named as the measure group by default, and the nested key for your model is Product. You specify the nested table as predictable.

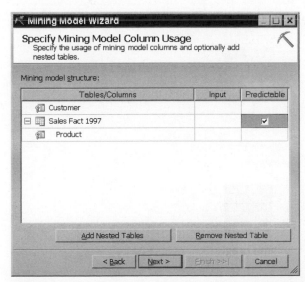

Figure 11.14 Mining structure for market basket analysis

When the mining structure is defined, the DMW asks you to slice the source cube if necessary. Your market basket model is for analyzing the cross-selling patterns in Washington. You use the cube slice to slice the customers based on the Country ➪ State ➪ City ➪ Customer hierarchy, and use the Filter expression drop-down list to select WA at the State level. (See Figure 11.15.) Now, the model definition is complete; you name the model in the last page of the wizard and process the model.

Creating a Sales Forecast Model

Forecasting is yet another important data mining task. A cube usually contains a time dimension. It is natural for cube users (those who consume cube information through queries and reports) to ask the outlook for cube measures, for example, how many bottles of red wine will be sold in Washington stores over the next three months? How much revenue can each store make over the next two years?

In this example, you build a mining model using Microsoft Time Series on the Sales cube. The objective of the model is to do monthly forecast about the Unit Sales, Store Sales, and Store Cost for each store.

Because the model is for forecasting sales for each store, the case dimension is Store. You choose the dimension key Store to be the case key as displayed in Figure 11.16.

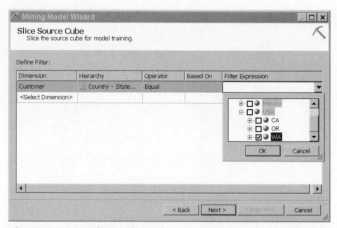

Figure 11.15   Slicing the cube

WORKING WITH TRANSACTIONS

The model just defined analyzes the products that customers tend to purchase together. If a customer bought a case of beer in March, and then purchased some diapers in September, this model considers beer and diapers to be correlated because no time constraints are specified. This sometimes doesn't satisfy the business requirements from the marketing department. There are two ways to address this issue. The first method is to use cube slices to limit the purchases to a given day. But you may miss some patterns, since your analysis is based on only one day. The second method is to add a transaction dimension on the cube so that each row in the fact table contains a transaction ID. You then specify the case dimension as `Transaction` and the nested dimension as `Product`. In this way, you analyze the purchase patterns within each transaction. If the same customer committed three transactions in the cube, these transactions are considered three independent cases.

Market basket analysis is not limited to customer purchases. You can model different business problems by specifying the correct sets of case and nest tables/dimensions. For example, if you want to analyze the series of stores in which a customer tend to shop, you can set `Customer` as case dimension and `Store` as nested dimension. If you want to analyze relationship among various promotions each store runs, you can set the `Store` as case dimension and `Promotion` as nested dimension.

Figure 11.16   Select Store as case key

You learned in Chapter 6 that there are different ways to model time series data. Since the case dimension Store doesn't contain time information, the time information is modeled in the nested table. Click the Add Nested Table button in the Mining Model Column Usage page, as displayed in Figure 11.17.

You select the Time by Day time dimension to be the nested dimension. Now you need to specify a dimension attribute to be the nested key. You can choose any time attribute, for example, Quarter. In this case, your model will give the quarterly forecast for each store. Since your forecast time unit is month, you specify the dimension attribute The Month as the nested key, which is modeled as the key time. (See Figure 11.18.)

In the Select Nested Table Columns page, shown in Figure 11.19, you select all the measures to be both input and predictable. As you learned in Chapter 6, one of the unique features of the Microsoft Time Series algorithm is cross-prediction among series. For example, if the previous month's Store Sales has a strong correlation with this month's Store Cost, the algorithm will discover this pattern and use Store Sales to forecast Store Cost.

Figure 11.17 Mining model columns

Figure 11.18   Specify The Month as nested table key

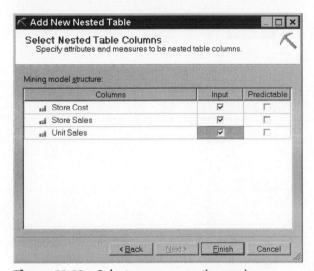

Figure 11.19   Select measures as time series

Figure 11.20 displays the mining structure for the forecasting model. The case key is `Store`, the nested key is `Month`, and the three measures are included in the nested table. There are two dozen stores in the Store dimension of the Sales cube, and each store has three selected measures. There is a total of 72 time series in this forecast model.

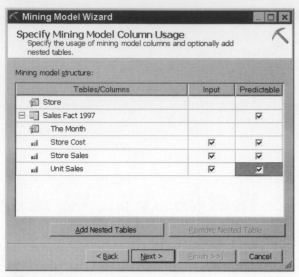

Figure 11.20   The mining structure for a time series

Before creating the forecasting model, you need to specify the time frame for the training data. A cube may contain many years of data, and you don't need to feed all the historical data for model training. Some data may be too old and won't have any impact on the forecast. Consider stock data, if a stock ticker has over 10 years of trading history, the initial 5 years of data is mostly likely useless for prediction. You can slice the cube on the time dimension, using only last two years data as displayed in Figure 11.21.

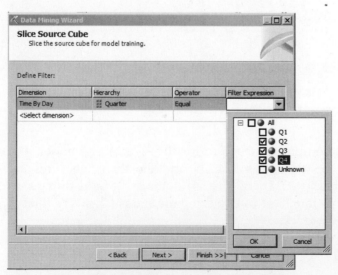

Figure 11.21   Slice the cube — specify time frame

TIP Most cubes have time dimensions. Most time dimensions contain members representing future time units. Slicing the cube on the time dimension is a necessary step for time series models. If you don't slice the time dimension, you will have future time members included in the training data. Since there are not yet values for these future members, by default, these null values are replaced with 0 for OLAP mining models during the processing. Without slicing the cube, the model you build is not the one you really want.

Using the Data Mining Editor

After defining the mining model in DMW, you find yourself in the Mining Model Editor. We explained how to build relational mining model using the Mining Model Editor in Chapter 3. Figure 11.22 displays the Mining Model Editor with the market basket model you just defined on the Sales cube. The editor is very similar to the Relational Mining Model Editor; the difference is in the Structure pane at right. It displays the OLAP cube in a relational way, similar to the right part of Figure 11.8. There are two "tables" for this model: the case table at the left represents the case dimension Customer, with all the Customer properties and a set of measures. The nested table at right represents the fact table. It has many more attributes than just original fact table. The original fact table contains a set of foreign keys and measures. The nested table in the editor displays all the dimension attributes under the dimension keys and the set of measures. You can add these dimension attributes to the nested table of your mining structure.

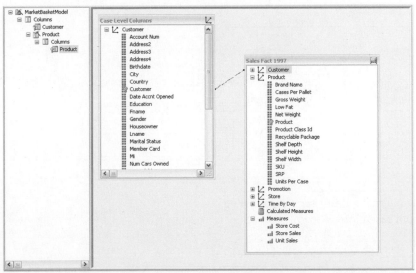

Figure 11.22   Data mining editor for the OLAP mining model

Understanding Data Mining Dimensions

You may have noticed on the last page of DMW, there is an option to create a data mining dimension. So, what is a data mining dimension?

We discussed the Model_Content schema rowset in Chapter 2. After processing a model, the pattern discovered by the algorithm is persisted in the Model_Content schema rowset. In a decision tree model, each tree node is stored as a row in this schema rowset; in a clustering model, each cluster is a row in this schema rowset. The Model_Content schema rowset is like a parent-child dimension, where each node has a parent node.

If you ask to create a data mining dimension in the DMW, after processing the mining model, Analysis Services creates a new dimension based on the mining model content. For example, for a clustering model, the data mining dimension has to levels, the *All* level and individual cluster levels. For a decision tree model, the dimension hierarchy structure is the tree-shaped. Meanwhile, the server creates an internal index structure, which maps each individual case in the case dimension to the members in the data mining dimension, as illustrated in Figure 11.23.

In the last page of DMW, you can also ask the server to create a new cube that contains the set of existing dimensions in the source cube plus the data mining dimension. You can browse the new cube by slicing and pivoting the data mining dimension.

Not all Microsoft data mining algorithms support data mining dimensions. For example, it doesn't make business sense to create a data mining dimension for time series model. Three algorithms currently support this feature: Microsoft Clustering, Microsoft Decision Trees, and Microsoft Association Rules.

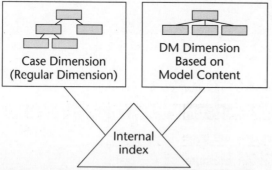

Figure 11.23 Internal indexes for a data mining dimension and a case dimension

INTERPRETING MEMBERS OF A DATA MINING DIMENSION

The interpretation of the members of a data mining dimension depends on the algorithm the source model uses.

For clustering, the members of the dimension represent each cluster, so slicing by the dimension restricts the output to cases in each cluster.

For decision trees, the dimension members represent the tree nodes, so slicing by the dimension divides your data by the rules that are most important in determining the target variable of the model.

For association rules, the dimension members represent the size 1 itemsets found in the model. Slicing by this type of data mining dimension allows you to determine sales and profit figures from *baskets* containing a particular item as opposed to the sales and profits of that item alone.

The following is a special type of DMX query designed for the data mining dimension feature:

```
Select * from myModel.dimension_Content
```

The query result is similar to the query Select * from myModel.content. However, it has only a subset of content columns, for example, the distribution chapter is not included, and the content may be modified to more appropriately map to an OLAP dimension. The query result represents the parent-child structure of the data mining dimension. For example, for a clustering model with 10 clusters, the query contains 11 rows: 1 for the model root and 10 for each individual cluster. The root node is the parent of the 10 individual cluster nodes. When creating a data mining dimension based on this cluster model, the new dimension contains a parent-child hierarchy: All and Node_Unique_Name. The All level represents all clusters in which Node_Unique_Name represents individual cluster.

Table 11.2 shows the list of columns returned by the model.dimension_content query and the usage of each column in the data mining dimension.

Table 11.2   Columns Returned by the model.dimension_content Query

COLUMNS	FUNCTION IN DM DIMENSION
ATTRIBUTE_NAME	Dimension attributes
NODE_NAME	Dimension attributes
NODE_UNIQUE_NAME	Dimension key attribute
NODE_TYPE	Dimension attributes

(continued)

Table 11.2   *(continued)*

COLUMNS	FUNCTION IN DM DIMENSION
NODE_CAPTION	`CaptionColumn` for key attribute
CHILDREN_CARDINALITY	Dimension attributes
PARENT_UNIQUE_NAME	`RelatedAttribute` for key attribute (`ParentAttribute` in parent-child hierarchy)
NODE_DESCRIPTION	Dimension attributes
NODE_RULE	Dimension attributes
MARGINAL_RULE	Dimension attributes
NODE_PROBABILITY	Dimension attributes
MARGINAL_PROBABILITY	Dimension attributes
NODE_SUPPORT	Dimension attributes

TIP   After you create a DM dimension based on customer segmentation model, the new dimension doesn't contain each customer as a dimension member. This is so because the data mining dimension is purely based on model content and doesn't drill though to the individual training cases.

However, the internal index maps the relationship of the content node and training cases. You can still find the customers for each cluster and their related measures by slicing the cube based on the DM dimension.

Using MDX inside DMX Queries

DMX is the SQL language for data mining. We have shown you many examples throughout the book. Up to now, all DMX prediction query examples you have seen have been prediction join statements with a trained mining model and a relational SQL query.

In SQL Server 2005, DMX is much enhanced and supports prediction join statements with a MDX query. When embedded inside a DMX query, the MDX query returns rowsets instead of a multidimensional cellset. The rowsets may be nested, depending on the query.

The mining model is not required to be an OLAP mining model. It is possible to prediction join a relational mining model with a MDX query, as long as your query specifies the mapping between the mining model columns and the columns returned by your MDX query.

The following statement returns the cluster ID for each member in the Customer dimension. The prediction is based on three member properties (`Occupation`, `HouseOwner`, `Member Card`) and one measure, `Store Sales`.

```
Select
  t.Customer, Cluster()
From
  [CustomerSegmentations]
PREDICTION JOIN

(with member measures.Occupation as Customer.Customer.Properties("Occupation")
member measures.HouseOwner as Customer.Customer.Properties("HouseOwner")
member measures.[Member Card] as Customer.Customer.Properties("Member Card")
Select { Measures.Occupation, Measures.HouseOwner, Measures.[Member Card],
Measures.[Store Sales] } on columns,
customer.customer.customer.members on rows
from [FoodMart 2000] ) as t

on
[CustomerSegmentations].Occupation = t.[[Measures]].[Occupation]]]
And [CustomerSegmentations].Houseowner = t.[[Measures]].[HouseOwner]]]
and [CustomerSegmentations].[Member Card] = t.[[Measures]].[Member Card]]]
and [CustomerSegmentations].[Store Sales] = t.[[Measures]].[Store Sales]]]
```

Using Analysis Management Objects for the OLAP Mining Model

In Chapter 14, you learn to program with Analysis Management Objects (AMO). There, we show you the code examples for creating mining models on relational tables. In this section, you learn how to create a mining model based on a cube using AMO. You may want read Chapter 14 and then revisit this section after learning the basics of AMO.

In SQL Server 2000, relational mining models and OLAP mining models are two different types of objects. In SQL server 2005, we no longer need this object. We still use the term OLAP mining model as a short notion to indicate that the mining model is created and processed based on a cube. Mining models defined based on a relational source and a multidimensional source have the same structure and metadata. The only difference is the way the models are bound to data and processed. In fact, a model created and processed with relational tables can be reprocessed with new bindings to a cube.

To create a mining model based on the cube, you need to define bindings to cube attributes, measures, and fact tables. In this section, we show you some sample code for defining mining structure columns based on cube attributes and measures.

The following procedure `CreateMiningStructureColumn` creates a `ScalarMiningStructureColumn` based on a dimension attribute. It has two parameters: a dimension attribute and a Boolean indicating whether the column is a key column.

```
public static ScalarMiningStructureColumn
CreateMiningStructureColumn(CubeAttribute attribute, bool isKey)
{
  ScalarMiningStructureColumn column = new ScalarMiningStructureColumn();
  column.Name = attribute.Attribute.Name;
  //cube attribute is usually modeled as discrete except for key column
column.Content = (isKey ? MiningStructureColumnContents.Key :
MiningStructureColumnContents.Discrete);
  column.IsKey = isKey;
  //bind column source to a cube dimension attribute
  column.Source = new CubeAttributeBinding(attribute.ParentCube.ID,
                    ((CubeDimension)attribute.Parent).ID,
attribute.Attribute.ID,
                    AttributeBindingType.Name);
  //Get the column data type from the attribute key column binding.
column.Type = MiningStructureColumnnTypes.GetColumnType
(attribute.Attribute.NameColumn.DataType);
   return column;
 }
```

Besides dimension attributes, an OLAP mining model may have measures as input columns. The following procedure `CreateMiningStructure-Column` has one parameter: a cube measure. It creates a mining structure column and binds it to a cube measure.

```
public static ScalarMiningStructureColumn CreateMiningStructureColumn(Measure
measure)
{
 ScalarMiningStructureColumn column = new ScalarMiningStructureColumn();
 column.Name = measure.Name;
 //Set the content type to continuous for measures.
 column.Content = MiningStructureColumnContents.Continuous;
 column.Source = new MeasureBinding(measure.ID);
 column.Type =
     MiningStructureColumnTypes.GetColumnType(measure.Source.DataType);
 return column;
}
```

Using the previous two procedures based on AMO, you can create the Customer Segmentation model of the previous section programmatically. In Listing 11.1, the procedure `CreateProcessSegmentationModel` creates a mining structure and clustering mining model based on two dimension attributes: `Member Card` and `Total Children` and one measure `Store Sales` of the FoodMart cube.

```
Public void CreateProcessSegmentationModel()
{
 //connecting the server and database
 Server myServer = new Server();
 myServer.Connect("DataSource=localhost;Catalog=FoodMart");
 Database myDatabase = myServer.Databases["FoodMart"];
 Cube myCube = myDatabase.Cubes["FoodMart 2000"];
 CubeDimension myDimension = myCube.Dimensions["Customer"];
 MiningStructure myMiningStructure =
myDatabase.MiningStructures.Add("CustomerSegment","CustomerSegement");
 //Bind the mining structure to a cube.
 myMiningStructure.Source = new CubeDimensionBinding(".",
                    myCube.ID, myDimension.ID);

 // Create the key column.
 CubeAttribute customerKey =
myCube.Dimensions["Customer"].Attributes["Customer"];
 ScalarMiningStructureColumn keyStructureColumn =
Utilities.CreateMiningModelColumn(customerKey, true);
 myMiningStructure.Columns.Add(keyStructureColumn);

//Member Card attribute
 CubeAttribute memberCard =
myCube.Dimensions["Customer"].Attributes["Member Card"];
 ScalarMiningStructureColumn memberCardStructureColumn =
Utilities.CreateMiningModelColumn(memberCard, false);
 myMiningStructure.Columns.Add(memberCardStructureColumn);

//Total Children attribute
 CubeAttribute totalChildren =
myCube.Dimensions["Customer"].Attributes["Total Children"];
 ScalarMiningStructureColumn totalChildrenStructureColumn =
Utilities.CreateMiningModelColumn(totalChildren, false);
 myMiningStructure.Columns.Add(totalChildrenStructureColumn);

//Store Sales measure
 Measure storeSales = myCube.MeasureGroups[0].Measures["Store Sales"];
 ScalarMiningStructureColumn storeSalesStructureColumn =
Utilities.CreateMiningModelColumn(storeSales);
 myMiningStructure.Columns.Add(storeSalesStructureColumn);

 //Create a mining model from the mining structure. By default, all the
 //structure columns are used. Nonkey columns are with usage input
 MiningModel myMiningModel = myMiningStructure.CreateMiningModel(true,
"CustomerSegment");
 //Set the algorithm to be clustering.
 myMiningModel.Algorithm = MiningModelAlgorithms.MicrosoftClustering;
```

Listing 11.1 CreateProcessSegmentationModel creates a mining structure and clustering mining model based on two dimension attributes. *(continued)*

```
//Process structure and model
try
{
  myMiningStructure.Update(UpdateOptions.ExpandFull);
  myMiningStructure.Process(ProcessType.ProcessFull);


}
catch (Microsoft.AnalysisServices.OperationException e)
{
  string err = e.Message;
}


}
```

Listing 11.1 *(continued)*

An OLAP mining model may contain nested tables. In an OLAP mining model, a case table is always bound to a dimension, while a nested table is always bound to a measure group/fact table. For example, in the Market Basket Analysis model we created in the previous section, the case table is bound to the Customer dimension, while the nested table is bound to the Sales Fact table. In AMO, you can create a TableMiningStructureColumn and then bind the column to the measure group, as displayed in the following code example:

```
public static TableMiningStructureColumn
CreateMiningStructureColumn(MeasureGroup measureGroup)
{
 TableMiningStructureColumn column = new TableMiningStructureColumn();
 column.Name = measureGroup.Name;
 column.SourceMeasureGroup = new MeasureGroupBinding(".",
 ((Cube)measureGroup.Parent).ID, measureGroup.ID);
 return column;
}
```

The following code creates a Market Basket Analysis model based on a cube.

```
private void CreateMarketBasketModel()
{
cubeAttribute basketAttribute;
CubeAttribute itemAttribute;

Server myServer = new Server();
myServer.Connect("DataSource=localhost;Catalog=FoodMart");
Database myDatabase = myServer.Databases["FoodMart"];
```

```
Cube myCube = myDatabase.Cubes["FoodMart 2000"];
CubeDimension myDimension = myCube.Dimensions["Customer"];
MiningStructure myMiningStructure =
myDatabase.MiningStructures.Add("MarketBasket","MarketBasket");
myMiningStructure.Source = new CubeDimensionBinding(".", myCube.ID,
myDimension.ID);

basketAttribute = myCube.Dimensions["Customer"].Attributes["Customer"];
itemAttribute = myCube.Dimensions["Product"].Attributes["Product"];

//basket structure column
ScalarMiningStructureColumn basket =
Utilities.CreateMiningModelColumn(basketAttribute, true);
basket.Name = "Basket";
myMiningStructure.Columns.Add(basket);

//item structure column - nested table
ScalarMiningStructureColumn item =
Utilities.CreateMiningModelColumn(itemAttribute, true);
item.Name = "Item";
MeasureGroup measureGroup = myCube.MeasureGroups[0];
TableMiningStructureColumn purchases =
Utilities.CreateMiningModelColumn(measureGroup);
purchases.Name = "Purchases";
purchases.Columns.Add(item);
myMiningStructure.Columns.Add(purchases);

MiningModel myMiningModel = myMiningStructure.CreateMiningModel();
myMiningModel.Name = "MarketBasket";
myMiningModel.Columns["Purchases"].Usage =
MiningModelColumnUsages.PredictOnly;
myMiningModel.Algorithm =
MiningModelAlgorithms.MicrosoftAssociationRules;
}
```

Summary

In this chapter, you learned about several important OLAP concepts, including cubes, dimensions, hierarchies, measures, and UDM. You also learned about the relationship between OLAP and data mining. They are both powerful tools for data analysis with different focuses. They are complementary to each other.

The second half of the chapter taught you how to apply data mining on a cube. You learned how to build OLAP mining models using the Data Mining Wizard and Editor. We gave you several examples of models that represent some popular scenarios in OLAP mining. We also discussed data mining dimensions, which enable you to optimize your dimension hierarchy designs and allow you to perform more advanced cube explorations.

The last part of the chapter taught you how to build OLAP mining models programmatically using AMO. Now it is time for you to apply these techniques to discover patterns on your own cubes.

Data Mining with SQL Server Integration Services

In a typical data mining project, the most resource-consuming step is data preparation. Creating and tuning mining models may represent only 20 percent of the total project effort. However, before creating these models, your data needs to be in the right format. Data preparation consists of multiple steps, including data gathering, cleaning, and transformation. You can prepare the data using SQL scripts, but there is a better tool for this: SQL Server Integration Service (SSIS), formerly named Data Transformation Services (DTS).

SSIS provides a workflow environment for you to build data transform packages. You can extract data from different data sources and perform a sequence of operations on the data. These operations are predefined and provided as components in SSIS Toolboxes. After transforming your data, you can process the data mining model or execute a prediction query directly inside the SSIS environment.

In this chapter, we will first give you an introduction to SSIS. We will then teach you how to perform data mining tasks in SSIS environment.

In this chapter, you will learn about:

- The basic concepts of SSIS, including control flow and data flow
- Performing data-mining-related transforms and tasks in SSIS, and their usages
- The text mining solution based on term extract and term lookup transforms

Introducing SSIS

SSIS was first introduced in SQL Server 7.0 in 1997 with the name Data Transformation Services. SSIS belongs to the ETL, which stands for Extraction, Transformation, and Loading, product family.

More and more enterprises have data warehouses nowadays. ETL is an indispensable tool for loading data from OLTP databases into data warehouses on a regular basis. In the first two releases — SQL Server 7.0 and SQL Server 2000 — SSIS mainly focused on extraction and loading. It allowed you to extract and load data to or from any data source. In SQL Server 2005, SSIS is reengineered and enhanced. It provides control flow and data flow. Control flow is also called job flow or task flow. It is more like a work flow, where each component is a task. These tasks are executed in a predefined sequence. There may be branches in task flow. The execution result of current task determines the branch to follow.

Data flow is a new concept. It is also called a pipeline. It mainly addresses the issue of data transformation. A data flow is composed of a set of predefined transforms. The starting point of a data flow is usually a data source (source table); the ending point of a data flow is usually a data destination (destination table). You can think of data flow execution as a pipeline process with each row of data as the part to be processed and each transform as the processing unit in the assembly line.

Figure 12.1 shows the SSIS Designer. You can invoke the SSIS Designer by launching Business Intelligence Development Studio and creating an Integration Services project. There is a Toolbox window on the left. The Toolbox window contains predefined control flow tasks and data flow transforms. The middle view pane contains four views: Control Flow, Data Flow, Event Handler, and Package Explorer. The Control Flow view providers a design environment for building control flows using the control flow items in the Toolbox. The Data Flow view provides a design environment for building data flow using the data flow items in the Toolbox. Event handler view allows you to define follow-up actions triggered by certain execution events. Package Explorer view provides a tree-style view of the flow.

Understanding SSIS Packages

A *package* is the basic deployment and execution unit of an SSIS project. All the work performed by SSIS tasks occurs within the context of the package. An SSIS package is the container for SSIS flows. You can create an SSIS package by right-clicking the SSIS Package folder in the Integration Services project folder and selecting the New SSIS Package menu item.

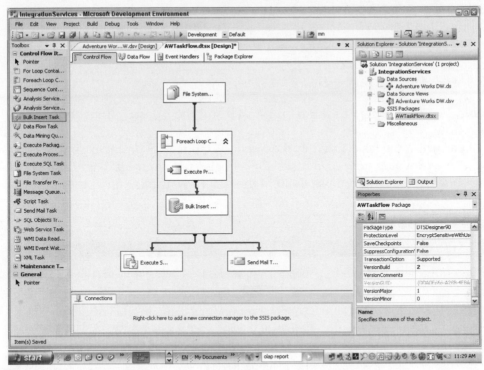

Figure 12.1   SSIS Designer

An SSIS project may contain multiple packages. A package contains only one control flow, which may contain one or more data flows.

Besides control flow and data flow, a package contains SSIS connections and package variables. Variables can have different scopes, for example, global to the whole package or local to a sequence of tasks.

The connections and variables are displayed in the tray, as shown at the bottom part of the SSIS Designer. (Refer to Figure 12.1.) The connection can be either to a relational database or to an Analysis Services database.

Task Flow

An SSIS package contains one control flow, which is composed of a set of tasks. These tasks define the job of the package, such as loading the data, executing SQL statements, processing scripts, or invoking other processes. Tasks are listed in the Toolbox. You can add a task to the package by dragging it from the Toolbox and dropping it into the package designer.

A package usually contains multiple tasks in a task flow. Multiple tasks are organized in sequential order with precedence constraints. Precedence constraints link two tasks in a sequence, where the result of executing the first task determines whether the second task is run. You can use precedence constraints to build conditional branches in a workflow. Multiple precedence constraints can be combined and evaluated as one constraint.

Standard Tasks in SSIS

Table 12.1 lists some of the prebuilt tasks and their descriptions in the SSIS task flow.

Apart from the tasks listed in the previous table, SSIS provides simple APIs for you to develop your own tasks. Once registered, your tasks will appear in the Toolbox, and you can use them in the task flow just like any prebuilt task.

Table 12.1   SSIS Tasks

TASK	DESCRIPTION
Bulk Insert Task	Loads large amounts of data from a text file into a SQL Server table.
Data Flow Task	Supports copying and transformation of data between heterogeneous data sources. A data flow task contains a data flow pipeline.
Execute Package Task	Runs subpackages.
Execute Process Task	Runs a program or a batch file as part of a package.
Execute SQL Task	Runs SQL statements during package execution and optionally saves the results of those queries.
File System Task	Performs file system operations.
File Transfer Protocol Task	Downloads data files from a remote server or an Internet location as part of a package workflow.
Message Queue Task	Uses message queuing to send and receive messages between SSIS packages.
Script Task	Uses a script to perform functions that are not available in prebuilt SSIS tasks. The Script task enables you to write script in Visual Basic .NET using the Microsoft Visual Studio for Applications (VSA) environment.
Send Mail Task	Sends an email message.
XML Task	Merges, filters, and transforms data in XML documents.

Containers

Containers are SSIS objects that provide structures to a package. Each package has a container, which stores the flows of a package. A package container may have other types of containers such as `Sequence Container`, `Foreach Loop Container`, and `For Loop Container`, which are available in the Control Flow Toolbox. You can define a subflow in these containers. Containers enrich the runtime execution model of control flow. For example, not all the tasks are executed in a sequential order. The subflow within a `Foreach` loop container will be executed multiple times based on the iterator defined in the container.

Debugging

Debugging the SSIS control flow is a new feature introduced in SQL Server 2005. You can set a breakpoint by simply pressing F9 while selecting a task in the designer. Debugging enables you to examine the values of package variables and the states of a task during the execution. Breakpoints can be set based on the events. For example, you can set one or more breakpoints on the following events of a task:

- `OnPreExecute`
- `OnPostExecute`
- `OnError`
- `OnWarning`
- `OnProgress`

The SSIS runtime pauses during the package execution when it reaches a breakpoint event. The experience is similar to debugging your C# code in Visual Studio.

Exploring a Control Flow Example

Figure 12.2 shows an example of a simple control flow. It starts with an FTP task to download compressed data files. Once files are downloaded, the runtime reaches a `Foreach` loop container that has two tasks inside: an Execute Process task, which calls the unzip application to unzip the data file, and a Bulk Insert task, which inserts the data file data into SQL server. The loop stops when the data file is unzipped and the data is loaded into SQL Server. If there is an error during the loop, the flow will execute the Send Mail task to send an email to the DBA. If every task is executed correctly, it will execute a SQL task to create some views on the new dataset. A breakpoint is set on the Execute SQL task at `OnPreExecute` event so that the DBA can verify the data before creating views.

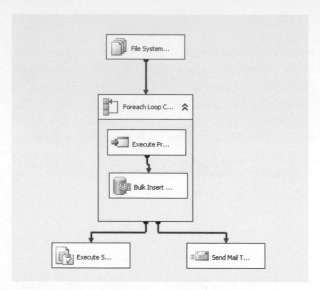

Figure 12.2 A control flow example

Data Flow

While control flow is an old concept that has existed since the first release of SSIS, data flow is a new concept introduced in SQL Server 2005. A data flow is a workflow that is very specific to data operations.

A data flow is also called a pipeline. You can think a data flow as an assembly line that contains multiple operations in a sequential order. Each node in the data flow is called a *transform*. A data flow usually starts with a source transform and ends with a destination transform. In between, predefined data flow transforms are applied to the data in a sequential order. Some transforms are *synchronous*, for example, Lookup, Conditional Split, and Data Conversion. These synchronous transforms can be executed in parallel.

Once a transform has been applied to a data row, the next transform can start to operate on it without waiting until the entire dataset is processed in the upstream transform. Some transforms are *asynchronous*, for example, Aggregation and Sort. These transforms need to get all the rows from the previous output in order to process and produce outputs for the following transforms.

In addition to the list of prebuilt transforms, SSIS provides APIs to help you build your own data flow transforms. For example, you can build a Numeric Processing transform to apply mathematical calculations and transformations on the pipeline data.

Data flow is always included in a task flow. There is one special task named Data Flow task, which is a container to host a data flow. You need to add the Data Flow task to the designer before building a data flow.

Transforms

While tasks are the basic components of task flows, transforms are the basic components of data flows. Transforms are predefined data operations. They are the machines in an assembly line that operate on the input data. Table 12.2 displays a list of popular transforms in SSIS data flow environment.

Table 12.2 SSIS Transforms

TRANSFORMS	DESCRIPTIONS
Aggregate Transformation	Performs aggregations such as average, sum, and count
Character Map Transformation	Applies string functions to character data
Conditional Split Transformation	Routes data rows to different outputs based on specified criteria
Copy/Map Transformation	Adds copies of input columns to the transformation output
Data Conversion Transformation	Converts the data type of a column to a different data type
Derived Column Transformation	Generates new columns that derives from existing columns using expressions
Dimension Processing Transformation	Processes Analysis Services dimensions
Fuzzy Grouping Transformation	Performs data-cleansing tasks by identifying rows of data that are likely to be duplicates and choosing a canonical row of data to use in standardizing the data
Fuzzy Lookup Transformation	Looks up values in a reference table using a fuzzy match
Lookup Transformation	Looks up values in a reference table using an exact match
Merge Transformation	Merges two sorted data sets
Merge Join Transformation	Joins two sorted data sets using a FULL, LEFT, or INNER join
Multicast Transformation	Distributes data sets to multiple outputs
Partition Processing Transformation	Processes Analysis Services partitions
Pivot Transformation	Creates a less normalized version of a normalized table

(continued)

Table 12.2 (continued)

TRANSFORMS	DESCRIPTIONS
Sort Transformation	Sorts pipeline data
Union All Transformation	Creates a union of multiple datasets
UnPivot Transformation	Creates a more normalized version of a nonnormalized table

Viewers

Viewers are designed for data flow debugging purposes. You can use viewers to visualize the rows in the pipeline during the execution. Viewers can be attached on the lines between transforms. To add a viewer, you simply right-click on a line and select the menu item Data Viewers. The default viewer is Grid. You can also add histogram, scatter plot, and column charts as graphic viewers. If these predefined viewers don't match your needs, you can even build you own viewers.

Exploring a Data Flow Example

Figure 12.3 displays a data flow example. The flow starts with an OLE DB Source transform, which loads a fact table containing retail sales transactions. The second transform is Lookup, which looks for the first and last name of customer from the customer dimension table. These two columns are added to the pipeline data. The next transform is Derived Column, which creates a new Full Name column based on the first and last name. Afterwards, the data enters the Aggregate transform, which sums the total sales for each customer. Based on the sales amount, the Conditional Split transform routes the customer to two destination tables, one for important customers and the other for normal customers.

Data Mining in SSIS Environment

SSIS provides a flow environment for data extraction, loading, and transformation with a set of built-in tasks and transforms.

As you have already learned, the most resource-consuming work in a data mining project is data cleaning and transformation. Naturally, SSIS can be a good complement to a data mining project. You can use this powerful tool to load data from various sources, join them together, normalize column values, remove dirty records, replace missing values, split data into training and testing datasets, and so on.

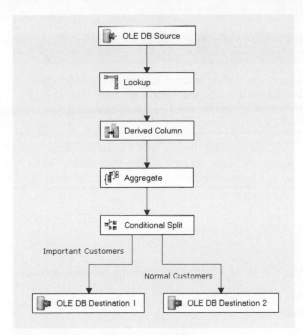

Figure 12.3   A data flow example

More than just an ETL tool for data mining, SSIS actually provides a few built-in data mining components in the control flow and data flow environment. In particular, there are a few data-mining-specific tasks and transforms listed in Table 12.3.

Table 12.3   Tasks and Transforms for Data Mining

DATA MINING TASK OR TRANSFORM	DESCRIPTION
Data Mining Query Task	Runs prediction queries based on data mining models.
Analysis Services Processing Task	Processes analytic objects such as cubes, dimensions, partitions, and data mining models.
Analysis Services Execute DDL Task	Runs Data Definition Language (DDL) code that can create, modify, delete, and process analytic objects.
Data Mining Query Transformation	Executes data mining prediction queries.
Data Mining Model Training Transformation	Processes data mining models using the pipeline data as input.

(continued)

Table 12.3 *(continued)*

DATA MINING TASK OR TRANSFORM	DESCRIPTION
Term Extraction Transformation	Processes the textual column to extract the key terms (either single word or short noun phrase). The extracted terms can be used as the dictionary for the Term Lookup transform.
Term Lookup Transformation	Searches and extracts the key terms from the input textual column based on a dictionary. The result of Term Lookup can be used as the training data for text mining.

Data Mining Tasks

In this section, we will take a closer look at a few data mining related tasks.

The Data Mining Query Task

Data Mining Query task is used for executing data mining queries, mainly prediction queries in SSIS control flow.

Figure 12.4 displays the Mining Model tab of the dialog box used to edit the properties of the Data Mining Query task. In this tab, you first specify the connection to a live Analysis Services database. Then you need to specify the mining structure and mining model on which your query is based.

Figure 12.4 Data Mining Query task — select mining model

Figure 12.5 shows the Query tab of Data Mining Query task. In this tab, you need to input the data mining query statement. You can write the query directly in the text box, or you can click the Build New Query button to invoke the Prediction Query Builder. The Prediction Query Builder provides a graphic environment, which helps you to build the DMX query. You learned how to use this tool in Chapter 3.

Your DMX query may contain parameters. These parameters can be mapped to SSIS variables. For example, you might want to write a query that returns those customers whose probability of having a gold membership card is greater than a given value. The value is set by an SSIS variable: `Probability`.

The ResultSet tab provides you an option to map the result to an SSIS variable such as collection.

Figure 12.6 displays the Output tab of Data Mining Query task. In this tab, you specify the connection destination database where the query result will be stored. It could be the same database as the source data or a different database. You also need to give name of the result table.

NOTE Your DMX query may produce nested results, for example, if you use the `PredictHistogram` function in your `Select` clause, the Data Mining Query task will automatically flatten the nested rowsets and insert the query result in a single table.

Figure 12.5   Data Mining Query task — build query

Figure 12.6 Data Mining Query task — specify output

Analysis Services Processing Task

The Analysis Services Processing task is a task for processing major objects in the Analysis Services database. The objects can be dimensions, cubes, mining structures, and mining models.

Figure 12.7 displays the editor for this task. You can select objects using the Add button. You can also specify the process options and settings in the Process Options column.

EXECUTING DMX QUERIES IN THE PREDICITON QUERY BUILDER

Apart from DMX prediction query, you can also execute other types of DMX queries in the Prediction Query Builder. For example, you can type the following content query:

Select * from myAssociationModel.Content

Where Node_Type = 7

You can also call a stored procedure:

Call mystoreproc

Actually, you can also specify a DMX Creation statement and Insert Into statement in Data Mining Query task. You can use this task to create and process a mining model.

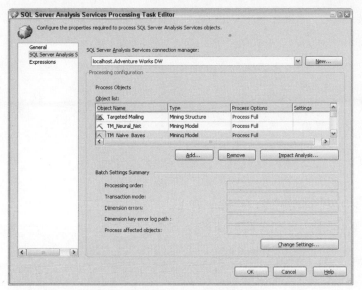

Figure 12.7   Analysis Services Processing task

Analysis Services Execute DDL Task

DDL stands for Data Definition Language. It is XML. In Analysis Services 2005, all the objects (mining models, mining columns, dimensions, cubes, roles, and so on) are defined with DDL. (You learn the principle concepts of DDL in Chapter 14.)

Besides object definition, DDL also contains a set of commands. These commands facilitate creating, updating, processing, and deleting objects.

When you use graphic tools such as mining model editors to create mining models, these tools produce DDL scripts that are sent to the server.

At times, you may want to create/update these objects without using data mining editors. You can copy or write these DDL scripts and execute them with the Execute DDL task.

Figure 12.8 displays the editor for the Execute DDL task. First, you need to specify a connection to the Analysis Services. Then you click on the Source-Direct property, which invokes a text box for DDL commands. The DDL in the figure is to create a mining structure *DM Customers* in the *Adventure Works DW* database.

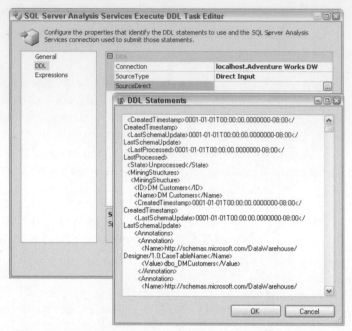

Figure 12.8 Analysis Services Execute DDL task

An Example of a Control Flow Using Data Mining

Figure 12.9 displays an example of control flow using the Data Mining Query task. The control flow first downloads a dataset of new customers through the FTP task, then it loads the data to a SQL Server database using the Bulk Insert task. If there is an error during the data loading, it sends an email to the DBA. If the data is loaded successfully, it executes the Data Mining Prediction task to find those customers who might be interested in a special promotion. The result of the prediction is saved in a table. After the prediction, it sends emails to the identified customers.

Data Mining Transforms

In this section, we will have a closer look at transforms related to data mining.

Data Mining Model Training Transform

The Data Mining Model Training transform (DM Training transform for short) is used for processing a mining structure and its associated mining models in the data flow environment.

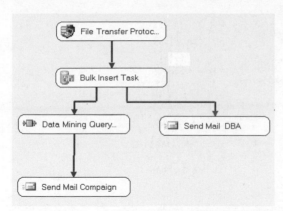

Figure 12.9 A control flow using a data mining query

The Analysis Services Process task can also process mining models, but you need to specify the input table in the task. During the execution, the AS server pulls data from the source table where the training data is stored. However, in the data flow environment, the DM training transform pushes data from the pipeline to Analysis Services during the execution. The AS server gets the training data in push mode. The pipeline data is wrapped by the DM training transform in an XML rowsets format before it is sent to the AS Server.

Figure 12.10 displays the Connection tab of the Properties dialog box for the DM training transform. In this tab, you specify the connection to an AS Server database and select the mining structure you want to process using the pipeline data.

You can also create a new mining structure using the New button. It launches the Data Mining Wizard. The wizard works you through the model creation process in the same way as it does in the Data Mining Editor environment. However, there are a few differences. First, the columns are from a pipeline, not from a relational table. Certain features, such as autodetect content type and correlation suggestions, are not available. This is because these features require scanning and sample the input data, which is not feasible in the pipeline environment.

Figure 12-11 shows the Columns tab of the DM training transform, where you specify the mappings between pipeline columns and mining structure columns. By default, the tool automatically does mapping based on column names.

Figure 12.10 DM Training transform — Connection tab

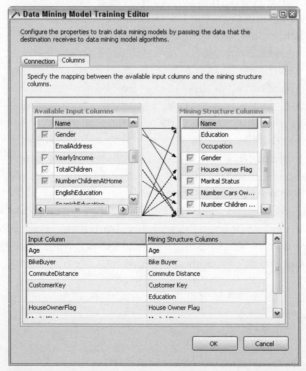

Figure 12.11 DM Training Transform — Mapping tab

TIP Although the DM Training transform allows you to create a model, it is rather difficult to edit it, for example, to change the model parameters.

One solution is to have two BI projects in the same solution: the SSIS project and the AS project. In this case, you can use the Mining Model Editor in the AS project for full editing functionality for mining models.

Data Mining Query Transform

Data Mining Query transform (DM Query transform), as the name suggests, is a transform for executing data mining queries. In Chapter 2, you learned about the various types of DMX queries including prediction, content, model creation, and model training. Among them, the prediction query is the most common.

To execute a prediction query, you need a trained mining model and an input dataset. In the pipeline environment, the input dataset is pushed from the pipeline. The DM Query transform wraps the input data from the pipeline into XML rowsets and sends them to the AS server through the XML/A protocol. The AS server executes the query and returns XML results to the transform. The transform then unwraps the results and pushes them into the pipeline for the next transform to consume. When the input data is large, this process is done in chunks each time a set of rows is sent to the AS server for prediction.

Figure 12.12 displays the Mining Model tab of the transform, where you specify the connection to a database of a live AS server. You also need to select a mining structure and one of its models.

Figure 12.13 displays the Query tab of the transform, where you can input the DMX query. You can either manually write the query or click the Build New Query button to launch the Prediction Query Builder. The input table for the prediction is the pipeline input, which is denoted as @InputRowset. Your DMX query result may contain nested results. For example, you use the PredictionHistogram function in the Select statement. In this case, the nested rowsets will automatically be flattened.

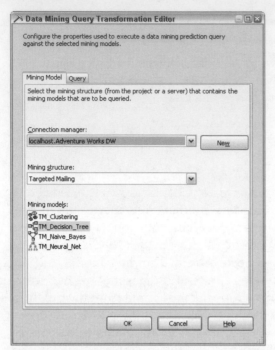

Figure 12.12   DM Prediction transform — Mining Model tab

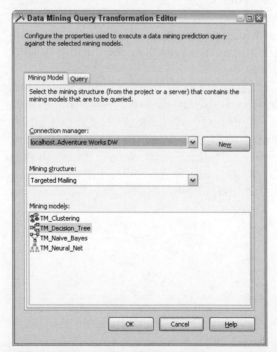

Figure 12.13   DM Prediction transform — Query tab

NOTE In SQL Server 2005, SSIS data flow doesn't support nested rowsets natively. This creates technical challenges for data mining training and prediction, which may require nested inputs and produce nested outputs. To address this issue, the DM Query transform will automatically flatten the results if there are nested rowsets. However, for nested input, it is more problematic. We recommend that you use the DM Training task and DM Query task when your model or query requires nested input.

Example Data Flows

Figure 12.14 shows an example of a data flow for model training. It starts with an OLE DB Data Source transform, which selects the FoodMart Customer table. The next transform is the Derived Column transform, which creates a new column, Age, derived from the Birthdate column. Once the new column is added to the pipeline, the data is sent to the DM Training transform, which processes the mining structure and its associated mining models in parallel.

Figure 12.15 displays a data flow using the DM Query transform. The pipeline starts with an OLE DB Source transform, which loads the NewCustomer table. The next transform is Derived Column, which adds the Age column derived from Birthdate. The third transform is DM Query, which uses a trained decision tree model to predict the most likely membership card for each new customer. The result of the prediction is sent to the Conditional Split transform, which splits the data into three pipeline branches based on the membership card type. The left branch contains only gold members, the middle branch contains only silver members, and the right branch contains bronze and normal members. Each branch leads to an OLE DB Destination transform, which stores the VIP customers, important customers, and normal customers, respectively.

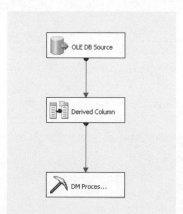

Figure 12.14 A data flow example for model training

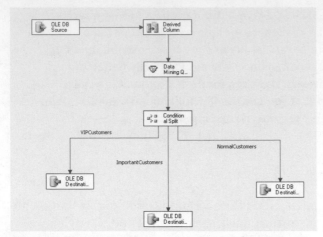

Figure 12.15 A data flow example with prediction

This example also demonstrates that data mining techniques can be applied as advanced ETL processes. It enables data splitting not only based on the existing attributes but also based on predictable attributes.

Term Extraction Transform

The Term Extraction transform is used to build a glossary of key terms for a specific domain. This is usually the first step of a text mining project. One of the columns in the input pipeline buffer contains text data with types such as `ntext` or `nvarchar`. The purpose of this transform is to analyze this column and build a dictionary of key terms based on its content. The output of the transform is a table with a single column. Extracting key terms is not as simple as you may think; there are sophisticated techniques such as word stemming and grammar parsing involved. The transform extracts nouns and noun phrases such as data mining.

The UI of the Term Extraction transform is quite simple. In the first tab, you need to specify the textual column. You can also name the output columns for key terms and their associated scores, as shown in Figure 12.16. The score is based on TFIDF, which stands for Term Frequency and Inverse Document Frequency. It is a statistical technique used to evaluate how important a word is to a document. The importance increases proportionally to the number of times a word appears in the document but is offset by how common the word is in all of the documents in the collection.

REMOVING OUTLIERS IN A DATA FLOW

You can apply data mining techniques to remove outliers in a data flow. As explained in Chapter 7, the Microsoft Clustering algorithm provides a prediction function, `PredictCaseLikelihood`, that returns the likelihood of a case being fit in a given model. Those cases with very low likelihood score are the anomalies. You can use the DM Query transform to execute prediction queries against the pipeline data and filter out the anomalies based on the query result. The following query identifies the top 50 outliers from the dataset based on the likelihood score.

```
SELECT Top 50  t.CustomerKey,
  PredictCaseLikelihood()
From
 MyClusterModel
PREDICTION JOIN
 @InputRowset AS t
ON
 ...
Order by PredictCaseLikelyhood() Desc
```

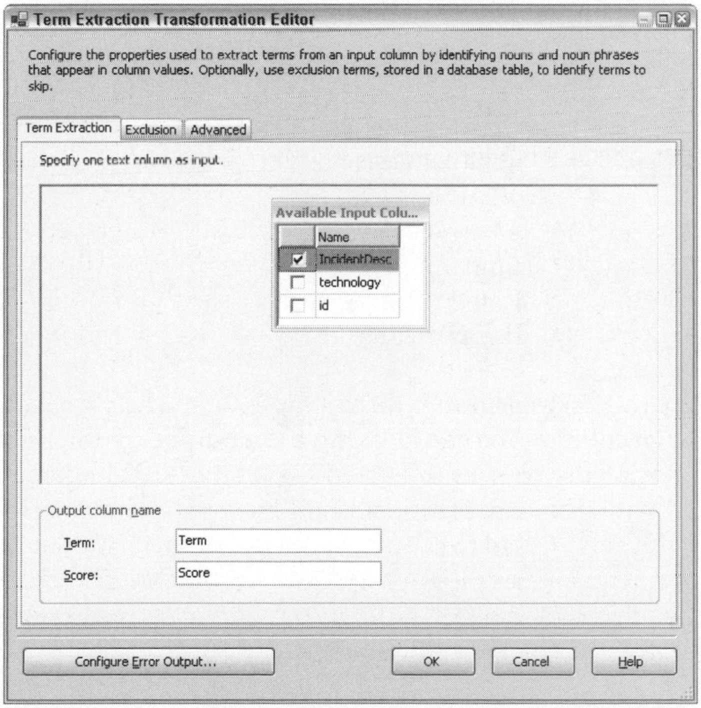

Figure 12.16 Term Extraction transform — Term Extraction tab

The second tab (see Figure 12.17) gives you the option to specify inclusion and exclusion terms. You may already have a list of predefined terms that must be included and a list of terms that you don't want to be extracted. You can specify these two term lists in this tab.

The Term Extraction transform also provides options for the terms; for example, you can specify that terms must be single words or noun phrases. In case of noun phrase, you can also mention the maximum length.

Term Lookup Transform

The Term Lookup transform is used to search for key terms from the input textual column, based on a dictionary. The dictionary is usually generated by the Term Extraction transform. Since the dictionary is just a table, you can write SQL queries to modify the list by adding or removing terms when necessary.

The editor for the Term Lookup transform is quite simple. The first tab is used for specifying the reference table (dictionary), as shown in Figure 12.18.

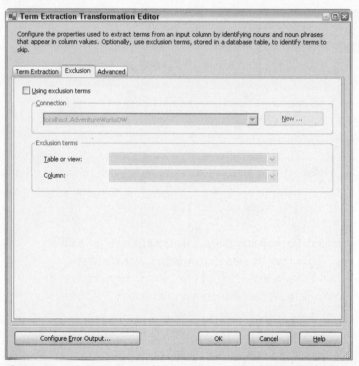

Figure 12.17   Term Extraction transform — Inclusion/Exclusion tab

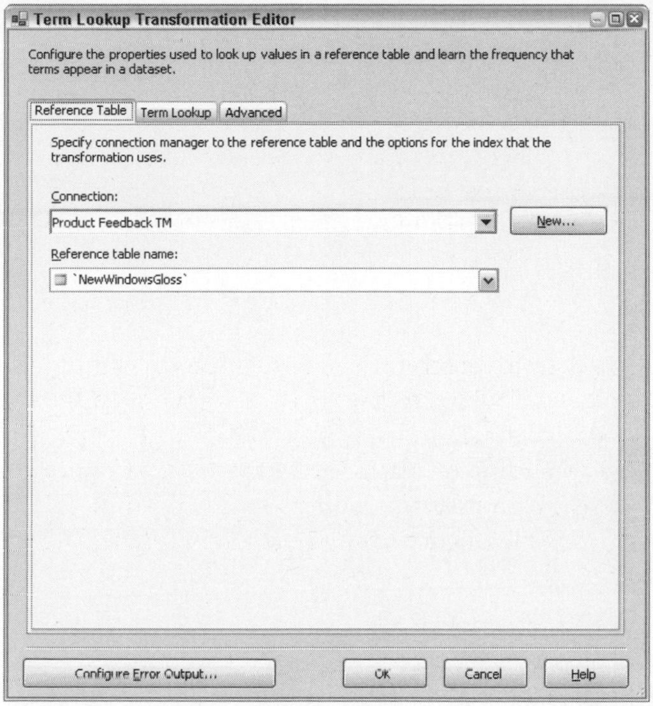

Figure 12.18 Term Lookup transform — Reference Table tab

The second tab is used to specify the column mapping, for example mapping the input textual column to the dictionary. (See Figure 12.19.) You can also pass through some input columns such as the document ID.

The Term Lookup transform produces two new columns as output: Term and Frequency. You can think of the output of this transform as a fact table with a large number of rows, containing the document ID, key terms, and associated frequency.

TIP In many cases, the Term Lookup transform generates more terms than you need for text mining. There may be some noisy terms. We strongly recommend that you browse the output table of the Lookup transform and remove those terms that you believe are useless before feeding the data to your mining models.

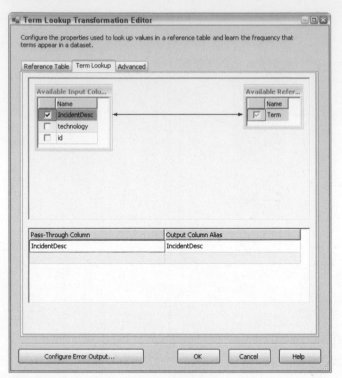

Figure 12.19 Term Lookup transform — Term Lookup tab

Example of Text Mining Project

There is much more unstructured data than structured data around us. Think about the Internet, which contains billions of Hypertext Markup Language (HTML) documents that are not structured. Analyzing text documents is becoming more important. Two popular data mining tasks for text mining are classification and segmentation. One of the popular text mining domains is customer support. In the classification example, you have lots of customer feedback from the Web and email, and you want to assign priorities to each feedback instance. In the segmentation example, you want to group similar feedback together and forward them to the right department.

With SQL Server 2005, you can implement a text mining project using SSIS and data mining. A typical flow starts with using Term Extraction to build a dictionary for your business domain. The second step is to use Term Lookup to search for key terms from the textual column, thus converting unstructured data to structured output. The third step is to apply data mining techniques such as Naïve Bayes, Neural network, clustering, and decision trees to build models on the output of Term Lookup. Usually the output of Term Lookup is served as a nested table in the mining model.

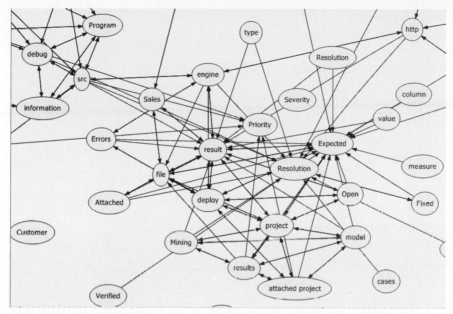

Figure 12.20 A Term Association model based on a software bug database

Figure 12.20 shows an example of a text mining model using an association algorithm. It analyzes the bug description database of a software development project and identifies the relationship among the key terms.

Summary

In this chapter, you learned the basic concepts of another important SQL Server component: SQL Server Integration Services. We gave you an introduction to control flow and data flow. We also discussed a few important tasks and transforms. SSIS is an important tool for data cleaning and transformation, which is a time-consuming step for any data mining project.

The second half of the chapter focused on the data-mining-specific features in the SSIS environment. We went through each of the data-mining-related tasks and transforms. We gave you some examples of control flow and data flow using these DM tasks and transforms. Finally, we show you the two text-mining-related transforms and a typical text mining project example based on SQL Server 2005.

Data mining and SSIS mutually benefit from each other. SSIS provides a data processing environment for data mining, while data mining techniques can be used as part of data transform process. It makes SSIS smarter and, thus, places it ahead of other classic ETL products.

By now, you should have a clear understanding of the relationship between SSIS and DM, as well as the type of DM projects that you can complete in the SSIS environment.

SQL Server Data Mining Architecture

This chapter discusses, in some detail, the architecture of Analysis Services and, in particular, the data mining side of things. It covers the communication mechanisms used between the client and the server, the server components and how they are used, server configuration, and how different options impact memory and disk usage. This chapter is intended for those who will be administering a data mining server or programming against it. Readers who are interested only in performing analysis with SQL Server Data Mining can skip this chapter.

In this chapter, you will learn about:

- The Analysis Services architecture
- Using XML for Analysis
- Processing architecture
- Server administration
- Data mining security

Introducing Analysis Services Architecture

Analysis Services works in a simple client-server architecture, allowing clients to connect through a TCP/IP connection or using IIS to connect through HTTP through the Internet. Analysis Services provides a variety of clients, such as

OLE DB, ADOMD.Net, and more. Rather than introducing a new communication mechanism for each client, each client is merely a thin shim that communicates with the server by producing and consuming the core Analysis Services interface, which is XML for Analysis (XMLA). XMLA is a simple XML protocol for communicating with analysis servers regardless of the source or destination platform. XMLA is covered in more detail in the next section.

When a request is received by the server, Analysis Services determines whether the request is an OLAP request or a data mining request and routes the request appropriately. In the end, a data mining request invokes a data mining algorithm that can be one created by Microsoft and included with the product, or can be a custom third-party plug-in algorithm loaded into the Analysis Services server. Additionally, a user-defined stored procedure can be invoked that uses a server-side version of the client ADOMD.Net interface to access server objects and model content directly.

A *diagram* of the data mining client architecture is displayed in Figure 13.1. The shaded boxes represent components that are part of Analysis Services, and, where appropriate, identify the files necessary to use the component. Programming with these components will be explained in Chapters 14 through 16.

XML for Analysis

XML for Analysis (XMLA) is an XML API based on the Simple Object Access Protocol (SOAP) designed to standardize and facilitate the interaction between clients and data providers across the Web. Traditional data access technologies require the installation of client components that are tightly coupled to the data provider. This coupling creates limitations such as platform- and language-dependence, as well as versioning issues between the client and server components. XMLA is built on the open standards of HTTP, XML, and SOAP and, therefore, is not bound to any specific language or platform.

XMLA defines the mechanism for communicating with analytical data providers, such as data mining or OLAP providers, over the Web. It takes the concepts defined in other specifications such as OLE DB, OLE DB for Data Mining, and OLE DB for OLAP, and extends them to be accessible via XML. Because of the flexibility this allows, XMLA is the core communications protocol for all clients to the Analysis Services server.

Here, we will cover only the most basic aspects of XMLA. For those readers wishing to learn more, the complete specification is available at http://www.xmla.org. The architecture diagram in Figure 13.1 demonstrates how all client interfaces communicate through the XMLA protocol.

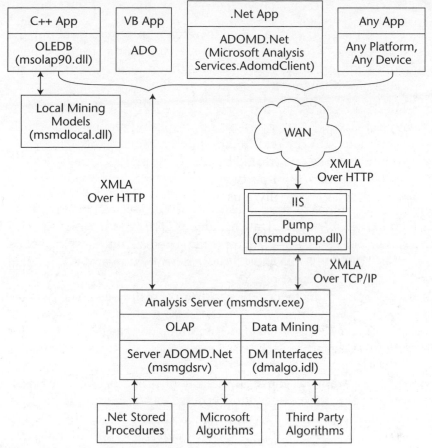

Figure 13.1 Data Mining architecture

XMLA APIs

XMLA accomplishes all that it does with only two APIs — *Discover* and *Execute*. Discover retrieves schema information from the data provider, and Execute executes queries or commands on the server.

Examples in this section refer to the XMLA ThinMiner sample application available at `wiley.com/go/tang/Chapter13`. ThinMiner uses XMLA to display a list of models on a remote server and presents a Web interface allowing the user to query the model.

Discover

The `Discover` method allows the caller to receive information about the capabilities and the state of the data provider. The caller indicates the type of information requested, and the provider returns that information in the form of a rowset, analogous to schema rowsets in OLE DB or ADO.

The prototype for a `Discover` call is:

```
Discover(IN RequestType as EnumString,
         Restrictions as Array,
         Properties as Array,
     OUT Resultset as Rowset)
```

The `RequestType` indicates the requested schema. This can be any of the schema defined in the OLE DB for Data Mining or OLE DB for OLAP specifications, or it can be one of the six XMLA specific schema from the XML specification, such as `DISCOVER_DATASOURCES`, which enumerates the data sources the XMLA provider is exposing.

The `Restrictions` parameter contains an array of restrictions. The possible restrictions for each schema are specified in the `DISCOVER_SCHEMA_ROWSETS` schema rowset. In Figure 13.2, from XMLA ThinMiner, you can see a request for the mining columns schema rowset (`DMSCHEMA_MINING_COLUMNS`) that is restricted to the Demographics model.

The `Properties` parameter contains an array of properties — the possible options indicated in the `DISCOVER_PROPERTIES` schema. Listing 13.1 shows a properties array, indicating that we are accessing a model that exists in the MovieSurvey2 database on the data source DataMiner. Additionally, the code specifies that the results should appear in a tabular format (the only option for schema rowsets) and that the result contain the schema that was used plus the data returned.

```
<SOAP-ENV:Envelope
  xmlns:SOAP-ENV="http://schemas.xmlsoap.org/soap/envelope/"
  xmlns:xsi=http://www.w3.org/2001/XMLSchema-instance
  xmlns:xsd="http://www.w3.org/2001/XMLSchema">
<SOAP-ENV:Body>
    <Discover xmlns="urn:schemas-microsoft-com:xml-analysis"
      SOAP-ENV:encodingStyle=
               "http://schemas.xmlsoap.org/soap/encoding/">
    <RequestType>DMSCHEMA_MINING_COLUMNS</RequestType>
    <Restrictions>
      <RestrictionList>
         <MODEL_NAME>Demographics</MODEL_NAME>
      </RestrictionList>
    </Restrictions>
```

Listing 13.1   XMLA Discover for mining columns

```
      <Properties>
        <PropertyList>
           <DataSourceInfo>DataMiner</DataSourceInfo>
           <Catalog>MovieSurvey2</Catalog>
           <Format>Tabular</Format>
           <Content>SchemaData</Content>
         </PropertyList>
      </Properties>
    </Discover>
  </SOAP-ENV:Body>
</SOAP-ENV:Envelope>
```

Listing 13.1   *(continued)*

After submission of the request, the XMLA server returns an XMLA rowset. The rowset contains a schema section, describing the columns returned, and a data section containing the data. If the schema is known, you can set the Content property to Data to eliminate the schema section from the response. Listing 13.2 displays a segment of the response from the query in Listing 13.1 that contains a single row. You can see that a row simply contains the column names as tags with the column data as the data.

```
<row>
  <MODEL_CATALOG>MovieSurvey2</MODEL_CATALOG>
  <MODEL_NAME>Demographics</MODEL_NAME>
  <COLUMN_NAME>Age Disc</COLUMN_NAME>
  <ORDINAL_POSITION>1</ORDINAL_POSITION>
  <COLUMN_HAS_DEFAULT>false</COLUMN_HAS_DEFAULT>
  <COLUMN_FLAGS>16</COLUMN_FLAGS>
  <IS_NULLABLE>true</IS_NULLABLE>
  <DATA_TYPE>20</DATA_TYPE>
  <NUMERIC_PRECISION>10</NUMERIC_PRECISION>
  <CONTENT_TYPE>DISCRETIZED(AUTOMATIC,5)</CONTENT_TYPE>
  <MODELING_FLAG></MODELING_FLAG>
  <IS_RELATED_TO_KEY>false</IS_RELATED_TO_KEY>
  <IS_INPUT>true</IS_INPUT>
  <IS_PREDICTABLE>false</IS_PREDICTABLE>
  <PREDICTION_SCALAR_FUNCTIONS>RangeMax,RangeMid,RangeMin
    </PREDICTION_SCALAR_FUNCTIONS>
  <IS_POPULATED>true</IS_POPULATED>
  <PREDICTION_SCORE>0</PREDICTION_SCORE>
  <SOURCE_COLUMN>Age Disc</SOURCE_COLUMN>
</row>
```

Listing 13.2   Excerpt from Discover response

Execute

Where `Discover` retrieves information about the server, `Execute` allows you to send queries or commands. The function prototype is:

```
Execute (IN   Command as String,
              Properties as Array,
         OUT  Resultset as Resultset)
```

The parameters for `Execute` are simply the command string and the properties array, which is identical to that of a `Discover` call. Listing 13.3 shows a singleton prediction query generated by XMLA ThinMiner to predict theater-going frequency based on marital status and number of children. The resultant rowset is identical to that of a `Discover`.

```
<SOAP-ENV:Envelope
  xmlns:SOAP-ENV="http://schemas.xmlsoap.org/soap/envelope/"
  xmlns:xsi=http://www.w3.org/2001/XMLSchema-instance
  xmlns:xsd="http://www.w3.org/2001/XMLSchema">
<SOAP-ENV:Body>
    <Execute xmlns="urn:schemas-microsoft-com:xml-analysis"
      SOAP-ENV:encodingStyle
        ="http://schemas.xmlsoap.org/soap/encoding/">
      <Command>
        <Statement>SELECT Flattened
                    PredictHistogram([Theater Freq])
                  FROM [Demographics]
                  NATURAL PREDICTION JOIN
                    (SELECT 'Married' as [Marital Status1],
                        '2' as [Num Children1])
                  AS T
        </Statement>
      </Command>
      <Properties>
        <PropertyList>
          <DataSourceInfo>DataMiner</DataSourceInfo>
          <Catalog>MovieSurvey2</Catalog>
          <Format>Tabular</Format>
          <Content>SchemaData</Content>
        </PropertyList>
      </Properties>
    </Execute>
  </SOAP-ENV:Body>
</SOAP-ENV:Envelope>
```

Listing 13.3 XMLA Execute package

TIP The Template Explorer in SQL Management Studio contains XML for Analysis templates for performing common operations against Analysis Services.

XMLA and Analysis Services

XMLA is the core communication mechanism for Analysis Services. Regardless of which API you are using to connect to the server, the payload of the request and the response is essentially XMLA, as described by Figure 13.1. In the case of OLE DB and ADOMD.Net, these clients enhance XMLA with compression and encryption and allow communication with binary XML.

Since XMLA is platform- and language-independent, and XMLA is the one native protocol, all the functionality of the server is accessible from any platform. No limitations are imposed on any client running on any device using any operating system and language.

Analysis Services extends XMLA to include the Data Definition Language (DDL) it uses to create server objects. This DDL is directly accessible and editable in both the BI Development Studio and the SQL Management Studio. To access the DDL of an object in the BI Development Studio, right-click the object in the Solution Explorer and choose View Code. To access from SQL Management Studio, right-click in Object Explorer and choose Script to CREATE, as shown in Figure 13.2.

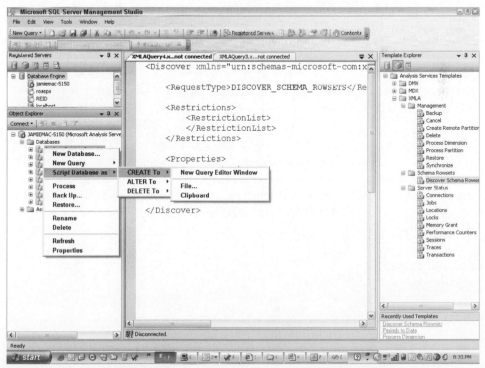

Figure 13.2: Scripting a database in SQL Server Management Studio

TIP After you become familiar with it, many edits are faster to accomplish in the DDL rather than with the user interface. Using the SQL Management Studio, you can easily modify existing objects (with ALTER) or clone objects with small modifications by editing the DDL and submitting to the server.

Processing Architecture

SQL Server Data Mining is built from the ground up for performance and scalability, sharing many components with the OLAP portion of Analysis Services. Processing occurs in basically three stages: querying the source data, determining raw statistics, and finally using the model definition and the data mining algorithms to train your mining models.

To process a mining structure and the contained models, Analysis Services issues several queries to the source database. As the engine queries the data, it builds an index of all of the discrete and discretized columns in the mining structure. Additionally, another query is issued if there are any continuous-valued columns in the structure.

For models with nested tables, Analysis Services first issues one query per discrete-valued column in each nested table to generate an index, then issues an additional query per nested table in your mining structure to process the relationships between the nested tables and the case table.

TIP Analysis Services issues many queries against the source database. You can limit the number of simultaneous queries to your relational store by setting the server property OLAP\Process\DatabaseConnectionPoolMax in the server properties in SQL Management Studio. (See the "Server Configuration" section later in this chapter.)

The reason for all of these queries is to process a specialized OLAP cube that is contained inside the mining structure and is not user-accessible. This cube and its associated dimensions index and cache the case data. Once this cube is processed, the server creates independent threads to train each of the models in the structure that read the pretokenized and indexed data from the OLAP cache into their respective algorithms. In the Enterprise Edition of SQL Server, all models are trained in parallel, whereas in the Standard Edition, they are trained serially.

Data Mining Administration

Most administration information is well documented in Books Online, accessible through the help menu of BI Development Studio or SQL Management Studio. However, some points are specific to data mining and are worth repeating or are not sufficiently covered. These topics are server configuration and data mining security.

Server Configuration

The variables that control server behavior are modified in SQL Management Studio. To access server properties, you need to connect to the server in Object Explorer, and then right-click the server and select Properties from the context menu. Modifying these properties allows you to tune your server for the way you use it and also to control how the server is used by clients for security issues. Properties are divided into two categories: Basic and Advanced. By default, you will only see the basic properties. To see the advanced properties, you need to check the Show Advanced (All) Properties check box at the bottom of the Properties window. All data-mining-specific entries start with "Data-Mining." The server properties dialog is shown in Figure 13.3

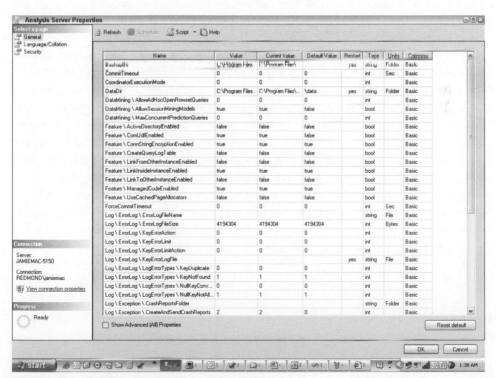

Figure 13.3   Analysis Services Properties dialog

The properties AllowAdHocOpenRowsetQueries and AllowedProviders InOpenRowset allow you to control ad hoc access to OLE DB providers during prediction or training (INSERT INTO) queries. Since OLE DB providers are loaded directly into the server's memory space, it is theoretically possible that a security hole in the provider could manifest in Analysis Services. Setting AllowAdHocOpenRowsetQueries to true allows the execution of OpenRowset queries by those who are not server administrators, but opens a potential security hole. Leaving this property false, the default value, limits your users to browsing models, executing singleton queries, and executing statements containing OPENQUERY clauses against data sources for which they have permission.

If you choose to allow ad hoc OPENROWSET access, you still can limit your security exposure. The advanced property AllowedProvidersInOpen Rowset allows you to select exactly which OLE DB providers can be loaded. This parameter takes a comma-delimited list of providers, or you can specify [All] to indicate that all installed providers are allowed. It is recommended that you set this property to the specifically allowed providers if you turn on AllowAdHocOpenRowsetQueries.

Another property, MaxConcurrentPredictionQueries, allows you to control the load on the server caused by predictions. The default value, zero, allows the server to simultaneously process as many queries as are allowed by the edition of SQL Server Analysis Services that is installed, that is five for Standard Edition, and unlimited for Enterprise Edition. Queries sent to the server above and beyond this number are serialized and may time out.

Two sections of advanced properties control which algorithms are available to users and what their default parameters are. The first section, Algorithms, allows you to control which algorithms are available. For example, if you wanted only analysts to use a particular server for Time Series analysis, you could enforce this by setting the Enabled flag for all the other algorithms to 0.

The last section, Services, describes the defaults for all of the installed algorithms. Changing these parameters changes the processing of all future models created with the associated algorithm. For example, setting the cluster count parameter on the Microsoft Clustering algorithm to 0 causes the algorithm to automatically pick the best number of clusters for predictive purposes. If you wanted this to be the default behavior, you would set the ClusterCount entry under Microsoft Clustering to 0.

Setting the enabled state and default parameters of plug-in algorithms is not supported through the SQL Management Studio user interface. These properties can be changed through code using Analysis Management Objects (AMO), which is described in Chapter 14.

Data Mining Security

The word "security" when used in conjunction with data mining has a tendency to raise some eyebrows. The Data Mining Moratorium Act of 2003 introduced by Senators Feingold and Wyden exemplifies the type of mistrust much of the populace has with this rather innocent technology. This being the case, Analysis Services has many options for controlling access to the information stored inside mining models. The types of permissions that can be assigned are described in Table 13.1.

TIP If you want to expose a model directly as a Web service through XMLA for predictive purposes, you can protect the content of your model by assigning Read permission but not the Browse permission.

Security in Analysis Services is *role-based*, that is, you create a role that defines a set of permissions you would like to provide and then you assign users to that role. All users in a role have all the permissions of that role, and their permissions are automatically updated as the role permissions are modified using the dialog shown in Figure 13.4. Roles can be created and edited in both the BI Development Studio and SQL Management Studio.

Table 13.1 Data Mining Permissions

PERMISSION	EFFECT
Read	User can perform prediction queries on the mining model
Write	User can update node captions in the model content
Browse	User can access the learned content of the model
Drillthrough	User can access the source data from which the model was trained
Read Definition	User can see the DDL representing the model metadata
Process (mining structure only)	User can process the mining structure

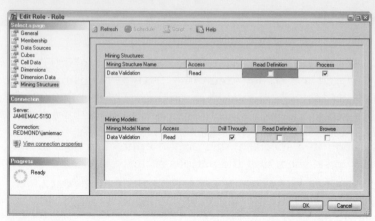

Figure 13.4   Role properties dialog showing Mining Structure permissions

NOTE Analysis Services has only the ability to permit premissions and not to deny permissions as the SQL Server relational engine does. Therefore, a user's permissions are the union of the permissions of all of the roles to which the user belongs. For example, Mary belongs to the Database Processors role, which allows her to process all database objects but not query them. She also belongs to the Data Miners role, allowing her to query models but not process them. Mary has the permission to both process and query models.

Additionally, permissions are nested; a role must have the same permission (if applicable) on the parent object to perform that action on the target object. For instance, using the Data Miners role, the role would have to have Access Read permissions on the database and the mining structure containing the mining model to be queried as well as permission on the model itself.

Additional areas of concern for the security conscious are stored procedures and plug-in algorithms. Although users must be administrators to install either one, you should ensure the source of the code and that the authors are security-conscious.

Summary

In this chapter, you learned where SQL Server Data Mining fits into Analysis Services. The native protocol of Analysis Services is XML for Analysis, which allows clients on any device, any platform, and using any language to connect and perform analytical queries. Analysis Services comprises many APIs, but all client communication, including management, has XMLA at its root.

Also, you learned about the special configuration options of SQL Server Data Mining and how to set them and the various security options that are available to secure your models.

Programming SQL Server Data Mining

The concept of data mining as a platform technology opens up the doors for the possibility of a new breed of "intelligent applications." An intelligent application is one that does not need custom code to handle various circumstances; rather it learns business rules directly from the data. Additionally, as business rules change, intelligent applications are updated automatically by reprocessing the models that represent the business logic. Examples of intelligent applications are cross-sales applications that provide insightful recommendations to your users, call center applications that show only customers with a reasonable chance of making a purchase, and order-entry systems that validate data as it is entered without any custom code. These are just the tip of the iceberg; the flexibility and extensibility of the SQL Server Data Mining programming model will excite the creativity of the developer, leading to the invention of even more types of intelligent applications.

In the last chapter, we demonstrated that the core communication protocol for Analysis Services is XML for Analysis (XMLA). This protocol provides a highly flexible, platform-independent method for accessing your data mining server. Everything that can be done between the client and the server can be done through XMLA. However, as is true in the rest of your life, just because you can do it the hard way doesn't mean that you have to.

In this chapter, you review programming interfaces and object models that make it easy to write data mining applications using Analysis Services. You see examples in Visual Basic .NET, demonstrating how to implement typical data mining tasks using the appropriate interface for each task, and explore some special features of SQL Server data mining that you can use to exploit data mining programming to the fullest. The sample code, along with versions in Visual C# .NET, is available at wiley.com/tang/Chapter14.

In this chapter, you learn about:

- APIs and their application to data mining
- Using Analysis Services APIs
- Creating and managing data mining objects using AMO
- Data mining client programming with ADOMD.NET
- Writing server-side stored procedures with Server ADOMD.NET

Data Mining APIs

Listing the various application programming interfaces (APIs) for SQL Server Data Mining, you get a dizzying array of acronyms. To make things even more confusing, many of the names were chosen not because of their function, but to provide brand affinity with existing technologies. Table 14.1 describes the major APIs used in Analysis Services programming and their descriptions.

Table 14.1   SQL Server Mining APIs

API	COMPLETE NAME	DESCRIPTION
ADO	ActiveX Data Objects	Provides access to data objects, including data mining, from native languages such as Visual Basic
ADOMD.NET	ActiveX Data Objects (Multidimensional) for .NET	Provides access to Analysis Services data objects from managed languages such as Visual Basic .NET, C#, and J#
Server ADOMD	Server ActiveX (r) Data Objects (Multidimensional)	Provides access to Analysis Services data objects from user-defined functions running inside the server
AMO	Analysis Management Objects	A management interface for Analysis Services providing objects to perform operations such as creation, processing, and so on
DSO	Decision Support Objects	The Analysis Services management interface from SQL Server 2000. Maintained for backward compatibility

Table 14.1   *(continued)*

API	COMPLETE NAME	DESCRIPTION
DMX	Data Mining Extensions	Extensions to SQL to support data mining operations
OLE DB/DM	Object Linking and Embedding for Databases for Data Mining	The name of the specification that defines the DMX language and introduces the concept of data mining models as database objects
XMLA	XML for Analysis	A communication protocol and XML format for communicating with an analytical server independent of any platform

ADO

Active Data Objects (ADO) was created to assist the Visual Basic programmer in accessing data residing in databases. The ADO libraries wrap the OLE DB interfaces into objects that are easier to program against. Because OLE DB for Data Mining specifies that a data mining provider is first an OLE DB provider, ADO can be used to execute data mining queries just as it does relational database queries.

ADO reduces the complexity of OLE DB interfaces to three essential objects: the connection, the command, and the record set. The *connection object* is used to connect to the server and to issue schema rowset queries. The *command object* is used to execute DMX statements and optionally retrieve their results, and the *record set object* contains the result of any data returning queries.

ADO.NET

ADO.NET is the managed data access layer. It was created to allow managed languages, such as Visual Basic .NET and C#, to access data, much as ADO was created for native languages. The philosophy of ADO.NET is somewhat different from that of ADO in that ADO.NET is designed to work in a "disconnected" mode, where data can be accessed and manipulated without maintaining an active connection to the server. When work is completed, a connection can be established, and all the appropriate updates will be propagated to the server, providing that there is server support for such behavior.

ADO.NET is more modular than ADO is. ADO works in one way and that way only, and contains special code to interact with the SQL Server provider better than other providers. ADO.NET provides generic objects that work with any OLE DB provider, but also allows providers to create their own managed providers for data interaction. For example, SQLADO.NET contains objects optimized for interacting specifically with SQL Server, and similar managed providers can be written for any data source.

Similarly to ADO, ADO.NET contains connection and command objects. However, ADO.NET introduces the dataset object for data interaction. A dataset is a cache of the server data contained in a set of datatables that can be independently updated or archived as XML. Datasets are loaded using dataadapters — either the generic adapter that is supplied with ADO.NET or a provider-specific adapter such as the SQLDataAdapter. For direct data access, ADO.NET uses a datareader, which is similar in concept to the ADO record set, returned from its command object.

ADOMD.NET

ADOMD.NET (ADO.NET – Multidimensional) is a managed data provider implementing the dataadapter and datareader interfaces of ADO.NET specifically for Analysis Services, making it faster and more memory-efficient than the generic ADO.NET objects. In addition to the standard ADO.NET interfaces, ADOMD.NET contains data mining and OLAP-specific objects, making programming data mining client applications easier.

The `MiningStructure`, `MiningModel`, and `MiningColumn` collections make it easy to extract the metadata describing the objects on the server. The `MiningContentNode` object allows for the programmatic browsing of mining models and can be accessed from the root of the content hierarchy or randomly from any node in the content.

> **NOTE** There also exists a native version of ADOMD.NET, appropriately named ADOMD. This interface is maintained mostly for backward compatibility with SQL Server 2000 and does not contain any objects or interfaces for data mining programming.

Server ADOMD

Server ADOMD is an object model for accessing Analysis Server objects, both data mining and OLAP, directly on the server. It is intended for use in user defined functions, described later in this chapter.

AMO

AMO, or Analysis Management Objects, is the main management interface for Analysis Services. It replaces the SQL Server 2000 interface, Decision Support Objects (DSO), which is still maintained for backward compatibility, but has not been updated to take advantage of all the new features of SQL Server 2005.

Like ADOMD.NET, AMO contains the `MiningStructures`, `Mining-Models`, and `MiningColumns` collections, and the like. However, whereas ADOMD.NET is for browsing and querying, AMO is for creating and managing. All the operations you perform in the user interfaces of the BI Workbench or SQL Workbench are possible to perform programmatically using AMO; in fact, the management operations of both user interfaces were written using AMO.

TIP You should use ADOMD.NET when writing data mining client applications except when .NET is not available. Otherwise, use ADO (or OLE DB) for Windows applications, or plain XMLA for thin client applications. For applications in which you will be creating new models or managing existing models, use AMO.

NOTE See Books Online for full documentation and samples of all APIs used by Analysis Services.

Using Analysis Services APIs

Whenever you need to access any of the APIs for Analysis Services, you have to make sure that you add the appropriate references to your project. Table 14.2 lists many of the APIs with the required references:

Table 14.2   Analysis Services References

API	TYPE	REFERENCES
ADO	Native	Microsoft ActiveX Data Objects
ADOMD.NET	Managed	`Microsoft.AnalysisServices.AdomdClient`
Server ADOMD	Managed	`Microsoft.AnalysisServices.AdomdServer`
AMO	Managed	`Microsoft.AnalysisServices` `Microsoft.DataWarehouse.Interfaces`
DSO	Native	Microsoft Decision Support Objects 9

To make your coding easier you can add code like the following to the top of your source files so that you don't have to specify the fully qualified name for every object.

VB.NET

```
Imports Microsoft.AnalysisServices
```

C#

```
Using Microsoft.AnalysisServices
```

Using Microsoft.AnalysisServices to Create and Manage Mining Models

In this section, we will use AMO to create and manage models using the MovieClick database to analyze premium channel use across different generations of customers. If your programming interest lies only in embedding data mining into client applications, you can skip this section.

The simplest way to create mining models is to use DMX statements such as CREATE MINING MODEL and INSERT INTO with any of the command interfaces such as ADO, ADO.NET, or ADOMD.NET. While that method has the advantage of simplicity, features such as Data Mining Drillthrough and custom column bindings, among others, are not accessible through the command-based APIs. Therefore, to ensure that your application can take advantage of all that SQL Server Data Mining has to offer, the recommended API for creating mining models is AMO. In fact, the creating, editing, and managing tools included in the BI Development Studio and SQL Management Studio were written with AMO. Chapter 16 describes a scenario in which it is appropriate to use DMX for model creation and processing.

Figure 14.1 shows the major AMO objects used for data mining programming. These objects will be used in the code samples throughout the AMO section of this chapter.

AMO Basics

AMO is a rather straightforward object model placed on top of the XML representation of Analysis Services objects. In addition to providing a convenient API, AMO also provides basic validation and methods to update, change, and monitor objects on the server.

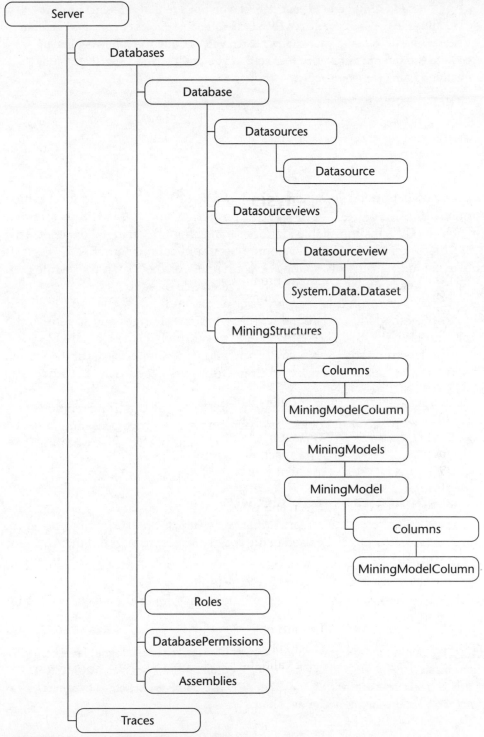

Figure 14.1:   Partial AMO object hierarchy

NOTE To add AMO code to your project, you need to add references to two assemblies: `Microsoft.AnalysisServices` and `Microsoft.DataWarehouse.Interfaces`. To make your coding easier, you can add the following line of code to the top of your source files so that you don't have to specify the fully qualified name for every object.

VB.NET

```
Imports Microsoft.AnalysisServices
```

C#

```
Using Microsoft.AnalysisServices
```

Every object in AMO implements the `NamedComponent` interface, which supplies `Name`, `Id` and `Description` properties and a `Validate` method. An object's ID is its immutable identifier that cannot be changed once set. This is useful, for instance, when developing user applications with fixed objects. It allows users to arbitrarily change object names for their own use, while providing a consistent way for your code to reference objects.

`MajorObject` inherits `NamedComponent` and adds the `Update` and `Refresh` methods to update the server with local changes and to refresh the local model with the server contents, respectively. Additionally `Major-Objects` has methods to access referring and dependant objects and contains an `Annotations` collection for arbitrary user extensions. The `Role` object is an example of a `MajorObject`.

`ProcessableMajorObject` inherits `MajorObject`, adding methods and properties to process the object and determine the processed state and last processed time. `MiningStructure` is an example of a `Processable-MajorObject`.

AMO Applications and Security

Because AMO is generally a management API, certain permissions must be present for users to use any AMO-based application. Obviously, any user with Administrator permissions will have access through AMO, but users with more restrictive permissions can also have limited access.

Table 14.3 describes the permissions necessary for a user to perform any function through AMO.

NOTE Some operations, such as iterating objects, require a higher level of permission using AMO than when using a command API, such as ADOMD.NET. This is because ADOMD.NET and other APIs use database schemas to access objects rather than metadata definitions.

Table 14.3   AMO Permissions

IN ORDER TO . . .	YOU NEED THE PERMISSION . . .
Iterate objects	Access and Read Definition
View object definitions	Access and Read Definition
Modify objects	Administrator
Process objects	Access, Read Definition, and Process
Add or delete objects	Administrator
Set permissions	Administrator
Receive traces	Administrator

TIP You can test security in your application by impersonating roles or specific users. Set the Effective Roles property in your connection string to a comma-delimited set of roles you want to impersonate, or set the Effective Username connection string property to the name of the user. Note that only server administrators can connect with these properties.

For example:

```
svr.Connect("location=localhost;" _ &
    "Initial Catalog=MyDatabase;Effective Roles=LimitedAccessRole")
```

Object Creation

To create mining models programmatically using AMO, you perform all the same steps you would do if you were creating and managing the models in the user interface. That is, as described in Chapter 3, create a database, data source, data source view, mining structure, and finally a mining model.

To create any object on the server, you generally perform the following steps:

1. Instantiate the object
2. Set object Name and ID properties
3. Set object-specific properties
4. Add object to its parent container
5. Call Update to the object or its parent

For example, Listing 14.1 demonstrates how to connect to a local server and create a database.

```
Sub CreateDatabase()
    Dim svr As Server
    Dim db As Database

    ' Create server object and connect
    svr = New Server()
    svr.Connect("location=localhost")

    ' Create database and set properties
    db = New Database()
    db.Name = "MovieClick"
    db.ID = "MovieClick"

    ' Add database and commit to server
    svr.Databases.Add(db)
    db.Update()

    ' Disconnect from server
    svr.Disconnect()
End Sub
```

Listing 14.1   Database creation

Creating Data Access Objects

After you have a database object, the next step is to create `Datasource` and `DatasourceView` (DSV) objects. The `Datasource` object is fairly trivial, consisting of little more than a connection string to your database. The DSV is a bit more complicated. The main element of the DSV is the *schema*, which is a standard `Dataset` object augmented with custom properties.

To load a schema into a DSV, you create data adapters for each of the tables you wish to load and add their schemas into a dataset. You then add any relationships necessary and finally add the dataset to a DSV, which is then added to the AMO database. Listing 14.2 demonstrates this procedure by creating a `Datasource` for the MovieClick data and a DSV that can be used to create mining models with a nested table needed for analysis of movie channels.

```
Sub CreateDataAccessObjects(ByVal db As Database)
    ' Create relational datasource
    Dim ds As New RelationalDataSource("MovieClick","MovieClick")
    ds.ConnectionString = "Provider=SQLOLEDB;Data Source=localhost;" & _
        "Initial Catalog=MovieClick;Integrated Security=True"
    db.DataSources.Add(ds)
```

Listing 14.2   Data Access Object creation

```
    ' Create connection to datasource to extract schema to dataset
    Dim dset As New DataSet()
    Dim cn As New SqlConnection("Data Source=localhost;" & _
        "Initial Catalog=MovieClick;Integrated Security=True")

    ' Create data adapters from database tables and load schemas
    Dim daCustomers As New SqlDataAdapter("Select * from Survey", cn)
    daCustomers.FillSchema(dset, SchemaType.Mapped, "Customers")
    Dim daChannels As New SqlDataAdapter("Select * from Channels", cn)
    daChannels.FillSchema(dset, SchemaType.Mapped, "Channels")

    ' Add relationship between Customers and Channels
    Dim drCustomerChannels As New DataRelation("CustomerChannels", _
            dset.Tables("Customers").Columns("SurveyTakenID"), _
            dset.Tables("Channels").Columns("SurveyTakenID"))
    dset.Relations.Add(drCustomerChannels)

    ' Create the DSV, add the dataset, and add to the database
    Dim dsv As New RelationalDataSourceView("MovieClick", "MovieClick")
    dsv.DataSourceID = "MovieClick"
    dsv.Schema = dset.Clone()

    ' Update the database to create the objects on the server.
    db.Update(UpdateOptions.ExpandFull)
End Sub
```

Listing 14.2 *(continued)*

The DSV of Listing 14.2 contains the customer table and the channels table, but
the models you want to build need more specific information than is present in
the raw data: the customers' "generation" and a list of only the premium movie
channels they watch. To accomplish this, you need to modify the code to add a
calculated column to the Customers table and swap out the Channels table with
a named query returning only the limited set of channels you are interested in.

Listing 14.3 contains `CreateDataAccessObjects` modified with a named
calculation and named query.

```
Sub CreateDataAccessObjects(ByVal db As Database)
    ' Create relational datasource
    Dim ds As New RelationalDataSource("MovieClick","MovieClick")
    ds.ConnectionString = "Provider=SQLOLEDB;Data Source=localhost;" & _
        "Initial Catalog=MovieClick;Integrated Security=True"
    db.DataSources.Add(ds)
```

Listing 14.3   Creating calculated columns and named queries *(continued)*

```
' Create connection to datasource to extract schema to dataset
Dim dset As New DataSet()
Dim cn As New SqlConnection("Data Source=localhost;" & _
    "Initial Catalog=MovieClick;Integrated Security=True")

' Create the customers data adapter with the
' calculated column appended
Dim daCustomers As New SqlDataAdapter("SELECT *, " & _
    "(CASE WHEN (Age < 30) THEN 'GenY' " & _
    " WHEN (Age >= 30 AND Age < 40) THEN 'GenX' " & _
    " ELSE 'Baby Boomer' END) AS Generation" & _
    "FROM Customers", cn)
daCustomers.FillSchema(dset, SchemaType.Mapped, "Customers")
' Add extended properties to the Generation column
' indicating to AnalysisServices that it is a
' calculated column.
dset.Tables("Customers").Columns("Generation"). _
    ExtendedProperties.Add("DbColumnName", "Generation")
dset.Tables("Customers").Columns("Generation"). _
    ExtendedProperties.Add("Description", _
    "Customer Generation")
dset.Tables("Customers").Columns("Generation"). _
    ExtendedProperties.Add("IsLogical", "True")
dset.Tables("Customers").Columns("Generation"). _
    ExtendedProperties.Add("ComputedColumnExpression", _
    "CASE WHEN (Age < 30) THEN 'GenY' " & _
    " WHEN (Age >= 30 AND Age < 40) THEN 'GenX' " & _
    " ELSE 'Baby Boomer' END")


' Create a 'pay channels' data adapter with a custom query
' for our named query.
Dim daPayChannels As New SqlDataAdapter("SELECT * FROM Channels "& _
    "WHERE Channel IN ('Cinemax', 'Encore', 'HBO', 'Showtime', " & _
    "'STARZ!', 'The Movie Channel')", cn)
daPayChannels.FillSchema(dset, SchemaType.Mapped, "PayChannels")
' Add extended properties to the PayChannels table
' indicating to AnalysisServices that it is a
' named query.
dset.Tables("PayChannels"). _
    ExtendedProperties.Add("IsLogical", "True")
dset.Tables("PayChannels"). _
    ExtendedProperties.Add("Description", _
    "Channels requiring an additional fee")
dset.Tables("PayChannels"). _
    ExtendedProperties.Add("QueryDefinition", _
    "SELECT * FROM Channels WHERE Channel IN ('Cinemax', " & _
    "'Encore', 'HBO', 'Showtime', 'STARZ!', 'The Movie Channel')")
dset.Tables("PayChannels"). _
    ExtendedProperties.Add("TableType", "View")
```

Listing 14.3 *(continued)*

```
        ' Add relationship between Customers and PayChannels
    Dim drCustomerPayChannels As New DataRelation("CustomerPayChannels",_
            dset.Tables("Customers").Columns("SurveyTakenID"), _
            dset.Tables("PayChannels").Columns("SurveyTakenID"))
    dset.Relations.Add(drCustomerPayChannels)


    ' Create the dsv, add the dataset, and add to the database
    Dim dsv As New RelationalDataSourceView("MovieClick", "MovieClick")
    dsv.DataSourceID = "MovieClick"
    dsv.Schema = dset.Clone()
    db.DataSourceViews.Add(dsv)


    ' Update the database to create the objects on the server.
    db.Update(UpdateOptions.ExpandFull)
End Sub
```

Listing 14.3   *(continued)*

Creating the Mining Structure

The next step in the data mining program is to create the mining structure that describes the domain of the problem in terms the data mining engine understands. You need to create MiningStructureColumns and specify their data types, content types, and data bindings to their source columns in the DSV. Listing 14.4 contains the code to create a mining structure that will allow you to analyze the relationships between generation and premium channels.

```
Sub CreateMiningStructure(ByVal db As Database)
    ' Initialize our Mining Structure
    Dim ms As New MiningStructure("PayChannelAnalysis", _
        "PayChannelAnalysis")
    ms.Source = New DataSourceViewBinding("MovieClick")


    ' Create the columns of the MiningStructure,
    ' setting the type, content, and data binding.


    ' UserID column
    Dim UserID As New ScalarMiningStructureColumn("UserId", "UserId")
    UserID.Type = MiningStructureColumnTypes.Long
    UserID.Content = MiningStructureColumnContents.Key
    UserID.IsKey = True
    ' Add data binding to the column.
    UserID.KeyColumns.Add("Customers", "UserId", OLE DBType.Integer)
    ' Add the column to the MiningStructure
    ms.Columns.Add(UserID)
```

Listing 14.4   Creating the mining structure *(continued)*

```
      ' Generation column
      Dim Generation As New ScalarMiningStructureColumn _
          ("Generation", "Generation")
      Generation.Type = MiningStructureColumnTypes.Text
      Generation.Content = MiningStructureColumnContents.Discrete
      Generation.KeyColumns.Add("Customers", "Generation", _
          OleDbType.VarChar)
      ' Add the column to the MiningStructure.
      ms.Columns.Add(Generation)

      ' Add Nested Table by creating a table column
      ' and adding a key column to the nested table.
      Dim PayChannels As New TableMiningStructureColumn _
          ("PayChannels", "PayChannels")
      Dim Channel As New ScalarMiningStructureColumn _
          ("Channel", "Channel")
      Channel.Type = MiningStructureColumnTypes.Text
      Channel.Content = MiningStructureColumnContents.Key
      Channel.IsKey = True
      Channel.KeyColumns.Add("PayChannels", "Channel", OleDbType.VarChar)
      PayChannels.Columns.Add(Channel)
      ms.Columns.Add(PayChannels)

      ' Add the MiningStructure to the database.
      db.MiningStructures.Add(ms)
      ms.Update()
End Sub
```

Listing 14.4   *(continued)*

NOTE You may wonder why you specify that the column content is `Key` and also have to set the `IsKey` property to `True`. This is due to the extensibility in the content types defined in the OLE DB for Data Mining specification. Currently Analysis Services supports three types of keys: Key, Key Time, and Key Sequence. Having a separate `IsKey` property allows you to take advantage of this extensibility in the future.

Creating the Mining Models

Finally, you are at the point where you can create the models you wish to use to analyze your customers. In addition to a collection of columns, a structure contains a collection of models. For each model, you add the columns you wish from the structure and set their usage to `Key`, `Predict`, or `PredictOnly`. Columns without a specified usage are assumed to be `Input`, so you do not need to explicitly set them. Columns that you want the algorithm to ignore, you simply do not add to the model.

Listing 14.5 demonstrates how to create two models inside the structure you previously built. A parameterized cluster model is created and then a tree model is built from a copy of that model.

```
Sub CreateModels(ByVal ms As MiningStructure)
    Dim ClusterModel As MiningModel
    Dim TreeModel As MiningModel
    Dim mmc As MiningModelColumn

    ' Create the Cluster model and set the
    ' algorithm and parameters.
    ClusterModel = ms.CreateMiningModel(True, _
        "Premium Generation Clusters")
    ClusterModel.Algorithm = "Microsoft_Clusters"
    ClusterModel.AlgorithmParameters.Add("CLUSTER_COUNT", 0)

    ' Add the case key - every model must contain the case key.
    mmc = ClusterModel.Columns.Add("UserID")
    mmc.SourceColumnID = "UserID"
    mmc.Usage = "Key"

    ' Add the Generation column.
    mmc = ClusterModel.Columns.Add("Generation")
    mmc.SourceColumnID = "Generation"

    ' Add the nested table.
    mmc = ClusterModel.Columns.Add("PayChannels")
    mmc.SourceColumnID = "PayChannels"

    ' Add the nested key - required for nested tables
    mmc = mmc.Columns.Add("Channel")
    mmc.SourceColumnID = "Channel"
    mmc.Usage = "Key"

    ' Copy the cluster model and change the necessary properties
    ' to make it a tree model to predict Generation.
    TreeModel = ClusterModel.Clone()
    TreeModel.Name = "Generation Trees"
    TreeModel.ID = "Generation Trees"
    TreeModel.Algorithm = "Microsoft_Decision_Trees"
    TreeModel.AlgorithmParameters.Clear()
    TreeModel.Columns("Generation").Usage = "Predict"
    TreeModel.Columns("PayChannels").Usage = "Predict"
    ms.MiningModels.Add(TreeModel)
```

Listing 14.5 Adding mining models to the structure *(continued)*

```
      ' Submit the models to the server.
      ClusterModel.Update()
      TreeModel.Update()
  End Sub
```

Listing 14.5 *(continued)*

Processing Mining Models

The code for processing an object is trivial, consisting only of the `Process` method called with the appropriate options. In the example program, you could process an individual model, the mining structure, or the entire database as you choose. However, because processing can be a rather lengthy task, it would be nice to receive progress messages from the server for the duration. Luckily, the AMO contains a `Trace` object to handle this type of server interaction. Listing 14.6 demonstrates setting up a progress trace for a processing operation.

```
Sub ProcessDatabase(ByVal svr As Server, ByVal db As Database)
    Dim t As Trace
    Dim e As TraceEvent

    ' Create the trace object to trace progress reports
    ' and add the column containing the progress description.
    t = svr.Traces.Add()
    e = t.Events.Add(TraceEventClass.ProgressReportCurrent)
    e.Columns.Add(TraceColumn.TextData)
    t.Update()

    ' Add the handler for the trace event.
    AddHandler t.OnEvent, AddressOf ProgressReportHandler

    Try
        ' Start the trace process of the database, then stop it.
        t.Start()
        db.Process(ProcessType.ProcessFull)
        t.Stop()
    Catch ex As Exception
    End Try

    ' Remove the trace from the server.
    t.Drop()
End Sub
```

Listing 14.6 Processing the database with progress reports

```
Sub ProgressReportHandler(ByVal sender As Object, _
        ByVal e As TraceEventArgs)
    lblProgress.Text = e(TraceColumn.TextData)
End Sub
```

Listing 14.6 *(continued)*

Deploying Mining Models

After creating your models, you may find that you need to move them around to different servers; for example, you may need to move them from an analytical server to a production server for embedding into line-of-business applications, or maybe simply to share a model with a colleague who cannot physically access your servers.

DETERMINING SERVER CAPABILITIES

When creating models on the server, it is useful to understand exactly what kinds of models you can create. The algorithm selection varies between Standard and Enterprise editions of SQL Server, plus there may be plug-in algorithms installed as well. Additionally, each algorithm supports a variety of parameters whose default values may vary depending on the server configuration.

The MINING_SERVICES and MINING_PARAMETERS schema rowsets described in Chapter 2 contain descriptions of the available algorithms and their capabilities. You can use any client command API to access these schemas, or, even better, you can use the object model provided in ADOMD.NET to iterate quickly through the server's data mining capabilities. The following code demonstrates how to iterate through the mining services and their respective parameters.

```
Sub DiscoverServices()
    Dim cn As New AdomdConnection("location=localhost")
    Dim ms As MiningService
    Dim mp As MiningServiceParameter
    cn.Open()
    For Each ms In cn.MiningServices
        Console.WriteLine("Service: " & ms.Name)
        For Each mp In ms.AvailableParameters
            Console.WriteLine("  Parameter: " & mp.Name & _
                "  Default: " & mp.DefaultValue)
        Next
    Next
    cn.Close()
End Sub
```

Analysis Services provides a robust backup and restore API in AMO. However, these APIs are geared more toward OLAP objects than toward data mining objects. The APIs contain many options that are unnecessary for data mining and at the same time operate solely at the database level, which is generally too coarse for most data mining operations.

Due to the mismatch in functionality provided and the functionality required in AMO, the deployment of data mining objects is handled through DMX using a command API. Using the DMX EXPORT and IMPORT commands, you can select the single model that performs best out of the forest of candidate models you created and deploy it alone, rather than deploying the entire database. Listing 14.7 demonstrates using ADOMD to transfer individual models from your current server to your production server.

```
Sub TransferModel()
    ' Create connections to the source and destination server.
    Dim cnSource As New AdomdConnection("location=localhost;" & _
        "Initial Catalog=MovieClick")
    Dim cnDest As New AdomdConnection("location=ProductionServer;" & _
        "Initial Catalog=MovieClick")

    Try
        ' Export the model to a share on the destination server.
        Dim cmdExport As New AdomdCommand
        cmdExport.Connection = cnSource
        cmdExport.CommandText = "EXPORT MINING MODEL GenerationTree " & _
            "TO '\\ProductionServer\Transfer\GenerationTree.abk' " & _
            "WITH PASSWORD= 'MyPassword'"
        cnSource.Open()
        cmdExport.ExecuteNonQuery()

        ' Import the model into the current database on the
        ' destination server.
        Dim cmdImport As New AdomdCommand
        cmdImport.Connection = cnDest
        cmdImport.CommandText = "IMPORT FROM " & _
                " c:\Transfer\GenerationTree.abk " & _
                " WITH PASSWORD= 'MyPassword' "
        cnDest.Open()
        cnDest.ExecuteNonQuery()
    Catch ex As Exception

    End Try
    cnSource.Close()
    cnDest.Close()
End Sub
```

Listing 14.7 Exporting and importing of mining models

In this example, you simply move one model between servers. The EXPORT command is flexible enough to export multiple models or entire mining structures as well. If you need to reprocess the models on the destination server, you can append INCLUDE DEPENDENCIES to the EXPORT command, and the necessary Datasource and DSV objects will be included in the export package.

NOTE Due to the fact that OLAP objects do not support object-level importing and exporting, OLAP mining models cannot be exported using the EXPORT command.

Setting Mining Permissions

After the models are built, processed, and deployed, you need to assign permissions so that they can be accessed by client applications. Permissions in Analysis Services are managed by the coordination of two objects: a Role object, which belongs to the database and contains a list of members, and a Permission object belonging to the protected object, which refers to a role and specifies the access permissions of that role. Listing 14.8 demonstrates creating a role and assigning permissions.

```
Sub SetModelPermissions(ByVal db As Database, ByVal mm As MiningModel)
    ' Create a new role and add members.
    Dim r As New Role("ModelReader", "ModelReader")
    r.Members.Add("MOVIECLICK\Jamiemac")
    r.Members.Add("MOVIECLICK\Zhaotang")

    ' Add the role to the database and update
    db.Roles.Add(r)
    r.Update()

    ' Create a permission object referring to the role.
    Dim mmp As New MiningModelPermission()
    mmp.Name = "ModelReader"
    mmp.ID = "ModelReader"
    mmp.RoleID = "ModelReader"

    ' Assign access rights to the permission.
    mmp.Access = Access.Read
    mmp.AllowBrowsing = True
    mmp.AllowDrillThrough = True
    mmp.AllowPredict = True

    ' Add permissions to the model and update
    mm.MiningModelPermissions.Add(mmp)
    mm.Update()
End Sub
```

Listing 14.8 Assigning mining model permissions

Browsing and Querying Mining Models

Creating and deploying models is only the beginning. The real fun starts when you take the power of the learned knowledge of your models and embed that directly into your applications. You can recommend products, manage inventory, forecast revenue, validate data, and perform countless other tasks limited only by your data and your imagination.

Predicting Using ADOMD.NET

Let's start with an example of a basic prediction query using ADOMD.NET. Listing 14.9 demonstrates a typical example of query execution. Readers familiar with ADO.NET will notice that the only differences between the APIs thus far are the names of the data access classes. In fact, it is equally possible to use the ADO.NET classes to perform simple queries against Analysis Services, however ADOMD.NET is optimized to work with the Analysis Services server and allows you to take advantage of additional Analysis Services features.

```
Private Sub SingleResultQuery()
    ' Create connection and command objects.
    Dim cn As New AdomdConnection("location=localhost; " & _
        "Initial Catalog=MovieClick")
    Dim cmd As New AdomdCommand()

    ' Initialize command with query
    cmd.Connection = cn
    cmd.CommandText = "SELECT Predict(Generation) " & _
        "FROM [Generation Trees] NATURAL PREDICTION JOIN " & _
        "SELECT (SELECT 'HBO' AS Channel UNION " & _
        "SELECT 'Showtime' AS Channel) as PayChannels as t"

    ' Open connection and write result to debug window
    cn.Open()
    Debug.WriteLine(cmd.ExecuteScalar().ToString())

    ' Close connection
     cn.Close()
End Sub
```

Listing 14.9 Executing a simple singleton prediction query

TIP Use `ExecuteScalar` when executing singleton queries that return a single column in a single row.

Use ExecuteReader when executing queries returning multiple columns or rows as in Listing 14.10, which performs the same prediction as in Listing 14.9 but returns the flattened result of PredictHistogram, so you can see the likelihood of all possible prediction results.

```
Private Sub MultipleRowQuery()
    ' Create connection and command objects.
    Dim cn As New AdomdConnection("location=localhost;" & _
        "Initial Catalog=MovieClick")
    Dim cmd As New AdomdCommand()

    ' Initialize command with query
    cmd.Connection = cn
    cmd.CommandText="SELECT FLATTENED PredictHistogram(Generation) " & _
        "FROM [Generation Trees] NATURAL PREDICTION JOIN " & _
        "SELECT (SELECT 'HBO' AS Channel UNION " & _
        "SELECT 'Showtime' AS Channel) as PayChannels as t"

    ' Open connection and execute query
    Dim reader As AdomdDataReader
    cn.Open()
    reader = cmd.ExecuteReader()

    ' Write field names to debug window
    Dim i As Integer
    For i = 0 To reader.FieldCount - 1
        Debug.Write(reader.GetName(i) & "\t")
    Next
    Debug.WriteLine("")

    ' Iterate results to debug window
    While reader.Read
        For i = 0 To reader.FieldCount - 1
            Debug.Write(reader.GetValue(i).ToString())
        Next
        Debug.WriteLine("")
    End While

    ' Close reader and connection
    reader.Close()
    cn.Close()
End Sub
```

Listing 14.10 Iterating a multiple-row result

In the last example, you flatten the results of a nested table query for ease of iteration. In some situations, however, flattening the results is not practical, for example when you have a query returning multiple nested tables, or even nested tables inside nested tables. Listing 14.11 demonstrates how to iterate the results of the previous example with the FLATTENED keyword removed.

```
Dim nestedreader As AdomdDataReader
While reader.Read()
    nestedreader = reader.GetReader(0)
    While nestedreader.Read()
        Debug.WriteLine(nestedreader.GetValue(0).ToString())
    End While
    nestedreader.Close()' Be sure to close the nested readers!
End While
```

Listing 14.11   Iterating the Attribute column of the nested PredictHistogram result

So far, everything you have done could have been done, albeit less efficiently, with ADO.NET. Next, you learn to expand your application's functionality by using a parameterized query to change the prediction input. ADO.NET does not support named parameters for providers other than the SQL Server relational engine. To use named parameters in your query, you are forced to use ADOMD.NET. Listing 14.12 demonstrates your data mining query using named parameters.

```
' Initialize command with parameterized query
cmd.CommandText = "SELECT PredictHistogram(Generation) " & _
    "FROM [Generation Trees] NATURAL PREDICTION JOIN " & _
    "SELECT (SELECT @Channel1 AS Channel UNION " & _
    "SELECT @Channel2 AS Channel) as PayChannels as t"

' Initialize parameters and add to command
Dim Channel1 As New AdomdParameter()
Dim Channel2 As New AdomdParameter()
Channel1.ParameterName = "@Channel1"
Channel2.ParameterName = "@Channel2"
cmd.Parameters.Add(Channel1)
cmd.Parameters.Add(Channel2)


' Set parameter values
cmd.Parameters("@Channel1").Value = "HBO"
cmd.Parameters("@Channel2").Value = "Showtime"
```

Listing 14.12   Data mining query with named parameters

Listing 14.12 assumes that you know that you only allow and require two channels to perform the prediction. Obviously, this is not always the case. ADOMD.NET allows you use a parameter to pass an entire table as the input data source. This allows you to easily perform predictions using data that is on the client or otherwise unavailable to the server. Listing 14.13 demonstrates using shaped table parameters as prediction input.

```
' Create table for case
Dim caseTable as new DataTable
caseTable.Columns.Add("CustID", System.Type.GetType("System.Int32"))
caseTable.Rows.Add(1)

' Create nested table
Dim nestedTable as new DataTable
nestedTable.Columns.Add("CustID", _
     System.Type.GetType("System.Int32"))
nestedTable.Columns.Add("Channel", _
     System.Type.GetType("System.String"))
nestedTable.Rows.Add(1,"HBO")
nestedTable.Rows.Add(1,"Showtime")
' Initialize command with parameterized query
cmd.CommandText = "SELECT PredictHistogram(Generation) " & _
    "FROM [Generation Trees] NATURAL PREDICTION JOIN " & _
    "SHAPE { @CaseTable } " & _
    "APPEND ({ @NestedTable } " & _
        "RELATE CustID to CustID) AS Channels " & _
    "as t"

' Initialize parameters and add to command
Dim caseParam As New AdomdParameter()
Dim nestedParam As New AdomdParameter()
caseParam.ParameterName = "@CaseTable"
nestedParam.ParameterName = "@NestedTable"
cmd.Parameters.Add(caseParam)
cmd.Parameters.Add(NestedParam)

' Set parameter values
cmd.Parameters("@CaseTable").Value = caseTable
cmd.Parameters("@NestedTable").Value = nestedTable
```

Listing 14.13   Data mining query with table parameters

Browsing Models

As described in Chapter 2, all the model metadata and content is accessible through schema rowsets. However, using ADOMD.NET, you can browse the server and models using a rich object model instead. Figure 14.2 shows the major data mining objects of ADOMD.NET.

As you can see from the object model, you can simply connect to the server and iterate over any of the data mining objects without having to resort to schema queries. A nice benefit to application developers is that if a connected user does not have access to a particular object, that object will simply not appear in its collection, as if it didn't exist.

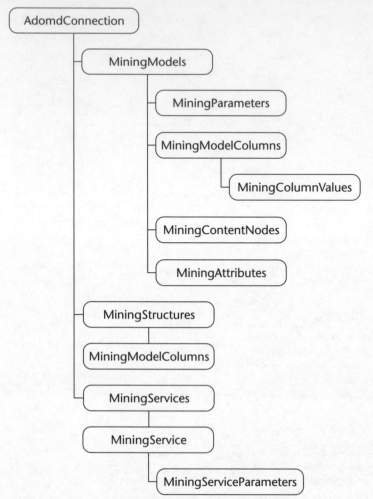

Figure 14.2   Data mining object hierarchy in ADOMD.NET

The most interesting ability you gain by using the ADOMD.NET object model is the ability to iterate mining model content in a natural, hierarchical, manner using objects instead of trying to unravel the flat schema rowset form. Using this object model makes it easy to write complex programs to explore or display the content to your users. For example, an interesting problem for the Microsoft Decision Trees algorithm is: given an attribute, find all of the trees that contain a split on that attribute.

Listing 14.13 demonstrates using the content object model to explore trees to find splits on a specified attribute. First, you identify all child nodes of the root that represents trees and then recursively check the children of the trees to see whether their marginal rule contains the requested attribute. By looking at the node type rather than at the algorithm used, this function will work against any model containing trees, whether it uses the Microsoft Decision Trees algorithm, the Microsoft Time Series algorithm, or any third-party tree-based algorithms.

```
' Identify all the attributes that split
' on a specified attribute.
Sub FindSplits(ByVal cn As AdomdConnection, _
        ByVal ModelName As String, ByVal AttributeName As String)
    ' Find the specified model.
    Dim model As MiningModel
    model = cn.MiningModels(ModelName)
    If IsDBNull(model) Then Return

    ' Look for the attribute in all model trees.
    Dim node As MiningContentNode
    For Each node In model.Content
        If node.Type = MiningNodeType.Tree Then
            FindSplits(node, AttributeName)
        End If
    Next
End Sub

' Recursively search for the attribute among content nodes
' Return when children exhausted or attribute is found
Sub FindSplits(ByVal node As MiningContentNode, _
        ByVal AttributeName As String)
    ' Check for the attribute in the MarginalRule.
    If node.MarginalRule.Contains(AttributeName) Then
        ' The attribute column contains the
        ' name of the tree.
        Debug.WriteLine(node.Attribute)
        Return
    End If

    ' Recurse over child nodes
    Dim childNode As MiningContentNode
    For Each childNode In node.Children
        FindSplits(childNode, AttributeName)
    Next
End Sub
```

Listing 14.13 Exploring content using ADOMD.NET

You can also use the content to find the reason for a prediction by using the `PredictNodeId` function. For example, you can use this query

```
SELECT Predict(Generation), PredictNodeId(Generation) ...
```

to retrieve the ID of the node used to generate the prediction, and feed the result into a function like that in Listing 14.14.

```
Function GetPredictionReason(ByVal model As MiningModel, _
      ByVal NodeID As String) As String
   Dim node As MiningContentNode
   node = model.GetNodeFromUniqueName(NodeID)
   If IsDBNull(node) Then Throw New System.Exception("Node not found")

   return node.Description;
End Function
```

Stored Procedures

ADOMD.NET provides an excellent object model for accessing server objects and browsing content. However, there are some major drawbacks. For the `FindSplits` method in Listing 14.14, you need to bring the entire content from the server to the client to determine the list. A model with 1,000 trees and 1,000 nodes per tree would require the marshaling of over 1,000,000 rows, even if only a handful of trees referenced the desired attribute. Also, in the `GetPredictionReason` function, even though you can access the desired node directly using `GetNodeFromUniqueName`, you are still causing a round trip to the server on each call; performing this operation in batch is not recommended.

There is a solution to these problems. Analysis Services in SQL Server 2005 supports stored procedures that can be written in any managed language such as C#, VB.NET, or managed C++. The object model, ADOMD+, is almost identical to that of ADOMD.NET, making conversion between the two models simple. The clear advantage of ADOMD+ is that all of the content is available on the server, and you can return only the information you need to the server. You can call UDFs by themselves, using the `CALL` syntax or as part of a DMX query. For example, the following query:

```
CALL MySprocs.TreeHelpers.FindSplits('Generation Trees','HBO')
```

calls a stored procedure directly and simply returns the result, whereas the query:

```
SELECT Predict(Generation),
  MySprocs.TreeHelpers.GetPredictionReason(PredictNodeId(Generation))
...
```

calls a stored procedure for every row returned from the prediction query. In this case, the query will return the prediction result plus the explanation of the result for every row.

CALLING VBA AND EXCEL FUNCTIONS AS STORED PROCEDURES

If you have Microsoft Office installed on the same machine as your Analysis Services server, you can leverage the functions of Visual Basic for Applications (VBA) and Excel as stored procedures inside your DMX queries.

For example, you can convert the prediction output to lowercase like this:

```
SELECT LCase(Predict(MyModel.[Home Ownership])) FROM MyModel
PREDICTION JOIN ....
```

If a function exists in both Excel and VBA, you need to prefix the function name with the name of the function. For example, to get the base 10 log of a prediction from Excel, and the natural log of the prediction from VBA, you would issue a query like this:

```
SELECT Excel!Log(Predict(Sales)), VBA!Log(Predict(Sales))
From MyModel ....
```

If an Excel or VBA function also exists in MDX or DMX or contains a $ character, you need to escape the function name with square brackets ([ ]). For example to format a prediction as currency, for example $20.56, you would issue a query like this:

```
SELECT [Format](Predict(Sales), '$d.dd') FROM MyModel ....
```

The supported functions from VBA and Excel are listed in Appendix B.

Writing Stored Procedures

After you reference the required assembly — Microsoft.AnalysisServices .AdomdServer — you have access to a global object called the Context. This object, similar to the ADOMD.NET connection object contains all the collections of major objects, such as MiningModels, that you can access in your stored procedure. Stored procedures can also take advantage of the Current-MiningModel property of the Context object that refers to the model that is the subject of the query.

Stored procedures can take any simple type as a parameter and can return simple types or even a DataTable or DataSet in response. A client using CALL to call a stored procedure returning a simple type will not receive a value, although the stored procedure will be executed. A client calling a stored procedure inside a prediction query that returns a DataTable or DataSet will receive a nested table containing the returned rows.

Stored Procedures and Prepare

When writing a procedure to be executed on the server, you need to know when you are being called to return a result, and when you are being called simply to gather schema information during a prepare call. Additionally, you

SENDING COMPLEX TYPES TO STORED PROCEDURES

If you need to send complex types, such as structures or arrays, to a stored procedure, you can serialize them using the XMLSerializer on the client and send them as an XML string. On the server side, deserialize the structure or array, and call an overloaded function using the complex types you are interested in. For example, you may have a function that requires an array of the following type:

```
Public Structure MyType
    Public a As Integer
    Public b As String
End Structure
```

You could write the following function to serialize the array into an XML string and send that string as a parameter to the stored procedure:

```
Function SerializeMyType(ByVal MyArray As MyType()) As String
    Dim s As New
System.Xml.Serialization.XmlSerializer(MyArray.GetType())
    Dim sw = New System.IO.StringWriter()
    Dim str As String
    s.Serialize(sw, MyArray)
    Return sw.ToString()
End Function
```

On the server side, you would duplicate the type definition and write a stub function to deserialize the array and call the real function.

```
Public Function MySproc(ByVal xmlString As String) As DataTable
    Dim MyArray() As MyType
    Dim s As New
System.Xml.Serialization.XmlSerializer(MyArray.GetType())
    Dim sr = New System.IO.StringReader(xmlString)
    MyArray = s.Deserialize(sr)
        Return MySproc(MyArray)
        End Function
Function MySproc(ByVal MyArray As MyType()) As DataTable
        ... ' Function body
End Function
```

This strategy will allow you to pass complex types and will prepare you for future versions that may allow naturally passing complex types

need to indicate that your procedure is safe to call during a prepare operation and that calling it won't have any undesirable side effects; you wouldn't want to create the same object twice, for instance.

The `Context` object contains an `ExecuteForPrepare` property that you can check before performing any time-consuming operations in your procedure. If you are returning a `DataTable` or `DataSet`, you should fully define the objects and return them empty of data so the client will know the schema. In general, you should not raise errors during preparation, especially for missing objects, because the prepare call could be called during a batch query, and the objects may exist by the time the procedure is called to return a result.

To indicate that your procedure does not have any unwanted side effects, you must add the custom attribute `SafeToPrepare`.

A Stored Procedure Example

Listing 14.15 demonstrates a stored procedure written in VB.NET. The methods are the same as in Listing 14.13 and 14.14 but is modified to operate on the server, taking into account the presence of the `Context` object and properly handling situations where the procedure is called during a prepare operation.

```
Imports Microsoft.AnalysisServices.AdomdServer
Imports System.Data

Public Class TreeHelper
    <SafeToPrepare(True)> _
        Public Function FindSplits(ByVal ModelID As String, _
            ByVal AttributeName As String) As DataTable

        ' Create the result table and add a column.
        ' for the attribute
        Dim tblResult As New DataTable()
        tblResult.Columns.Add("Attribute", _
            System.Type.GetType("System.String"))

        ' If this is a prepare statement, return the empty
        ' table for schema information.
        If Context.ExecuteForPrepare Then Return tblResult

        ' Access the model and throw an exception if not found.
        ' Error text will be propagated to the client.
        Dim model As MiningModel
        model = Context.MiningModels(ModelID)
        If IsDBNull(model) Then Throw _
            New System.Exception("Model not found")

        ' Look for the attribute in all model trees.
        If model.Content.Count > 0 Then
            Dim node As MiningContentNode
            For Each node In model.Content(0).Children
                If node.Type = MiningNodeType.Tree Then
                    FindSplits(node, AttributeName, tblResult)
                End If
            Next
        End If
```

Listing 14.15 Data mining stored procedures *(continued)*

```
             ' Return the table containing the result.
         Return tblResult
     End Function


     Private Function FindSplits(ByVal node As MiningContentNode, _
             ByVal AttributeName As String, _
             ByRef tblResult As DataTable) As Boolean


         ' Check for the attribute in the MarginalRule
         ' and add row to the table if found
         If node.MarginalRule.Contains(AttributeName) Then
             Dim row() As String = {node.Attribute.Name}
             tblResult.Rows.Add(row)
             Return True
         End If


         ' Recurse over child nodes
         Dim childNode As MiningContentNode
         For Each childNode In node.Children
             If (FindSplits(childNode, AttributeName, tblResult)) Then
                 Return True
             End If
         Next
         Return False
     End Function


     <SafeToPrepare(True)> _
     Public Function GetPredictionReason( _
             ByVal NodeID As String) As String
         ' Return immediately if executing for prepare
         If Context.ExecuteForPrepare Then Return ""

         ' Return the node description.
         Return Context.CurrentMiningModel. _
             GetNodeFromUniqueName(NodeID).Description
     End Function
 End Class
```

Listing 14.15   *(continued)*

Executing Queries inside Stored Procedures

A common use of a stored procedure is to encapsulate a query for easy reuse.
For example, if your application needed to predict Generation, but you needed
the flexibility to change the model that was being used or add additional business logic, you could write a procedure that executes the query and redeploy
the procedure as necessary without changing the application layer.

Server ADOMD allows the execution of DMX queries using the same objects that you would use with ADOMD.NET, the only exception being that you do not have to specify a connection, since you are already connected. Results from the query can be copied into a `DataTable`, or you can simply return the `DataReader` returned by `ExecuteReader`. Listing 14.16 demonstrates the query from Listing 14.9 implemented as a UDF.

```
Imports Microsoft.AnalysisServices.AdomdServer
Imports System.Data

Public Class MyClass
 <SafeToPrepare(True)> _
Public Function PredictGeneration() as AdomdDataReader
    Dim cmd As New AdomdCommand()

    ' Initialize command with query
    cmd.CommandText = "SELECT Predict(Generation) " & _
       "FROM [Generation Trees] NATURAL PREDICTION JOIN " &
       "SELECT (SELECT 'HBO' AS Channel UNION  " & _
       "SELECT 'Showtime' AS Channel) as PayChannels as t"

    ' Return result to client
    Return cmd.ExecuteReader()
End Sub
```

Listing 14.16 Executing a DMX query inside a stored procedure

In this example, if you wanted to change the model that was performing the prediction, you would change the query inside the stored procedure, and you wouldn't have to change queries embedded inside your application. Of course, you can parameterize your query as demonstrated in Listing 14.12.

NOTE Stored procedures cannot be used to implement security in Analysis Services. The security context of the current user is used to determine the access to the objects inside the Analysis Services server. That is, any user calling a procedure that queries a mining model who does not read permission on that model will receive a permission error. Similarly, a user calling the `GetPredictionReason` UDF from Listing 14.15 who does not have browse permission on the model will also receive a permission error.

Deploying and Debugging Stored Procedure Assemblies

After you have compiled and built your stored procedure, you need to deploy the procedure to your Analysis Server so that you can call it from DMX. To add a .NET assembly to your Analysis Services project, you right-click the Assemblies folder in the Solution Explorer and select New Assemble Reference.

When you deploy your project, your assembly is encoded and sent to the Analysis Server, where it is available for use in the project database. When you need to update your assembly, you can simply redeploy it. If you are using a live project, the assembly is immediately deployed on the server. To update an assembly in a live project, delete the assembly and add it back to the project.

If you have a general-purpose assembly that you want to access across all databases on the server, you can use SQL Management Studio to deploy it at the server level. In the Object Explorer, right-click the Assemblies collection of the server. From there, you can select Add Assembly and pick your assembly to add.

Debugging assemblies is best done when running the server and client on the same machine; you can use a development license of SQL Server for this purpose. To debug the assembly in Visual Studio, select Attach To Process from the Debug menu. Select the executable `msmdsrv.exe` from the list, and make sure that the dialog box displays Common Language Runtime next to Attach To. Once you have followed these steps, you will be able to set breakpoints in your stored procedures.

Summary

In this chapter, you learned about the variety of APIs that can be used to access functionality of Analysis Services programmatically. Although many APIs are supported, the two most important APIs are AMO and ADOMD.NET. AMO is used for programmatically creating, processing, and managing mining models, structure, and your servers. ADOMD.NET is the general client API for browsing and prediction queries.

Using these APIs, you can create intelligent applications of your own. The logic of your application can involve dynamically creating mining models to solve user-defined problems. It can apply the predictive power of the data mining algorithms or examine the learned content of the mining models to provide new insights and new abilities to your users. And finally, you can leverage your server in your application by writing user-defined functions that have access to all of the server resources through a .NET programming model.

Implementing a Web Cross-Selling Application

Cross-selling is a very common business problem. It involves suggesting a list of new products based on those in the customer's current or previous shopping basket. For example, if you go to Amazon.com and put a book in your shopping cart, you get a set of other book recommendations. This list is based on the market basket analysis of thousands of customers with similar purchases. Good recommendations improve customers' shopping experiences and thus increase the overall sales. Bad recommendations annoy customers and eventually drive them away. The major challenge of cross-selling is how to give each customer the right set of recommendations. While the shop product catalog is small, it is relatively easy to give suggestions based on marketing experiences. However, when the number of distinct products is large, the problem is pushed to a new dimension.

Suppose that you are the owner of MoviePick.com, an online retail store that sells movies. You have thousands of movies at MoviePick.com. You want to increase movie sales by giving online shoppers personalized suggestions. In this chapter, we will help you to solve this business problem using data mining techniques.

In this chapter, you will learn about:

- Source data descriptions
- Building recommendation models with the Microsoft Decision Trees and Microsoft Association Rules algorithms.

- The difference between Microsoft Decision Trees and Microsoft Association Rules for cross-selling
- Integrating your predictions within Web applications

Source Data Description

Figure 15.1 gives the partial schema of the MoviePick.com data mart. Two tables are shown in the figure: Customers and Purchase. The Customers table contains the customer demographic information such as age, education, gender, income, and so on. It is a dimension table. The Purchase table stores the historical transactions of the customer's previous purchases. It is a fact table with two columns: CustomerID and Movie. Each customer has bought a set of movies. The relationship between these two tables is 1 to *n*.

Building Your Model

The first step in a data mining project is to understand the business requirement and identify the proper data mining task for this business problem. The list of data mining tasks includes classification, regression, association, segmentation, forecasting, and so on. Most of the data mining algorithms in SQL Server 2005 can be applied to multiple tasks. After you identify the data mining task, you can apply the set of algorithms that is suitable for this task to build mining models.

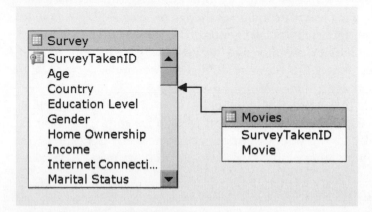

Figure 15.1 Schema of MoviePick.Com

Identifying the Data Mining Task

Before building any mining models, you need to identify the type of data mining task for the business problem. In this case, the goal is to analyze the movies customers tend to buy together. After you get these patterns, you can use them for making recommendations. Based on what was defined in the Chapter 1, this problem belongs to the data mining association task. There are a few Microsoft data mining algorithms that you can apply to the association task; the two most suitable ones are Microsoft Decision Trees and Microsoft Association Rules. In this chapter, we use these two algorithms to build models.

Using Decision Trees for Association

In Chapter 5, you learned how decision trees can be applied to association analysis. Usually there is a predictable nested table in the association model. Each nested key is modeled as a predictable attribute, and a decision tree is built for each of the nested keys during the process.

NOTE Nested tables need to be set as `Predict` if you want to analyze the relationship among the nested keys (Movies, Products, and so on). If you set the nested table to `Predict_Only`, you won't find splits based on other movies in the case of the Microsoft Decision Tree algorithm, and you won't find rules with other movies on the left side in the case of the Association Rules algorithm.

Figure 15.2 displays the model definition. The model has only one case-level attribute, which is the case key `CustomerID`. Purchase is a nested table, with `Movie` modeled as the nested key. The model will analyze the movie associations purely based on each customer's shopping cart. You can also include demographic information in the mining structure. The model will then analyze the associations among all the movies as well as the demographic information.

Figure 15.2 The Decision Tree model for movie association

After processing the model, you get a set of decision trees. Figure 15.3 displays one of the decision trees predicting the movie *Jaws*. Only about 2% of the customers purchase this movie. The first tree split is on *Jurassic Park*. Among those who like *Jurassic Park*, about 20% also like *Jaws*. This gives a lift of 10 times compared to the overall population. Among those who don't like *Jurassic Park* but like *E.T.*, about 10% also like *Jaws*. This tree tells us that *Jurassic Park* and *E.T.* are good predictors for *Jaws*. You can quantitatively measure the relationship between these predictors and the predictable attribute (*Jurassic Park*) based on the tree splitting scores at each level.

Figure 15.4 shows the dependency network of the tree model. This can be thought as a bird's eye view from the top of the forest. Each node is a decision tree. When you double-click any node you see the details of the underlying tree. Each edge represents the relationship between two trees. Each edge has a direction, which indicates the direction of the prediction. Each edge also has a weight, which represents the strength of the prediction. For example, from the figure you can see that *Jurassic Park* predicts *Jaws*. *E.T.* and *Jaws* predict each other. All information displayed in the Dependency Network viewer is derived from source trees.

Figure 15.3 Tree for *Jaws*

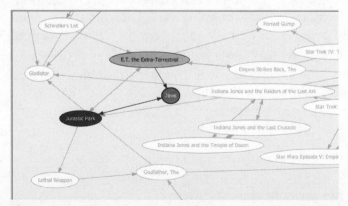

Figure 15.4 Dependency Network viewer of Decision Tree model

By default, the mining model builds 255 trees, even though there may be thousands of different movies. These 255 movies are chosen by the feature selection component in the Microsoft Decision Tree algorithm. As explained in Chapter 5, you can raise this limit by a setting higher value in `Maximum_Input_Attribute` and `Maximum_Output_Attribute` parameters. However, the processing time and tree loading time will be longer. If decision trees don't have enough splits due to the sparsity of the data, you can reduce the value of `Complexity_Penalty` to create reasonably sized trees. The default setting for `Complexity_Penalty` tends to be high when the data is not dense.

When there are hundreds of thousands of different movies, the Microsoft Decision Trees algorithm is clearly not the best choice.

In SQL Server 2005, the feature selection component is part of the algorithm. Different algorithms have different feature selection criteria.

TIP Depending on which algorithm you are using, the feature selection algorithm may be different. For Naive Bayesian and clustering, it uses entropy-based interestingness score, which tells how an attribute would be "interesting." For decision trees, it uses the same interestingness score for output attribute feature selection. Then, it calculates the split score for each input attribute versus the selected output attributes. Input feature selection is based on the calculated split score. This will effectively tells you which input attributes are worth consideration, and which ones are not, based on selected output attributes. There is no feature selection when using Association Rules, as it has no built-in feature selection component. You can specify the feature selection by setting the value for `Minimum_Support` and `Minimum_Probablity`.

Using the Association Rules Algorthim

The Association Rules algorithm is an efficient counting algorithm. It counts the support of each frequent itemset, meaning the number of distinct customers who purchase both Movie *A* and Movie *B*. This is the algorithm designed for market basket analysis.

Based on the same mining structure displayed in Figure 15.1, you can create a related mining model using the Microsoft Association algorithm. As explained in Chapter 9, you need to specify the two threshold parameters before processing the model. The first parameter, `Minimum_Support`, is used to filter unpopular itemsets. The other parameter is `Minimum_Probability`, which is used to restrict rules. Rules will be used for prediction. Rules are generated based on the frequent itemsets. The Association algorithm is very sensitive to `Minimum_Support`. If this parameter is set too high, there won't be enough itemsets and rules. If this parameter is set too low, the model processing time will increase exponentially.

In this example, we set the `Mininum_Support` to `0.01`, which means we are interested in only those itemsets that appear in at least 1% of all shopping carts. We set the `Minimum_Probability` to be `0.30`, which means that if 30% of the customers who purchase Movie *A* also purchase Movie *B*, we consider `A=>B` as a qualified rule. The model is shown in Figure 15.5.

The Association model and the Decision Tree model share the same mining structure. As the mining structure is processed while training the tree model, the source data has already been tokenized and the correlations among movies have been counted. This saves much time for Association model processing.

Figure 15.6 displays the dependency network view of the Association model. The dependency network is generated based on the pairwise rules. Usually, an association model has more rules than those displayed in the dependency network. By default, the dependency network displays only 60 popular nodes. The strength of each link represents the importance of the rule. Lowering the value of `Minimum_Probability` and `Minimum_Support` results in the model returning more rules.

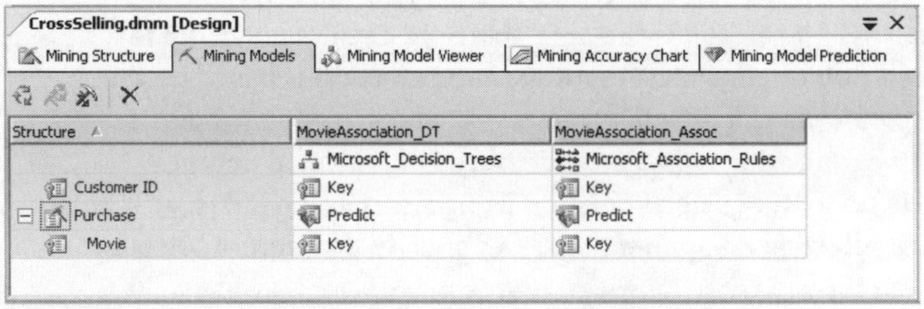

Figure 15.5   Association model for movie association

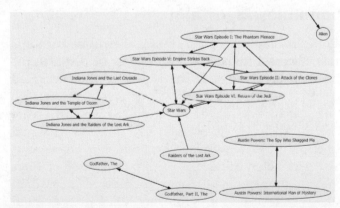

Figure 15.6   Dependency network for movie association

Comparing the Two Models

Both the Microsoft Decision Trees and Microsoft Association algorithms find the relationship among these movies. The discovered patterns are represented in different forms: one with decision trees and the other with a set of frequent itemsets and rules. Naturally, you have a question: which technique to use for the cross-selling model.

Table 15.1 gives a general comparison of the Microsoft Decision Trees and Microsoft Association Rules algorithms for association tasks. The Decision Trees algorithm has the advantage of showing deeper correlations. It is rather easy for the user to visualize all the patterns related to a given movie by browsing the decision tree. The Decision Tree algorithm also supports continuous inputs; for example, you can add continuous attributes such as age and income in the model. The drawback of using the Decision Trees algorithm is its scalability, since it builds one tree per movie.

The biggest advantage of the Microsoft Association algorithm is its performance and scalability. The drawback is that the algorithm is sensitive to the threshold parameter settings. You need to adjust these parameter values in order to have a good model.

> **NOTE** In many cases, the Microsoft Decision Trees algorihtm performs well for association tasks. However, decision trees may ignore patterns in some cases.
>
> For example, *The GodFather*, *GodFather II*, and *Godfather III* are highly correlated. In the tree of *GodFather III*, the first split is on *Godfather II*. The *Godfather* and *Godfather II* are highly correlated. Those who like *GodFather II* also like *The Godfather*. Since the split on *Godfather II* is almost equivalent to splitting on *The Godfather*, after the first split, there aren't any further splits on *The Godfather*. The dependency network is generated based on the top three levels of decision tree splits. As a consequence, no link exists between *The GodFather* and *Godfather III* in the depency network. For associative prediction queries given *The Godfather*, the predicted results won't contain *Godfather III*, since this pattern is covered by *Godfather II*.
>
> This phenomenon is due to the nature of decision trees. It may hide information if some input attributes are highly correlated. The general recommendation for this is to try using several different algorithms.

Table 15.1   Comparison of decision trees and association rules for the association task

	MICROSOFT DECISION TREES	MICROSOFT ASSOCIATION RULES
Pros	More detailed patterns for each item Support continuous input	Fast, scalable
Cons	Not scalable to large catalogs	Very sensitive to the algorithm parameters

TIP Apart from the Microsoft Decision Tree and Association algorithms, a few other techniques of SQL Server 2005 can be applied for association task. These techniques include Naïve Bayes, neural network, and even clustering algorithms. Generally speaking, any algorithm except the time series algorithm that allows nested tables to be predictable can be used for associative analysis. In the case of Naïve Bayes, it calculates the conditional probabilities for each movie given other movies during training. During prediction, it uses conditional probabilities to predict other associated movies for each movie in the shopping basket of the input case, and returns the top *n* most likely ones based on the probabilities.

In general, we don't recommend you use algorithms other than decision trees and association for cross-selling for the reason of scalability and accuracy. For a small dataset with a limited number of items (catalog) in the nested key, you may try these different techniques.

Making Predictions

After the models are processed, you can use their patterns to predict the list of movies in which new customers may be interested.

Making Batch Prediction Queries

MoviePick.com has two new tables: NewCustomer and NewCustomerPurchase. NewCustomer contains a list of new customers with their demographic information. NewCustomerPurchase contains the list of movies that each new customer has purchased recently. As store manager, you plan to do a mailing campaign, sending these customers a set of personalized movie recommendations.

You can get the best recommendations for your customers by using the following prediction query:

```
SELECT
  t.CustomerID
  (Predict(Purchase, $AdjustedProbability, 5)) as Recommendation
From
  MovieAssociation
PREDICTION JOIN
  SHAPE {
  OPENROWSET('SQLOLEDB.1',
    'Integrated Security=SSPI;Initial Catalog=MovieSurvey;Data
Source=localhost',
    'SELECT
      CustomerID
    FROM
      NewCustomer
     ORDER BY
      CustomerID')}
  APPEND ({
  OPENROWSET('SQLOLEDB.1',
    'Integrated Security=SSPI; Initial Catalog=MovieSurvey;Data
Source=localhost',
    'SELECT Movie, CustomerID
    FROM
     NewCustomerPurchase
    ORDER BY
      CustomerID')}
    RELATE
      CustomerID TO CustomerID)
    AS
      NewCustomerPurchase AS t
ON
  MovieAssociation.Purchase.Movie = t.NewCustomerPurchase.Movie
```

The preceding query can be generated using Prediction Query Builder in the
BI Dev Studio. Figure 15.7 displays the results of this prediction query.

TIP `Predict(Purchase, 5)` returns the five most likely products based on
the probability. Sometimes items with highest probiblities may not be the
best ones to recommend. For example, if every customer likes *Star Wars*,
recommending *Star Wars* may not be necessary. For this purpose, you can use
`AdjustedProbability Predict(Purchase, $AdjustedProbability, 5)`
instead. `AdjustedProbability` is derived from probability, but it penalizes
those items with high popularity. We recommend you try both `Probability`
and `AdjustedProbability` in your prediction query and pick the one that
makes more sense for your application.

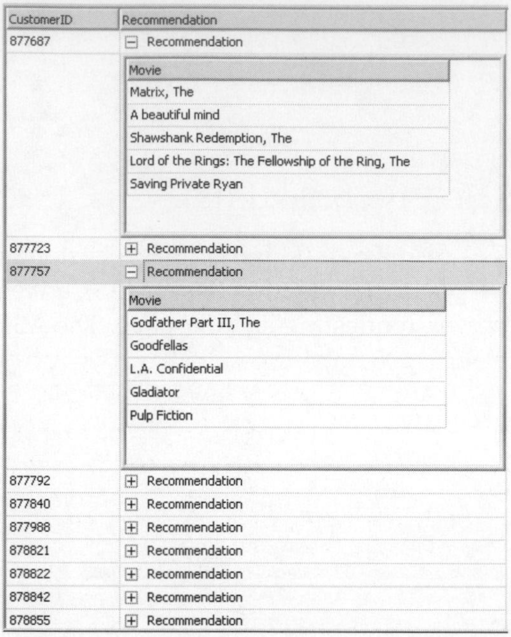

CustomerID	Recommendation
877687	⊟ Recommendation
	Movie
	Matrix, The
	A beautiful mind
	Shawshank Redemption, The
	Lord of the Rings: The Fellowship of the Ring, The
	Saving Private Ryan
877723	⊞ Recommendation
877757	⊟ Recommendation
	Movie
	Godfather Part III, The
	Goodfellas
	L.A. Confidential
	Gladiator
	Pulp Fiction
877792	⊞ Recommendation
877840	⊞ Recommendation
877988	⊞ Recommendation
878821	⊞ Recommendation
878822	⊞ Recommendation
878842	⊞ Recommendation
878855	⊞ Recommendation

Figure 15.7 Query result for movie recommendation

Using Singleton Prediction Queries

In many cases, the information about new customers has not yet been stored in the database. For example, if a Web customer visits MoviePick.com to purchase movies, you want to give the customer recommendations in real time based on what he/she has selected in the shopping cart. To do this, you can use the DMX singleton query:

```
SELECT
    (Predict(purchase, 6)) as [Recommendation]
From
  [MovieAssoc]
NATURAL PREDICTION JOIN
  (Select  (Select 'Jaws' as Movie)
     Union (Select 'Matrix' as Movie) as Purchase) as NewCustomer
```

Integrating Predictions with Web Applications

You have explored association patterns from the historical data of MoviePick .com using the decision trees and association algorithms. We also showed you the prediction queries you need to get the movie recommendation for each customer. In the next step, we add the recommendation feature in the Web site. In this section, we discuss the details about integrating data mining prediction features in a Web application.

Understanding Web Application Architecture

A Web application usually has *n* tiers as displayed in Figure 15.8. A customer uses a Web browser to connect to the Internet Information Server (IIS), a Web server integrated inside a Windows server, requesting an ASP page. The ASP page connects to the SQL Server relational database to display the list of movies so the customer can pick one. After the customer selects a movie, an ASP page generates a singleton prediction query based on the contents of this customer's shopping cart. The ASP page then connects to SQL Server Analysis Services through ADO.NET, ADOMD.NET, or OLE DB directly and sends the prediction query against a given mining model. The results of the prediction are displayed in the Web page as recommendations. A singleton prediction can be executed in real time.

The cross-selling mining model is retrained regularly, for example, once every two weeks. While the content of the model changes after each update, the model definition remains the same. Thus, the prediction query generated by the ASP page is always valid. No matter how frequently the model is reprocessed, you don't need to update the query embedded in ASP pages. In many large enterprises, mining models are built by data analysts, whereas applications are written by software developers. The server-side mining model architecture greatly reduces the dependency between them.

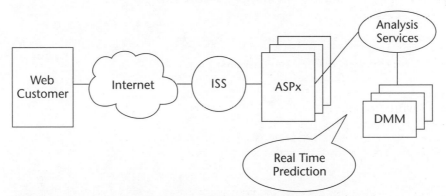

Figure 15.8   Architecture of a Web-based cross-selling application

Setting the Permissions

After the mining model is created, you need to assign the proper permissions for your Web customers. First, you create a new database role ASP in the Analysis Services server with Read permission on the database. You can use the Create Role dialog box in the SQL Workbench environment, as displayed in Figure 15.9.

After the ASP role is created, you then assign the permission on the mining model for this new role. In the Web recommendation application you need to assign only the Read right for the ASP role, because Web customers only query the model for recommendations. (See Figure 15.10.) Because ASP pages execute only prediction queries, you don't need to add Browse and Drill Through permissions for the role.

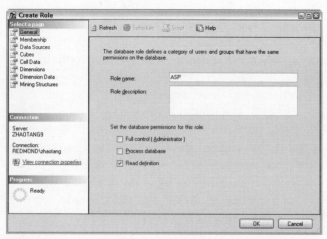

Figure 15.9   Creating a new role in the Analysis Services database

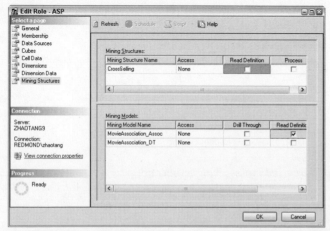

Figure 15.10   Assigning the permissions on mining model

The last step is to associate users to the newly created role. Because ASP has only the query right, you can assign `WebApplicationAccount` to this role as displayed in Figure 15.11.

Examining Sample Code for the Web Recommendation Application

In this section, you take a closer look at how to build a Web application that includes the recommendation feature. The code presented here is written in C# and is embedded in the ASP.NET page.

Listing 15.1 connects to Analysis Services through ADOMD.NET.

```
using System;
using Microsoft.AnalysisServices.AdomdClient;
using System.Data;

AdomdConnection con;

static bool CreateADOMDConnection()
{
  con = new AdomdConnection("Data Source=ASServer;
Catalog=MovieAssociation; Integrated Security=SSPI");
  try
  {
     con.Open();
  }
  catch (System.Exception e)
  {
     Log(e.Message);
     return false;
  }
  return true;
}
```

Listing 15.1   Connecting to Analysis Services through ADOMD.NET

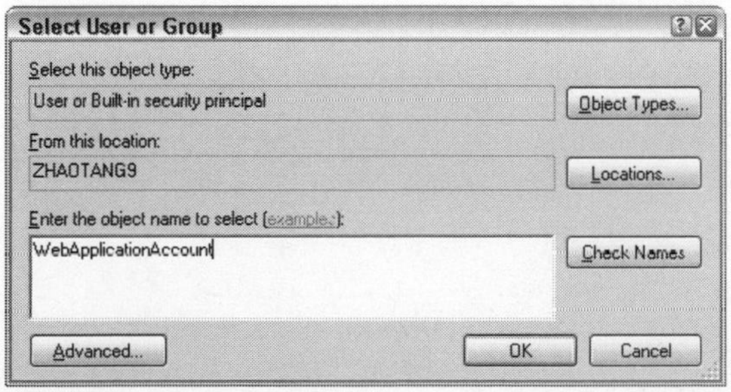

Figure 15.11   Add Everyone as a member of the new role

The Web application will dynamically generate a DMX singleton prediction query. The following `GenerateDMX` function is invoked each time a customer selects a movie in the shopping cart. `SelectList` is a list box for storing the list of movies the customer picked. When there is more than one movie in the shopping cart, the singleton query uses the `Union` operator to construct multiple rows of the table column Movies.

```
public string GenerateDMX()
{
    static string DMX1 = "Select Flattened Predict(Purchase,5) From
        MovieAssociation Natural Prediction Join (Select (";
    static string DMX2 = ") as Purchase) as input";
    int Count = SelectedList.Items.Count;
    string DMX = "";
    for (int i=0; i<Count; i++)
    {
    string movieName = SelectedList.Items[i].Text;
            DMX += "select '" + movieName + "' as Movie ";
            if (i<Count-1)
                    DMX += "UNION ";
    }
    DMX = DMX1 + DMX + DMX2;
    return DMX ;
}
```

The `ExecuteAndFetchSQL` function executes the prediction query through `AdomdCommand` object and fetches the query result using a `DataReader` object. Each predicted item in the record set is displayed in a list box of the recommendation Web page:

```
public bool ExecuteAndFetchSQL(string strCommand)
{
 AdomdCommand cmd = (AdomdCommand)
 con.CreateCommand();
 cmd.Text = strCommand;
 IDataReader dr - null;
 try
 {
    dr = cmd.ExecuteReader();

 }
 catch(Exception e)
 {
    Log(e.Message);
    return false;
 }
    ...
```

```
//display the result in the listbox
while(dr.Read())
{
    string val = dr.GetString(0);
SuggestedList.Items.Add(val);
}
...
return true;
}
```

Figure 15.12 is the MoviePick.com Web site with a cross-selling feature integrated. When a customer picks a movie from the move list, for example, *Forrest Gump*, he/she immediately sees a list of movie suggestions below the shopping cart. The recommendations are purely based on other customers' shopping patterns in similar cases. These patterns are stored in either a decision trees model or an association model.

The customer can then pick movies directly from the suggested list. Again, once an item is added or removed from the shopping cart, a new singleton prediction query is executed against the model, which returns a new set of recommendations.

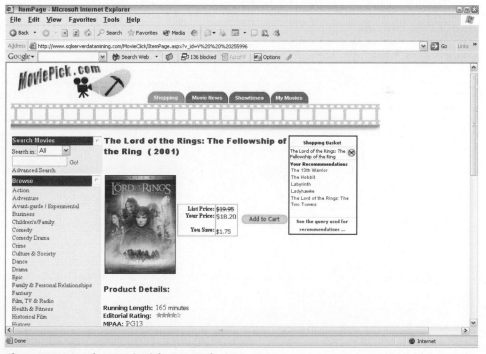

Figure 15.12   The MoviePick.com Web site

Summary

In this chapter, you learned how to build mining models to do market basket analysis. Several algorithms in SQL Server 2005 can be applied for data mining association tasks. The recommended ones are Microsoft Decision Trees and Microsoft Association Rules. You learned the pros and cons of these two algorithms.

The second half of the chapter talked about how to write associative prediction queries and how to integrate these queries into a Web cross-selling application. You learned about the architecture of such a Web application with data mining predictions.

Advanced Forecasting Using Microsoft Excel

For many people, Microsoft Excel is the beginning and end of data analysis. Excel is used to view data, perform simple calculations, build advanced financial models, and report the results. Forecasting is one of the most common tasks that analysts using Excel are tasked to perform, yet Excel's own tools for performing said forecasts are somewhat paltry. SQL Server Data Mining provides an excellent algorithm for predicting future values of time series; what if you could leverage that power directly inside Excel?

It turns out that you can. Using a feature called *session mining models*, you can programmatically create, train, and predict from the data mining engine using temporary models that automatically disappear when you disconnect. In this chapter, we explain how that works by implementing an advanced forecasting tool for Excel.

In this chapter, you will learn about:

- Configuring your server to accept session mining models
- Using the Advanced Forecasting sample add-in
- The architecture of an Analysis Services Excel add-in
- Generating XML for analysis rowsets from Excel
- Automatic creation and training of a session mining model
- Retrieving prediction results into an Excel worksheet

Configuring Analysis Services for Session Models

The Advanced Forecasting tool for Excel uses a feature of Analysis Services called *session mining models*. A session mining model is a model that is created in the context of a single connection. This model is accessible only from this session and is automatically deleted when the session ends. Since nonadministrators can create session models, thereby putting additional load on the server, this feature needs to be explicitly turned on by the Analysis Services server administrator before it can be used. The following steps outline how to turn session mining models on in Analysis Services:

1. Launch SQL Management Studio.
2. Connect to your Analysis Services server.
3. Right-click on your server in the Object Explorer and select Properties.
4. In the Properties editor, set the value of the Data Mining\AllowSession-MiningModels property to true.
5. Click OK in the Properties editor.

After these steps are completed, clients will be able to create session mining models and structures on that Analysis Services server.

Using the Advanced Forecasting Tool

Before getting into how to implement the forecasting tool, let's discuss what it does and how to use it. Many Excel worksheets contain what is essentially time series data — that is, a variety of columns or rows indicating values for some category and one additional column or row indicating the time of each value. For example, a retail firm may have a sheet indicating monthly sales and inventory for each product or category of products. A user in that situation may be using Excel simply as a data repository or reporting mechanism. That person may try to visualize figures through the built-in charting abilities. In many cases, Excel is used as a budgeting tool, where the user will manually impute budget appropriations according to what he/she believes his/her needs and resources will be in the future. Having accurate forecasts of these figures, for example sales and inventory, greatly enhances the budgeting scenario, allowing for more accurate allocations. Simple linear regressions or running averages are available in Excel, but the Microsoft Time Series algorithm allows one to make more precise predictions by looking at series periodicities and interrelationships between series. The Advanced Forecasting Add-in brings this functionality to Excel.

To get started with the Advanced Forecasting Add-in, first download the `ExcelTimeSeries.zip` file from `www.wiley.com/go/tang/Chapter16`. Extract the add-in (.xla) and the test file, `Census Sales Data.xls`. Next, run Excel and add the add-in by selecting the AddIns option from the Tools menu. From there, you can browse to the location where you extracted the add-in file and install it.

NOTE You must have your Excel macro security settings to Medium or Low to install and run the add-in. If you set macro security to Medium, make sure that you choose Enable Macros when prompted.

Inside Excel, you will now see an Advanced Forecasting option under the Tools menu. Selecting this option displays the Advanced Forecasting dialog box, as shown in Figure 16.1.

First, you specify the range and orientation of your data. In the sample file, the series are in columns — that is, the column headers specify the names of the individual time series, and time goes downward, as in Table 16.1. If your data series names were in rows, with time going across the worksheet, as in Table 16.2, you would specify the orientation as Series in Rows. Next, you must specify which column contains the date or time of each series entry, then choose how far into the future you wish to forecast. Finally, before submitting the dialog, click on the Connection button to specify the server and database you are working with. Although the model will automatically be deleted upon completion, you still need to specify a database you have permissions to access in order to perform the analysis.

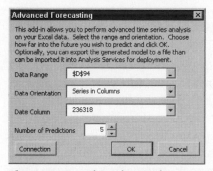

Figure 16.1:   The Advanced Forecasting Excel add-in

Table 1.1 Series in Columns

DATE	RETAIL	TOTAL	NEW CAR DEALERS	USED CAR DEALERS
Jan-92	$133,519	$24,057	$1,793	
Feb-92	$134,085	$25,040	$2,046	
Mar-92	$145,771	$28,018	$2,237	
Apr-92	$150,669	$27,981	$2,670	
May-92	$156,030	$28,924	$2,229	
Jun-92	$155,487	$30,591	$2,266	

Table 16.2 Series in Rows

Date	Jan-92	Feb-92	Mar-92	Apr-92	May-92
Retail Total	$133,519	$134,085	$145,771	$150,669	$156,030
New Car Dealers	$24,057	$25,040	$28,018	$27,981	$28,924
Used Car Dealers	$1,793	$2,046	$2,237	$2,670	$2,229

When you click OK after making your selections, the add-in creates a model and trains it with the selected data. It then populates the cells adjacent to your data with the specified number of forecasts, plus a comment containing the standard deviation of the forecast.

ExcelTimeSeries Add-In Architecture

The ExcelTimeSeries add-in is written using the Visual Basic for Applications (VBA) subsystem of Microsoft Excel. VBA allows you to add your own custom functionality and user interfaces to Microsoft Office applications. Since VBA code is executed natively (that is, not using the common language runtime [CLR] for managed code), you are required to use a native interface to Analysis Services. Analysis Services uses OLE DB as its native interface, which is rather difficult to program. Visual Basic programmers, however, use Active Data Objects (ADO), which wraps OLE DB in a simpler, more convenient interface.

The add-in itself comprises three pieces of code. The ExcelTimeSeries form provides the user interface and logic to fill the worksheet with the forecasted values. The ExcelTimeSeriesMining module communicates with the Analysis Services on the server to build, train, and predict from time series models. Finally the XMLARowsetGen module creates the input training set for the mining model in XML for Analysis rowset format. Figure 16.2 shows the modules and the client components used by the add-in.

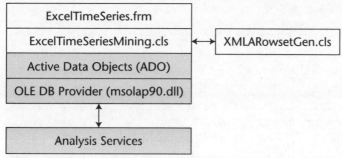

Figure 16.2: ExcelTimeSeries add-in architecture

Building the Input Data Set

The trickiest problem with data mining inside Excel is how to move the data from Excel to the server for training. Typically, you assume that the data is accessible to the mining engine through an OLE DB provider. In fact, you could use the Microsoft Jet provider to access the data in the Excel spreadsheet. This would work, however, only if your data was in the proper format and accessible to the Analysis Services server. If your data was pivoted, as in the Series in Rows columns, the Jet provider wouldn't work.

Luckily the SQL Server 2005 engine supports the option of accepting a rowset as a parameter for data mining input. This allows you to specify a training or prediction query and, in the place of the source data query, put a parameter (such as `@InputRowset`) in its place. The mining engine supports only rowset parameters that are standard XML for Analysis (XMLA) rowsets, as described in Chapter 13, and are specified in a particular way. However, the OLE DB provider allows you to send the rowset to the mining engine in a few different ways. The OLE DB provider automatically serializes `IRowset` parameters. Additionally, if you provide a binary large object (BLOB) parameter to the OLE DB provider that is an XMLA rowset in a `bstring` (BSTR), the OLE DB provider will recognize this and generate the correct XMLA package. The latter method is the only way accessible through ADO, and therefore, inside Excel.

> **NOTE** The ability to push data from the client to the server allows you to train and predict from models using data from the client or any other source not directly accessible by the server. This also permits training on arbitrary data that may not exist in any particular source. This is how SQL Server 2005 Integration Services moves data from the pipeline to analysis services.

Creating the XMLA Rowset

Having the functionality to send data via XMLA is one thing, actually creating the rowset from the contents of an Excel worksheet is another. Luckily, the XMLA rowset format is straightforward, so it is easy to make the translation.

The XMLA rowset format has three parts: the header, the schema, and the data. The header is constant, so you can simply insert that into your stream. That leaves you with the schema and the data. The schema for an Excel worksheet again will be relatively simple. The flat nature of Excel enables you to ignore the possibility of nested tables so your schema generation is simplified. Practically speaking, you simply need to take the name and data type of a column and generate the schema fragment.

Converting from Excel to XMLA

To get the name and type of an Excel column or row, you look at the header cell and the adjacent cell. As a simplification, assume that all cells in each column or row are the same type. If a cell in the range is not convertible to the type of the first cell, an error will be raised either by the XMLARowsetGen component or the mining engine itself. The code to get the name and type of a column looks like this:

```
colName = col.Cells(1, 1).Value
colType = TypeName(col.Cells(2, 1).Value)
XMLARowset.AddColumn(colName,colType)
```

For a row-based series, the indices are reversed.

The XMLARowsetGen class converts that column into a fragment that looks like this:

```
<xsd:element sql:field='Retail Total' name='Retail_d32_Total'
    type='xsd:double' minOccurs='0'/>
```

Similarly, the class converts rows into equivalent XMLA rowset fragments. For instance, once the column addition is complete, the following statement:

```
XMLARowset.AddRow 1/1/92, 149252, 33519
```

Results in this XMLA:

```
<row>
  <Date>1992-01-01T00:00:00</Date>
  <Retail_d47_Food_d32_Total>149252</Retail_d47_Food_d32_Total>
  <Retail_d32_Total>33519</Retail_d32_Total>
</row>
```

For convenience, if you pass an array as the first element of the AddRow parameter, the method will unwind that array to create the XMLA row.

Building the XMLA Rowset

You want to create an XMLA Rowset from a user selection — that is, an Excel range. This is performed by the XMLARowsetGen method FillRowset, as shown in Listing 16.1. When reading the listing, note that columns and rows refer to XMLA columns and rows, and not Excel columns and rows. Therefore, when transposing, the code is identical except for how the range is indexed.

```
Public Sub FillRowset(DataRange As Range, RowsAsRows As Boolean)
    Dim iRow As Integer
    Dim iCol As Integer
    Dim col As Range
    Dim colName As String
    Dim colType As String
    Dim colCount As Integer
    Dim rowCount As Integer
    Dim arValues() As Variant

    If DataRange.Areas.Count > 1 Then
        Err.Raise vbObjectError + 1, , "XMLA Rowset generation on " _
            & "multiple-area ranges not allowed."
    End If

    If RowsAsRows Then
        ' Handle Series as Rows case
        colCount = DataRange.Columns.Count
        rowCount = DataRange.Rows.Count - 1

        ' Add each column with the header row name
        ' and the type of the first column value.
        For Each col In DataRange.Columns
            colName = col.Cells(1, 1).Value
            colType = TypeName(col.Cells(2, 1).Value)
            AddColumn colName, colType, True
        Next

        ' Allocate rows and add each row in the range.
        PreAllocateRows (rowCount)
        ReDim arValues(colCount - 1)
        For iRow = 1 To rowCount
            For iCol = 1 To colCount
                arValues(iCol - 1) = DataRange(iRow + 1, iCol).Value
            Next
```

Listing 16.1   XMLARowsetGen.FillRowset *(continued)*

```
                AddRow (arValues)
            Next
        Else
            ' Handle Series as Columns case
            colCount = DataRange.Rows.Count
            rowCount = DataRange.Columns.Count - 1
            For Each col In DataRange.Rows
                colName = col.Cells(1, 1).Value
                colType = TypeName(col.Cells(1, 2).Value)
                AddColumn colName, colType, True
            Next
            PreAllocateRows (rowCount)
            ReDim arValues(colCount - 1)
            For iRow = 1 To rowCount
                For iCol = 1 To colCount
                    arValues(iCol - 1) = DataRange(iCol, iRow + 1).Value
                Next
                AddRow (arValues)
            Next
        End If
    End Sub
```

Listing 16.1   *(continued)*

Once the rowset is filled, calling `XMLARowsetGen.GenerateRowset` creates the string you need to provide to the data mining engine. The details of the remaining code of the `XMLARowsetGen` class are omitted due to space considerations. The full code is included with the add-in.

Creating and Training the Mining Model

The `ExcelTimeSeriesMining` class handles the interactions with the data mining engine. To create and train a mining model, you have to perform three steps. First, connect to the data mining engine, then create and execute a `CRE-ATE MINING MODEL` statement, and finally create and execute an `INSERT INTO` statement.

Connecting to the Data Mining Engine

You connect to the Analysis Services server using the standard ADO methodology. The client machine must have the Analysis Services OLE DB provider (`MSOLAP90.DLL`) installed As mentioned before, this server must be configured to accept session mining models, and the user must have permissions on at least one database on the server.

The simple VBA code using ADO to connect to a server looks like this:

```
Dim conn As New ADODB.Connection
Conn.Open "Provider=MSOLAP90;Location=MyServer;" & _
        "Initial Catalog=MyDatabase"
```

Creation and Training

The `ExcelTimeSeriesMining` class performs model creation and training in a single step. The model created here has one column for every column (or row) in the data selection. This model will indicate the date column as the KEY TIME and every other column will have the content type CONTINUOUS and usage PREDICT. A sample creation statement would look like this:

```
CREATE MINING MODEL ExcelTimeSeriesModel
(
    [Date]                DATETIME  KEY TIME,
    [Retail Food Total]   DOUBLE    CONTINUOUS PREDICT,
    [Retail Food]         DOUBLE    CONTINUOUS PREDICT
) USING Microsoft_Time_Series
```

INSERT INTO is simplified as there is no input query. Instead, you simply need to list the columns and specify the named parameter for the input XMLA rowset.

```
INSERT INTO ExcelTimeSeriesModel
    ([Date],[Retail Food Total],[Retail Food])
@InputRowset.
```

ExcelTimeSeriesMining.CreateModel Implementation

The implementation of `ExcelTimeSeriesMining.CreateModel` takes advantage of the selecting preprocessing performed by `XMLARowsetGen.FillRowset` (shown in code Listing 16.3. Using `FillRowset` as a starting point allows you to ignore issues relating to series orientation, because the `XMLARowsetGen` object is always Series as Rows. The code in Listing 16.2 demonstrates how to create the creation and insertion commands, add a XMLA named parameter to a command, and execute those commands. Note the string generation uses helper functions to ensure column name correctness and to convert from Excel data types to OLE DB for Data Mining data types.

```
''''''''''''''''''''''''''''''''''''''''''''''''''''''''''''''''''''''
Public Sub CreateModel(ModelName As String, Key As String, _
    DataRange As Range, RowsAsRows As Boolean)
'
' Build and train a time series mining model from an Excel selection.
''''''''''''''''''''''''''''''''''''''''''''''''''''''''''''''''''''''
On Error GoTo onerror
    Dim strCreate As String
    Dim strInsert As String
    Dim cmd As New ADODB.Command
    Dim param As ADODB.Parameter
    Dim i As Integer
    Dim xmla As New XMLARowsetGen
    m_strModelName = ModelName

    ' Create XMLA rowset from specified range
    xmla.FillRowset DataRange, RowsAsRows

    ' Initalize creation and insertion commands.
    strCreate = "CREATE SESSION MINING MODEL " & ModelName & "( "
    strInsert = "INSERT INTO " & ModelName & " (  "

    ' Add columns.
    For i = 0 To xmla.ColumnCount - 1
        If i > 0 Then
            strCreate = strCreate & " ,"
            strInsert = strInsert & " ,"
        End If
        strCreate = strCreate & _
                    "[" & NormalizeName(xmla.ColumnName(i)) & "]"
        strInsert = strInsert & _
                    "[" & NormalizeName(xmla.ColumnName(i)) & "]"
        strCreate = strCreate & " " & _
                    BuildOLEDBDMType(xmla.ColumnType(i))
        If Key = xmla.ColumnName(i) Then
            strCreate = strCreate & " KEY TIME"
        Else
            ' If connection to a standard edition server
            ' use PREDICT ONLY instead of PREDICT
            strCreate = strCreate & " CONTINUOUS PREDICT"
        End If
    Next

    ' Complete creation command.
    strCreate = strCreate & ") USING Microsoft_Time_Series"

    ' Complete Insertion command.
    strInsert = strInsert & ") @InputRowset"

    ' Execute Creation command.
    cmd.ActiveConnection = m_cnAS
```

Listing 16.2 CreateModel code listing

```
      cmd.CommandText = strCreate
      cmd.Execute

      ' Execute Training command.
      cmd.CommandText = strInsert
      cmd.NamedParameters = True

      ' Add named parameter to command object.
      Set param = cmd.CreateParameter
      param.Name = "InputRowset"
      param.Type = adBSTR
      param.Direction = adParamInput
      param.Attributes = adParamLong
      param.Value = xmla.GenerateRowset
      cmd.Parameters.Append param

      cmd.Execute

      GoTo finally
onerror:

finally:
      Set cmd = Nothing
      ' Resend error to top level.
      If Err.Number <> 0 Then
          Err.Raise Err.Number, Err.Source, Err.Description, _
              Err.HelpFile, Err.HelpContext
      End If
End Sub
```

Listing 16.2   *(continued)*

Forecasting the Series

Now that the model has been created and trained, it is time to perform the prediction query that will forecast your data into the future. For each series in the selection, you want to predict the specified number of data points along with the standard deviation of the result so that you have an idea of how accurate your answers are. Additionally, you need to fetch the date labels of the future time slices for the key column.

The prediction query you will use for each series looks like this:

```
SELECT FLATTENED (SELECT $TIME,
                     [Retail Food],
                   PredictStdev([Retail Food])
                 FROM PredictTimeSeries([Retail Food], 5))
FROM [ExcelTimeSeriesModel]
```

The code for executing such a query is quite straightforward, as illustrated in Listing 16.3.

```
Public Function DoPredict(PredictCol As String, _
                          numPredictions As Integer) As ADODB.Recordset

    Dim szQuery As String
    Dim cmd As New ADODB.Command

    szQuery = "SELECT FLATTENED (select $TIME, [" & _
        NormalizeName(PredictCol) & "], PredictStdev([" & _
        NormalizeName(PredictCol) & "]) from PredictTimeSeries([" & _
        NormalizeName(PredictCol) & "], " & numPredictions & _
        ")) from [" & m_strModelName & "]"
    cmd.ActiveConnection = m_cnAS
    cmd.CommandText = szQuery
    Set DoPredict = cmd.Execute
End Function
```

Listing 16.3   DoPredict code listing

The caller can iterate through the resultant recordset to extract the forecast using helper functions CurrentDate, CurrentValue, and CurrentStdev that simply return the appropriate column from the current row.

Bringing It All Together

So far, you have seen code to create an XMLA input rowset from an Excel range, create and train a mining model based on that selection, and predict a specified number of time slices on a series in that model. Now, you need to put all these pieces together with the user interface to insert the predicted results into the worksheet.

The code in Listing 16.4 handles the click on the OK button action in the Advanced Forecasting dialog box. This handler updates a status window while initializing the data mining connection, training the model, and predicting the results. For each nonkey column in the selection, the handler calls ExcelTimeSeriesMining.DoPredict and iterates the results to put the forecast into the worksheet. Comments containing the standard deviation are added as well. The cell population code is duplicated to handle both column orientation possibilities. Note that the date column is repopulated for every series. This can easily be avoided with a small additional code condition.

```
'''''''''''''''''''''''''''''''''''''''''''''''''''''''''''''''''''''''
Private Sub btnOK_Click()
'
' Handle OK by creating and training a model, forecasting results,
' and placing the resultant forecast into the worksheet's cells.
'''''''''''''''''''''''''''''''''''''''''''''''''''''''''''''''''''''''

    On Error GoTo onerror

    Dim status As New frmStatus
    Dim ets As New ExcelTimeSeriesMining
    Dim RowsAsRows As Boolean
    Dim DataRange As Range
    Dim DateColumn As Range
    Dim Forecast As ADODB.Recordset
    Dim col As Range
    Dim i As Integer

    Set DataRange = GetRange
    ' Set the wait cursor, hide the dialog, and show the status window.
    Application.Cursor = xlWait
    Me.Hide
    DoEvents
    status.Show vbModeless

    ' Initialize data mining
    status.lblStatus = "Initializing..."
    status.Repaint

    RowsAsRows = (cbOrientation.Value = "Series in Columns")
    ets.Init

    ' Analyze data.
    status.lblStatus = "Analyzing Data..."
    status.Repaint
    ets.CreateModel "ExcelTimeSeriesModel", cbKey.Value, _
            DataRange, RowsAsRows

    ' Populate Results.
    status.lblStatus = "Forecasting..."
    status.Repaint

    ' Find the date column.
    If RowsAsRows Then
        For Each col In DataRange.Columns
            If col.Cells(1, 1).Value = cbKey.Value Then
                Set DateColumn = col
                Exit For
            End If
        Next
    Else
```

Listing 16.4   OK handler code listing *(continued)*

```
            For Each col In DataRange.Rows
                If col.Cells(1, 1).Value = cbKey.Value Then
                    Set DateColumn = col
                    Exit For
                End If
            Next
    End If


    ' Populate the forecast.
    If RowsAsRows Then
        For Each col In DataRange.Columns
            If col.Cells(1, 1).Value <> cbKey.Value Then
                iRow = DataRange.Rows.Count + 1
                Set Forecast = ets.DoPredict(col.Cells(1, 1).Value, _
                                    numPredictions)
                Forecast.MoveFirst
                While Not Forecast.EOF
                    With col.Cells(iRow, 1)
                        If Not .Comment Is Nothing Then
                            .Comment.Delete
                        End If
                        .AddComment
                        .Comment.Visible = False
                        .Comment.Text "Standard Deviation:" & _
                                ets.CurrentStdev(Forecast)
                        .Interior.Color = vbYellow
                        .Value = ets.CurrentValue(Forecast)
                    End With
                    DateColumn.Cells(iRow, 1) = _
                                ets.CurrentDate(Forecast)
                    Forecast.MoveNext
                    iRow = iRow + 1
                Wend
            End If
        Next
    Else
        For Each col In DataRange.Rows
            If col.Cells(1, 1).Value <> cbKey.Value Then
                iRow = DataRange.Columns.Count + 1
                Set Forecast = ets.DoPredict(col.Cells(1, 1).Value, _
                                        numPredictions)
                Forecast.MoveFirst
                While Not Forecast.EOF
                    With col.Cells(1, iRow)
                        If Not .Comment Is Nothing Then
                            .Comment.Delete
                        End If
                        .AddComment
                        .Comment.Visible = False
```

Listing 16.4 *(continued)*

```
                        .Comment.Text "Standard Deviation:" & _
                            ets.CurrentStdev(Forecast)
                        .Interior.Color = vbYellow
                        .Value = ets.CurrentValue(Forecast)
                    End With
                    DateColumn.Cells(1, iRow) = _
                                ets.CurrentDate(Forecast)
                    Forecast.MoveNext
                    iRow = iRow + 1
                Wend
            End If
        Next
    End If

    GoTo finally
onerror:
    MsgBox Err.Description

finally:
    status.Hide
    Application.Cursor = xlDefault
End Sub
```

Listing 16.4   *(continued)*

Summary

The ExcelTimeSeries example scrapes the tip of the iceberg as to what can be done with data mining and Excel. Just considering the forecasting example in this chapter, the flexibility of the XMLARowsetGen class provides unlimited opportunities. For example, you can preprocess the data prior to prediction — such as building a model using derivatives rather than the actual values. You could even easily populate the XMLARowsetGen class from data from an external data source, not requiring the source data even be in the Excel worksheet to begin with.

The ExcelTimeSeriesMining class can easily be extended beyond forecasting by using any algorithm in SQL Server Analysis Services. Clustering could be used to identify anomalous rows in the worksheet, or decision trees can fill in missing cell values. Your imagination and business needs can invent new and unique ways to leverage the session mining scenario from the Excel platform.

If a user has administrative permissions on an Analysis Services database, Excel could be used as a complete front end for SQL Server Data Mining.

Persistent models can be created using VBA code that could later be deployed into production environments and managed using all of the standard SQL Server tools.

Finally, this code can be taken out of Excel and modified to add data mining functionality to any other client application. Examples include forecasting in Microsoft Project, or rendering decision trees using Microsoft Visio. Outside the Microsoft Office family, the code can be used in standard Visual Basic applications to add data mining to any application you can imagine.

CHAPTER 17

Extending SQL Server Data Mining

One of the drawbacks of any data mining tool is that no matter how many features and algorithms the tool provides, the tool immediately becomes useless the moment you require features and algorithms not provided by the tool. SQL Server Data Mining addresses this problem by providing extensibility mechanisms, allowing you to augment the functionality of the server and tools. There are four main ways to extend the SQL Server Data Mining system:

- Using stored procedures to add business logic or enhanced intelligence on top of SQL Server Data Mining

- Using the Visual Studio extensibility mechanisms to extend and enhance the data mining tools

- Developing plug-in algorithms that extend the algorithm set available on the server

- Writing new viewers to visualize data mining models

The use and implementation of stored procedures is detailed in Chapter 14. Extending Visual Studio is out of scope for this book. Details, white papers, and samples are available at http://msdn.microsoft.com/vstudio/extend.

This chapter will briefly describe the potential and mechanisms developing plug-in algorithms and viewers. This chapter will cover the topics in enough detail for you to understand the basic architecture of each extensibility method, and how and why you would use such method. The precise details of the interfaces involved are described in white papers and tutorials that are available by selecting Documentation and Samples ⇨ Samples ⇨ Microsoft SQL Server 2005 Samples from the Microsoft SQL Server 2005 section of the Start menu.

In this chapter, you learn about:

- The plug-in algorithm framework
- How to implement data mining viewers

Understanding Plug-in Algorithms

SQL Server 2005 is unique in that it provides the mechanisms and allows third parties to develop and integrate their own algorithms that run inside Analysis Services. The Analysis Services tools and server architecture is arranged in such a way that they are agnostic to the actual algorithms that exist on the server. As shown in Chapter 13, it is possible to disable server algorithms; likewise, you can add new algorithms to each server. These algorithms operate using essentially the same interfaces as the built-in algorithms provided by Microsoft, so they can take advantage of all the platform features provided by the server without performance penalties.

A *plug-in algorithm* is a COM object that implements and understands a set of interfaces specified by the SQL Server Data Mining team. From an end-user perspective, plug-in algorithms are no different than the built-in algorithms. They appear in the tools as an algorithm you can select to build a model. Their functions show in the function lists in the query builders. You can add them to your mining structures and compare them using the standard lift charts. End users of plug-in algorithms can stop reading this chapter here. Those of you interested in implementing your own, read on.

Plug-in Algorithm Framework

The plug-in algorithm framework makes it very easy to create and deploy fully functional enterprise-ready data mining algorithms. Since algorithm development takes place at the lowest possible level, the algorithm developer gets for free all the platform abilities of SQL Server Data Mining. The framework takes care of:

- DMX language processing
- Client and Server APIs such as ADOMD.Net, AMO, and XMLA
- Transaction management

- Object management
- Security
- Data access and tokenization
- Modeling
- Remoting
- Integration with:
  - BI Development Studio
  - SQL Management Studio
  - OLAP
  - SQL Server Integration Services
  - SQL Server Reporting Services

Plug-in Algorithm Concepts

When creating a plug-in algorithm you need to implement two distinct objects. The first, the algorithm factory, creates algorithm objects and exposes the capabilities of the algorithm through the metadata interface, `IDMAlgorithmMetadata`. The second object is the algorithm object itself. Analysis Services creates one instance of an algorithm object for each mining model using that algorithm. This object is responsible for handling processing, prediction, and content navigation requests, and contains the in memory representation of the learned content of the mining model.

At the most basic level, a plug-in algorithm receives a stream of data from which it must extract patterns and store these patterns onto disk. It then receives requests to describes these patterns and apply them to new data streams to perform predictions.

The data stream that is provided to the algorithm is a stream of attribute-value pairs representing a set of cases. This stream is called the *Case Set* and from the algorithm point of view, the case set is same independent of the data source. Relational, OLAP, streams from Integration Services, and so on, are all delivered to the algorithm using the same mechanism. An attribute can be either numerically valued or nominally valued. Attribute-value pairs for numeric attributes, such as income, contain an attribute index and a double containing the value. Attribute-value pairs for nominal attributes, such as gender, contain the attribute index along with an index representing the state of the attribute. The set of attributes that are available to an algorithm, along with their metadata, are described in the Attribute Set. An example of a potential case set and an attribute set are shown in Figure 17.1.

Case Set

1	2	2	34	3	35000	4	2	8	1	10	1		
1	1	2	25	3	24000	4	1	5	1	7	1	9	1
1	1	2	47	3	75500	4	3	8	1	6	1		
1	2	2	31	3	52300	4	1						

Attribute Set

Index	Name	Data Type	Content Type	Cardinality	States
1	Gender	Text	Discrete	3	Missing, Male, Female
2	Age	Long	Continuous	2	Missing, Value
3	Income	Long	Continuous	2	Missing, Value
4	Marital Status	Text	Discrete	5	Missing, Never Married, Married, Divorced, Widowed
5	Milk	Text	Key	2	Missing, Existing
6	Bread	Text	Key	2	Missing, Existing
7	Cereal	Text	Key	2	Missing, Existing
8	Eggs	Text	Key	2	Missing, Existing
9	Bacon	Text	Key	2	Missing, Existing
10	Coffee	Text	Key	2	Missing, Existing

Figure 17.1 Case set and attribute set

The data stream illustrated in Figure 17.1 demonstrates many issues that algorithm developers need to be aware of. For instance, this data contains both numerical and nominal data. This data set has a case table with four attribute columns (and a key column that doesn't show in the data stream), and a nested table containing a single key column. It is important when implementing an algorithm that you keep in mind the capabilities of your algorithm and accurately represent your functionality by exposing the correct algorithm metadata. Algorithms such as Microsoft Decision Trees and Microsoft Clustering support all content types and expose such in their metadata. If your algorithm cannot handle numerical data, do not indicate that it supports CONTINUOUS as a content type, if it can't handle nominal data, don't indicate DISCRETE. If your algorithm does not understand cases of varying lengths, don't support the content type TABLE. The data mining infrastructure validates models based on the metadata you expose to ensure that the user model conforms to the basic requirements of your algorithm. Additionally, your algorithm meta-data class is called to validate the attribute set in the case that you have more complex requirements that can't be represented by metadata. For instance, if you have an algorithm that requires two continuous inputs and one discrete output, you can guarantee the model meets your algorithm requirements.

After a model is processed, an algorithm must be able to respond to prediction and content navigation requests. All requests are handled in the context of the attribute set. For prediction, the algorithm is provided a set of inputs in the same format as provided for training. The algorithm is required to evaluate the inputs and return a data structure containing the predicted results with supporting statistics. Content is assumed to be a set of nodes organized in a tree hierarchy and is navigated by Analysis Services in a preorder fashion: first the content of one node is requested and then Analysis Services requests all of the children of that node.

Model Creation and Processing

Model creation from the algorithm perspective begins when Analysis Services calls the algorithm factory's `IDMAlgorithmMetadata` interface to validate the model structure against the metadata exposed by the algorithm. During model creation, Analysis Services calls `IDMAlgorithmMetadata::ValidateAttributeSet`. In `ValidateAttributeSet`, your algorithm receives an unpopulated attribute set that describes the structure of the model. This attribute set contains the descriptions of the attributes as described by the model metadata. For example, you will be able to tell what the content type and usage of each attribute is, and if there is a nested table, but you won't be able to determine the number of states of each discrete attribute, or even the total number of attributes when there is a nested table.

When a process command is sent to a mining model, the algorithm factory is called to instantiate a new algorithm object. This object is initialized with the model's attribute set and an object called the `DMContext`. `DMContext` provides services such as memory allocators, locale information, and methods for sending progress notifications among other things. It is important that the algorithm use the memory management interfaces of the `DMContext` *exclusively* so that Analysis Services can properly manage memory usage for all of the objects currently loaded in the server. The `DMContext` object comes in two flavors. The first, the context provided at model initialization, provides memory allocators for memory that should be allocated for as long as the model stays in memory. This context is guaranteed to exist for the life of your algorithm object and should be cached. The second is an execution context that is provided to every other interface call. This context is a user-request context allowing you to allocate memory that is freed by the end of the current operation.

Algorithm processing begins when Analysis Services calls the algorithms `IDMAlgorithm::InsertCases` method with an execution context and the case set. Inside `InsertCases`, your algorithm processes any algorithm parameters and then calls `IDMPushCaseSet` to start the flow of training cases, providing a pointer to an `IDMCaseProcessor` interface (usually on the same algorithm object). As the case sets streams cases from the source, it calls `ProcessCase` for each case it reads. It is up to the algorithm to determine how to process each case. For example, an algorithm can update its learned model as each case is fed, or it can cache a subset of the case set to process a larger number at one time or to set cases aside for validation purposes. The case set allows your algorithm to optionally determine the memory location of each case, allowing you to avoid copying if you are caching the cases. During `ProcessCase` your algorithm is also responsible for periodically sending feedback notifications through the execution context. The return value of `ProcessCase` is used to indicate success, failure, or if you simply want to abort the current case iteration. During `InsertCases`, your algorithm is free to call `StartCases` as many times as it needs to iterate the input cases.

Note that the Analysis Services data mining architecture allows for an unlimited number of attributes and an unlimited number of discrete states per attribute. Since many data mining algorithms are very sensitive to these cardinalities, it is up to your implementation to gracefully handle circumstances where high cardinalities would indicate undesirable memory usage or processing time. Strategies to alleviate this problem are intelligent feature selection or simply returning descriptive error conditions.

By the end of `InsertCases`, your algorithm should have all of its learned content stored in memory allocated from the model context, and should have freed any temporary memory allocated using the execution context. If you return success, your algorithm object will be queried for the `IDMPersist` interface. `IDMPersist::Save` is called with an `IDMPersistanceWriter` pointer to be used to archive in the in-memory representation of your model. It is recommended that you use a forward compatible file format such that future versions of your algorithm will be able to load the models.

If any part of the processing procedure fails, including saving the models, the architecture will automatically rollback the transaction to preserve the server state.

Prediction

The primary method for predicting attribute values is `IDMAlgorithm::Predict`. The plug-in architecture also allows for algorithm-specific prediction methods in custom interfaces such as `IDMClusteringAlgorithm::Cluster` to determine cluster membership in clustering-type algorithms, or

IDMDispatch where you can implement custom functions for your algorithm needs. The main Predict method is used for predicting a specific attribute value, retrieving statistics about a predicted value, retrieving statistics about all possible predicted values (as in PredictHistogram), and to predict sets of attributes (as in predicting nested table membership).

Regardless of the method used, all prediction works in a similar way. Analysis Services parses DMX statements and prepares input cases in a manner similar to training. For each input row, Analysis Services calls Predict or the appropriate method as indicated by the DMX statement. Predict indicates that the algorithm provide predictions for a group of attributes, specifies how many predictions to return, how many states to return for each prediction, and provides a set of modifiers to control how the algorithm should return the values. Predict is optimized for batch predictions in that it allows you to place predictive results in the same memory space for each call to avoid the continual reallocation of memory.

As an example, to predict the most likely state of a discrete attribute, Predict would be called with the attribute group containing a single attribute with the maximum number of predictions and states set to one. To predict the top five movies in a nested table, the attribute group in the Predict call would contain the list of possible attributes in the nested table, and the maximum number of predictions would be set to five. Additional flags sent to Predict would indicate what criteria to use to rank the results (such as support or probability) and what additional information to include or exclude. If called in batch mode, for example using a query as the prediction input, Predict would be called with a preallocated output buffer so your implementation wouldn't have to allocate it.

The white paper and plug-in tutorial provide in-depth implementation details for Predict.

Content Navigation

The final required area of implementation detail is content navigation. As described throughout this book, SQL Server Data Mining exposes learned content as a parent-child nested rowset. Each row represents a node in the model's content and specifies, among other things, the node's unique ID, parent ID, node type, and a set of distributions in a nested table. This schema allows for a wide range of content types to be represented in a generic way.

How your algorithm represents its content is a personal design decision. If you are implementing algorithms with structures similar to the Microsoft algorithms, it is recommended that you mimic the content structure of those algorithms as closely as possible. Doing so will allow models built using your algorithm to be browsed using the standard Microsoft viewers. The viewers and associated stored procedures tolerate to some degree variations in content.

In particular, if the viewers encounter node types they don't recognize, they will simply skip them.

Content navigation is initiated by a call to `IDMAlgorithm::GetNavigator` to return an object implementing `IDMAlgorithmNavigation`. Since many clients may be browsing a model simultaneously, this method should create a new object every time it is called. As mentioned previously, navigating the entire model content is done in a preorder fashion, but navigation can be initiated from any node in the model. When designing your content layout and data structures to store the in-memory representation of your model, it is important to keep in mind how the content is exposed to the user, especially for performance reasons. For example, our initial design of the Microsoft Association Rules content had each rule being the child of the left-hand side itemset. However, in practice, we determined that this hierarchy made it extremely expensive to retrieve a simple list of rules. The final design has all itemsets and rules as children of the model root node.

Managed Plug-Ins

As described previously, a plug-in is a COM object. It is possible to wrap the COM interfaces with .NET and write managed plug-ins in languages such as C# and Visual Basic .NET. Microsoft even provides a sample wrapper to facilitate the development of managed plug-ins. However, the ease of development provided by .NET does not come without cost. There are performance penalties in training and prediction related to the cost of marshaling data between native C++ and managed code, although the Microsoft-supplied wrappers do their best to alleviate this. Additionally, all memory used by a managed plug-in is not allocated using the Analysis Services allocators. This raises the potential for the server to be unable to optimize memory utilization under stress situations. For these reasons, the decision to create and use managed plug-ins in a production environment should be taken with care and only after extensive testing using simulated server loads.

Installing Plug-in Algorithms

To install a plug-in algorithm, you need to register the COM and update the server's .ini file. Details on the exact registry and .ini file settings are specified with the sample plug-in.

Using Data Mining Viewers

Another way of extending SQL Server Data Mining is to add data mining visualizations. The visualization architecture in the Data Mining Designer allows you to add viewers for any or all algorithms. For example, you could write an additional viewer for the Microsoft Decision Tree algorithm that displays line charts for continuous targets, or you could create a Neural Net viewer that displays the actual nodes of the network, or, of course, you can add viewers specifically designed to display your custom plug-in algorithms.

The Microsoft supplied visualization controls are simply .NET WinForm controls that implement the `IMiningModelViewerControl` interface. To implement your own visualization, you simply need to do the same. Launch Visual Studio, create a new .NET class library, and add the controls you want to your class. BI Dev Studio initializes your control by setting the `Mining-Model` and `ConnectionString` properties of the `IMiningModelViewer-Control` interface and then calling `LoadViewerData`.

`LoadViewerData` is called immediately after your WinForm control is initialized and displayed. Your implementation of `LoadViewerData` opens a connection to the server and queries the model for at least enough information for the initial display of the model. For instance, the Decision Tree viewer retrieves the list of trees in the model plus the complete first tree. Depending on the expected time to load, your interface should indicate that loading is occurring.

As an example, Listing 17.1 shows an implementation of `LoadViewerData` that populates a list box with the unique name and caption of all model nodes.

```
public  bool LoadViewerData(object context)
{
    AdomdConnection connection = new AdomdConnection();
    AdomdCommand command = new AdomdCommand();
    AdomdDataReader reader;

    // Open a new connection to the server.
    connection.ConnectionString = this.ConnectionString;
    connection.Open();

    // Initialize the command.
    string commandText = string.Format("SELECT NODE_UNIQUE_NAME, " +
        "NODE_CAPTION FROM [{0}].CONTENT",
        this.MiningModelName);
    command.Connection = connection;
    command.CommandText = commandText;

    // Execute the command.
    reader = command.ExecuteReader();

    // Extract information from the schema here.
    while (reader.Read())
    {
```

Listing 17.1   LoadViewerData Implementation *(continued)*

```
        string uniqueName = "";
        string caption = "";

        if (!reader.IsDBNull(1))
            uniqueName = reader.GetString(1);
        if (!reader.IsDBNull(2))
            caption = reader.GetString(1);

        ListBox1.Add(uniqueName + "  " + caption);
    }
    reader.Close();
    connection.Close();

    return true;
}
```

Listing 17.1   *(continued)*

It is left to your discretion whether you keep an open connection to the server or reconnect as necessary to fetch additional data based on user interaction. If you maintain a live connection, your code should handle the situation where the connection is dropped and be sure to close the connection when the control is destroyed.

After implementing your viewer, there are a number steps involved to strongly name your assembly and register and place your viewer. All of these steps are detailed in the Data Mining viewer tutorial included with the plug-in sample. If your viewer, like the Microsoft viewers, makes use of custom stored procedures, your installation procedure will have to include installing these procedures on servers you intend to access with the viewer. You can use SQL Management Studio to generate the DDL required to deploy the necessary assemblies.

Summary

This chapter covered the basic concepts behind extending SQL Server Data Mining. In addition to extending the server by creating stored procedures as described in Chapter 14, or extending Visual Studio as described at `http://msdn.microsoft.com/vstudio/extend`, you can add your own custom data mining algorithms and viewers to SQL Server Data Mining. The concepts covered in this chapter enhance and extend the plug-in white papers and tutorials provided in the Analysis Services samples.

Conclusion and Additional Resources

In this chapter, we will review the highlights of data mining features in SQL Server 2005. We will talk about the new business opportunities in data mining. We will also point you to resources for further reading and discussions.

Recapping the Highlights of SQL Server 2005 Data Mining

You learned about a wide range of data mining topics throughout the book. We started with an overview of data mining, and then we showed you how to use data mining tools of SQL Server 2005. We discussed in depth each of the seven Microsoft data mining algorithms and their typical usages. We introduced the two important APIs for data mining: DMX and XML for Analysis. We described the SQL Server Data Mining architecture. We also talked about the integration with other BI components, including OLAP, SSIS, and Reporting Services. Finally, we gave you a few data mining project cases studies.

Data Mining in SQL Server 2005 presents a marked advancement since its addition to the SQL Server family in SQL Server 2000. With the advanced data mining functionality, tools, and APIs packaged with a popular database at a low price point, we believe that SQL Server 2005 will result in a paradigm shift in the data mining industry. Now let's go over the highlights of the SQL Server 2005 data mining features as a summary.

State-of-the-Art Algorithms

SQL Server Data Mining contains seven world-class data mining algorithms covering the following areas:

- **Microsoft Naïve Bayes(Chapter 4):** Naïve Bayes is a simple and efficient algorithm for classification. It analyzes pairwise relationships between each input attribute and the predictable one.

- **Microsoft Decision Trees (Chapter 5):** This is a state-of-the art decision tree algorithm, including both classicization and regression. It can also build multiple trees in a single model to performance association analysis. This algorithm is also packaged as Microsoft Linear Regression for those who want to do simple linear regression analysis.

- **Microsoft Time Series (Chapter 6):** Time Series is a unique forecasting algorithm based on the AutoRegression Tree technique.

- **Microsoft Clustering(Chapter 7):** This algorithm includes two different clustering techniques: EM (expectation and maximization) and K-means. It automatically detects the number of natural clusters in the dataset.

- **Microsoft Sequence Clustering (Chapter 8):** This algorithm is a hybrid between clustering and sequence techniques. It can group similar cases together based on normal attributes as well as sequence attributes.

- **Microsoft Association Rules (Chapter 9):** This is the most frequently requested algorithm since the SQL Server 2000 data mining release. It provides a powerful correlation counting engine. It can perform scalable and efficient market basket analysis.

- **Microsoft Neural Network (Chapter 10):** This algorithm can perform deeper analysis and find complicated patterns. It can be used for both classification and regression tasks. This algorithm is also packaged as Microsoft Logistic Regression when the hidden layer is removed.

- **Text Mining (Chapter 12):** With SSIS term extraction and term lookup transforms, unstructured data can be converted to structured format. This enables classification and clustering textual documents with data mining algorithms.

If your needs require you to go beyond the standard capabilities, SQL Server Data Mining is fully extensible through .NET stored procedures and plug-in algorithms that embed seamlessly to take advantage of all the platform abilities and integration.

Easy-to-Use Tools

The lack of model building and tuning tools is another limitation of SQL Server 2000. In SQL Server 2005, data mining tools are largely enhanced. The set of tools available includes model composition, training, browsing, comparison, and prediction query generation.

The Data Mining Wizard is a handy yet powerful tool to help you build data mining models from any data source. It helps you pick the most relevant input columns related to the predictable one. It can also be used to mine OLAP cubes. With a few mouse clicks, you can build a very sophisticated mining model. The Data Mining Editor allows you to tune your models by specifying parameter settings. Additionally, lift and profit charts are provided, so you can compare and contrast the quality of your models before you commit to deployment.

Simple Yet Powerful API

When it comes to applying models, SQL Server opens a new chapter in data mining. The creation of DMX (Data Mining Extensions to SQL) provides a rich SQL language already familiar to the throngs of developers and DBAs already close to their data. Performing complex predictions against data mining algorithms is now reduced to a join in a familiar SQL query. For the first time, those responsible for creating applications and handling data are empowered to leverage data mining technology using tools they already understand.

Integration with Sibling BI technologies

Rarely can a data mining problem be solved with only a data mining tool. SQL Server Data Mining sits among a family of BI technologies that can be leveraged together to enhance and develop this new breed of intelligent applications.

- **SSIS Integration:** Integration with SQL Server Integration Services injects the power of data mining into your operational data flows.

- **OLAP Integration:** Integration with OLAP allows you to mine against complex multidimensional calculations and use the results to create self-organizing cubes.

- **Reporting Services Integration:** Integration with Reporting Services provides a user-friendly presentation layer to display and distribute interactive reports driven by your data mining models.

Exploring New Data Mining Frontiers and Opportunities

As a relatively young field, data mining's current market size is still less than $1 billion dollars. Most data mining users (data miners) are analysts holding advanced degrees in statistics. Here is the typical usage scenario. First, the IT department builds the data warehouse or data mart, and data miners pull out a sample set to analyze. After the model is built, data miners publish a report with the findings to their business managers. The data mining process usually takes a few months. Data mining is considered as a reserved area for power analysts.

With SQL Server 2005, this perception will be changed. SQL Server Data Mining is designed for the vast developer populations, not statisticians. Its goal is to make developers and applications smarter.

- **Make developers smarter:** Ordinary developers will be empowered with easy-to-use yet powerful analysis tools. This will enable them to dig inside their own databases and discover the gold mine of previously hidden data patterns and relationships

- **Make applications smarter:** Data mining will make your applications smarter. Data mining is not only for decision support systems. Data mining can be integrated with line of business applications for daily operations. Data mining can be completely embedded, while consumers of data mining don't even need to know the results are from data mining. For example, an online DVD retail site can automatically give you suggestions based on your profile or your shopping basket. If you enter a new customer into the CRM system, the application will tell you in real time the personalized products/services you can provide to this customer. In an ERP application, the system will give you the forecast number of products for future production. If you browse a cube, with a single click, the tools will show you the anomalies in the cube. All these wonderful applications will become possible with data mining in SQL Server 2005. With its simple APIs, embedding data mining is possible with just a few lines of code.

Further Readings

To learn more about data mining, you can use some of the resources listed here.

Microsoft Data Mining Resources

- SQL Server Books Online is the official document of the product. It contains details about concepts, references, samples, and tutorials.

- The SQL Server Web site (`microsoft.com/sql`) contains useful information and case studies of different components of SQL Server, including data mining and other BI features.

- XML for Analysis (`xmla.org`) is an industrial standards body to define XMLA Specifications. The council is co-chaired by Microsoft, Hyperion, and SAS. The specification is implemented in Analysis Services 2005.

- OLE DB for Data Mining specification can be found `Microsoft.com` Web site. It contains the official definition of DMX language and a set of data mining schema rowsets.

- Microsoft Research has made significant contribution to SQL Server 2005 Data Mining. Several algorithms in SQL Server 2005 are implemented based on research articles from Microsoft researchers. These articles are listed on the Microsoft Research Web site.

- Almost every Microsoft product has its newsgroup. The official news group of SQL Server Data Mining is `Microsoft.public.sqlserver .datamining`. This is by far the best place for you to reach Microsoft data mining product team members.

- `SQLServerDataMining.com` is a non-official Web site dedicated to SQL Server data mining. It is partially maintained by the product team members. There are many important resources such as articles, white papers, case studies, FAQs, and also live demos.

More on General Data Mining

The following is a list of recommended data mining books for your further reading:

- *Data Mining Concepts and Techniques* by Jiawei Han and Micheline Kamber, Morgan Kaufmann Publishers, 2000.

- *Principles of Data Mining (Adaptive Computation and Machine Learning)* by David J. Hand, Heikki Mannila, and Padhraic Smyth, MIT Press, 2001.

- *The Elements of Statistical Learning* by T. Hastie, R. Tibshirani, and J. H. Friedma, Springer Verlag, 2001.

- *Data Mining: Practical Machine Learning Tools and Techniques with Java Implementations* by Ian H. Eibe Frank, Morgan Kaufmann, 1999.

- *Data Mining Techniques: For Marketing, Sales, and Customer Support* by Michael J. A. Berry, and Gordon Linoff, John Wiley & Sons, 1997.

Popular Data Mining Web Site

KDNuggets.com (`www.kdnuggets.com`) is perhaps the most popular data mining portal site. It contains the information about most data mining products, training courses, conferences, FAQ, publications, and also jobs announcements. It also provides a mailing list for data-mining-related news.

Popular Data Mining Conference

ACM SIGKDD (ACM Special Interest Group on Knowledge Discovery in Data and Data Mining) is the most important data mining annual conferences. It is the premier international conference on knowledge discovery and data mining. The conference provides a forum for academic researchers and industry and government innovators to share in their results and experience. The program usually includes keynote presentations, oral paper presentations, poster presentations, workshops, tutorials, and panels, as well as the KDD Cup competition.

Importing Datasets

This appendix describes the various datasets used throughout the chapter and how to import them into SQL Server.

Datasets

All datasets are provided in Access (.mdb) format. Since most descriptions in this book assume the data is located in a SQL Server, you should use the technique described later in this chapter to import the datasets. The datasets are found at `wiley.com/tang/datasets`.

MovieClick Dataset

The MovieClick dataset consists of almost 3,200 survey results by Microsoft employees taken in November 2002. Respondents were asked about their movie-watching behavior, demographics, hobbies, movies, actors, and directors. The following list shows the questions that were asked in the survey. The results of the survey were used to test and exercise the data mining capabilities of SQL Server 2005 while in development.

1. What is your preferred format for prerecorded movies?

2. How often do you watch prerecorded movies?

3. How often do you rent prerecorded movies?

4. How often do you watch Pay-Per-View events or movies?

5. How often do you purchase prerecorded movies?

6. How often do you watch movies in theaters?

7. How often do you watch movies on a movie network (television)?

8. Which criteria are most important in choosing a particular movie?

9. Which movie channels do you watch most frequently?

10. How do you watch broadcast television?

11. How many televisions do you have in your home?

12. Who generally picks the movies you watch?

13. Enter your favorite movies:

14. Enter your favorite actors and actresses:

15. Enter your favorite directors:

16. Age:

17. Gender:

18. Marital Status:

19. Number of children:

20. What level of education have you completed?

21. Do you currently own or rent your home?

22. How many bedrooms do you have in your home?

23. How many bathrooms do you have in your house?

24. How many cars do you own?

25. How do you connect to the Internet from home?

26. Which of the following technologies do you own?

27. What are your favorite hobbies/areas of interest?

The survey resulted in eight tables, one for the main survey responses, and one each for questions 8, 9, 13, 14, 15, 26, and 27. The main table results in the case table for data mining analysis and the additional tables become nested tables. A data source view representing the relationships between these tables is shown in Figure A.1.

NOTE As the survey results were examined, some flaws in the survey methodology were discovered. Favorite movies, actors, and directors were selected from an alphabetical list. This resulted in an unexpected number of selections starting with the letter "A," which can be seen in the resulting mining models.

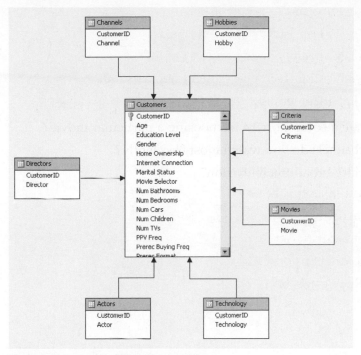

Figure A.1   Movies Data Source View

Voting Records Dataset

The Voting Records dataset contains selected issues presented for voting in the House of Representatives in 2002. In addition to the results for each vote, "Y," "N," or abstain (null), each row contains the name and party affiliation of each representative.

The issues that are captured in the dataset are presented in the following list.

1. Bankruptcy Abuse Prevention and Consumer Protection Act

2. To reduce preexisting PAYGO balances

3. Homeland Security Act

4. Help America Vote Act

5. To Authorize the Use of United States Armed Forces Against Iraq

6. Child Abduction Prevention Act

7. Help Efficient, Accessible, Low Cost, Timely Healthcare Act of 2002

8. Abortion Non-Discrimination Act

9. Consumer Rental Purchase Agreement Act

10. Consumer Rental Purchase Agreement Act

11. Improving Access to Long-Term Care Act

12. National Aviation Capacity Expansion Act

13. Fed Up Higher Education Technical Amendments of 2002

14. Cyber Security Enhancement Act

15. Arming Pilots Against Terrorism Act

16. Inland Flood Forecasting and Warning System Act

17. Social Security Program Protection Act

18. Permanent Death Tax Repeal Act

19. Investing in America's Future Act

20. Customs Border Security Act

21. Afghanistan Freedom Support Act

22. Highway Funding Restoration Act

23. Farm Security Act

24. Child Custody Protection Act

25. Pension Security Act

26. Class Action Fairness Act

27. Higher Education Act Amendments

FoodMart 2000 Dataset

The FoodMart 2000 dataset is the sample dataset included with SQL Server 2000 and 2005. Refer to the product documentation for a description of this dataset.

College Plans Dataset

The College Plans dataset comprises real data from a Midwest college concerning high school students' intentions to attend college based on a number of factors. These factors are parental encouragement, parental income, IQ, and gender. The original dataset contained all columns as discrete variables, with the income and IQ variables bucketed into ranges. In the supplied dataset, continuous values for income and IQ have been imputed from the original ranges. Artifacts from this imputation can be observed by analyzing the data.

Importing Datasets

While it is easy to mine directly against the Access databases we supply when in an experimental situation where the client tools and server reside on the same machine, in general you will be performing your data mining activities against data inside an actual database server. The main reason for this is that users of the development and other client tools in general do not have physical access to the server machine. To mine against an Access database, you need to place the Access database on the server machine or provide a path to the data relative to the server machine, which may not be possible. Another good reason to import the data into SQL Server is that you will have access to the tools in SQL Management Studio to manage and perform ad hoc queries against the data for exploration purposes. Luckily, it is a fairly simply operation to import the data into a SQL Server database.

To import data from Access files into SQL Server, you use the SQL Server Integration Services (SSIS) Import and Export Wizard. This is available in SQL Server Management Studio. Right click on a SQL Server database and select Task⇨Import Data. Upon selecting this item, the wizard appears as shown in Figure A.2.

Click Next to advance to the next page of the wizard, where you select the data source and specify the filename. Select Microsoft Access as the filename and enter or browse to your file, as shown in Figure A.3.

Figure A.2 SSIS Import and Export Wizard

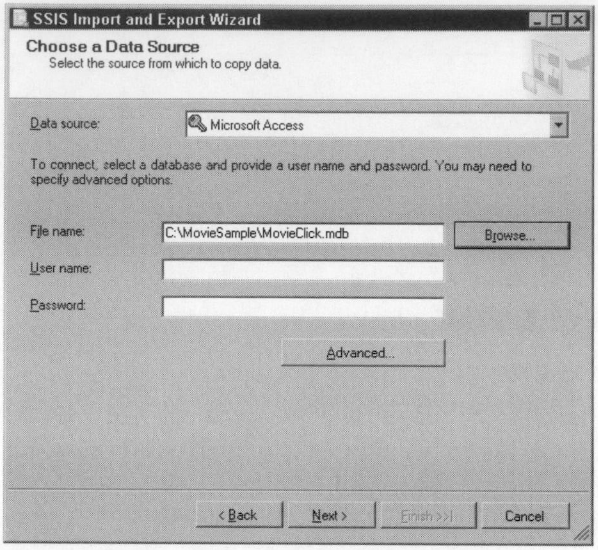

Figure A.3   Choosing an Access Data Source in the Import and Export Wizard

On the next page you specify the destination for the data. On this page, you should choose SQL Native Client as the destination and choose your database server and authentication method, as shown in Figure A.4. At that point you can choose the destination database or click the New button to create a new database on the destination server.

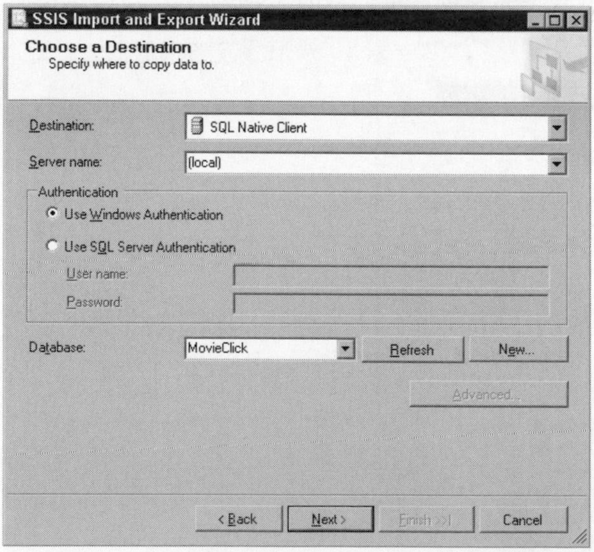

Figure A.4   Choosing a SQL Server destination in the Import and Export Wizard

On the next page, you select how the data is to be copied (see Figure A.5). Leave the Copy data from one or more tables or views default selected, and click Next.

On the next page, Select Source Tables and Views, check the box next to all tables you want to import from the source database. Optionally, you can check the optimization and transaction boxes as in Figure A.6 for performance benefits and to prevent partial transfers in event of an error.

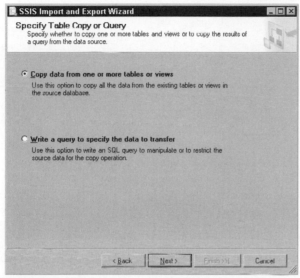

Figure A.5 Selecting import method in the Import and Export Wizard

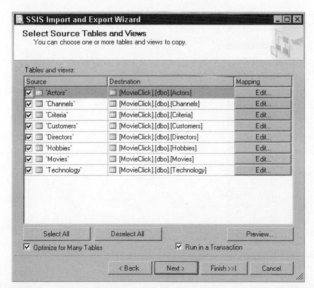

Figure A.6 Selecting a table in the Import and Export Wizard

The final page of the wizard, shown in Figure A.7, allows you to run or save the generated package. Choosing Run immediately and clicking Finish will import the data into your database.

Supported VBA and Excel Functions

This appendix lists the Visual Basic for Applications (VBA) and Excel functions that can be called as stored procedures from the DMX language, as described in Chapter 14. Table B.1 lists the supported VBA functions.

Table B.1 Supported VBA Functions

aBS	cDBL	cOS	datePart
array	choose	cSNG	dATESERIAL
aSC	cHR	cSTR	dATEVALUE
aSCB	cHR$	cVAR	day
aSCW	cHRB	cvDate	dDB
aTN	cHRB$	cVErr	error
cBOOL	cHRW	date	error$
cBYTE	cHRW$	dATE$	eXP
cCUR	cINT	dATEADD	fix
cDATE	cLNG	dateDiff	format

(continued)

Table B.1 *(continued)*

format$	mIDB	space$
fv	mIDB$	sqr
hex	mINUTE	str
hex$	mIRR	str$
hOUR	mONTH	strComp
iIF	nOW	strConv
iMEStatus	nPER	string
inStr	nPV	string$
iNT	oct	switch
iPMT	oct$	sYD
iRR	partition	tAN
isDate	pMT	tIME
isEmpty	pPMT	tIME$
iSERROR	pV	timer
isNull	qBColor	timeSerial
isNumeric	rATE	tIMEVALUE
isObject	rGB	tRIM
lCase	rIGHT	tRIM$
lCase$	rIGHT$	typeName
lEFT	rIGHTB	uCase
lEFT$	rIGHTB$	uCase$
lEFTB	rnd	val
lEFTB$	round	varType
lEN	rTrim	wEEKDAY
lENB	rTrim$	yEAR
lOG	sECOND	
lTrim	sgn	
lTrim$	sIN	
mID	sLN	
mID$	space	

Table B.2 lists the supported Excel functions.

Table B.2   Supported Excel Functions

Acos	Acosh	And	*Application
Asc	Asin	Asinh	Atan2
Atanh	AveDev	Average	BetaDist
BetaInv	BinomDist	Ceiling	ChiDist
ChiInv	ChiTest	Choose	Clean
Combin	Confidence	Correl	Cosh
Count	CountA	*CountBlank	*CountIf
Covar	*Creator	CritBinom	*DAverage
Days360	Db	Dbcs	*DCount
*DCountA	Ddb	Degrees	DevSq
*DGet	*DMax	*DMin	Dollar
*DProduct	*DStDev	*DStDevP	*DSum
*DVar	*DVarP	Even	ExponDist
Fact	FDist	Find	FindB
FInv	Fisher	FisherInv	Fixed
Floor	Forecast	*Frequency	FTest
Fv	GammaDist	GammaInv	GammaLn
GeoMean	*Growth	HarMean	*HLookup
HypGeomDist	*Index	Intercept	Ipmt
Irr	IsErr	IsError	IsLogical
IsNA	IsNonText	IsNumber	Ispmt
IsText	Kurt	Large	*LinEst
Ln	Log	Log10	*LogEst
LogInv	LogNormDist	*Lookup	Match
Max	*MDeterm	Median	Min
*MInverse	MIrr	*MMult	Mode
NegBinomDist	NormDist	NormInv	NormSDist

(continued)

Table B.2 *(continued)*

NormSInv	NPer	Npv	Odd
Or	*Parent	Pearson	Percentile
PercentRank	Permut	Pi	Pmt
Poisson	Power	Ppmt	Prob
Product	Proper	Pv	Quartile
Radians	*Rank	Rate	Replace
ReplaceB	Rept	Roman	Round
RoundDown	RoundUp	RSq	Search
SearchB	Sinh	Skew	Sln
Slope	Small	Standardize	StDev
StDevP	StEyx	Substitute	*Subtotal
Sum	*SumIf	SumProduct	SumSq
SumX2MY2	SumX2PY2	SumXMY2	Syd
Tanh	TDist	Text	TInv
Transpose	*Trend	Trim	TrimMean
TTest	USDollar	Var	VarP
Vdb	*VLookup	Weekday	Weibull
ZTest			

Index